# HOW TO WRITE EFFECTIVE

# LAW ENFORCEMENT REPORTS

## RUSSELL L. BINTLIFF

**PRENTICE HALL**
Englewood Cliffs, New Jersey 07632

Prentice-Hall International (UK) Limited, *London*
Prentice-Hall of Australia Pty. Limited, *Sydney*
Prentice-Hall Canada, Inc., *Toronto*
Prentice-Hall Hispanoamericana, S.A., *Mexico*
Prentice-Hall of India Private Limited, *New Delhi*
Prentice-Hall of Japan, Inc., *Tokyo*
Simon & Schuster Asia Pte. Ltd., *Singapore*
Editora Prentice-Hall do Brasil, Ltda., *Rio de Janeiro*

10  9  8  7  6  5  4  3  2  1

**Library of Congress Cataloging-in-Publication Data**

Bintliff, Russell L.
   How to write effective law enforcement reports/by Russell L. Bintliff.
      p.   cm.
   Includes index.
   ISBN 0-13-400920-7
   1. Police reports.   2. Report writing.   I. Title.
HV7936.R53B56   1991
808'.066363—dc20                                           90-47807
                                                              CIP

ISBN 0-13-400920-7

**PRENTICE HALL**
**BUSINESS & PROFESSIONAL DIVISION**
**A division of Simon & Schuster**
**Englewood Cliffs, New Jersey 07632**

Printed in the United States of America

# Dedication

*To my family*

# About the Author

**Russell L. Bintliff** has worked at almost every level of law enforcement: county, as deputy sheriff; state, as a police lieutenant, Arkansas; special tax and crime investigator, Florida Department of Revenue; 15 years as a criminal investigator, Department of the Army. At present he is a licensed private investigator and runs his own agency which conducts extensive financial and white collar crime investigations for law firms, and major corporations on request. He has compiled a number of law enforcement courses offered by the FBI, Department of the Army, DEA and U. S. Secret Service, among others. He has been awarded degrees in Business Administration (University of Maryland) and Law (LaSalle University). He is the author of TRAINING MANUAL FOR LAW ENFORCEMENT OFFICERS, Prentice Hall, 1990.

# Acknowledgments

Special thanks for contributions to this book:

The Arkansas State Highway Police

The New Hampshire State Police

The New Hampshire Department of Motor Vehicles

Crp, Incorporated

G. A. Thompson Company, Inc.

Bear-Aide, Inc.

Sirchie Finger Print Labs, Inc.

# Contents

How this Book Can Improve Your Image as a Law Enforcement Professional ♦ xiii

ONE How Effective Information Management Saves You Valuable Time, Makes You a Dynamic Law Enforcement Report Writer, and Gives Your Career Upward Mobility ♦ 1

Are You Sure You Know What Business You're In? ♦ 2

How Negative and Positive Tradition Can Harm or Help Your Information Management ♦ 2

When Do You Begin Writing Your Law Enforcement Report? ♦ 3

A Quick Reference Guide for Beginning to Write Your Report on the Way to a Crime Scene, a Vehicle Collision Scene, or Other Situation ♦ 5

Your Information Collection and Management Depends on Equipment ♦ 6

TWO How to Develop an Information Management System That Will Force You to Be Effective, Efficient, and Professional ♦ 11

Develop a Personalized Information Management System for Your Case Files In Five Easy Steps ♦ 12

Information Management System Forms, Worksheets and Checklists ♦ 14

THREE How to Create an Information Management System with a Case File Based on Your Report Format ♦ 69

Eight Steps to Creating a Personalized Information Management System Designed for Writing Dynamic Law Enforcement Reports ♦ 70

Organize Your Professional Image by Writing Dynamic Reports ♦ 73

About Your Equipment ♦ 86

Develop the Resources Needed to Write Effective, Efficient, Dynamic Law Enforcement Reports—A Reference Checklist ♦ 86

**FOUR   How to Develop Your Law Enforcement Report Writing Strategy: Narrative versus Expository ♦ 89**

Make Sure You Have All the Information in Your Report in Six Important Steps ♦ 91

What You Should Do when the Conclusion Is Written ♦ 95

Break with Tradition by Changing Some Old Attitudes ♦ 95

Five Important Objectives and Advantages Your Expository Report Writing Should Achieve ♦ 96

Report Writing Guidelines ♦ 96

Four Causes of Heavy Writing in Law Enforcement Reports ♦ 99

**FIVE   How Structuring Provides You with the Key to High-Impact Law Enforcement Reports ♦ 101**

Think First about Your Readers ♦ 101

Substantiate Your Conclusion ♦ 104

List Victims and Witnesses in Your Report ♦ 106

List Exhibits in Your Report ♦ 108

How to Write and Attach Your Investigator's Statement ♦ 109

A Quick Review ♦ 110

An Important Tip on Writing Your Report Quickly ♦ 110

The Myths and Truth about Written Statements ♦ 110

The Art of Taking Written Statements ♦ 111

How to Use Written Statements as Your Investigative Notes ♦ 112

Listen to What People Say: A Critical Step in Statement Taking and Report Writing Excellence ♦ 123

Seven Telltale Body Language Signs to Watch for when Interviewing ♦ 126

How to Sketch and Photograph the Scene ♦ 127

A Picture Is Worth a Thousand Words ♦ 136

Quick Reference Checklist ♦ 137

**SIX   Investigative Report Techniques for Law Enforcement Detectives ♦ 141**

The Complex Criminal Investigation Report Writing Formats and Techniques System of Information Management ♦ 142

Organize Your Criminal Investigation with Visual Network Planning: An Eight-Step Planning Process ♦ 146

What a First Progress Report Looks Like ♦ 147

Make an Investigative Activity Log ♦ 149

Second and Subsequent Progress Reports ♦ 150

Third Progress Report ♦ 152

Completed Report of Investigation ♦ 152

A Quick Reference Guide for Criminal Investigation Reports ♦ 161

**SEVEN   Information Management Systems for Complex Criminal Investigation Reports ♦ 163**

Undeveloped Leads Report ♦ 163

Supplemental Reports of Investigation ♦ 164

The Importance and Benefits of Written Statements ♦ 167

**EIGHT    Criminal Intelligence Report Writing Systems ♦ 187**

Intelligence versus Information ♦ 187

The Criminal Intelligence Cycle ♦ 188

Dissemination of Criminal Intelligence Data ♦ 188

Terminology Is Important to Your Criminal Information and Intelligence Report Systems ♦ 189

How Information and Intelligence Reports Differ from Preliminary and Criminal Investigative Reports ♦ 190

The Craft of Writing Intelligence Reports ♦ 191

Examples and Critiques of Incorrectly and Correctly Written Intelligence Reports ♦ 193

How to Manage Intelligence Report Information Effectively ♦ 199

Glossary of Criminal Intelligence Terms ♦ 203

**NINE    How to Write Effective Vehicle Collision Investigation Reports ♦ 205**

Essential Elements of a Vehicle Collision Investigation ♦ 206

Vehicle Collision Investigation Report Writing Style ♦ 206

Classification, Terminology, Factors, and Stages of Vehicle Collisions ♦ 207

Glossary of Vehicle Collision Investigation Terms ♦ 207

Factors Associated with Vehicle Collisions ♦ 208

Stages of Vehicle Collisions ♦ 209

Effective Vehicle Collision Report Writing Requires Efficient Information Management ♦ 210

Five Important Steps in Making a Vehicle Collision Scene Sketch ♦ 213

How to Write a Vehicle Collision Investigation Report ♦ 217

How to Write a Supplemental Vehicle Collision Investigation Report ♦ 221

**TEN    How to Write Crime Prevention Reports a Businessperson Can Understand ♦ 239**

Use a Worksheet to Develop Your Systems Approach Concept for Crime Prevention Inspections and Surveys ♦ 240

How to Write a Crime Prevention Inspection Report ♦ 251

Model Crime Prevention Inspection Report ♦ 252

**ELEVEN    Guidelines on Outlining, Grammar, Spelling, and Writing Style ♦ 261**

Benefits of Outlining ♦ 261

Advantages of Making an Outline before Writing Your Report ♦ 262

Guidelines for Spelling ♦ 267

Abbreviations ♦ 270

Numbers ♦ 272

Punctuation ♦ 273

**TWELVE    Model Reports ♦ 277**

Model 1: Crimes against Persons—A Misdemeanor Report ♦ 283

Model 2: Crimes against Persons—A Felony Report ♦ 287

Model 3: Crimes against Persons ♦ 290

Model 4: Crimes against Persons ♦ 293

Model 5: Drug Trafficking ♦ 301

APPENDIX A    High-Tech Information Management and Report Writing: Computers in Law Enforcement Applications ♦ 315

APPENDIX B    How to Interview Suspects and Take Statements Legally ♦ 321

INDEX   ♦ 331

# How this Book Can Improve Your Image as a Law Enforcement Professional

The law enforcement profession continues to improve, moving into a high-tech world, increasing training requirement levels, tightening officer selection and standards criteria. Categories of criminals escaping arrest and prosecution a few years ago are regularly tracked down today with amazing skill. Improvements are primarily credited to computerized systems, collating vast amounts of information in a fraction of time needed by previous methods and linking departments nationally and internationally with immediate communications. Some credit must go to the law enforcement profession itself, which abounds with professional officers desiring improvement, removing law enforcement from the category of a job and giving it professional career status. Most states now have minimum standards of candidate selection and performance certification programs that go a long way to ensure that men and women carrying badges and guns are competent.

With technology, greater enforcement success, and the increasing diversity and complexities that accompany modernization and improvement come heavier burdens on the individual officer to provide reports which are exact, comprehensive, and totally relevant. In past years as well as today, many cases are unsolved, never prosecuted, or lost in grand jury and court proceedings solely because information supplied by the officers investigating a case isn't presented clearly. Unfortunately, report writing is one area which hasn't kept pace with law enforcement modernization.

Several law enforcement departments are moving into sophisticated lap-top computerized systems which officers take to the scene of a crime or complaint and prepare a report at the scene. This is done with preprogrammed forms in the computer's memory that can be filled in quickly and transmitted via telephone to the department. The idea behind this technology is that an officer can handle complaints quickly, spend more time on the street, and dispense with traditional agonizing over filling out reports at the end of a shift.

The computer in the field reminds of innovative moves to standardized forms three decades past. About 1960, a modernization began to take shape in the law enforcement profession, calling for uniformity in forms, reporting procedures, and policies; now technology allows that effort to transfer into computers in the field. The only problem with those laudable efforts is that technology improves capability and saves valuable time; *it doesn't perform the task of writing.*

Unfortunately, a tainted perception about report writing which probably began in the 1960s with the increase of fill-in-the-blanks forms continues today. Filling out a form, either manually or on a lap-top computer, is considered the cure-all for poor report writing. The truth of the matter, which presents a nagging problem for most departments, is that technology and innovative progress don't replace a need for writing comprehensive reports. The ill-formed perceptions are a product of trying to find an easy solution to an often monumental problem. Law enforcement officers, despite their education levels, abilities, and other attributes, aren't likely to be lauded for writing award-winning prose. In today's society we can trace the problem back to widely publicized education problems, including a marked deficiency in reading and writing skills. Somehow, in the beginning, extraordinary advances in technology lulled us into believing computers would do it for us, and now we're learning that that was an erroneous perception. The problem still looms, but this book will enable you, whether chief or patrol officer, to trim it down to size and eventually eliminate it.

Having studied this problem of law enforcement report writing for thirty years, participating both as an officer and investigator writing reports about everything from vandalism to complicated murder investigations, I've decided it's time for a definitive, inclusive book each officer, patrol to chief, can use as a guide for developing his or her writing skill, producing comprehensive, dynamic, and success-oriented law enforcement reports. This bold step moves report writing from the dusty corners of stagnation and tradition to a level worthy of the times, enabling officers now and later to excel by writing precise, action-producing, information-managed reports.

A few years ago while investigating serious criminal activity within a major corporation, I had the opportunity to browse through several corporate departments. I found much emphasis placed on information management, an important area for corporations dealing in billions of dollars, since lack of clear information can mean financial decline. What I found had nothing to do with the case but always impressed me, because its application plainly applies to law enforcement report writing. I also found much information about management and marketing. That information boiled down to making a point of how critically important it is to define exactly what business you're in. When you know that, amazing perceptions develop, management competence occurs, and problems are successfully solved. Applying that question to our profession of law enforcement at first seems odd, since we're obviously enforcing the law. However, giving some thought about that vague definition brings us some interesting answers. Although often not recognized in training and on the job, law enforcement officers today are managers—more specifically, managers of law enforcement and situations and for the most part information managers. Despite our activity, whether at the scene of a crime, a traffic accident, a complaint of some kind, or taking part in gathering intelligence involving criminal activity, our purpose is investigating or, in other words, controlling the situation, collecting information, and, at some point, filling out forms and writing reports. Being a peace officer who walks or rides around ensuring that the general public behaves according to the law is an ever-decreasing percentage of professional effort. In today's modern diversity of law enforcement responsibilities, we spend most, if not all, of our active law enforcement time as managers of situations and information. We take notes, write daily activity reports, fill out forms, explain what happened, take written statements, write affidavits, and so on. When this definition is clear in our mind, we can define our business, able to recognize that management success or failure relies on how well the process applies to both separate and general situation. We can accept that our law enforcement role of management is broad, reaching into every facet of a diverse society, coupled with an ever-increasing complexity of laws. How effectively we collect information and what we do with it later has an important effect on the criminal justice purpose.

While reading this book, think of yourself as an information manager. Law enforcement reports are the single permanent and often public record of your competence and expertise. This is one area of professional management you can't afford to overlook.

# ONE

## How Effective Information Management Saves You Valuable Time, Makes You a Dynamic Law Enforcement Report Writer, and Gives Your Career Upward Mobility

The best reason for managing time is to get things you don't like to do out of the way so you can devote more time to things you enjoy doing. Probably one of the things you don't like to do is write reports; few if any law enforcement officers I know enjoy the task. It's normally reserved for the last item of duty, when you're tired and have a number of things you would rather be doing. Or, you try to squeeze it in during duty and turn in mediocre or incomplete reports.

The best way to manage your time is to manage effectively the information collected for your reports. Information can be your most valuable professional asset or the greatest curse, depending on how well it's managed. Most of us in the law enforcement profession don't recognize that one of the key elements of our job is collecting information and organizing it into a comprehensive and complete report. In fact, your law enforcement report is the most vital task you perform on a daily basis. Many reports are routine and mundane tasks, but one of the traps we can easily fall into is categorizing all reports as routine; therein lies the most significant problem. Any report you create which has or may have an impact on the lives of others is very important.

Beyond routine information that is obviously pure statistics or recordkeeping, there are reports of your investigative findings at the scene of a crime, a traffic collision, or other situations such as a construction accident, domestic disturbance, fire, or any of several kinds of problems requiring your intervention or presence. The information you collect and report is vitally important to someone, often many people. Your report may precipitate action leading to jail or prison terms, disrupt and separate families, cause children to be taken from parents, initiate lawsuits, provide protection for those otherwise ignored, and so on. When a patrol officer responds to the scene of a robbery or burglary, for instance, information he or she collects and reports can make the difference of identifying one or more perpetrators, obtaining an indictment, successfully prosecuting the persons responsible for the crime, and exacting appropriate punishment, or none of the foregoing. Far too many crimes remain unsolved and/or unresolved because the officer responding to the scene failed to collect and accurately report all the information available. Writing your report effectively is important, but always remember that it is not your version of what happened. It is your report about all the information which you were able to collect. How to collect and manage information at a crime or other kind of scene is the point where this book begins.

## ARE YOU SURE YOU KNOW WHAT BUSINESS YOU'RE IN? _____

A number of years ago I conducted a long, tiresome, but successful investigation into a so-phisticated white-collar crime operation within a major corporation. The case involved em-bezzlement of money and theft of property over a period of years and amounted to many millions of dollars. During the investigation, I discovered information which had nothing to do with the case but provided insights into our law enforcement profession from a fresh per-spective: effective ways of managing information and managing anything in general. Al-though the information concerned the world of business, something clicked in my mind that a part of that advice could apply to our profession. Readers were told that effective manage-ment requires a first step of defining exactly what business you are in. I thought about that for some time, and that one piece of advice changed my mind about new, effective ap-proaches for a lot of old problems. This story does have a significant impact on some of the concepts in this book.

In past years, whenever the opportunity arose, I related that same story to randomly selected law enforcement officers of all ranks and positions across the country. The answers I received are interesting and pointed out what I believed to be true. A common answer was, "Well, we keep the peace." Another common answer was, "We enforce the law." Of the hun-dred or so officers I talked with about defining what we do from their point of view, not once did I receive a clear answer. Perhaps because we are vague about our own profession, our success percentages across the board aren't exactly extraordinary.

Not once did an officer of any rank or position say that our job is primarily managing information. Perhaps at one time officers of the law were primarily peace officers, but how often have you kept the peace during your career? Maybe a parking lot dispute outside a bar, or a domestic disturbance, is as close as contemporary law enforcement gets to keeping the peace. It's not on the top of department priority lists. The phrase *enforcing the law* is vague. What laws? There are libraries filled with all kinds of laws, federal, state, county, local, and international.

The truth is, law enforcement officers use a vast majority of their duty time collecting and managing information, which culminates in writing a report. When officers are not collecting and managing information, they're on the streets looking for information to col-lect and manage. That's the business we're in a vast majority of the time. It's commonly referred to within the profession as investigation and intelligence, which is really informa-tion management.

## HOW NEGATIVE AND POSITIVE TRADITION CAN HARM OR HELP YOUR INFORMATION MANAGEMENT _____

One of the first steps you'll need to make when writing your law enforcement reports is to break with negative traditions. This is one of the most difficult elements of training officers to write effective reports because, for some unknown reason, little emphasis is placed on this vitally important part of the profession. Have you noticed that the most prevalent part of law enforcement training focuses on firearms? I have no fault with that; I've been a firearms in-structor, designed courses, and I insist on every officer being an expert with any firearm car-ried or used. However, I also know that a vast majority of officers have never used their handgun in the line of duty. I recently read an article about a small department that had three days training with automatic rifles. The article stated that officers should be well trained in their use. I know the department and officers well, that they have no automatic weapons, and that in the past twenty years the only incident involving an officer using firearms on duty resulted from accidental firing. Added to those statistics is the crime rate in the department's precinct, which in twenty years comprised two armed robberies, both involving a knife and drunks. I also know that the greatest problem in the department's jurisdiction is burglary, theft, and similar situations, most of which are never solved. Having read reports filed by the officers, I conclude that their time and money would be far better spent on training the officers to manage information. This is not singling out one small department; it's prevalent across the country.

The key reason I've found for less than competent information management, which includes report writing, is that academies place little emphasis on it, departments even less. The result is a diligently followed tradition of writing which is substandard.

### How Positive Tradition Helps Make Reporting Better

The law enforcement profession has a number of traditions which are positive and provide esprit de corps: parades, honoring deceased officers, taking care of fellow officers and their families, and taking an interest in schools, children, and the like. Other traditions are paramilitary and involve appearance, demeanor, procedure, and so forth.

### How Negative Tradition Hinders Effective Reporting

Negative traditions are those which go on for years without any definable purpose. Often they continue either because someone in an authoritative position within a department doesn't want anything to change, normally because of personal insecurities; because no one has the courage to change something even though the added benefit is apparent; no one has found a way to improve something which is clearly deficient; or no one really cares.

A common excuse I've heard about report writing and information management is, "We've always done it that way." If everyone followed that negative approach, we would still be patrolling the streets in Model A Fords, would have no radios and hand-cranking sirens, and would be selected based on our size or who we knew.

As this book progresses, I'll show you the negative traditions you'll probably have to confront and trash if you want your information management to excel. We'll begin with the idea about when to write your reports.

## WHEN DO YOU BEGIN WRITING YOUR LAW ENFORCEMENT REPORT? _____

The craft of writing effective, dynamic, action-getting law enforcement reports requires a clean break with negative tradition in several ways. The first break involves when you write your reports, at least in concept. Writing isn't purely a mechanical process, as we often characterize it. Your reports are the only part of your professional performance that becomes a permanent and often public record. How well you perform dozens of other law enforcement-related tasks on the street is known by few—your supervisor and a few others who recognize your skill but soon forget it. An officer's performance on the job is usually not remembered beyond, "He (or she) does a good job." But every officer is expected to do a good job. Your report, however, is your chance to shine and to be remembered by those who count in your career advancement. It is a clear, consistent record not only of how well you write, but of how competent you perform as a law enforcement officer overall. It is your one, constantly recurring opportunity to make your expertise known to many. Of course, your reports also reveal your shortcomings and lack of expertise and often project an inaccurate and unfavorable image to others because of poor information management and writing skill. For example, a prosecutor, a defense attorney, the press, insurance companies, and in some states anyone in the general public can read, scrutinize, and often criticize your reports. Not only is your writing style and the composition of the report under a magnifying glass, but what you say happened and how well you support it is examined carefully. You may have conducted a superb, thorough investigation, but if your report doesn't reflect the information accurately, completely, and clearly, readers think of you as incompetent. Remember, a report reader's perception of you comes from what you write, not from on-the-scene or on-the-job performance.

To project your real expertise, you must not only perform well on the job, but you must carry that performance through to your writing. To do that, you must begin writing your report mentally the moment you are dispatched to the scene of a crime, a traffic collision, or other situation. At that point you are beginning the all-important process of information management. Not long after we enter the law enforcement profession, the words *relevant* and *admissible* become a daily part of our thoughts and vocabulary, along with several others. As you begin thinking about your report, those two key words play an important role. If, for instance, you are collecting information about a residential burglary that occurred last weekend, the fact that the owner of the house had been in a distant city at a specific hotel attending a business convention can be relevant. The fact that he had a headache, ate trout for dinner, and didn't sleep well is not relevant to your investigation. It may sound ridiculous, but I have read thousands of law enforcement reports over three decades, and you would be surprised at what information officers include in their reports.

Each crime has essential elements of proof which cause a situation to be either a crime (misdemeanor or felony) or an unfounded complaint. If the elements are not present in their entirety there is no crime. On your way to investigate a complaint, think about the essential elements and focus your information collection and management on them. Doing so will save you valuable time and effort that might be used better elsewhere. For example, you're dispatched to a convenience store where an armed robbery allegedly occurred. On arrival, the clerk, still nervous, tells you that a man walked into the store, pointed a pink water pistol at him, and told him to put all the money from the cash register into a bag. The clerk complied, putting the money in a paper bag, and the man left the store without saying anything further.

One of the essential elements of armed robbery or robbery in general is the kind of force applied and if the victim was in fear of harm or losing life. In this case, the store clerk would have a difficult time convincing me that a water pistol could have created that kind of fear. One or more of the essential elements is missing, and the crime is unfounded. If, on the other hand, the man had told the clerk that the water pistol was filled with a caustic acid and he would spray it in his face or on his body, the essential element probably existed and the crime did occur.

Vehicle collisions are another common investigative task. You'll notice I don't call them traffic accidents, which is a misnomer. All vehicle collisions aren't accidents, just as all suicides aren't always what they appear to be. For example, I know of a case that involved what appeared to be a routine collision. However, the investigation evolved into a case of criminal assault with a vehicle. The trial resulted in conviction on charges of attempted murder. A man I'll call John Doe was fired from a job held for fifteen years. His termination came from a reorganization by a new plant manager, Mr. Smith, who admittedly had little regard for the plight or loyalty of others. A year later, after Doe had lost his house, new car, and credit, his wife announced that she wanted a divorce and left with their two children, moving to a distant city. During this time, Doe, having worked at the plant most of his adult life, found it impossible to get another meaningful job. Once a shirt-and-tie supervisor expecting promotion to the executive offices, Doe now washed dishes for a local restaurant, did menial odd jobs, and drove a broken-down old car. He lived in a cheap boarding house in a low-income section of the city. On the day of the collision, Doe was driving his old car to a day labor job and noticed his old boss, Smith, leaving a parking lot in his new Mercedes. Something snapped in Doe, and as Smith turned onto the street, Doe drove his car at high speed into Smith. Smith was severely injured (although later recovered after a lengthy stay in the hospital), and Doe told the investigating officer that Smith came onto the street apparently without noticing Doe's vehicle traveling in a direct collision line. Doe said he slammed on the brakes, but it was too late and a collision took place. Doe had minor injuries, was treated at a hospital and released. Had the officer treated it routinely, the matter would undoubtedly have shown that Smith's inattentive driving caused a traffic accident, and Doe would not only have collected insurance money but went on his way pretending to be the victim. This officer, however, always traveled to the scene of crimes and collisions, believing that a crime probably occurred unless the information conclusively proved otherwise. That should be your approach to information management. It prevents overlooking evidence which may only be available at that precise point in time. This is true with any crime scene, but doubly so at the scene of a vehicle collision.

Vehicle collisions take on a whole set of information collection problems beyond the identification of a crime, if one occurred. Your skill and precision in the information collection and management process, including writing a report, is critical. Often, collisions involve injuries or fatalities, and beyond the criminal aspects which may or may not be a factor are the civil lawsuits, insurance inquiries, or settlements that normally follow the event. Regardless of the outcome, you may be certain your report will be circulated among a number of persons and agencies. The outcome of your investigation is important to victims and others, and normally your report will be the deciding factor on the outcome. Often, a collision case isn't resolved for years, depending on its complexity and seriousness of damage. Your report, coupled with court testimony based on the information you placed in the report, will be foremost in final decisions.

When you arrive at the scene of an alleged crime, a vehicle collision, or other situation with no direction or focus, your information collection effort will have no direction or focus. You will invariably collect a great deal of useless information, use a lot of time, and often neglect relevant facts. That's not being overcritical, it's being realistic based on decades of experience in the field. I had to learn over the years, with the help of a few excellent supervisors, who systematically tore my reports in half and told me to do it right, on my time. One of them provided a bit of wisdom I've never forgotten: "It takes less time to do something right than it takes to explain why you did it wrong."

## A QUICK REFERENCE GUIDE FOR BEGINNING TO WRITE YOUR REPORT ON THE WAY TO A CRIME SCENE, A VEHICLE COLLISION SCENE, OR OTHER SITUATION

1. Sort out the essential elements of proof for the complaint enroute to the scene.

2. Be alert at the scene for other or lesser crimes that are often associated, and think about their essential elements of proof.

3. Think about the information likely to be relevant and irrelevant.

4. Organize your thoughts, determine your direction and focus before you arrive at a scene, and your information collection will have direction and focus.

5. Think about your readers—who will be receiving your information via your report and basing their decisions on your report.

## YOUR INFORMATION COLLECTION AND MANAGEMENT DEPENDS ON EQUIPMENT

A traditional means of recording information is the handy pocket notebook. I can't disagree with the convenience of carrying a small notebook, especially on foot patrol. I agree that each officer should always carry a pocket notebook and pen or pencil. However, the notebook serves a limited purpose, such as noting a name or license number. It is for brief notes, not investigating crime scenes, vehicle collisions, or other situations which result in a report.

The kind of equipment you select for your personalized information management kit does make a difference. Old ideas or rhetoric about scribbling on whatever is available, jotting down a few facts and relying on memory for the rest, field expediency, and so on are fodder for the inexperienced, ineffectual, or rookie who heard it's the way things are done in police work. A true professional, in any profession, selects his or her equipment with considerable care. Professional ability which excels requires capability, and that's where select equipment comes into the picture. The idea here is not a standardized set of items, but a set of personalized tools enabling you to perform investigative duties effectively, efficiently, and with maximum information management capability. Setting out to collect and manage information without the right tools is like carrying a handgun that works now and then. You depend on your handgun to protect you and others under life-and-death attack situations; you must also depend on other equipment for its dependability.

### Building Your Information Management Tool Box

In generic terms, you should have the following items as a minimum in your information management kit:

1. *A briefcase.* Select your briefcase carefully, in accordance with your needs. In addition, consider the weather. I like leather, but climates with excessive humidity or rain may make other materials more feasibile. I like hard briefcases opposed to soft simply because they function well as a hard writing surface, which is valuable in some cases, especially when a scene is in a rural area, such as in the woods or a field, or in a warehouse. Your briefcase should be large enough to accommodate easily not only all your information management tools but the information you collect on several cases. Expandable briefcases are available and work well for law enforcement officers. You may want to consider them before you buy or replace the one you have.

2. *A clipboard.* A variety of styles are available including the old standby—a fiberboard with a large clip. A viable option, however, is a durable yet thin lightweight aluminum clipboard with a small rubber-coated clip. This version is less bulky, and I've found it to work better.

3. *Two or more ballpoint pens.* Most office supply houses sell good quality ballpoint pens in a box of a dozen or so, a good idea for your kit. Always use black ink, for better readability, better copies, and official appearance.

4. *Two or more pencils.* A couple of good mechanical pencils or wooden pencils with a sharpener should be included in your kit. Often, especially when making sketches or drawings, a pen is unsuitable. Number 4 lead works best.

5. *A wood or metal ruler.* This is an inexpensive but useful tool for sketches, separating notes, measuring short distances, and using as a comparison item when taking photographs of possible evidence found at a scene. Laying a ruler alongside before photographing provides a better perspective of size when you or others view the picture later.

*How Effective Information Management Saves You Valuable Time, Makes You a Dynamic*
*Law Enforcement Report Writer, and Gives Your Career Upward Mobility*

7

6. *A twelve-foot tape.* I suggest the small version, metal and encased in a retractable housing. For vehicle collision investigation you'll need measuring tapes of considerable length, but most departments equip patrol vehicles with that item. They are too clumsy for measuring a room or other shorter distances.

7. *Graph paper pads.* Graph paper is best for making crime or collision scene sketches because the equal squares can often be used to indicate inches or feet. Later, when you need to use the sketch either as a reference or basis for a scale drawing, your task is much easier and more professional.

8. *White or yellow lined pads.* These are the old standby for note taking, obtaining written statements, and lots of other uses. White with black ink copies best.

9. *Vehicle collision templates.* This is an invaluable item for sketching the scene and making detailed sketches later.

10. *Crime scene templates.* This is another invaluable item for doing a professional job, accuracy, and saving time if you're not an artistic person. In most cases, office supply stores have a large selection of templates, many of which can be adapted to use for crime scene templates; however, most law enforcement equipment catalogs or stores have the real thing available.

11. *Stick-on tabs.* Made under two or three brand names, these items are often invaluable and come in a variety of sizes. I suggest the 3" × 5" for notes or reminders, which can be pasted on nearly anything (including paper) and removed easily without any damage to the item or document. For tabbing documents, a 1" × 2" and 3" × 3" work fine. Once you are used to having them in your information management system, it's hard to do without them.

12. *Document protectors.* Several kinds are available, and I suggest those made for executive offices in which administrative assistants pass letters to executives for signatures. I like them because they are heavier grade and resist transferring ink to the plastic or sticking to the document. If you're working in a humid climate and the document will be in the protector for a while, it may be best to use paper folders. Under normal conditions, however, the document protectors prevent anything from happening to a statement, affidavit, questioned document, or item of evidence. You can also label the document by writing with a marker on the protector or using a stick-on tab.

13. *Zip-lock sandwich bags.* A few of these can save lots of problems later. Labeled the same way as the document protectors, they can safely contain a pen or pencil that might be suspected evidence, matchbooks, or a variety of other items that don't fit anywhere else but are important and need protection. You can even attach them to your report when the item is bulky but must accompany your report.

14. *Department forms.* These include reporting forms, statement forms, property receipts, inventory forms, and others. They can be used as worksheets if necessary, or in cases of statements, property, and so on requiring signatures. Always have an ample supply available according to your department's procedures and policies.

15. *Worksheets.* These will be discussed later in the book and are by far the best way to collect and manage information.

16. *Camera and film.* As the saying goes, a picture is worth a thousand words. You can save a great deal of time by referring to your "work photographs" when writing a report. For your information management kit, you should have a small,

inexpensive camera, preferably Polaroid® type. Remember, this is for collecting information you'll use to write and support your report, not for taking admissible crime scene photographs, although in some cases they may suffice.

17. *Other items.* Depending on your circumstances, other items are always considered, such as paper clips, Scotch® tape, and so forth. Think of everything you'll need under all circumstances when building your personalized kit. Most departments furnish crime scene and vehicle collision investigation kits that include latent fingerprint collection items, along with other equipment. If for some reason those kits are not sufficient for your needs, supplement them with additional items in your personalized kit.

This collection of information management equipment can easily be tailored and expanded to your liking. My point is that you must have something to work with if you truly are intent on doing a professional job and writing dynamic reports. I am computer oriented; in other words, I like to use computer or word processing equipment anytime it's feasible. However, while talking to an officer recently, he proudly described his department's innovative move to using lap-top computers loaded with all the report forms. He told me that now, right at the scene, he can fill in and write all his reports. It is the trend in law enforcement and probably a good trend, except, as I mentioned to the officer, who told me he wouldn't have to carry around a kit of items any longer, "What if you arrive at a scene and the computer doesn't work?" He thought about it for a minute, smiled, and commented that maybe he ought to throw the old briefcase in the trunk after all. If your department switches to field computers, throw the briefcase full of personalized information management equipment in the car, too; you might save a lot of problems and embarrassment. I've never found a computer that will take photos, bag a book of matches I found at the scene, label evidence, take measurements, tag evidence, and so on. Computers are great, but think of them only as a sophisticated ballpoint pen when it comes to doing your job at a scene.

### Define Your Task Carefully

I talked about defining our business earlier in this book. Now it's time to talk about defining our task.

What you do is often defined by your department. For example, if you're a patrol officer in a large city with specialized teams, your task when dispatched to a crime scene may be only to secure the scene and wait for detectives to arrive. However, keep in mind that often the first officer to arrive will observe things that may not be there later, even a few minutes later. An officer once told me about a similar situation when in the heat of summer a chunk of ice was found alongside a deceased body at a local fish market, and the body had a head wound. All logic told the officer the chunk of ice was probably the weapon used to bash the man's head, which probably killed him or contributed to his death. The officer had a camera in his car, took a picture of the scene, and then moved the ice carefully to a freezer to prevent it from melting in the heat. Twenty minutes later when the detectives arrived, he told them what he observed, gave them his film, and pointed out the ice, now preserved in a freezer, which he and other officers verified and watched to maintain integrity of the evidence. As it turned out, the case was solved and successfully prosecuted because of the officer's quick thinking and because he had his equipment with him.

Although the officer was not expected or required to investigate or process the crime scene, he defined his task of securing the scene as preserving evidence rather than as just standing around waiting for detectives.

*How Effective Information Management Saves You Valuable Time, Makes You a Dynamic*
*Law Enforcement Report Writer, and Gives Your Career Upward Mobility*

**9**

In a vast majority of locations you are expected to do far more than just secure the scene and wait for specialists to arrive. However, always remember that your task is to do whatever necessary to manage the available information, either in total or in part, and you'll have to write a report. If you allow evidence or any other part of a crime scene to deteriorate or disappear, how will you explain that in your report? What will readers of your report think about your competence? Your task is always information management, regardless of what level you work at. It's your responsibility as a law enforcement officer.

## Quick Reference Guide and Reminder

1. Begin writing your report before you arrive at the scene of a crime, vehicle collision, or other situation.
2. Begin writing your report before you start collecting information.
3. Make certain you have the proper tools to investigate a scene effectively and manage information efficiently.
4. Define your task, depending on your situation.
5. Remember that the difference between failure and success is doing a job nearly right and doing a job exactly right.

# TWO

## How to Develop an Information Management System that Will Force You to Be Effective, Efficient, and Professional

It's been a busy day; you arrive at the department an hour before your shift ends and sit down at a writing table. Opening your bulging briefcase and removing a sheaf of notes, papers, and assorted junk, depression and fatigue set in. This is not an uncommon scene; it happens nearly every day in thousands of law enforcement departments across the country. We've all been the person sitting there sorting out a day's worth of notes, trying to make sense of them, and looking for a way to get home on time. You figure the paperwork will take at least two hours, and since the chief cracked down on overtime, probably the best thing to do is use your own time. After a call home to break the bad news and apologize, you begin tackling the awesome task of writing reports.

Your problem is information management. You have the information, but it's not managed. It's easy for any of us in the law enforcement profession to arrive at a crime, collision scene, or other situation and believe that hours later we'll remember every detail. The reality is, after a busy day all the cases we were covering during a shift tend to run together. There's always the problem of forgetting to ask a question and thus a major piece of information wasn't collected. That can mean a telephone call if you're lucky and perhaps a lot of running around to track down the person if you're unlucky. Either way, valuable time, energy, and motivation is lost.

You sort your notes and papers and find scribbles and words, numbers, and doodles here and there made hours before that defy any real meaning now. But it's getting late, and they probably aren't important anyway, so you sort them into a pile of information that isn't understood. About two hours past the end of your shift, you toss a handful of reports in your supervisor's "in" box and drive home.

If all or part of the preceding scenario is true in your case, you need an information management system that enables you to collect information efficiently and effectively and understand it completely when it comes time to write reports. Some of the advantages of this system will be a lack of stress, not being late getting home, and promotions.

## DEVELOP A PERSONALIZED INFORMATION MANAGEMENT SYSTEM FOR YOUR CASE FILES IN FIVE EASY STEPS _____

### *Step 1: Use Containers*

The idea of "containerizing" your information serves several purposes: (1) It enables you to isolate all the information from one case to one container; (2) it allows you to file the information for court appearances often one, two, or more years after the fact; (3) it forces you to focus on one case at a time when reports have to be written; and (4) it causes you to write dynamic reports that get favorable attention and criminal justice action.

Although your personal preference may differ from mine, I suggest the following ways to contain your information.

*In the field.* Use wallet file folders, which are available at most office supply stores for a couple dollars. Use the kind with a flap and elastic fastener, and preferably legal size, which accommodate all sizes of documents. In addition to insuring that nothing is lost and everything from a particular investigation is in one place, this kind of container is durable and can be used for an extended period of time. At report writing time, just open up a folder, remove its contents, and everything you'll need for your report is there for a quick review before you start writing. When finished, you're ready for the next step.

*For your personal file.* Use large, heavy-duty manila envelopes. Some departments may require your notes to be filed with your report. In such cases, always make a copy of everything, including your report, and place it all in a large brown envelope, label it, and take it home for your personal work files. Some years ago I worked on a vehicle collision investigation that also involved some criminal activity. One driver was intentionally negligent, and that contributed to a collision which disabled a lady who was a passenger in the other car. She happened to be a surgeon, and her injuries prevented her from continuing her career. The criminal case went to trial about eight months later after a number of delays, and the lawsuit resulting from the collision went to trial nearly two years later. All together, a span of about three years passed from the actual event and the conclusion of court activity. All the notes, worksheets, sketches, and other information were filed along with the completed report one day after the event. When the first court case was pending, I asked for the case file as a review procedure before testifying, and after a few days of frantic searching it was determined that the file was lost or destroyed by accident. That department had a policy of destroying old case files five years after the fact if no reason was determined for keeping them. Somehow, this case and several others were mixed in the annual destruction box and incinerated. Fortunately, the original report and exhibits were safe with the prosecutor; however, my notes, very important in this case, were not available. Because of that I was unable to have a few small but significant facts available, and the criminal case was dismissed. The civil lawsuit was less favorable for the victim than it would have been if I could have testified about facts that were in the notes.

Since that time, I've kept copies of everything, regardless of how insignificant it may seem, even after a case has passed through all the courts. The records are secured in a locked file but could at some point in time many years later be of significant importance.

### *Step 2: Develop Personalized Worksheets*

I know you use forms at your department and you like to fill them out at the scene, because it saves time. I also know that even with the best intentions, officers regularly file the same form filled out at the scene, complete with mistakes and often missing information. Filling out a form at the scene and trying to write a report in that kind of environment is sloppy and clumsy at best. It may save time, but it doesn't save your career from stagnation. Forms were designed over the years as a cure-all for busy officers, and they are helpful to collect all the information. There are merits attached to using fill-in-the-blanks forms, but they fall far short of being a cure-all or substitute for developing report writing skills. Unfortunately, every shortcut has its price, and forms have led to a lack of interest in requiring officers to become proficient report writers.

The best way I've found to meet the fill-in-the-blanks form requirements and continue to develop my investigative and writing skills is designing and using worksheets. The information required by the endless stream of tiny blanks that normally ask for more information than there is space to write is contained on the worksheet, leaving adequate space to write notes that might be important. For example, if you're receiving information from a person and have the feeling it's not accurate, such as a date of birth, you can make a note to yourself to check it more thoroughly later, perhaps through driver's license records or some other source. It's embarrassing and makes you appear incompetent when you place erroneous information on a form and it is later pointed out in court. Even if you had a chance to explain, an opportunity a diligent defense attorney would not allow, you would still lack credibility and open the door for being attacked and questioned. Use a worksheet, fill in the blanks in a quiet environment, and make certain the information is accurate. An example of fill-in-the-blanks forms is shown in Exhibits 2-1 through 2-7. Worksheets you can develop are shown in Exhibits 2-8 through 2-13.

### Step 3: Develop and Use Personalized Checklists

Regardless of how skilled we are, it's easy to overlook an important item at a crime scene, vehicle collision, or other situation being investigated. For about twenty years I've used checklists, and they have regularly proved invaluable. When it comes time to write a report, the checklist ensures that we've managed the information available expertly. It's important while taking notes, statements, and performing other investigative functions to ensure that all the elements are covered before leaving the scene. Prosecutors have nightmares about law enforcement reports coming in which fail to document and itemize elements needed to continue taking action. Remember that each checklist you create must correspond with the specific laws of your state. Although such laws are similar across the country, some have slightly different essential elements of proof. Often prosecutors also have certain requirements to determine if evidence is sufficient to move forward with a case. Whatever the reason, personalize your checklist to satisfy local legal requirements.

### Step 4: Make a Personalized Identification Notebook

One of the most frustrating parts of managing investigations at a scene is obtaining an accurate description of assailants, perpetrators, weapons, and even vehicles. I've found over the years that ten witnesses will provide ten versions, often far different from each other although each looked at the same person, object, or vehicle. There's good reason, since a number of factors come into play: where the person was at the time of an observation; eyesight; not actually seeing something, but rather glimpsing and associating the glimpse with a memory or rationalization; and so on. Although you may question a victim or witness and they provide a sincere description, it may not be accurate. When you write your report, that inaccurate information is included. But when it comes time to investigate further, perhaps by detectives or specialists, or the matter comes to trial, some questions arise concerning your competency. For example, you say in your report that the assailant in a robbery, according to a witness, was over 6 feet tall, weighed over 200 pounds, was muscular, had a deep voice and a full beard. Later, a suspect is arrested, and there is no doubt that he is the perpetrator;

| 1. Name of ☐ Victim ☐ Complainant ☐ Business | 2. Case Number | | |
|---|---|---|---|
| 3. Offense or Incident | 4. Offense Number | | |

| 5. Address of ☐ Victim ☐ Complainant ☐ Business | 6. Telephone No ☐ R ☐ B | ☐ **OFFENSE** ☐ **INCIDENT** |
|---|---|---|
| 8. Person Reporting and Address | 9. Telephone No ☐ R ☐ B | 7. Time Ofcr. Arrived at Scene: ☐ A.M. ☐ P.M. |

10. Burglary Report ONLY 11. Reported By____
☐ Res. D.T. ☐ Non-Res. D.T. ☐ Phone ☐ Officer
☐ Res. N.T. ☐ Non-Res. N.T. ☐ In Person ☐____

| | 12. OCCURRED | | | | | 13. REPORTED | | | | 14. Type of Property | 15. Value of Property | 16. Value of Recovered Property |
|---|---|---|---|---|---|---|---|---|---|---|---|---|
| On or btwn. and | Month | Day | Year | Day Wk. | Time | Month | Day | Year | Time | ☐ Lost ☐ Stolen ☐ Recovered | | |
| | | | | | | | | | | A. Currency, Notes, Etc. | | |
| | | | | | | | | | | B. Jewelry and Precious Metals | | |
| 17. Place of Occurance ☐ inside ☐ outside | | | | | 18. Type of Premises... | | | | | C. Clothing and Furs | | |
| | | | | | | | | | | D. Locally Stolen Motor Vehicles | | |
| 19. Victim's Occupation - & | | Race | Sex | Age | 20. Person Who Discovered Crime or Incident | | | | | E. Office Equipment | | |
| | | | | | | | | | | F. Televisions, Radios, Stereos, Etc. | | |
| 21. Trademark or Unusual Event | | | | | 22. Address of Number 20 | | | | | G. Firearms | | |
| | | | | | | | | | | H. Household Goods | | |
| 23. Tool(s) Used (Described) | | | | | 24. Knife or Other Means Used | | | | | I. Consumable Goods | | |
| | | | | | | | | | | J. Livestock | | |
| 25. WEAPONS USED ☐ Revolver ☐ Semi-Automatic ☐ Rifle ☐ Shotgun Caliber — | | | | | 26. How Entrance-Exit Gained? | | | | | K. Miscellaneous | | |
| | | | | | | | | | | L. Auto Recovered ☐ For other Authority | | |

**Offender / Missing person / Runaway** ☐ ☐ ☐

| 27. | Last Name | First Name | MI | Address | 28. Arrested/Located ☐ Yes ☐ No |
|---|---|---|---|---|---|

| Height | Weight | Hair | Eyes | Compl. | Hat | Coat | Shoes | Sweater | Blouse/Shirt | Skirt/Trousers | Jewelry |
|---|---|---|---|---|---|---|---|---|---|---|---|

| 29. Possible Cause of Absence | 30. Possible Destination | 31. Past Record, Other Data-ID, Money Carried, Etc. |
|---|---|---|

**VEHICLE**

| 32. ☐ UBO ☐ stolen ☐ Entered | 33. Color | 34. Yr. | 35. Make | 36. Body Style | 37. St. | 38. License No. | 39. VIN Number | 40. Stored At: |
|---|---|---|---|---|---|---|---|---|

**PROPERTY**

| 41. Qu. | 42. Article (Name Only) See No. 14 | 43. Value | 44. Description (Size-Color-Model-Serial No.-Style-Material-Condition-Etc.) |
|---|---|---|---|
| | | $ | |
| | | $ | |
| | | $ | |
| | | $ | |

**WITNESS PARENT GUARDIAN** ☐ ☐ ☐

| 45. Name (Last, First and Middle) | Age | Best Contact Address | Residence Telephone | Business Telephone |
|---|---|---|---|---|
| 1. | | | | |
| 2. | | | | |

**EVIDENCE**

| 46. Evidence ☐ None ☐ Personal Belongings ☐ Tools ☐ Drugs ☐ Other | Description of Physical Evidence Obtained |
|---|---|

47. Details as Reported by the Victim, Person Reporting, and/or the initial investigating Officer(s).

Use Supplementary Report if Needed

| 48. Status of the Case ☐ Active ☐ Cleared by Arrest ☐ Inactive ☐ Exceptionally Cleared ☐ Closed ☐ Unfounded | 49. Date | 50. Investigating Officer(s) | 53. Emp # | 54. Dist # | 55. UCR # | Page ____ |
|---|---|---|---|---|---|---|
| | 51. Date | 52. Approving Supervisor | | | | |

☐ Supplementary Report(s) Attached

FORM #OI-1

G.A. THOMPSON, P.O. BOX 64681, DALLAS, TEXAS 75206

EXHIBIT 2-1

# OFFENSE REPORT

NO. _____    _____    NO. _____
Classification

| 1 COMPLAINANT'S OR VICTIM'S NAME (Firm name if business) | | 2 AGE | DESCENT/RACE | SEX | DOB | 3 PHONE (Business) |
|---|---|---|---|---|---|---|
| 4 COMPLAINANT'S OR VICTIM'S ADDRESS | | 5 CITY | | STATE | | 6 PHONE (Residence) |

| COMPLAINANT'S OR VICTIM'S BUSINESS, EMPLOYMENT OR SCHOOL | 8 OBJECT OF ATTACK (Burglary, theft, assault, etc.) |
|---|---|
| 9 PLACE WHERE OFFENSE OCCURRED | 10 TYPE OF BUILDING (Residence, store, bank, etc.) |

| 11 REPORTED BY | PHONE | 12 REPORTED TO | OFFICER'S ARRIVAL TIME |
|---|---|---|---|

| 13 DAY, DATE AND TIME OF OFFENSE | 14 DAY, DATE AND TIME OF REPORT |
|---|---|

| 15 BODILY INJURIES TO | HOSPITAL? | 16 HOW REPORTED (In person, phone, on view, other) |
|---|---|---|

17 M/O (How done - force used - at what point - with what tool or weapon - other acts or trademarks)

17A EXACT WORDS USED BY OFFENDER

18 VEHICLE INVOLVED IN OFFENSE (Year - color - make - model - auto license no. - year - state)                    Complainant's □ Suspect's □

| 19 DIRECTION OF FLIGHT STREET OR ROAD | □ N □ E □ S □ W | □ AUTO □ FOOT | 20 WILL COMPLAINANT PROSECUTE? |
|---|---|---|---|
| | | □ UNK. □ OTHER | |

| 21 NAME AND ADDRESS OF SUSPECT(S) - OR AGE DESCENT SEX DESCRIPTION | 22 CIRCLE IF SUSPECT IS |
|---|---|
| 1 | Employee - Relative - Acquaintance |
| 2 | |

| 23 WITNESSES NAME, | BEST CONTACT ADDRESS | AGE | BEST PHONE | OTHER PHONE | PARENT OR GUARDIAN? |
|---|---|---|---|---|---|
| 1 | | | | | |
| 2 | | | | | |

24 NARRATIVE (Write in any available details not covered above)

25 INVESTIGATING OFFICER(S) _____ 26 REPORT MADE BY _____ DATE_____

| 27 CASE FILED | | 28 THIS CASE IS | | Active □ | 29 APPROVED BY |
|---|---|---|---|---|---|
| Yes □   No □ | Cleared by arrest □ | Unfounded □ | Inactive □ | Other □ | |

FORM # OR-1
PRICE GROUP "C"

Use supplementary report for additional information not covered above.
G. A. THOMPSON, P. O. BOX 64681, DALLAS, TEXAS 75206

EXHIBIT 2-2

## STATE OF NEW HAMPSHIRE
## INITIAL INVESTIGATION REPORT

| 1. CASE NO. | 2. INVESTIGATING OFFICER | 3. ID | 4. TOWN OF CRIME | 5. CODE | 6. DATE OF REPORT |
|---|---|---|---|---|---|

**CRIME**

| 7. CRIME ( ) | 8. RSA # | 9. CRIME (SECOND, IF ANY) ( ) | 10. RSA # |
|---|---|---|---|
| 11. CRIME (THIRD) ( ) | 12. RSA # | 13. CRIME (FOURTH) ( ) | 14. RSA # |

**VICTIM**

| 15. VICTIMS NAME DOB. | 16. RACE | 17. SEX | 18. AGE | 19. VICTIMS HOME ADDRESS | 20. TEL. NO. |
|---|---|---|---|---|---|

**TIME AND PLACE**

| BETWEEN (HR. &DATE) | 21. HOUR | 22. DAY OF WK. 1. MON. 5. FRI. 2. TUES. 6. SAT. 3. WED. 7. SUN. 4. THUR. | 23. DAY | 24. MONTH | 25. DATE | 26. YEAR | 27. LOCATION OF CRIME INCIDENT |
|---|---|---|---|---|---|---|---|
| AND(OR AT) (HR. &DATE) | 28. HOUR | | 29. DAY | 30. MONTH | 31. DATE | 32. YEAR | |

**REPORTED BY**

| 33. NAME | 34. DATE RPT. | 35. TIME | 36. HOME ADDRESS | 37. TEL. NO. |
|---|---|---|---|---|

**M. O.**

| 38. TYPE OF PREMISES | 39. CODE | 40. WEAPONS — TOOLS | 41. CODE |
|---|---|---|---|

42. HOW ATTACKED (MO)

**VEHICLE**

| 43. 1. STOLEN 4. RENTAL 2. SUSPECT 5. N/A 3. KNOWN | 44. CODE | 45. YEAR | 46. MAKE | 47. TYPE | 48. COLOR | 49. REGISTRATION | 50. STATE | 51. VIN |
|---|---|---|---|---|---|---|---|---|

**VALUE OF STOLEN PROPERTY**

| 52. LARCENY CODE A B C D E F G H I J K L | 53. AMOUNT $ | 54. BURGLARY CODE 1 2 3 | 55. AMOUNT $ | 56. AMT. M/V $ | 57. MISC. AMT. $ |
|---|---|---|---|---|---|

| 58. TOTAL AMT. STOLEN $ | 59. TOTAL AMT. RECOVERED $ | 60. WEATHER 1. CLEAR 2. CLOUDY 3. RAIN 4. SNOW 5. SLEET 6. FOG 7. OTHER 8. UNKNOWN | 61. CODE |
|---|---|---|---|

| 62. UCR CODE | 63. STATUS OF CRIME 1. ACTIVE 3. X-CLEARED 2. CL. ARREST 4. UNFOUNDED 5. NO CRIM. ASPECT | 64. CODE | 65. STATUS OF CASE 1. INVEST. 2. CLOSED | 66. CODE | 67. AGE OF OLDEST |
|---|---|---|---|---|---|

List accused - List and identify additional victims - Describe perpetrators or suspects - Action taken including findings and observations of investigator - Personal evidence found - Where - By whom - Disposition and technical services performed - Interview of victims - Witnesses - Persons contacted - Suspects - List - Describe stolen property - Value - Court Action - Attach statements. If narrative is such that it will require continuation pages (UCR-102), place a synopsis below and entire narrative on continuation pages.

| 68. ACCUSED ARRESTED SUSPECTED | 69. NAMES AND ADDRESS | 70. CHARGE | 71. DOB | 72. RACE | 73. SEX | 74. AGE |
|---|---|---|---|---|---|---|

| 75. NCIC/TT | PAGE NO. OF PGS. | SIGNED (INVESTIGATING OFFICER) | ID NO. | DATE | CASE NO. |
|---|---|---|---|---|---|

INITIAL INVESTIGATION REPORT
UCR-101

APPROVED _____ DATE _____

GRANITE STATE BUSINESS FORMS, INC. Goffstown, N.H. 03045 (603)622-4480

EXHIBIT 2-3

## STATE OF NEW HAMPSHIRE
## CONTINUATION OF INVESTIGATION/ARREST REPORT

| 1. CASE NO. | 2. INVESTIGATING OFFICER | 3. ID | 4. TOWN OF CRIME | 5. CODE | 6. DATE OF REPORT |
|---|---|---|---|---|---|
| | | | | | |

CASE NO.

| | | page ____ of ____ pages | signed | date / / |
|---|---|---|---|---|

CONTINUATION OF INVESTIGATION/ARREST REPORT
UCR-102

GRANITE STATE BUSINESS FORMS, INC. Goffstown, N.H. 03045 (603)622-4480

MASTER FILE

EXHIBIT 2-3

## COMPLAINT REPORT

| COMPLAINANT'S NAME | NATURE OF COMPLAINT | SERIAL NUMBER |
|---|---|---|

| COMPLAINANT'S ADDRESS | PHONE NUMBER | LOCATION OF OFFENSE OR INCIDENT |
|---|---|---|

| REPORTED BY | ADDRESS | PHONE NUMBER |
|---|---|---|

| RECEIVED BY | TIME | DATE | OFFICERS ASSIGNED | HOW REPORTED |
|---|---|---|---|---|

DETAILS OF COMPLAINT, OR INCIDENT

PERSONS ARRESTED _____NO._____  _____NO._____

CASE CLOSED:_____UNFOUNDED:_____CLEARED BY ARREST:_____ OTHER_____

APPROVED_____SIGNED_____DATE_____

## OFFENSE REPORT

DESCRIPTION OF PROPERTY

| ESTIMATED VALUE | RECOVERED | |
|---|---|---|
| | DATE | VALUE |
| | | |
| | | |
| | | |
| | | |
| | | |
| TOTAL | | |

I HEREBY ACKNOWLEDGE RECEIPT OF THE ABOVE RECOVERED ARTICLES DELIVERED TO ME

BY_____  SIGNED_____  DATE_____

DESCRIPTION OF SUSPECTS OR PERSONS WANTED:

G. A. THOMPSON, P. O. BOX 64581, DALLAS, TEXAS 75206  FORM NO. LE 9-1

Exhibit 2-4

# SUPPLEMENTARY REPORT

NO. _____      _____      NO. _____
Classification

Name of Complainant          Address          Phone No.

Offense

DETAILS OF OFFENSE, PROGRESS OF INVESTIGATION,ETC.:
(Investigating Officer must sign)

Page No._____          Date_____19____

25 INVESTIGATING OFFICER(S) _____ 26 REPORT MADE BY _____ DATE_____

27 CASE FILED      28 THIS CASE IS      Active ☐   29 APPROVED BY

Yes ☐    No ☐      Cleared by arrest ☐    Unfounded ☐    Inactive ☐    Other ☐   |_____

FORM 6-1 R          G. A. THOMPSON, P. O. BOX 64681, DALLAS. TEXAS 75206

EXHIBIT 2-5

NO. _____     NO. _____

NO. _____     NO. _____

## ARREST REPORT

| NAME OF PERSON ARRESTED | | | | | | ALIAS OR NICKNAME(S) | ARREST DATE |

| ADDRESS OF SUSPECT | | OCCUPATION | TIME | ☐ AM ☐ PM |

| SOCIAL SECURITY NO. / / | STATE | DRIVER'S LICENSE INFORMATION LICENSE NUMBER | TYPE | EXPIRES |

| AGE | RACE | SEX | EYES | HAIR | HEIGHT | WEIGHT | DATE OF BIRTH | PLACE OF BIRTH | TATTOOES OR ID. MARKS |

| WHERE ARRESTED | HOW ARREST MADE: ☐ ON VIEW  ☐ CALL  ☐ WARRANT |
| | WARRANT NO.  WARRANT DATE |

OFFENSE(S) SUSPECTED OR CHARGED

| DATE OFFENSE COMMITTED | TIME ☐ A.M. ☐ P.M. | COURT |

| WHERE OFFENSE COMMITTED | TYPE PREMISES | BUSINESS TRADE NAME |

| ARMED  ☐ YES  ☐ NO | CHECK ALL ITEMS WHICH APPLY |
| TYPE WEAPON | ☐ DRUNK  ☐ DRINKING  ☐ CURSED  ☐ RESISTED  ☐ OTHER |
| PREVIOUS ARRESTS | OTHER PERSONS ARRESTED FOR SAME OFFENSE |

| VEHICLE | YEAR | MAKE | MODEL | STYLE | COLOR | LICENSE # | STATE | EXP. | IMPOUNDED ☐ YES | ☐ NO |
| INVOLVED | | | | | | | | | WHERE | |

PROPERTY PLACED IN PROPERTY ROOM

| NAME OF COMPLAINANT | RELATION OF COMPLAINANT & SUSPECT - IF ANY? |

| ADDRESS OF COMPLAINANT, | BEST PHONE | OTHER PHONE |

| WITNESSES NAME | BEST CONTACT ADDRESS | AGE | BEST PHONE | OTHER PHONE | PARENT OR GUARDIAN? |
| 1 | | | | | |
| 2 | | | | | |

NOTE FACTS OF ARREST NOT INCLUDED ABOVE.

| ARRESTEE'S RIGHTS GIVEN BY | DATE | TIME | PLACE |

| RESULTS OF INVESTIGATION | NCIC # |

| ARRESTING OFFICER(S) | REPORT MADE BY | FINAL DISPOSITION |

Use supplementary report for additional information not covered above.

FORM LE 7-1R

G. A. THOMPSON, P.O. BOX 64681, DALLAS, TEXAS 75206

Exhibit 2-6

# LAW ENFORCEMENT INVESTIGATION/COMPLAINT WORKSHEET

## (EXAMPLE ONLY)

DATE: _____ TIME PREPARED: _____

CRIME/COMPLAINT: (1) _____

(2) _____

(3) _____

LOCATION OF CRIME/COMPLAINT: _____

_____

_____

VICTIM(S): _____

_____

_____

SUSPECT(S): _____

_____

_____

EXHIBIT 2-7

# CHECKLIST

- ♦ **Attach detailed statement of victim(s).**

- ♦ **Attach detailed statement of witness(es).**

- ♦ **Attach sketch of the crime/complaint scene.**

- ♦ **Attach photographs of the crime/complaint scene.**

- ♦ **Attach list of stolen/damaged property.**

- ♦ **Attach list of evidence developed/collected.**

- ♦ **Attach information about vehicles involved.**

- ♦ **Attach draft report summary/conclusion.**

EXAMPLE: **About 10:20 A.M., at Joe's Convenience Store, 3286 South Elm Street, Any City, Any State, three men wearing ski masks and jump suits entered the store and used handguns to force a clerk and customers to give them money and jewelry valued at about $5,000. The three men fled, and the clerk, Mr. John Overby, called the police.**

Exhibit 2-8

# CHECKLIST

This summary, written at the scene after your investigation, will provide you with a conclusion, important in report writing (and discussed later in this book). Hours later, this summary will bring your focus to the situation quickly and is the basis for assembling the supporting notes, statements, and other information.

This worksheet can, of course, be in much more detail, according to your situation. The idea of a worksheet is to provide plenty of space for specific information as noted and a few notes which may be important later. All of the blanks required to be filled in on your department's report forms need not be duplicated on your worksheet. As noted in forms, addresses and telephone numbers are called for. It is obvious that anytime you interview a victim, witness, or suspect, you obtain more than a name. You should obtain every shred of identifying data possible. Of course, if you feel a reminder is needed, put it on the worksheet; it is, after all, your personalized way of effectively and efficiently managing the information collected.

EXHIBIT 2-8

# CRIME SCENE WORKSHEET

**TIME AND DATE OF INVESTIGATION:** _____

**LOCATION OF INVESTIGATION:** _____

**INVESTIGATED BY:** _____

**CRIME(S):** _____

**FOUNDED/UNFOUNDED:** _____

**WEATHER CONDITIONS:** _____

**TIME CRIME OCCURRED:** _____

# CHECKLIST

| | |
|---|:---:|
| **LIST ALL VICTIMS (NAME/ADDRESS/TEL NO./EMPLOYER/DL/DOB/POB)** .................................. | |
| **LIST ALL WITNESSES (NAME/ADDRESS/TEL NO./EMPLOYER/DL/DOB/POB)** ............................ | |
| **CRIME SCENE SKETCH** ............................................................................. | |
| **CRIME SCENE PHOTOGRAPHS (EXTERIOR/INTERIOR)** ............................................ | |
| **PHYSICAL EVIDENCE** .............................................................................. | |
| **VICTIM/WITNESS STATEMENTS** ................................................................. | |

EXHIBIT 2-9

# CRIME SCENE SKETCH WORKSHEET

**TIME AND DATE OF INVESTIGATION:** _____

**LOCATION SKETCHED:** _____

**SKETCHED BY:** _____

**CRIME(S):** _____

# CHECKLIST

SKETCH KEYED TO PHOTOGRAPHS ............................................................

MEASUREMENTS KEYED TO SKETCH ............................................................

DIRECTION NORTH INDICATED ............................................................

EVIDENCE LOCATION KEYED TO SKETCH ............................................................

NOT DRAWN TO SCALE—ROUGH SKETCH

LEGEND

NORTH INDICATOR & PHOTOGRAPH KEY

EXHIBIT 2-10

# CRIME SCENE EXHIBITS/EVIDENCE WORKSHEET

**TIME AND DATE OF INVESTIGATION:** ───────────────────────────────

**LOCATION EVIDENCE COLLECTED:** ───────────────────────────────

**EVIDENCE COLLECTED BY:** ───────────────────────────────

**EXHIBITS COLLECTED BY:** ───────────────────────────────

**CRIME(S):** ───────────────────────────────

# CHECKLIST

ALL EVIDENCE PACKAGED, MARKED WITH INITIALS, TIME, DATE, TAGGED ........................ ☐

ALL EXHIBITS COMPLETED, MARKED, SIGNED...................................................... ☐

PROPERTY RECEIPT PREPARED, ISSUED, AND SIGNED ............................................. ☐

Exhibit 2-11

# CRIME SCENE SKETCH WORKSHEET

**LEGEND**

Exhibit 2-12

# PACKAGING YOUR CRIME SCENE INVESTIGATION NOTES

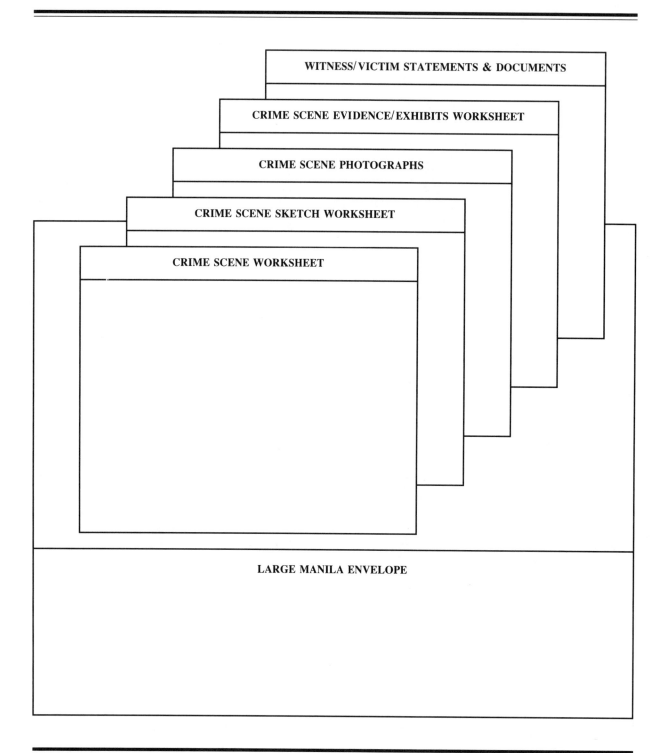

WITNESS/VICTIM STATEMENTS & DOCUMENTS

CRIME SCENE EVIDENCE/EXHIBITS WORKSHEET

CRIME SCENE PHOTOGRAPHS

CRIME SCENE SKETCH WORKSHEET

CRIME SCENE WORKSHEET

LARGE MANILA ENVELOPE

Exhibit 2-13

however, convincing a jury may be another matter. When the witness is called to testify, he or she is looking at the defendant and recognizes him. When you are called to the stand and are questioned by a defense lawyer looking for some technical reason to cause a jury to doubt, he or she will, if possible, play your information against that provided by the witness. If the jury isn't sure who is right, and the lawyer can convince them that an identification error happened, there's a good chance the case will be unsuccessfully prosecuted. Let's say the prosecutor asks you why you placed the description in your report. You answer that it is the same as provided by the witness. However, the lawyer points out that the witness identified the defendant in the court room and asks you how that could happen, since his client is 5 feet, 5 inches tall, weighs barely 150 pounds, has no beard, is not muscular, and does not have a deep voice. The lawyer will claim that some pretrial coaching must have occurred, along with coaching at a line-up prior to arrest, and a lot of other questionable information. Whether his allegations are allowed in the record is not important; the jury heard them, and they begin to wonder who's right. Few if any jurors are interested in convicting an innocent person regardless of the crime. If the case is lost, the witness isn't going to be blamed—you will be blamed, and besides the embarrassment, this can have a profound effect on your law enforcement career. Even within the department superiors question your competence. Maybe you exaggerate or forget and make something up. A prosecutor will hesitate when evaluating your information, wondering if it's accurate.

All that can easily be avoided, and even if a witness changes his or her description in court, you'll come out of it on top, rebutting any attempt by a defense lawyer to discredit your competence. If any question or blame is fixed, it will be on the witness—because you can clearly show how the identifying information was determined by having your identification notebook with you in court.

I suggest you use a three-ring notebook with plastic document protectors. In the notebook, include a basic description guide collection which you can use while interviewing the victims and/or witnesses to a crime, vehicle collision, or situation where descriptions of people, items, or vehicles are important.

Separate from the notebook, create an identification checklist which you can fill out using the notebook as a guide. The completed checklist is a part of your report-writing notes and if necessary can be attached as an exhibit. It can serve you well in court when supported by the notebook. An example of a basic identification checklist and notebook contents is shown in Exhibits 2-14 through 2-18. Remember, the exhibits are guidelines; make your notebook as detailed as you want. However, I don't recommend using actual photographs of people; that will get you into trouble. You can, however, use photographs or copies of photographs of firearms, vehicles, and other objects.

### Step 5: Information Management of Physical Evidence

Law enforcement officers would rarely consider physical evidence as information. It is, as is all evidence, comprised of *things*, and we see no relationship between evidence, especially physical evidence, and our report. It is merely used to solve the case and prove the case in court. That is logical, negative, traditional thinking, and I readily admit that in years past I shared the same viewpoint.

However, our learning and skill development comes to us in layers, not all at once, and at some point, I found that report writing and physical evidence are indeed related; in fact, evidence is essential to the effectiveness of your report. A rule of thumb is: Whatever you write in your report, include in your notes, photograph, or record in any other way, is information. Information is then organized into a comprehensive format, and that becomes your report.

# CHECKLIST EXAMPLE FOR THE IDENTIFICATION OF PEOPLE

From the victim and witnesses—determine: GENERAL DESCRIPTION (used primarily to broadcast immediately)

A description of the assailant(s) to include:

☐ Male (a)                              ☐ Female (b)

☐ Caucasian                            ☐ Black

☐ Oriental                             ☐ Other: _____

☐ Height _____             ☐ Weight _____

☐ Nationality _____        ☐ Complexion _____

☐ Build _____              ☐ Posture _____

☐ Eye Color _____          ☐ Eyeglasses _____

☐ Eyes Alert _____         ☐ Eyes Normal _____

☐ Eyes Droppy _____        ☐ Tattoos _____

☐ Marks, Scars _____       ☐ Age Estimate _____

☐ Hat _____                ☐ Hair Color _____

☐ Mustache _____           ☐ Beard _____

☐ Sideburns _____          ☐ Haircut Style _____

☐ Shirt _____              ☐ Necktie _____

☐ Jacket _____             ☐ Coat _____

☐ Suit _____               ☐ Blazer _____

☐ Trousers _____           ☐ Shoes _____

☐ Weapon _____             ☐ Other _____

SUPPLEMENT TO GENERAL DESCRIPTION (used primarily to enable an effective investigation effort)

Features and Other Characteristics

SEX OF SUSPECT:

☐ Male          ☐ Female

Race

☐ Black          ☐ Caucasian

☐ Oriental       ☐ Indian

EXHIBIT 2-14

# CHECKLIST EXAMPLE FOR THE IDENTIFICATION
# OF PEOPLE

Head Shape and Size

☐ Round     ☐ Flat on top

☐ Long     ☐ Broad

☐ Narrow     ☐ Flat in back

☐ Square     ☐ Bulging behind

☐ Small     ☐ Egg-shaped

Hair and haircut

☐ Long     ☐ Short

☐ Full     ☐ Thinning

☐ Bald     ☐ Curly

☐ Kinky     ☐ Crew Cut

☐ Straight     ☐ Wig/Toupee

☐ Red     ☐ Hazel

☐ Black     ☐ Blond

☐ Brown     ☐ Gray

☐ White     ☐ Neatly Combed

☐ Mussed     ☐ Other: _____

Complexion

☐ Normal     ☐ Scarred

☐ Blotched     ☐ Pock marked

☐ Pale     ☐ Florid

☐ Acne     ☐ Fair

☐ Medium     ☐ Dark

Exhibit 2-14

# CHECKLIST EXAMPLE FOR THE IDENTIFICATION
# OF PEOPLE

Eye Specifics

- ☐ Blue
- ☐ Black
- ☐ Green
- ☐ Large
- ☐ Medium
- ☐ Round
- ☐ Cocked
- ☐ Sunken
- ☐ Albino
- ☐ Glassy
- ☐ Piercing
- ☐ Close-set

- ☐ Brown
- ☐ Hazel
- ☐ Crossed
- ☐ Squint
- ☐ Small
- ☐ Slanted
- ☐ Bloodshot
- ☐ Multicolored
- ☐ Protruding
- ☐ Blinking
- ☐ Dull
- ☐ Bags under

Eyeglasses

- ☐ Plastic
- ☐ Plain lens
- ☐ Thick
- ☐ Bifocal

- ☐ Wire frame
- ☐ Dark lens
- ☐ Normal
- ☐ Monocle

Eyebrows

- ☐ Heavy
- ☐ Dark
- ☐ Bushy
- ☐ Average

- ☐ Thick
- ☐ Light
- ☐ Thin
- ☐ Other: _____

Exhibit 2-14

# CHECKLIST EXAMPLE FOR THE IDENTIFICATION
# OF PEOPLE

Nose

- ☐ Large
- ☐ Wide
- ☐ Narrow
- ☐ Turn-up
- ☐ Short
- ☐ Pug

- ☐ Small
- ☐ Medium
- ☐ Hooked
- ☐ Long
- ☐ Flat
- ☐ Pointed

Mouth Size and Features

- ☐ Small
- ☐ Large
- ☐ Normal
- ☐ Dry lips
- ☐ Lipstick

- ☐ Medium
- ☐ Thin lips
- ☐ Thick lips
- ☐ Moist lips
- ☐ Color _____

Beard and Mustache

- ☐ Mustache/color _____
- ☐ Beard/color _____
- ☐ Long
- ☐ Trimmed
- ☐ Full

- ☐ Short
- ☐ Unkept
- ☐ Other: _____

Teeth

- ☐ Normal
- ☐ Large
- ☐ Cracked
- ☐ Irregular
- ☐ Braces
- ☐ Stained
- ☐ Gaps

- ☐ Missing _____
- ☐ Small
- ☐ Protruding
- ☐ Wide Spaced
- ☐ Close Spaced
- ☐ Fillings
- ☐ Other: _____

Exhibit 2-14

# CHECKLIST EXAMPLE FOR THE IDENTIFICATION OF PEOPLE

Ears

    ☐ Small     ☐ Medium

    ☐ Large     ☐ Other: _____

Chin

    ☐ Jutting     ☐ Receding

    ☐ Pointed     ☐ Normal

    ☐ Square     ☐ Double

    ☐ Dimpled     ☐ Short

Neck

    ☐ Short     ☐ Long

    ☐ Thick     ☐ Slender

    ☐ Other: _____

Shoulders

    ☐ Small     ☐ Medium

    ☐ Broad     ☐ Stooped

Hands and Fingers

    ☐ Small     ☐ Average

    ☐ Large     ☐ Short fingers

    ☐ Stubby     ☐ Long fingers

    ☐ Rings _____

    ☐ Missing _____

Trunk of Body

Chest   ☐ Large     ☐ Average

       ☐ Narrow     ☐ Sunken

Back   ☐ Straight     ☐ Curved

       ☐ Humped     ☐ Bowed

Exhibit 2-14

# CHECKLIST EXAMPLE FOR THE IDENTIFICATION
# OF PEOPLE

Waist
- ☐ Small
- ☐ Large
- ☐ Average
- ☐ Protruding stomach

Hips
- ☐ Broad
- ☐ Thin
- ☐ Average
- ☐ Other: _____

Legs
- ☐ Long
- ☐ Average
- ☐ Straight
- ☐ Short
- ☐ Bowed
- ☐ Muscular

Feet
- ☐ Small
- ☐ Large
- ☐ Average
- ☐ Other: _____

Marks/Scars/Tattoos
- ☐ Tattoos: _____
- ☐ Scars: _____
- ☐ Marks: _____

Speech
- ☐ Normal
- ☐ Coarse
- ☐ Whisper
- ☐ Soft
- ☐ Deep
- ☐ High
- ☐ Vulgar
- ☐ Rough
- ☐ Lisp
- ☐ Strained
- ☐ Harsh
- ☐ Average
- ☐ Raspy
- ☐ Accent
- ☐ Cultured
- ☐ Articulate
- ☐ Drawl
- ☐ Dumb sounding
- ☐ Explain: _____

EXHIBIT 2-14

# CHECKLIST EXAMPLE FOR THE IDENTIFICATION
# OF PEOPLE

Dress/Appearance

☐ Hat or Cap, kind and color

_____

☐ New ☐ Old ☐ Faded

☐ Blouse, kind and color

_____

☐ New ☐ Old ☐ Faded

☐ Dress or Skirt (female), kind and color

_____

☐ New ☐ Old ☐ Faded

☐ Purse/Other (female), kind and color

_____

☐ New ☐ Old ☐ Faded

☐ Trousers, kind and color

_____

☐ New ☐ Old ☐ Pressed

☐ Shoes, kind and color

_____

☐ New ☐ Old ☐ Shined

☐ Shirt ☐ Sweater ☐ T-shirt
Color: _____
☐ New ☐ Old ☐ Worn

Exhibit 2-14

# CHECKLIST EXAMPLE FOR THE IDENTIFICATION
# OF PEOPLE

☐ Necktie    ☐ Bandana    ☐ Ascot

Color: _____

☐ New    ☐ Old    ☐ Worn

☐ Suit    ☐ Blazer    ☐ Jacket

Color: _____

☐ New    ☐ Old    ☐ Worn

Prosthetic Devices

☐ Crutches    ☐ Hearing Aid

☐ Cane    ☐ Braces

☐ Other: _____

Overall Appearance

☐ Neat    ☐ Unkept    ☐ Rumpled

☐ Dirty    ☐ Clean    ☐ Cologne

☐ Groomed    ☐ Mannered    ☐ Crude

Overall Build

☐ Large    ☐ Average

☐ Small    ☐ Tall

☐ Short    ☐ Straight

☐ Stooped    ☐ Agile

☐ Clumsy    ☐ Muscular

Exhibit 2-14

# CHECKLIST EXAMPLE FOR THE IDENTIFICATION
# OF PEOPLE

Mannerisms and habits

☐ Calm          ☐ Nervous

☐ Twitches      ☐ Facial tics

☐ Smokes        ☐ Chews Tobacco

Subconscious mannerisms

☐ Pulling an ear

☐ Scratching or pulling nose

☐ Jingling keys or change

☐ Hitching up pants

☐ Running hand through hair

☐ Other: _____

NOTES AND MEMORANDUMS:

_____

_____

_____

_____

_____

_____

Exhibit 2-14

# ARKANSAS HIGHWAY POLICE
Arkansas State Highway and Transportation Department
## – DESCRIPTION OF SUBJECT –

ROI NO. _____

NAME: _____

ALIAS: _____ SSN: _____

ADDRESS: _____ PHONE: _____

RACE: _____ SEX: _____ DOB: _____ AGE: _____ D.L. NO.: _____

HT: _____ WT: _____ EYES: _____ HAIR: _____ WHERE BORN: _____

SCARS & MARKS: _____

PECULIARITIES: _____ COMPLEXION: _____

OCCUPATIONS: _____

EMPLOYER: _____

EDUCATION: _____

MARITAL STATUS: _____

PARENT'S NAME & ADDRESS: _____

RELATIVES: _____

_____

VEHICLE: _____

PREVIOUS ARRESTS: _____

DATE ARRESTED: _____ PLACE ARRESTED: _____

CHARGE: _____ ARRESTED BY: _____

DISPOSITION: _____

PHOTOGRAPHED: _____ DATE: _____ AGENCY: _____

FINGERPRINTED: _____ DATE: _____ AGENCY: _____

OTHER INFORMATION: _____

_____

_____

_____        _____
INVESTIGATOR                                                            REPORT NUMBER

_____        _____
DATE SUBMITTED                                                         TYPE OF REPORT

A.H.P. FM 6

– FOR OFFICIAL USE ONLY –

Exhibit 2-15

# CRIMINAL DESCRIPTION SHEET

## Physical Description

HEIGHT_____

WEIGHT_____

NATIONALITY (IF KNOWN)_____

COMPLEXION_____

EYES — COLOR — EYEGLASSES
(ALERT — NORMAL — DROOPY)

_____

VISIBLE SCARS, MARKS, TATTOOS

_____

AGE_____

## Method of Escape

DIRECTION_____

LICENSE_____

VEHICLE DESCRIPTION_____

_____

## Remarks _____

_____

_____

HAT

HAIR  COLOR - CUT

BEARD OR MOUSTACHE
SIDEBURNS

SHIRT

NECKTIE

JACKET
OR
COAT

WEAPON

RIGHT
OR
LEFT
HANDED

TROUSERS

SHOES

EXHIBIT 2-16

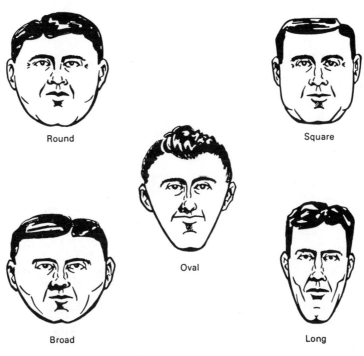

Round

Square

Oval

Broad

Long

## Shapes of Faces

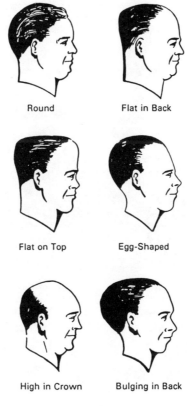

Round

Flat in Back

Flat on Top

Egg-Shaped

High in Crown

Bulging in Back

## Head Shapes

EXHIBIT 2-17

# EYE SHAPES

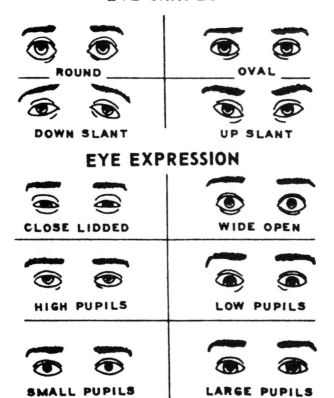

ROUND      OVAL

DOWN SLANT      UP SLANT

# EYE EXPRESSION

CLOSE LIDDED      WIDE OPEN

HIGH PUPILS      LOW PUPILS

SMALL PUPILS      LARGE PUPILS

# EYE BROWS

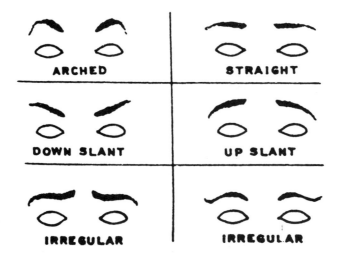

ARCHED      STRAIGHT

DOWN SLANT      UP SLANT

IRREGULAR      IRREGULAR

Exhibit 2-17

SLOPE

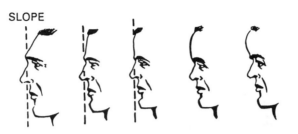

Receding • Medium • Vertical • Prominent • Bulging

WIDTH

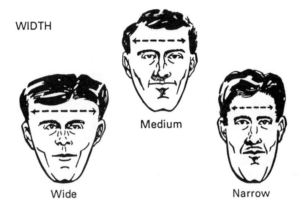

Wide          Medium          Narrow

Types of Foreheads

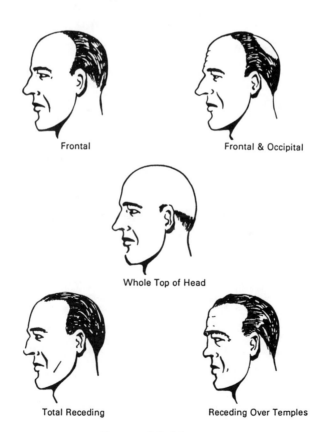

Frontal          Frontal & Occipital

Whole Top of Head

Total Receding          Receding Over Temples

Types of Baldness

Exhibit 2-17

# Types of Noses

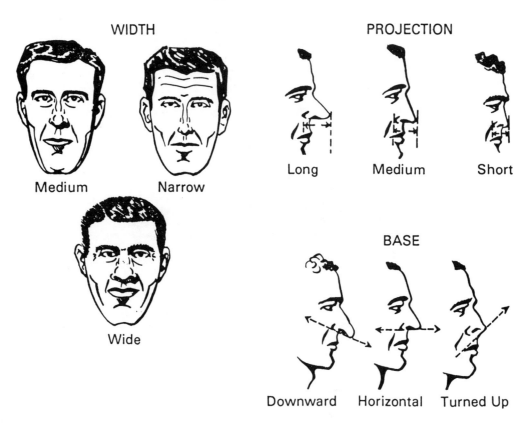

WIDTH

Medium     Narrow

Wide

PROJECTION

Long    Medium    Short

BASE

Downward   Horizontal   Turned Up

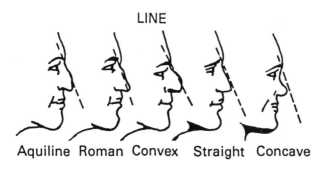

LINE

Aquiline   Roman   Convex   Straight   Concave

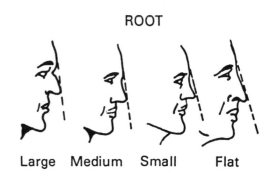

ROOT

Large    Medium    Small    Flat

Exhibit 2-17

## Shapes of Ears

Round

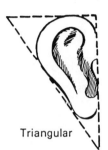
Triangular

Rectangular

## Ear Lobe Characteristics

Descending

Square

Medium

Gulfed

## Setting of Ears

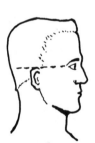
Low

Normal

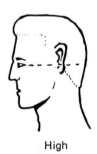
High

Exhibit 2-17

# Types of Mustaches

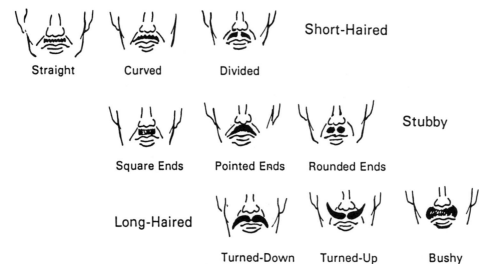

Straight    Curved    Divided    Short-Haired

Square Ends    Pointed Ends    Rounded Ends    Stubby

Long-Haired    Turned-Down    Turned-Up    Bushy

Special Styles    Handlebar    Mandarin    Kaiser

# Types of Beards

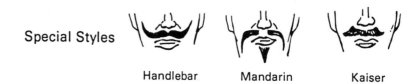

Pointed    Squared    Rounded    Chin Whiskers (Goatees)

Full Beards

Rounded    Squared    Double-Pointed

Special Styles

Van Dyke    Henry VIII    Side Whiskers

Exhibit 2-17

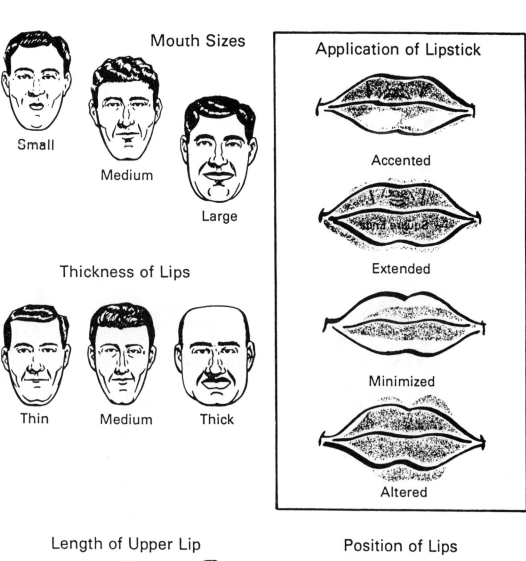

## Mouth Sizes

Small

Medium

Large

## Thickness of Lips

Thin

Medium

Thick

## Application of Lipstick

Accented

Extended

Minimized

Altered

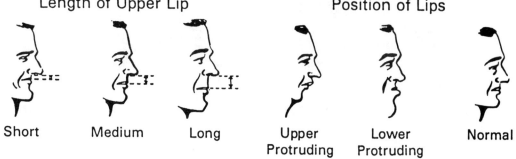

## Length of Upper Lip

Short

Medium

Long

## Position of Lips

Upper
Protruding

Lower
Protruding

Normal

Exhibit 2-17

# Chin Shapes and Characteristics

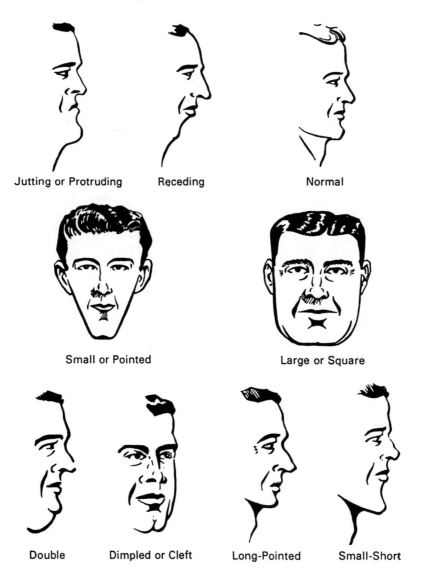

| | | |
|---|---|---|
| Jutting or Protruding | Receding | Normal |

Small or Pointed

Large or Square

| | | | |
|---|---|---|---|
| Double | Dimpled or Cleft | Long-Pointed | Small-Short |

Exhibit 2-17

# Chest Characteristics

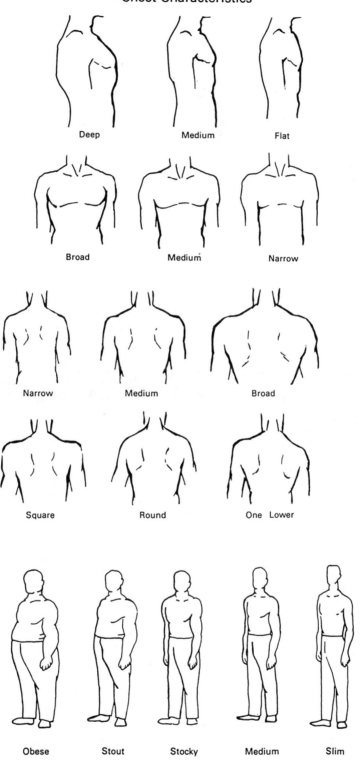

Exhibit 2-17

Exhibit 2-18

Exhibit 2-18

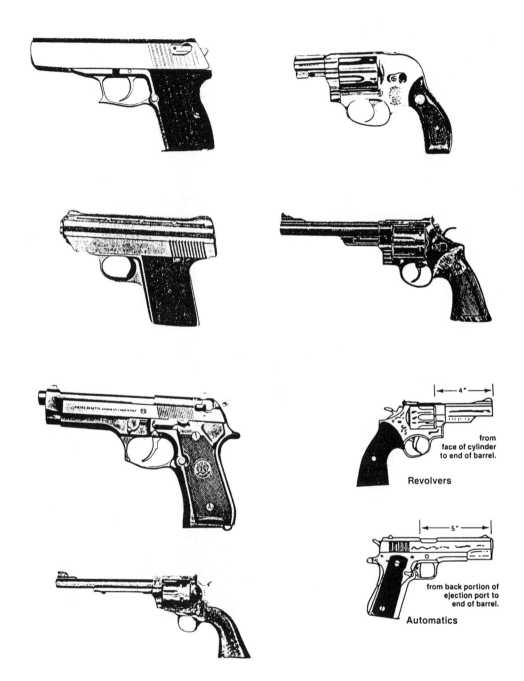

from face of cylinder
to end of barrel.

**Revolvers**

from back portion of
ejection port to
end of barrel.

**Automatics**

EXHIBIT 2-18

We've already mentioned the importance of your report being well written, containing accurate information, and portraying the image of expertise through your writing. Evidence of all kinds, whether it is testimony in written or oral statements you recount, documents, observations, or tangible items collected at the scene of a crime, vehicle collision, or other situation is vital to your report and how you support what you are saying in it.

There may have been a time when a law enforcement officer could build a case and see it through a successful prosecution based on what he or she said happened. Evidence, such as it was, bore no resemblance to our contemporary definition. Today, everything a law enforcement officer says or does is likely to be scrutinized by (1) the department, which does not want to get in a position of libel or create bad politics with the community; (2) the prosecutor, who has no intention of trying cases he or she knows is doomed to failure from the onset, and is adamant about being professionally embarrassed; (3) the courts, which, starting some years ago with the Miranda and similar decisions, accept that officers of the law do not always say what is accurate, make omissions, and may not perform as they should; and finally, (4) the media, always waiting in the wings for a law enforcement error, intentional or incidental. Police mistakes sell papers and make for good ratings for television news programs. In all fairness, perhaps all of these factors have caused law enforcement to become a profession filled with greater competence, which in turn creates greater public confidence.

Remember, your best defense and demonstration of your professionalism depends on how well you manage information, including what you write in your reports. Once you say it in a written report which you sign and date, there's no way to turn back. That's why everything you say in the report must be completely supported, and that's why evidence in any form is important to what you write. It not only solves cases and proves cases in court, but it first proves the information contained in your report.

A good trial lawyer in a court environment can normally defeat the testimony of a witness or victim unless you have physical evidence to support not only what you are saying in your report but to support the testimony of witnesses and victims equally. For example, a witness tells you that one of the men participating in an armed robbery fired a shot into the air inside the store. You receive their story, put it into a written statement, and include it in your report. No other witnesses recalls hearing a shot fired. Your investigation at the scene reveals a plausible reason for others not hearing the shot, such as that one witness has a marked hearing problem, the gun used was .22 caliber and doesn't make noise when fired, music was playing on the store's speakers at the time, refrigeration units were running, and all other witnesses were lying on the floor near the refrigeration units. One witness hears the shot, tells you, puts it in writing, and six others say that nothing like that happened as far as they know. What are you going to write in your report? Armed robbery is a serious crime, but its seriousness and impact increase when the assailant fires shots. You'll probably answer my question by shrugging and commenting that you'll just say it like it is: One says a shot was fired and six deny it. But are you sure that's a prudent way to respond?

Two suspects of the robbery case are identified, arrested, and brought to trial. They also found enough money someplace, probably from other robberies, to hire a skilled criminal defense lawyer. The lawyer's first strategy is your report, because his experience has taught him that somehow he must discredit witnesses, including you, and create a doubt in the jurors' minds that his clients are guilty of the crime as charged. The prosecutor can place them in the store, and a gun was found in their apartment during a warrant search after their arrest. But they deny the whole event, saying it's a mistake in identity. They both claim to have made a purchase and left the store prior to the robbery, and that's why the witnesses have remembered them. Since they live in the vicinity of the four witnesses, their lawyer will claim that's a contributing factor in his clients' identification. The defense lawyer will get you on the stand, and one of the first questions will be about the shot fired. He knows that your report says nothing about finding any evidence of that happening, and if you say there is, he'll ask why it isn't in the report. Whatever you say from then on is only going to make it worse—I've been in such a situation, and I took the lesson seriously.

However, let's change the scenario slightly and say that you take the time to validate the story of the one out of seven witnesses. You find a tiny hole, and you photograph it. You crawl into the attic space and find a .22 caliber slug lodged in thick insulation. Regardless of what the other witnesses say, you can support the one and explain in your report why others probably didn't hear the shot being fired. Most important, however, your report says something and backs it up with supporting information, combining testimony, observation, photographs, and physical evidence. It makes your report accurate, makes the case stronger, and you can be certain that the defense lawyer, on reading the expertise demonstrated in your report, will avoid having you say anything in court. Of course, it isn't up to the defense lawyer: The prosecutor will get a great deal of mileage from your competence.

Information management does include physical evidence. Collect it, document it, and, as you do, think about how to use that information to support other elements in your report. Remember, everything a law officer does is based on the need to convey information to others by writing a report.

As you collect physical evidence, remember that it must have integrity from the time you find it until it's introduced as an exhibit in court. That point is critical. It does no good to convert an item of physical evidence into information in your report if its integrity is lost. Make sure you tag it, mark it, and make out a chain of custody document like the one shown in Exhibit 2-19.

Exhibits 2-20 through 2-23 provide you with helpful and valuable guidance for evaluating your field procedure, writing accurate reports and evaluating physical evidence as you convert it into information.

# ARKANSAS HIGHWAY POLICE

Arkansas State Highway and Transportation Department

## — PROPERTY RECEIPT —

| ITEM NO. | DESCRIPTION OF ITEMS | DATE | ROI NO. |
|---|---|---|---|
| | | | |
| | | | |
| | | | |
| | | | |
| | | | |
| | | | |
| | | | |
| | | | |
| | | | |
| | | | |
| | | | |
| | | | |

| ITEM NO. | RELINQUISHED BY: | DATE/ TIME | LOCATION | | DATE |
|---|---|---|---|---|---|
| | RECEIVED BY: | | PURPOSE | | DATE |
| | RELINQUISHED BY: | | RECEIVED BY: | | |
| | | | | | |
| | | | | | |
| | | | | | |
| | | | | | |
| | | | | | |
| | | | | | |

A.H.P. FM 2

**— FOR OFFICIAL USE ONLY —**

Exhibit 2-19

56

| ITEM NO. | RELINQUISHED BY: | DATE | RECEIVED BY: | DATE |
|---|---|---|---|---|
| | | | | |
| | | | | |
| | | | | |
| | | | | |
| | | | | |
| | | | | |
| | | | | |
| | | | | |
| | | | | |
| | | | | |
| | | | | |
| | | | | |
| | | | | |
| | | | | |
| | | | | |
| | | | | |
| | | | | |
| | | | | |
| | | | | |

**A.H.P. FM 2A**

**– FOR OFFICIAL USE ONLY –**

Exhibit 2-19

# GUIDEPOSTS FOR LAW ENFORCEMENT OFFICERS

## PRELIMINARY INVESTIGATION AND DIRECT ACTION TIPS
### (A Memory Aid to Patrol Officers at a Crime Scene)

**P**  Proceed to the scene with safety and dispatch.

**R**  Render assistance to the injured.

**E**  Effect arrest of perpetrator when present.

**L**  Locate and identify witnesses.

**I**  Interview complainant and witnesses.

**M**  Maintain scene and protect evidence.

**I**  Interrogate suspects when appropriate.

**N**  Note all conditions, events, and remarks.

**A**  Arrange for collection of evidence.

**R**  Report incident fully and accurately.

**Y**  Yield responsibility to detectives when directed.

Exhibit 2-20

58

# PHYSICAL EVIDENCE CATEGORIES

## BASIC INVESTIGATIVE REMINDERS

1. TOOLMARKS. Include all physical conditions where it was evident that one object, serving as the tool, acted on another object, creating impressions, friction marks, or other striations. A screwdriver, pry bar, automobile fender, or gun barrel all might produce toolmarks.

2. FINGERPRINTS AND PALMPRINTS. All such prints, latent or visible, including footprints and prints from gloves or other fabric.

3. ORGANIC, BOTANICAL, ZOOLOGICAL MATERIAL. Excreta, residues from botanical sources, and food stains are typically classified in this category.

4. GLASS AND PLASTIC FRAGMENTS. Broken, chipped, or splintered glass or plastic discovered in locations suggesting that it was the result of an offender's actions or was transferred to such persons.

5. TRACKS AND IMPRESSIONS. Skid and scuff markings, shoe prints, depressions in soft soil or vegetation, and all other forms of tracking. Toolmarks would not be included in this category.

6. PAINT. Liquid or dried paint in positions where it could have been transferred to individuals passing by. Freshly painted areas, cracked and peeling surfaces on window sills, and automobile collisions are frequent examples.

7. CLOTHING. Items of clothing which were left, carried, removed, or discarded by offenders. Individual fiber characteristics would be included in this category.

8. WOOD FRAGMENTS. The fragmenting and splintering of wood (prying, kicking, and chapping actions at entry points are the most frequent examples).

9. DUST. Instances where dust (all forms of surface contamination) was disturbed by an offender in the criminal act.

10. CIGARETTES, MATCHES, AND ASHES. Discovery of any of these combustible materials, or their remains, in positions which suggest their relationship to offenders.

11. PAPER. Cases where the paper itself may be traced to its original position or orientation, and where latent prints or other contaminating substances may be present on the surface of the paper.

12. SOIL. The presence of soil or soil-like material in locations where identification or individualization seemed possible.

13. FIBERS. Includes both natural and synthetic fibers, discovered primarily on sharp corners or edges, or on surfaces where electrostatics or mechanical forces caused a transfer.

Exhibit 2-21

# PHYSICAL EVIDENCE CATEGORIES

## BASIC INVESTIGATIVE REMINDERS

14. TOOLS AND WEAPONS. Instances where tools and weapons are found at crime scenes or in automobiles and where there exists a strong possibility that such objects were involved in a criminal act.

15. GREASE AND OIL. Any lubricant or fatty substance, sometimes possessing environmental contamination. Position might suggest its relevance to a crime scene.

16. CONSTRUCTION AND PACKING MATERIAL. All those substances found in work areas and not belonging in any other category.

17. DOCUMENTS. Written or printed paper capable of being traced to a particular person or instrument, including suicide and robbery notes—as well as cases involving the theft of equipment, such as check protectors—where a document could be traced back to that instrument.

18. CONTAINERS. All bottles, boxes, cans, and other containers which held substances or other residues of an informative nature.

19. METAL FRAGMENTS. Materials found near industrial machinery and scenes of collisions, and other scrap with high probability of being transferred to offenders.

20. HAIR. Any suspected animal or human hair found in an environment with reasonable probability of being traced to an offender.

21. BLOOD. Any suspected blood, liquid or dried, animal or human, present in a form suggesting a relationship to the offense or the individuals involved.

22. INORGANIC AND MINERALOGICAL MATERIAL. Inorganic substances not falling in any other categories.

23. MISCELLANEOUS. All other physical phenomena.

Exhibit 2-21

# A CHECKLIST FOR LAW ENFORCEMENT OFFICERS ON THE COLLECTION AND PRESERVATION OF PHYSICAL EVIDENCE

DEFINITION OF EVIDENCE:

A. *Webster's* (Third International Edition): That which is legally submitted to a competent tribunal as a means of ascertaining the truth of any alleged matter of fact under investigation before it.

B. *Black's Law Dictionary* (5th Edition): Any species of proof, or probative matter, legally presented at the trial of an issue, by the act of the parties and through the medium of witnesses, records, documents, exhibits, concrete objects, etc. for the purpose of inducing belief in the minds of the court or jury as to their contention. (Taylor v. Howard, 111 R.I. 527, 304 A.2d 891, 893)

C. *Relevant evidence*: Evidence having any tendency to make the existence of any fact that is of consequence to the determination of the action more probable or less probable than it would be without the evidence (Fed. Evid. R. 401). Evidence, including evidence relevant to the credibility of a witness or hearsay declarant, having any tendency in reason to prove or disprove any disputed fact that is of consequence to the determination of the action (Calif. Evid. Code). Evidence which bears a logical relationship to the issues in a case trial.

D. *Physical*, *real*, *tangible*, *laboratory*, *latent* are all adjectives to describe the type of evidence which the FBI laboratory and identification divisions examine.

E. *Essential elements of proof* (*evidence*): Indispensably necessary; important in the highest degree; requisite. That which is required for the continued existence of a thing (Black's).

F. Anything which a suspect leaves at a crime scene or takes from the scene or which may be otherwise connected with the crime is physical evidence.

PURPOSE OF COLLECTION AND EXAMINATION OF PHYSICAL EVIDENCE

A. Aid in solution of case:

    1. Develop (MO's) or show similar MO's.

    2. Develop or identify suspects.

    3. Prove or disprove an alibi.

    4. Connect or eliminate suspects.

    5. Identify loot, contraband, illegal whiskey.

    6. Provide leads.

Exhibit 2-22

# A CHECKLIST FOR LAW ENFORCEMENT OFFICERS ON THE COLLECTION AND PRESERVATION OF PHYSICAL EVIDENCE

    B.  Prove an element of the offense:

        1.  Safe insulation, glass, or building materials on suspect's clothing may prove entry.

        2.  Stomach contents, bullets, residue at scene of fire, semen, blood, toolmarks may all prove elements of certain offenses.

        3.  Safe insulation on tools may be sufficient to prove violation of possession of burglary tools statutes.

    C.  To prove a theory of a case:

        1.  Footprints may show how many were at scene.

        2.  Auto paint on clothing may show that person was hit by car instead of otherwise injured.

## CRIME SCENE SEARCH

Defined as a planned, coordinated legal search by competent law enforcement officers to locate physical evidence or witnesses to the crime under investigation. To be effective:

    A.  Conduct preliminary examination of crime scene—protect the area.

    B.  Photograph the scene.

    C.  Sketch the scene.

    D.  Conduct search and collect the evidence.

## COLLECTION OF PHYSICAL EVIDENCE: FIVE THINGS TO KEEP IN MIND

    A.  Obtain it legally:

        1.  Warrant

        2.  Consent

        3.  Incidental to arrest

    B.  Describe it in notes:

        1.  Location, circumstances, how obtained

        2.  Date, chain of custody

        3.  How identified

Exhibit 2-22

# A CHECKLIST FOR LAW ENFORCEMENT OFFICER ON
# THE COLLECTION AND PRESERVATION OF PHYSICAL EVIDENCE

C. Identify the property:

   1. Use initials, date, case number.

   2. Preferably on evidence itself. Liquids, soils, tiny fragments must be placed in suitable container, sealed and marked on outside.

D. Package it properly. One case to one box:

   1. Use suitable containers such as round pillboxes, plastic vials, glass or plastic containers, strong cardboard cartons.

   2. Seal securely against leakage.

   3. Package each item separately—avoid appearance of leakage or contamination.

   4. If wet or bearing blood, air dry before packaging (except arson cases where hydrocarbons are present).

E. Maintain chain of custody—keep it as short as possible:

   1. Same person or persons should find, seal, initial, and send evidence, if possible.

   2. Maintain in locked vault, cabinet, or room until shipped.

   3. Send by traceable, registered means (i.e., railway express, air express, registered mail, personal delivery or bonded courier service).

## HOW TO REQUEST AN FBI LABORATORY OR FINGERPRINT EXAMINATION

A. All requests should be made by letter, in duplicate.

   1. If evidence is for laboratory or combined laboratory-fingerprint examination, it should be marked, "Attention: FBI Laboratory."

   2. If evidence is exclusively for fingerprint examination, mark it, "Attention: FBI Identification Division, Latent Fingerprint Section."

B. Use additional copies of this letter of request as invoices for separate shipments of evidence.

Exhibit 2-22

# A CHECKLIST FOR LAW ENFORCEMENT OFFICERS ON THE COLLECTION AND PRESERVATION OF PHYSICAL EVIDENCE

C. Information in letter should include:

1. Complete names of all suspects and victims for indexing purposes.

2. Nature of violation or type of crime (character of case).

3. Date and place of crime.

4. Brief facts of case insofar as they pertain to the requested examinations—such as whether soil is from a filled area, whether evidence was weathered or otherwise altered, whether preservative was added to blood, or whether evidence is in the form in which it was at the time of crime. Include photos if you feel they will assist.

5. How evidence is being sent (herewith or under separate cover).

6. List of evidence correlated with notes on wrappings of individual items if appropriate.

7. What examinations or comparisons are to be conducted.

8. Whether to be compared with evidence in other specific cases.

9. Reference to previous correspondence in this or related cases.

10. What disposition would be made of the evidence.

11. If submitted for laboratory examination, include statement certifying that same evidence has not and will not be subjected to examination by other experts for prosecution in the same scientific field. (This statement not required regarding fingerprint evidence.)

12. Statement as to whether any civil action has been specifically indicated by interested parties.

13. Whether expeditious examinations is needed.

DEPENDENT ON SIZE AND TYPE, EVIDENCE MAY BE SUBMITTED

A. Herewith.

1. Certain small items of evidence, such as fraudulent check or latent lifts, may be submitted along with the letter of request. This method is limited to items not endangered by transmission in an envelope.

2. Letter of request would state, "Submitted herewith are the following items of evidence."

Exhibit 2-22

# A CHECKLIST FOR LAW ENFORCEMENT OFFICERS ON
# THE COLLECTION AND PRESERVATION OF PHYSICAL EVIDENCE

B.  Under separate cover.

Generally used for shipment of numerous and/or bulky items of evidence. Letter of request would state, "Submitted under separate cover by (method of shipment) are the following items of evidence."

1.  Submit letter of request, in duplicate, by appropriate mailing method (i.e., registered).

2.  Pack bulky evidence securely in box.

3.  Seal box and mark as evidence. Mark "Latent" if necessary.

4.  Place copy of transmittal letter (letter of request) in envelope and mark "Invoice."

5.  Attach envelope containing invoice to outside of sealed box.

6.  Wrap sealed box in outside wrapper and seal with gunned paper. Attach any necessary labels.

7.  Address to:   Director
Federal Bureau of Investigation
Washington, D.C. 20535

or to appropriate addressee if a state laboratory is used.

8.  If packing box is wood, tack invoice envelope to top under a clear plastic cover.

### STEPS AN OFFICER SHOULD TAKE BEFORE CALLING AN FBI LABORATORY OR LATENT FINGERPRINT EXPERT TO TESTIFY

A.  Ascertain whether the expert is a necessary witness. Is his or her testimony material? Can report be stipulated to by defense?

B.  Advise the bureau when and where the trial is to be held as far in advance as possible to avoid conflicts with other commitments.

C.  Advise regarding the expected duration of the trial and the exact date on which the expert will be needed.

D.  Arrange for a conference between the prosecutor and the expert prior to the time the expert takes the stand and arrange for the expert's early release after testifying.

E.  Furnish the names of opposing experts, if any, and ascertain whether the prosecutor contemplates using any other experts.

Exhibit 2-22

# QUICK GUIDE
# FOR LAW ENFORCEMENT OFFICERS:
# LEADING DECISIONS ON SCIENTIFIC EVIDENCE

### PHOTOGRAPHS
Udderzook v. Commonwealth, 76 Pa. 340 (1874)
Held that photographs are admissible into evidence as an established means of
producing a correct likeness.

### HYPNOSIS
People v. Ebanks, 49 P. 1049 (Cal. 1898)
Held that testimony of hypnotist that defendant, while under hypnosis, denied
guilt, was properly excluded at the trial.

### FINGERPRINTS
People v. Jennings, 96 N.E. 1077 (Ill. 1911)
Held that experts in fingerprint identification may give opinions as to whether
fingerprints found at the scene of a crime correspond with those of the accused.

### PALMPRINTS
State v. Kuhl, 175 P. 190 (Nev. 1918)
Held that there is no basic difference between fingerprints and palmprints, and
that qualified fingerprint experts are competent to give opinion evidence on
palmprint comparisons.

### FINGERPRINTS
Commonwealth v. Loomis, 113 A. 428 (Pa. 1921)
Held that a defendant may introduce testimony to prove that a fingerprint found
at crime scene was not made by him or her.

### FINGERPRINTS
Lamble v. State, 114 A. 346 (N.J. 1921)
Held that fingerprints on door of stolen automobile may be shown by
photograph and door need not be produced.

### SCIENTIFIC TESTS
Frye v. United States, 293 F. 1013 (1923)
Held that in refusing to admit evidence of deception tests, in order for the results
of scientific tests to be admissible, the scientific principle involved must be
sufficiently established to have gained general acceptance in the particular field
to which it belongs.

EXHIBIT 2-23

66

# QUICK GUIDE
# FOR LAW ENFORCEMENT OFFICERS:
## LEADING DECISIONS ON SCIENTIFIC EVIDENCE

### TRUTH SERUM
State v. Hudson, 289 S.W. 920 (Mo. 1926)
Held that in excluding doctor's testimony of denial of guilt by defendant while under the influence of truth serum, truth serum testimony in the present state of human knowledge was unworthy of serious consideration.

### FIREARMS
Evans v. Commonwealth, 19 S.W. 2d 1091 (Ky. 1929)
Held that expert testimony of firearms identification was admissible for the purpose of establishing the guilt of the accused and the fact that it was highly technical was no bar.

### LIE DETECTOR
State v. Bohner, 246 N.W. 314 (Wis. 1933)
Held that although the lie detector technique "may have some utility at present or may ultimately be of great value in the administration of justice, it must not be overlooked that a too hasty acceptance of it during this stage of development may bring complications and abuses that will overbalance whatever utility it may be assumed to have."

### URINE ANALYSIS
Novak v. District of Columbia, 160 F.2d 588 (1947)
Held that a urine analysis was inadmissible in a drunken driving case where the prosecution did not show that the sample analyzed by the chemist was the same one which the police officer had left at the laboratory.

### PHOTOGRAPHS
McKee v. State, 44 So.2d 781 (Ala. 1950)
Held that the courts take judicial notice that the act of photography is generally relied on for depicting the resemblance of persons, objects, things, and places; and the fact that photographs of homicide victim were made after exhumation did not render them inadmissible.

### CORPUS DELICTI
People v. Cullen, 234 P.2d 1 (Cal. 1951)
Held that the rule that the corpus delicti must be established independently of admissions by the defendant is to protect him or her against the possibility of fabricated testimony.

EXHIBIT 2-23

# QUICK GUIDE
# FOR LAW ENFORCEMENT OFFICERS:
# LEADING DECISIONS ON SCIENTIFIC EVIDENCE

## MOVING PICTURES
People v. Hayes, 71 P.2d 321 (Cal. 1937)
Held that sound moving pictures of defendant making voluntary confession to
police officer was admissible.

## FOOTPRINTS
Commonwealth v. Vartollni, 13 N.E.2d 382 (Mass. 1938)
Held that footprints, like fingerprints, remain constant throughout life and furnish
an adequate and reliable means of identification.

## FINGERPRINTS
State v. Helms, 12 S.E. 2d 243 (N.C. 1940)
Held that evidence of identification of fingerprints found in a place where crime
was committed, under such circumstances that they could only have been
impressed at the time when the crime was committed, may be sufficient to support
a conviction in a criminal prosecution.

## BLOOD GROUPING
Beach v. Beach, 114 F.2d 479 (1940)
Held that blood grouping tests cannot prove paternity and cannot always disprove
it, but they can disprove it conclusively in a great many cases.

## LIE DETECTOR
State v. Kolander, 52 N.W.2d 458 (Minn. 1952)
Held that admission of evidence of defendant's refusal to take lie detector test was
error inasmuch as the lie detector has not yet attained such scientific and
psychological accuracy, nor its operators such sureness of interpretation of results
shown therefrom, as to justify submission thereof to a jury as evidence of the guilt
or innocence of a person accused of crime.

## LIE DETECTOR
Leek v. State, 245 P.2d 746 (Okla. 1952)
Held that "this does not exclude the lie detector as an instrument of investigation,
nor does it mean that its use may not be shown as a step leading up to a confession,
but the results should not be brought out by either the state or the defendant."

## BLOOD TESTS
Breithaupt v. Abrams, 352 U.S. 432 (1957)
Held that evidence of taking blood test by hospital technician while intoxicated was
admissible over objection that it shocked the conscience or offended due process.

Exhibit 2-23

# THREE

## How to Create an Information Management System with a Case File Based on Your Report Format

Most of us in the law enforcement profession are comfortable with policies and procedures which create systems for effective control of situations we are likely to encounter on duty. For example, we must call for a back-up unit before we enter a building to investigate a suspicious activity. I've noted over the past thirty years that in the absence of clearly stated department procedure, officers tend to be less effective.

When you investigate a crime, vehicle collision, or other situation, the requirements should be spelled out in a procedural manual your department issues each officer. If no manual is provided, you rely on procedure unwritten or taught in an academy you attended, or word of mouth from a supervisor. The procedure may tell you what you're supposed to do at a scene and in what order you're to do it. I have read dozens of department-level manuals across the country over the years and talked to officers about what they do at a scene. I've found that department procedures, both written and unwritten, are rarely followed and are not designed with any continuity in mind, including the requirement of report writing. Ironically, word-of-mouth procedural instructions are the general rule, the rationalization being that written procedures are for eyewash, legal actions (lawsuits), and disciplinary action against an officer.

A high-ranking officer once recounted an experience he encountered some years ago regarding a state law enforcement agency. The chief called him to his office and told the officer, who was well educated and knowledgeable, to write a complete policy and procedural manual for the agency, replacing hit-and-miss memos and information handed out previously. The officer said that two months later he handed a draft to the chief, who readily approved it and, when it was printed and bound, told him to deliver it personally to each unit in the state and make certain each officer signed for a copy. A month later the task was complete, and the officer was promoted to an operational position within headquarters that involved supervising field operations and training. Some weeks later, he said the information coming from around the state indicated that no one was adhering to the policy and procedure manual he labored to compile, write, and distribute. He called the chief's attention to the disregard. The chief leaned back in his chair and laughed, explaining that the manual was just for show, that he ran the agency, and it would operate as he wanted it to, not what a book said to do. The officer is now retired, but his story is regrettably not uncommon. The prob-

69

lem is that a veiled appearance of competence creates negative traditions that are detrimental to the law enforcement profession.

However, you can create a procedural system of your own if one is lacking or not followed (the former is most prevalent, in my experience). Those which do exist are never consistent with the reports, which must support actions, and perhaps that's why they're ineffective.

## EIGHT STEPS TO CREATING A PERSONALIZED INFORMATION MANAGEMENT SYSTEM DESIGNED FOR WRITING DYNAMIC LAW ENFORCEMENT REPORTS _____

Teams of officers responding to investigate a crime or vehicle collision scene accompanied by laboratory technicians, photographers, and specialists is largely reserved for television and motion picture productions; in most departments officers go alone, or in pairs if they're lucky.

In some large city departments, special teams do exist but rarely become involved in cases other than homicides or some other significant crimes. In most cases, law enforcement budgets are not sufficient to field an army of specially trained officers. In the majority of departments, each officer is expected to handle most situations. The information in this chapter is intended for those officers. Of course, it is applicable to any law enforcement officer.

As noted in chapter 1, the concept of information management, mostly what contemporary law enforcement officers do, must be focused on the final management element—writing a report. The system discussed in this chapter is specifically designed to help you do that and to excel at the same time.

Most reports I've read are at best wishy-washy. They tend to be laboriously boring, ineffective, and confusing. Remember, your reports reflect a certain image to your readers. When I read an ineffective report, my first mental image is of an officer who fumbles around a great deal. To some degree our profession encourages that attitude, although I'm sure the suggestion is not intentional. I've even noted in reputable, long-time law enforcement equipment catalogs that a popular product sold is titled: "Patrol Latent Print Kit," which is a well-designed kit for developing latent fingerprints at a crime scene. It is the kind of kit you would be comfortable with and be able to do a good job with. The description of the item makes my point: "Designed for patrol officers who combine crime scene search with regular patrol duties. EXCELLENT PUBLIC RELATIONS TOOL." That suggests, at least to me, that the reason for buying and having the kit with you at a scene is for show, not for competent effort. Although our job involves a degree of public relations or helping the public to understand our profession and problems, it doesn't involve being sham artists. However, this ad is the best example I've found of a negative traditional attitude, especially in the treatment of burglary complaints. The sham involves talking to a few people, throwing some fingerprint powder around for effect, and filing a brief report. I hope that kind of activity is a shock to you and does not sound familiar, but I know if you've been around law enforcement for a while, it does.

This kind of attitude relates to traditional report writing: There's just not enough time to do it right, and there's so many burglaries, the perpetrators will never be caught anyway. However, there is plenty of time, and when you do the job right, writing dynamic reports, the percentage of solved cases increases. The way to save time and do an expert job at a scene is to develop a personalized system that is directly keyed to your written report.

Your system, in turn, organizes and manages your information. Your personalized procedure at the scene enables you to collect the information in the order of your report format. Not only will you be a good report writer, but you'll find that using this system increases your effectiveness and efficiency. Here are the suggested steps to follow at a crime scene—but you develop your own system that works for you and your reporting requirements; this is meant only as a thought-provoking guide.

*The scenario*: To avoid confusion, we'll set up a scenario for the following examples. You are on patrol and receive instructions on the radio to investigate a complaint of burglary at an office building.

*When you arrive*: Several employees of a small company are in the office suite where the burglary took place. They are milling around enjoying the excitement of being within a crime scene, and especially getting paid to mill around. The owner, looking as though the weight of the world were on his shoulders, meets you at the door and hurriedly tells you that someone broke into his private office over the weekend and stole expensive equipment, including typewriters, computers, software and computer files, and a lot of other items.

### Step 1: Control the Scene

Move all the people, including the owner, into a neutral area, such as an adjacent conference room or waiting area. Don't allow anyone to leave. Ask the owner if anyone who came to the office has already left; if so, obtain their identity first so you'll have it for later contact. Next, collect the driver's licenses of each witness at the scene. Once you have them or other suitable identification, you can safely ask the people to wait in another place until called for interview. You need not be concerned that they will slip away to avoid being involved or to avoid being identified. It's interesting to observe how differently people act from the point of law enforcement arrival to their actions just a few minutes later, especially when they believe their name will be recorded and questions asked. The idea is to find a place where each witness or potential witness can be interviewed privately. Witnesses overhearing each other's information are likely to conform their testimony, and you wind up with the same story or without any useful information at all. Once the witnesses are secured, you can move on to step two.

### Step 2: Satisfy the Essential Elements First

Remember that on the way to the crime scene, you began writing your report by thinking about the essential elements of proof the law requires to establish and prove that a burglary and theft actually occurred. You began making that determination by interviewing the owner and surveying the office suite. The owner shows you the entrance door to the office suite, and it is obvious that someone pried it open. Thus, element one of burglary is satisfied: forced entry. The owner shows you a storage room and explains the now-empty shelves contained computer systems and software, computer records, typewriters, administrative supplies, and other items. He has a sheaf of invoices and inventory sheets in his hand which contain serial numbers, costs, and companies where the items were purchased. Now you have the next element of proof: theft of something valuable. The owner points out his private office, which was rifled, and tells you about a number of expensive items that are missing. If the complainant hasn't already provided them, ask him or her for proofs of purchase—bills of sale, invoices, cancelled checks, or some other document. There is no question in the example presented here that burglary and theft occurred. Even if staged by the owner to collect insurance (always a possibility), a crime did occur.

### Step 3: Collect Information with Written Statements

Begin interviews with the owner, followed by the remaining witnesses, collecting that information in written statements. Don't waste time having the owner or any of the witnesses write their own statements; you'll be inundated with useless, irrelevant information that often raises more questions than are answered. Always obtain written statements, even if the person being interviewed says he or she knows nothing about the crime. I learned this lesson a long time ago, recounting what someone said to me in a report, only to learn later that they changed their story or denied having said what I recorded. Either way, you lose credibility. Always prove what you say in your report, and in the case of interviews, the best possible way is to include a written statement exhibit, signed and dated by the interviewee. If later they change their story, or deny telling you certain information, they are discredited because you have their signed statement. Comparing signed statements has also helped me solve a number of cases, since people involved or with knowledge often will get their stories confused or say something out of character to hide their involvement.

### Step 4: Collect Information with Photographs and Sketches

Always photograph the scene and specific items of evidence discovered before doing any other kind of processing. After interviewing the owner and employees and obtaining written statements from all, you're satisfied that a crime did occur and the items described were there at the close of the previous business day and missing on the beginning of the next business day. Since crime scenes normally contain some indication of who committed the crime, in generic terms at least, and since the scene will be entirely different five minutes after you leave, now is the time to record what you observed. Remember, support the information in your report. Written statements and photographs provide that kind of support. Since photographs hours or days later can be confusing, especially to those who have not been to the scene, make a rough sketch of the entire area and indicate the location of key evidence, different rooms, location from where you took a photograph, along with any other information that helps you remember or clarify some other information in your report. Depending on your artistic abilities, a rough sketch can be attached as an exhibit to your report; at a minimum, you'll have it for your notes file.

### Step 5: Search the Scene for Latent Fingerprints and Other Physical Evidence

With the office clear of people and distractions, you are able to envision what burglar(s) may have done and how they did it. Following that general pattern, beginning at the point of forced entry, you can spot any item left behind along with areas likely to have been touched or handled by the perpetrators. All the information should be developed and collected. Keep a good record, including photographs of items and developed finger, palm, or hand prints before moving them to your collection. (I once contributed to the conviction of a burglar, using glove prints that the laboratory matched to a pair of leather gloves found in possession of a suspect.) Each item, regardless of how small, can provide information leading to a successful effort. You're there to collect information, not just fill out a form and leave, as is too often the case in burglaries.

### Step 6: Collect Information from Molds and Casts

Forced entry marks made with prybars or other tools can be valuable information, along with footprints, tire tracks, or other items that provide strong support for your report. Each should be photographed before, during, and after a cast or mold is taken. In some cases, it's wise to take the entire object marked. Casts and molds are not attached as exhibits; instead you discuss them in your report, attach photographs, and explain they are in the department's evidence room or at the laboratory, whichever applies.

Investigation resource kits which help you collect information discussed in Steps Four and Five is reviewed in Exhibit 3-1.

### Step 7: Review Your Findings Before Leaving the Scene

The steps presented here reflect a simplistic crime scene processing procedure; however, this book is about writing your report, not how to conduct detailed investigations. I've tried here to point out the minimum steps to take which provide you with credible, competent information to write about in your report. I've pointed out that physical objects, as well as documentary and interviews, are indeed information. Before you leave, go back over the information you have and look over the scene. Once you leave, the scene will not be the same again, even a few minutes later.

### Step 8: Write Your Report

Your report should begin something like this:

> Between 5:00 P.M., Friday, July 10, 1990 and 8:00 A.M., Monday, July 13, 1990, at Acme Research and Development Company, Incorporated, 3492 South Elmwood Drive, Any City, Any State, person(s) unknown forced entry into an office suite and stole office equipment and other items valued at about $47,000.

With this statement or declaration, you've established your professional reputation and competence and, as you'll see in later parts of this book, everything else in your report supports or substantiates your declaration. A busy reader will appreciate your clarity and brevity. After you have learned to apply the information throughout this book, including the reporting format, readers will glance at your declaration and know that it is accurate and supported. They will have no reason to continue reading unless there is interest or a need to do so.

## ORGANIZE YOUR PROFESSIONAL IMAGE BY WRITING DYNAMIC REPORTS _____

Politicians and public figures often spend vast sums of money to perfect their image. In many cases, doing so is the only feasible way to satisfy public interest in an individual or organization he or she represents. Law enforcement officers should consider their image as well, but in different ways. Your concern is your personal and professional image. You want the public, your family, and friends to view you as an honest, professional law enforcement officer who gives 100% to fulfill your obligations and responsibilities. You also want to convey that same image to your superiors and others who influence your career. When I first entered the law enforcement profession, a seasoned officer gave me some negative, traditional advice which is often still heard today: "Look sharp, act like you know what you're doing, and you'll do okay. But don't do too good a job; higher-ups get nervous when officers steal their thunder." In those days, skill wasn't expected in any great degree; things were far different. Today, looking sharp is still a good part of the law enforcement positive tradition—no one wants to see a sloppy uniform, dirty patrol car, or run-down equipment. However, my advice after thirty years of international experience in this profession is: Young and old officer alike should look sharp, know exactly what they're doing at all times, and if they don't think they know what to do, find out fast. The days of "winging it" are long past. The fact that troubles me, from what I observe and interviews I conduct around the country, is that not all officers have discerned that expertise is what the taxpayer wants, and their career depends on it.

Earlier, we mentioned that reports are the one permanent and most important tool for letting superiors, the criminal justice system overall, and others (like the media) know how well you perform your job. Dynamic, forceful report writing coupled with looking sharp and being highly skilled will shape your image in a positive way. One without the others doesn't make the grade. You must always look as impeccably dressed as possible, be highly skilled,

# EQUIPMENT COMPONENT GROUPS

Effective criminal and other types of investigations call for proper tools used for the collection of information (including physical evidence) and information management. The following equipment component groups are suggested as a minimum, and as guidelines for developing effective capabilities. In cases where you believe some item should be added, space on the checklist is supplied for that purpose. Since each checklist in this book is designed to be independently copied and used, component groups may be repeated in several or all checklists, depending on the type of crime and items needed for your effective, complete investigative effort.

EXHIBIT 3-1

# INVESTIGATION RESOURCE KITS

**Photographic Equipment Kit. Components as a minimum:**

☐ 35mm Camera. Suggest compact types with features including, Day and Date imprint on negative, automatic focusing, exposure, flash, winding and rewinding, this model camera available from a variety of manufacturers should also have automatic adjustments for ASA or ISO settings by reading DX coded film commonly available.

☐ 35mm film. Suggest color film with a 100 ASA rating for normal light, 200 or higher according to lack of light. The higher a numerical ASA/ISO rating number, the less light needed to make an acceptable photograph. High speed film also tends to have more grain and lead to photographs that exclude small, important details.

☐ Instant photograph cameras, Polaroid which provides an immediate photograph and a backup should film not be exposed properly or defective. (With flash capability)

☐ Instant photograph film cartridges—suggest color (5 packs)

☐ Camera cleaning and maintenance kit (available at most camera equipment stores)

☐ Camera Tripod

Other items according to personal preference:

☐ _____

☐ _____

☐ _____

EXHIBIT 3-1

# INVESTIGATION RESOURCE KITS

**Evidence Collection Kit. Components as a minimum:**

- ☐ Ultra Violet (UV) light
- ☐ Stainless steel scissors
- ☐ Wire cutters
- ☐ Putty knife
- ☐ Liquid sampling jars
- ☐ Item container jars
- ☐ Stainless steel spatula
- ☐ Small Flashlight
- ☐ 6-foot steel tape
- ☐ Evidence tags
- ☐ Ball point pens
- ☐ Graph paper pads
- ☐ Lined paper pads
- ☐ Assorted plastic bags
- ☐ Diamond tip scribe
- ☐ 12 inch wooden ruler
- ☐ Traffic template

- ☐ Large stainless steel tweezers
- ☐ Needle-nose pliers
- ☐ Standard pliers
- ☐ China marking pencils
- ☐ White chalk
- ☐ Disposable syringes w/needles
- ☐ Pen knife
- ☐ Electric lantern, free-standing
- ☐ 50-foot steel measuring tape
- ☐ Evidence/property receipts
- ☐ Pencils, #4 or drawing
- ☐ Plain paper pads
- ☐ Clipboards
- ☐ Evidence sealer tape
- ☐ Assorted envelopes
- ☐ Crime scene template
- ☐ Evidence marker tape (ruler)

Personal preference items:

- ☐ _____
- ☐ _____
- ☐ _____

- ☐ _____
- ☐ _____
- ☐ _____

NOTES AND MEMORANDUM:

_____

_____

_____

Exhibit 3-1

# INVESTIGATION RESOURCE KITS

**Casts and Molds Kit. Components as a minimum:**

- ☐ Liquid silicone rubber
- ☐ Silicone rubber putty
- ☐ Dust and dirt hardener
- ☐ Oil coater
- ☐ Stainless steel mix bowl
- ☐ Spatula mixer
- ☐ Casting frames
- ☐ Clay
- ☐ Six-foot rule
- ☐ Spray power unit
- ☐ Stainless steel spoon

- ☐ Silicone rubber catalyst
- ☐ Plaster casting material
- ☐ Base builder
- ☐ Vertical surface brush
- ☐ Steel spatula
- ☐ Flexible rubber bowls
- ☐ Spray cleaner
- ☐ Reinforcement mesh
- ☐ Evidence Tags
- ☐ Gallon water can
- ☐ Stainless steel scribe

Personal preference items:

- ☐ _____
- ☐ _____
- ☐ _____

- ☐ _____
- ☐ _____
- ☐ _____

NOTES AND MEMORANDUM:

_____

_____

_____

_____

_____

_____

_____

EXHIBIT 3-1

# INVESTIGATION RESOURCE KITS

**Post Mortem Fingerprint and Cadaver Taking Kit (components)**

- ☐ Porelon post mortem tool.
- ☐ Post mortem porelon inking tool.
- ☐ Post mortem print card holder.
- ☐ Left hand post mortem cards.
- ☐ Right hand post mortem cards.
- ☐ Ink cleaner towelettes.
- ☐ Tissue builder solution.
- ☐ Tissue cleaner.
- ☐ 3cc molded hypodermic syringes.
- ☐ Absorbent cotton.
- ☐ Surgeon's gloves (disposable).

Exhibit 3-1

# INVESTIGATION RESOURCE KITS

**Latent Fingerprint Kit. Components as a minimum:**

- ☐ Black latent powder
- ☐ White latent powder
- ☐ Copper latent powder
- ☐ Black magnetic powder
- ☐ White magnetic powder
- ☐ Permanent magnetic wand
- ☐ White hinged lifters (12)
- ☐ White rubber lifters (12)
- ☐ Roll transparent lift tape
- ☐ Lifted print backing cards
- ☐ Towelettes (12)
- ☐ Scissors, stainless steel
- ☐ Tape measure, 12 foot
- ☐ Toothbrush, soft
- ☐ Small flashlight
- ☐ Envelopes, paper assorted
- ☐ Wooden ruler, 12 inch

- ☐ Gray latent powder
- ☐ Red latent powder
- ☐ Silver latent powder
- ☐ Gray magnetic powder
- ☐ Fiberglass filament brushes (6)
- ☐ Transparent hinged lifters (24)
- ☐ Black hinged lifters (12)
- ☐ Black rubber lifters (12)
- ☐ Roll frosted lift tape
- ☐ Fingerprint pad
- ☐ Large magnifying glass
- ☐ Tweezers, large, stainless steel
- ☐ Screwdriver set, assorted
- ☐ Pen knife
- ☐ Electric free-standing lantern
- ☐ Plastic bags, assorted sizes
- ☐ Ninhydrun aerosol spray

Personal preference items:

- ☐ _____
- ☐ _____
- ☐ _____

- ☐ _____
- ☐ _____
- ☐ _____

Exhibit 3-1

# DIAGRAMS

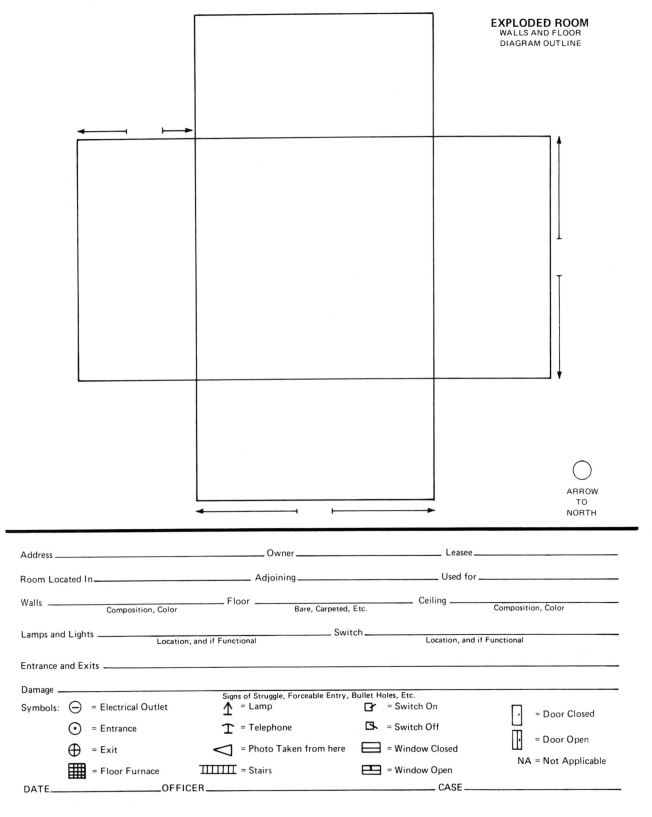

**EXPLODED ROOM**
WALLS AND FLOOR
DIAGRAM OUTLINE

ARROW
TO
NORTH

Address _____ Owner _____ Leasee _____

Room Located In _____ Adjoining _____ Used for _____

Walls _____ Floor _____ Ceiling _____
       Composition, Color         Bare, Carpeted, Etc.         Composition, Color

Lamps and Lights _____ Switch _____
       Location, and if Functional        Location, and if Functional

Entrance and Exits _____

Damage _____
       Signs of Struggle, Forceable Entry, Bullet Holes, Etc.

Symbols: ⊖ = Electrical Outlet    ↑ = Lamp    ☑ = Switch On    ▯ = Door Closed

⊙ = Entrance    ⊤ = Telephone    ☒ = Switch Off    ▯ = Door Open

⊕ = Exit    ◁ = Photo Taken from here    ▭ = Window Closed    NA = Not Applicable

▦ = Floor Furnace    ⅢⅢ = Stairs    ▱ = Window Open

DATE _____ OFFICER _____ CASE _____

EXHIBIT 3-2

82

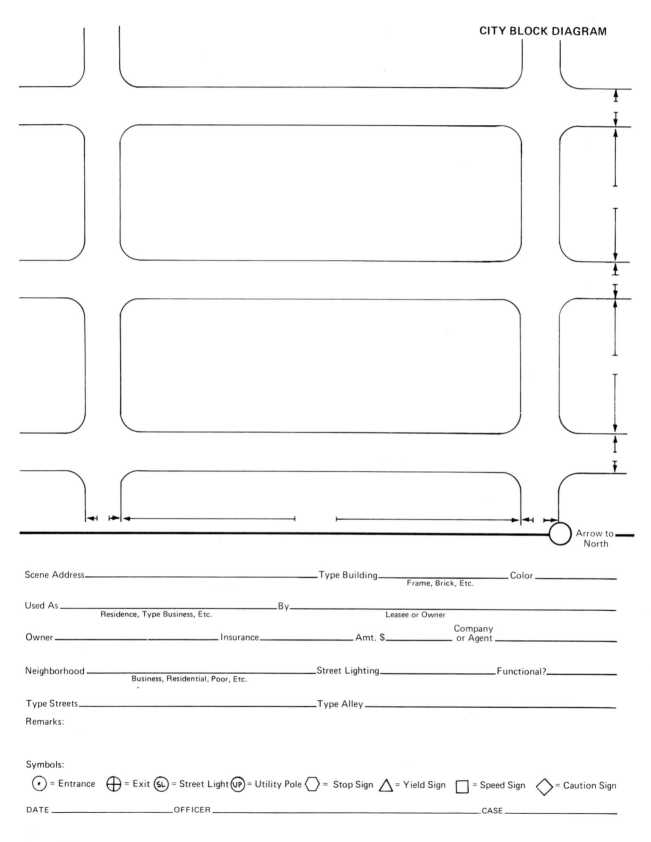

**CITY BLOCK DIAGRAM**

Arrow to North

Scene Address _____ Type Building _____ Color _____
Frame, Brick, Etc.

Used As _____ By _____
Residence, Type Business, Etc.                    Leasee or Owner

Owner _____ Insurance _____ Amt. $_____ Company or Agent _____

Neighborhood _____ Street Lighting _____ Functional? _____
Business, Residential, Poor, Etc.

Type Streets _____ Type Alley _____

Remarks:

Symbols:

(•) = Entrance  ⊕ = Exit  (SL) = Street Light  (UP) = Utility Pole  ⬡ = Stop Sign  △ = Yield Sign  ☐ = Speed Sign  ◇ = Caution Sign

DATE _____ OFFICER _____ CASE _____

EXHIBIT 3-2

Sirchie Labs Form No. CSD 11 ©

**Symbols:**  ⊙ = ENTRANCE  ⊖ = ELEC. OUTLET  ⊡ = SWITCH ON  ◀ = PHOTO TAKEN FROM HERE
⊗ = EXIT  🕯 = LAMP  ⊡ = SWITCH OFF  ⴲ = CENTER LINE

**DIRECTION**

╂

**Scale:** ¼″=

**Case:** .

1=_____  A=_____
2=_____  B=_____
3=_____  C=_____
4=_____  D=_____
5=_____  E=_____
6=_____  F=_____
7=_____  G=_____
8=_____  H=_____

ADDRESS
or Distance and
Direction to
Nearest Known
Point

Scene Used As:

Observations & Measurements Made:

Date: _____ Time: _____ To: _____

By: _____ Asst. by: _____

Drawing no.: _____ of _____ Part(s)

Drawn by: _____ Date: _____

**Weather:** Scene temp: _____ Outside: _____ Wind from: _____ Speed: _____ mph Sky: _____ Precipitation: _____ Road cond.: _____

EXHIBIT 3-3

84

## INJURY SYMBOLS

| IDENTIFYING MARKS | GUNSHOT WOUNDS | SHARP INSTRUMENT WOUNDS | BLUNT FORCE INJURY |
|---|---|---|---|
| (S) = Scar | ⠌⠄ = Shotgun Pellets | (—) = Stab | ⊥ = Fracture- broken bones |
| (T) = Tattoo | (·) = Entrance | (≡) = Incise - cut - slash | ⊗ = Laceration - tear |
| (D) = Deformity | ⊕ = Exit | (⠢) = Puncture(needle, nail, ice pick) | ⊗ = Fracture with laceration |
| | | | ⊜ = Abrasion-scrape-scratch |
| | | | (III) = Contusion - bruise |

### BODY DIAGRAM
**FRONT AND BACK VIEWS**

VICTIMS HT._____
in inches

SCALE _____

LOCATE EACH INJURY BY GIVING DISTANCE FROM TOP OF HEAD AND RIGHT OR LEFT OF MIDLINE

Victim _____ Location _____ Reported _____
Address or Location Found                    Time        Date

Scene                          Body                    Body
Temp._____ Time _____ Temp. _____ Time _____ Temp. _____ Time _____ Heat Loss _____
2 Hour Interval

Position of Body _____ Rigor Present? _____ Location _____ Time _____
Neck, Trunk, Arms, Legs

Lividity _____ Color _____ Time _____ Fixed? _____
Location

Last Ate                                    Last Seen                Death
What_____ Time _____ Date _____ Alive _____ Date _____ Noticed _____ Date _____
Time                        Time

Injury _____

Remarks: _____

**INVESTIGATION BEGAN** _____ DATE _____ OFFICER _____ DEPT. _____
Time                                                              (SEE OTHER SIDE)

EXHIBIT 3-4

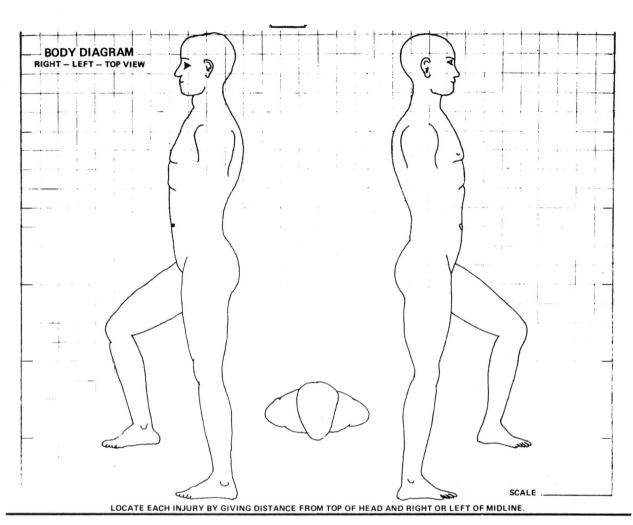

**BODY DIAGRAM**
RIGHT — LEFT — TOP VIEW

SCALE _____

LOCATE EACH INJURY BY GIVING DISTANCE FROM TOP OF HEAD AND RIGHT OR LEFT OF MIDLINE.

Name _____ A.K.A _____ S.S. # _____

D.O.B. _____ Age _____ Race _____ Sex _____ Ht. _____ Wt. _____ Hair _____ Eyes _____ Glasses? _____
                                                          in inches                    Length-Color

Marks
Scars, Tatoo's _____ Rt. -Left Handed _____

How Dressed _____
                          Describe clothing type, color, make, size, laundry mark, etc.

Address _____ Phone _____ Occupation _____ Hobby _____
                                                                                            or other interest

Recent Health
Complaints _____ Doctor _____ Phone _____ Last Seen _____

Medication                        Medication
Prescribed _____ Found At Scene _____
                                                  List Dr., Pharmacy, Date Prescribed & Amount found in each container

Recent Problems _____ Amount Insurance _____ Agent _____
                    Marital, Business, Financial, Social

Found By _____ Address _____ Res. Phone _____ Bus. Phone _____

Notified
Who? _____ Time _____ Date _____ Body moved by _____

                                                  Coroner, Dr.                          At
Time _____ Date _____ To _____ Medical Examiner _____ Scene? _____

                                                                          Probable cause
Autopsy? _____ By _____ Time: _____ Date: _____ of death _____

EXHIBIT 3-4

and always be receptive to formal, in-service, or self-help training. You demonstrate all your expertise when you write and file your reports.

A prosecutor, the courts, juries, insurance companies, the media, and the general public aren't primarily interested in your image from a viewpoint of uniform and resume. They are looking for a way to find out how you think, and that's done through reading what you write.

## ABOUT YOUR EQUIPMENT

Collecting and managing information requires the right equipment and tools. I've mentioned some of the requirements and suggested options. Items such as cameras, latent fingerprint kits, and taking casts and molds are all necessary for collecting and managing information.

I am aware that many departments are weak in the equipment area, primarily because of budget limitations. Convincing taxpayers that more and more money is needed for maintaining a highly professional department is not an easy task. So, in most departments, the capability isn't there at all, or limited. I've visited departments which have one latent print kit and nothing else except a broken-down camera. That department needs the items, recognizes it, but is forced to do without because the purse string holders aren't convinced of the requirements.

I recently observed a training class in which the trainer initiated a discussion about equipment. Several officers whimpered about the shortage of adequate equipment, and with obvious approval from a majority, one officer commented: "If the department don't care, I don't care. When the department issues the stuff, I'll use it. Until it's issued I'll just do what I can." If I had the authority, those officers would now be searching for a new profession. I'm well aware of the financial burdens always plaguing law enforcement officers, and I know that the problem exists for a majority of law enforcement departments. But is it really an excuse?

Over the years, I too grew weary and embarrassed about doing without needed equipment. However, the end result is not that your department will look incompetent: *You* are going to be branded as incompetent, not caring, and unprofessional. I came to realize that professional excellence must begin with my ability to demonstrate my competence, and that meant "personalizing" my equipment, another term for buying it yourself. With a family and a modest salary, it's difficult, but it can be accomplished with some planning effort.

It's vitally important to your career that you write dynamic reports. You can only do that with accurate and complete information resources. Acquiring that information and managing it properly, in part, requires specialized equipment. It might be difficult to find ways of acquiring what you need, but in the long run any sacrifices or creative budgeting will pay you back many times over. Somehow, if your department isn't able to supply all the equipment, then you'll have to "personalize" it if you're interested in remaining in the profession and moving up the career ladder.

## DEVELOP THE RESOURCES NEEDED TO WRITE EFFECTIVE, EFFICIENT, DYNAMIC LAW ENFORCEMENT REPORTS—A REFERENCE CHECKLIST

♦ *What business are we in?*

The majority of a law enforcement officer's duty time is used for information management.

- *Where does negative and positive tradition fit into information management?*

  Positive tradition supports cherished elements of the profession, while negative tradition interferes with information management, including reports.

- *When do you begin writing your law enforcement report?*

  Establishing accurate direction and focusing on the task at hand requires you to begin writing your report mentally enroute to the scene of a crime, vehicle collision, or other situation.

- *How does having the right equipment affect your ability to collect and manage information?*

  Having personalized equipment and tools that work for you helps to organize your procedure of collecting information and manage it right through report writing.

- *How will an excellent information management system force you to be effective, efficient, and professional?*

  Developing a personalized information management system for case file management in five steps enables dynamic report writing and recordkeeping.

- *How does creating a personalized information management system based on report requirements and formats make a difference?*

  Remember, the purpose of investigating a complaint or situation is not to solve the case, but to write a dynamic report. When you have sufficient information to write that kind of hard-hitting, factual, and complete report, the case is often solved through that information.

- *Why is your professional image important, and how does it relate to report writing?*

  Your reports are the only recurring, permanent means of demonstrating your consistent competence, professional growth, and devotion to your law enforcement career.

# FOUR

## How to Develop Your Law Enforcement Report Writing Strategy: Narrative Versus Expository

Traditional law enforcement writing styles are narrative and, as a result, lack impact and are inefficient for information management. Narrative writing, ironically, is a style used to tell stories, not convey factual information. Mystery writers use narrative style because it allows them to start at the beginning of a story and to have a controlled unfolding, releasing a clue and misdirection at nearly the same time. Whenever you want to tell a story, use the narrative style of writing. It's obvious that our reports should not be telling a story. Instead, we must present a forceful, dynamic summary of factual information collected on a specific event such as a crime, vehicle collision, or other situation.

The expository style of writing should always be used in law enforcement reports (there are exceptions, which I'll discuss later). The organization of an expository writing style is as follows: Start with your conclusion; then spend the rest of your report writing supporting that conclusion.

Those who read and act on information you provide in your report are busy and in a hurry to stop reading and take action. Your job as a law enforcement report writer is to organize information you collected during your investigation of a specific event as quickly, efficiently, and effectively as possible. Never make your readers wonder what you're getting at or spend their valuable time decoding what you do say. The following examples will clarify the need for you to adopt expository style report writing.

### A COMMON NARRATIVE-STYLE LAW ENFORCEMENT REPORT

On July 12, 1990, Mr. George Smith contacted this department on the 911 number and reported that a burglary had occurred at his residence located at 540 East Elm Street. When this officer arrived at the residence, I found Smith and his wife Linda Smith sitting on a porch. Mr. Smith explained to me that they own a small cabin on Loon Lake and often go there for the weekend. Last Friday night, about 9 P.M., George and Linda Smith left their resident on Elm Street and traveled to their cabin at Loon Lake, arriving about 10:30 P.M. Smith said that he personally checks the house on Elm Street before they leave, making sure all the windows and doors are locked, and the timers he installed on the lamps throughout the house are working and set properly for the season. He said that he always tries to have the lights come on and off inside the house in about the same way and same

89

time as they would if he and his wife were home. Smith said he always alerts a couple of neighbors, and they pick up newspapers and any other items delivered so passersby won't notice the house is vacant.

Smith took me to the north side of the house and pointed out a window that appeared to be damaged from a forced entry. The windowpanes above the lock located at the center of the window were broken out, and there were pry marks at the bottom of the window. The screen was lying on the ground. Smith said the window sticks, and probably after unlocking it, the perpetrator was still unable to get it open (which explains the pry marks). Since the window was still closed and probably stuck, the perpetrator apparently gave up trying to enter in this manner.

Smith then took me to a rear door which leads into a screened porch. He said that door is locked with a hook, and the door inside the porch which leads into the kitchen of the house is locked with a deadbolt lock. The screen on the porch door was ripped, probably with a knife (judging from the clean cut), and the perpetrator was able to reach in and unhook the hook. The inside door was pried with some kind of heavy prybar around the deadbolt area, causing extensive damage to the door. The perpetrator was successful in gaining entry through this door.

Inside the house, several kitchen cabinet doors were open, along with several drawers, indicating that the perpetrator was looking for silver flatware or anything else of value. Smith noted that the dishes and food on the kitchen table indicated that the perpetrator ate some of the food, which Smith indicated was kept in the refrigerator. Included on the table was a partially used quart of milk, a glass appearing to have been used to drink the milk, a partial loaf of bread, a jar of mayonnaise, a flatware knife and spoon, and an opened partial package of ham slices and a partial package of cheese slices.

Smith took me to the living room and showed me where a television set and stereo system had been, with the marks clearly shown on the carpet. Then he showed me the bedroom where several dresser drawers were opened and their contents scattered around on the floor. He pointed out that his wife kept her jewelry in one of the drawers whenever they left the house for the weekend, and it was missing. The jewelry was contained in a wooden jewelry box about the size of a cigar box, made of polished mahogany, which plays a tune when opened. It was a gift from Smith to his wife on their twenty-fifth anniversary. The jewelry, according to Smith, was worth about $5000, including several items of gold and a couple diamond rings.

Smith showed me through the rest of the house, which had apparently been searched by the perpetrators: Desk drawers were opened, papers were scattered on the rug, and in the dining room a server was rifled. Smith said that his wife kept a family heirloom chest of antique silver which had belonged to her grandmother and a silver serving set that his mother gave them as a wedding present. Both were missing and valued at about $5000. Smith said he didn't know what else might be missing but would carefully look through the house and drawers and report any further thefts.

This officer processed the scene for latent fingerprints but found none. Smith was asked to save the door and window casing which showed tool marks, since he remarked both would have to be replaced. No other evidence was found.

Smith said he would call his insurance company and also drop off a list of anything else found stolen along with the value. No suspects are known at this time.

For comparison, I'll replace this scenario written in traditional narrative style with expository style, as shown in the following example.

Between July 10 and July 12, 1990, at 540 East Elm Street, Any Town, Any State, persons unknown forced entry at a residence and stole personal property valued at more than $15,000; the property of Mr. George Smith.

All further information is contained in attached exhibits, including a written statement taken from George and Linda Smith separately. A list of stolen items, photographs, a sketch of the crime scene (both interior and exterior), closeup photographs of tool marks, molds taken (held in the evidence room but listed along with their location), and other pertinent information, such as statements of neighbors, are contained in the investigator's statement. (This procedure is discussed later in this book.)

If you are a busy reader, which would you prefer? All the people who read your report have dozens to read each day. If you're a patrol officer and crimes such as burglary are referred to a detective bureau for follow-up investigation, your report is forwarded to them. Whoever has to read and make decisions based on your information is interested in one thing: what happened, in as brief a manner as possible.

The first example, often in greater detail, goes on and on with useless information. Obviously, Mr. Smith contacted the department, or you wouldn't have been dispatched to investigate. Where the Smiths were when you arrived is not relevant to the case. The list goes on. My point is: Tell the reader the date, place, crime, and extent along with an arrest or identification of the perpetrator(s) or that they are unknown at the time of the report.

When your reader scans the second example, he or she knows what to do with the report in seconds. It's referred elsewhere, placed in an open case file, or whatever other action is normally taken at your department. If for some reason the reader wants to know all the details (for instance, a detective who is looking for patterns similar to other residential burglaries), he or she has the option of reading all your detailed exhibits. Give your readers the bare facts and let them decide whether to use valuable time to read the details.

Perhaps your reader wants to read your report selectively—for example, statements, your investigator's statement, or your sketch or photographs. With an expository-style report, that choice is easy because each supporting element is organized and listed.

Even when your reader intends to read every word of your reports, he or she is a better reader and can discern the case having received the conclusion first. Reading experts have found that an overview is important if the reader is to understand difficult or detailed information. They advise that it's unwise to provide isolated bits of information. First declare what information the reader is going to receive; then the bits of information are no longer isolated. Armed with an overview, it's far easier for your report readers to understand the details.

There is another important reason you should get to the point fast: If you don't tell your reader in advance what your important points are, he or she might arrive at some conclusion other than you intended. Remember, when presented with information, everyone has a different perception. Don't let that happen in your report writing. You control what your reader gets out of your writing by declaring early what he or she should get out of it.

## MAKE SURE YOU HAVE ALL THE INFORMATION IN YOUR REPORT IN SIX IMPORTANT STEPS

Expository writing style does not exclude information; instead, it's an effective, efficient system of managing information. Use the following guide, not only for your writing, but in every phase of your investigative effort.

## Who Questions

a.   Who discovered the crime?

b.   Who reported the crime?

c.   Who saw or heard anything of importance?

d.   Who had a motive for committing the crime?

e.   Who committed the crime?

f.   Who helped the perpetrator?

g.   With whom did the suspect associate?

h.   With whom are the witnesses associated?

## What Questions

a.   What happened?

b.   What crime was committed?

c.   What are the elements of the crime?

d.   What were the actions of the suspect?

e.   What do the witnesses know about the case?

f.   What evidence was obtained?

g.   What was done with the evidence?

h.   What tools were employed?

i.   What weapons were utilized?

j.   What knowledge, skill, or strength was necessary to commit the crime?

k.   What means of transportation were used in the commission of the crime?

l.   What was the motive?

m.   What was the modus operandi?

n.   What is the value of the stolen property?

## Where Questions

a.   Where was the crime discovered?

b.   Where was the crime committed?

c.   Where were the suspects seen?

d.   Where were the witnesses during the crime?

e.   Where was the victim found?

f.   Where were the tools and weapons obtained?

g.   Where did the suspect live?

h.  Where did the victim live?

i.  Where did the suspect spend his or her leisure time?

j.  Where is the suspect now?

k.  Where is the suspect likely to go?

l.  Where was the suspect arrested?

## When Questions

a   When was the crime committed?

b.  When was the crime discovered?

c.  When was notification received?

d.  When did police arrive at the scene?

e.  When was the victim last seen?

f.  When was the suspect arrested?

## How Questions

a.  How was the crime committed?

b.  How did the suspect get to the scene?

c.  How did the suspect get away?

d.  How did the suspect get the information necessary to enable him or her to commit the crime?

e.  How was the crime discovered?

f.  How did the suspect secure the tools and weapons?

g.  How were the tools and weapons utilized?

h.  How much damage was done?

i.  How much property was stolen?

j.  How much skill, knowledge, and strength was necessary to commit the crime?

## Why Questions

a.  Why was the crime committed?

b.  Why was the particular tool utilized?

c.  Why was the particular method employed?

d.  Why are the witnesses reluctant to talk?

e.  Why was the crime reported?

Your conclusion is not always written in the same order; in fact, it rarely is. I normally like to structure my conclusion in this order: *when, where, who, how, what, why.*

The following conclusion is written according to this structure, using the previous scenario:

> Between July 10 and July 12, 1990 (*when*); at 540 East Elm Street, Any Town, Any State (*where*); persons unknown (*who*); forced entry at a residence (*how*); and stole personal property (*what*); valued at more than $15,000 (*why*); close with the victim's identification if known, in this case Mr. Smith.

Each case has its own set of circumstances and degree of complexity. I've written reports which involved multiple offenses, locations, and circumstances. Strive to keep your reports succinct regardless of complexity, as in the following example:

> About 6:00 P.M., July 12, 1990, at Joe's Convenience Store, 1610 South Maple Street, Any Town, Any State, two unidentified men forced a clerk at gunpoint to give them monies contained in the cash register and safe totaling $28,000; the property of Joe's Convenience Store, Incorporated.

> About 6:15 P.M., July 12, 1990, at Joe's Convenience Store, same location, two unidentified men abducted Ms. Mary Jones, a customer in the store, and departed the scene in a late model van.

> About 7:00 P.M., July 12, 1990, at a gravel pit adjacent Route 16, south of Any Town, Any State, two unidentified men raped Ms. Mary Jones and later threw her from their van along Route 16 near Another Town. Ms. Jones was found by a passing motorist and taken to the Memorial Hospital at Another Town.

> At 9:00 P.M., July 12, 1990, on Route 421, north of Some Town, Any State, two men, identified as Carl Jones and Marty Smith, were arrested by State Police and confined in the Blank County Jail pending arraignment and further investigation.

Regardless of complexity and the number of separate crimes related to one initial crime or in some cases revealed during an investigation, each crime can be presented in an expository conclusion. I've had cases in which several pages of summaries are needed. However, as the example shows, your report reader can learn the entire sequence of events quickly and then decide which details to read that are contained in your supporting information and exhibits.

It's important to think about how courts in the criminal justice system operate. A charge or accusation is made first, followed by a step-by-step presentation of evidence supporting that accusation in the form of physical evidence and testimony of victims, witnesses, experts, and others relevant to the case. Your report is the beginning element in the criminal justice system and should always follow a similar pattern. When your report leaves your hands, it is used by the criminal justice system at various levels: by detectives (when applicable), the prosecutor, and the courts. Your report should never be a foreign element that has to be decoded and converted into information which can be used effectively in the system. Instead it must be a part of the system, with a similar format.

You may ask, "If the reader gets all the information in only a fraction of the report, why go to the trouble of writing the rest?" You write the rest of your detailed report to tell and show your reader how you arrived at the conclusion, and to prove it logically. You are also conveying the elements of proof and evidence your reader will use in taking further action. Without the supporting information and exhibits, a reader is not likely to trust your conclusion or perception of the case.

There is a part of your report which precedes your conclusion, but whether it's used depends on your department's forms. That part is the basis for investigation. If your department uses forms, like those shown earlier in this book, the basis for your being there is already described in the filled-in blanks. If, however, you are starting to write your information on a blank sheet of paper, you'll want to tell the reader *briefly*, as a matter of record, how you came to be the investigator in this case. For example, using the scenario of the Smith burglary, your basis for investigation would be as follows:

> At 10:00 A.M., July 12, 1990, Mr. George Smith, 540 East Elm Street, Any Town, Any State, contacted the Any Town Police Department and reported that a burglary was discovered at his residence.

All you're trying to do here is tell the reader that Smith called the department, which obviously sent you to the scene. On the other hand, you may have been driving along Elm Street and Smith flagged you down—in such cases, say that Smith contacted Patrol Officer John Doe instead of the Any Town Police Department.

## WHAT YOU SHOULD DO WHEN THE CONCLUSION IS WRITTEN

Your conclusion is supported with information you collected and is based on your perception of that information. The question your reader will ask is how you arrived at that conclusion, and that's the next step in your report. There are three ways you can organize the supporting information:

- In order of importance
- In logical order
- In chronological order.

Each case has its own personality. Burglaries, for example, are all the same crime, but even when committed by the same person, they are different and have a different set of circumstances. For that reason, you'll have to decide exactly which of the three ways to present supporting information is best for that particular case.

Remember, there is no need for a summary or wrap-up statement at the end of your expository report. Traditionally, law enforcement report writers tend to end their reports with a varying degree of drama—"the butler did it." Readers aren't impressed. In fact, using the expository style of report writing actually encourages readers to stop reading early, by making it easy to do with reliability. The best advice I can give on ending your expository report is: When you have nothing more to add, just stop.

## BREAK WITH TRADITION BY CHANGING SOME OLD ATTITUDES

It's tough to put aside traditions, even negative traditions that we are unable to rationalize, no matter how hard we try. Law enforcement officers often resist expository writing for that reason.

First, putting the conclusion at the beginning is probably opposite of your natural tendency. To do so requires a reversal in the order of your thinking, primarily because you are trained to investigate. When conducting an investigation, you start at the beginning and work your way through to a conclusion. Expository writing is the reverse order of that process. When you write a statement and testify in court, you also tend to say things in the order you learned about them, almost like a diary. However, there is no relationship between the order in which you learned information and the order in which your report reader should learn about it. If your thinking is open minded, you usually learn the supporting facts first and arrive at conclusions last. That is, however, generally the worst possible order for your report reader.

Second, law enforcement officers usually resist expository writing styles because their pride is hurt with the idea that a reader may not read every word of their report. This is especially true if you've done an outstanding job of investigation. You would like every reader to absorb every word, every brilliant action you took, and laud your investigative skill. The truth is, you'll gain far more interest and respect by helping the reader get through the day headache free. You gain far more being a part of the solution than being a part of the problem.

## FIVE IMPORTANT OBJECTIVES AND ADVANTAGES YOUR EXPOSITORY REPORT WRITING SHOULD ACHIEVE

1. ORGANIZATION. Your reports should be organized to tell as much as possible, as accurately as possible, in as few words as possible.

2. CLARITY. Your writing should be so clear that your reader cannot possibly misunderstand the information you're presenting.

3. SPEED. Using expository-style report writing and other information contained in this book, you'll be able to write your reports much faster, probably twice as fast as with traditional narrative writing, without wasting time fumbling over false starts and rewrites. A great deal of your report consists of exhibits already completed at the scene such as statements, lists, and other documents.

4. PROFESSIONAL IMAGE. You'll be able to present important information in a highly professional manner that highlights your attention to relevance, detail, and application of skills.

5. COMPLETENESS. Your reports will reflect a complete case file up to the point of writing, providing your reader with information needed to make decisions.

## REPORT WRITING GUIDELINES

### Organize Your Report

The first objective, organization or comprehensive information management, is an essential element of law enforcement report writing.

Readers of your reports are looking for information in the shortest possible time. It's your job to tell as much relevant information as possible, as clearly and accurately as possible, in as few words as possible. You do that by organizing your report so the reader gets the conclusion first, followed by information supporting your conclusion.

Remember, you're the first link in the criminal justice system, and recalling how cases are presented in court, with the accusation first, supported by the evidence, organize your report compatible with the system.

### Develop Clarity as Part of Your Report Writing Strategy

There's a widespread communications failure in our society. As a result of our improving education system, people can think better than ever before. But most successful, educated adults cannot write well enough to transmit their thoughts to others. The law enforcement profession now has officers with higher educational levels than ever before, due in part to many department-sponsored programs for higher education tuition assistance. State-supervised minimum standards and certification programs are constantly being upgraded; longer academy training and more stringent curriculum are instituted. Many departments fund in-house seminars, in-service training, and send as many officers as possible to a variety of specialized seminars around the country. Officers are required to think, are trained to think through tough situations; but noticeably lacking is an emphasis on report writing.

Most law enforcement officers have one of two problem tendencies: one to overwrite, and the other to underwrite. Both problems are stimulated by traditional narrative style writing, which forces an officer to tell a story rather than state the facts.

In any communication there is a sender and a receiver. The information being communicated exists in the sender's brain as electricity, not words. If communication succeeds, the same information will end up in the receiver's brain as electricity. But we can't transmit directly with electrical signals, so we convert the information from electricity to words, which can be written or spoken. Either way, it must be clear. Clarity ensures that the information is received in the same way it is intended to be sent.

Once you've grasped the concept of expository writing, you'll be writing with clarity and will begin reaping the benefits of pleased readers.

## Write with Accuracy and Speed and Save Valuable Time

It seems there is never enough time, and the more we are required to accomplish, the more valuable time becomes to us. Earlier in this book, we talked about the considerable amount of time law enforcement officers spend collecting and writing information, all under an umbrella of information management. However, much of the writing time is wasted because of traditional narrative style presentations coupled with the normal third-person portrayals found in law enforcement reports. Using a third-person approach not only slows you down, but also makes the writing heavy and detached. The following example demonstrates the problem of heavy writing:

> The Department has become cognizant of the necessity of eliminating undesirable vegetation surrounding the periphery of the police firing range.

Compare that sentence with the following:

> Please kill the weeds around the firing range.

Of course I'm exaggerating, but a heavy writing style usually uses about twice as many words as necessary, sometimes more, and that adds up to more time used and makes the message hard to understand. The words in the first example didn't come naturally. The writer had to wrestle with them and the sentence they form. Using unnatural language, which amounts to heavy writing, slows you and the reader down. Using words that come naturally to you makes writing easier and readers happier.

The third-person style of writing is a problem area in traditional law enforcement reports. The traditional belief is that third-person writing makes an officer appear impartial. It's like pretending you didn't conduct the investigation and failing to distinguish your identity. It is an ineffective way of writing. A common example is as follows:

> When this officer arrived at the scene, a subject in a red coat was observed running through an alley. This officer pursued and after subduing the subject found the money taken during the robbery. The subject was transported to the county jail and booked for armed robbery.

The following example of heavy, third-person writing coupled with confusion comes from actual report files:

It is expected that a court-ordered wire oral communications intercept will be initiated on the main target in accordance with the stature, and a large load of narcotics may be seized. Also approximately 40 co-conspirators may be arrested in the case. There is a very distinct possibility of spin-off investigations being initiated as a result of this case. At present, members of the Blank Sheriff's Office have an interest in a possible spin-off of this case. This case has very good R.I.C.O. possibilities, because of the large land ownerships by members of the enterprise.

In the first example, the officer writing the summary could have used the following words:

Arriving at the scene I noticed a man wearing a red coat running from the location of the armed robbery. I chased the man through an alley after he refused to obey my order to stop. After catching the man, I found money believed to be taken during the robbery along with a handgun and ski mask. I took him to the county jail pending further investigation.

In the second example, the officer could have written:

I believe the court approval for a telephone wire tap will result in the arrest of about 40 men and women involved in the drug trafficking case along with probable seizure of a large shipment of drugs. Our department, along with the Sheriff's Department, will attempt to develop additional cases which have strong R.I.C.O. possibilities because of real estate holding by the drug traffickers.

Trying to write in a style perceived by many to be official language always ensures more writing, more time, and considerable decoding.

### Consider How Your Readers Perceive Your Professional Competence

Your fourth objective of report writing concerns that intangible we call image or leadership. Your lasting contact in law enforcement is through writing. The way you write reports tells readers a great deal about your competence, an all-important prerequisite of a law enforcement officer. Your reader will decide from one or a series of reports whether the information should be accepted with confidence or caution.

It's no accident that outstanding law enforcement officers who move up the career ladder are also good communicators. Excelling in law enforcement writing is so important to your readers, the public you serve, and the criminal justice system that your ability can make the difference in the advancement of your career.

### Always be Accurate and Complete

The skill of writing dynamic law enforcement reports which are complete, but not book length, emerges almost automatically with expository writing styles. The key to complete, yet concise reports is allowing your exhibits to tell the story. Do not confuse the size of an investigation report with writing. Depending on the complexity, you may have to write more, but always concise declarations of each separate yet related event. Exhibits include written statements of victims and witnesses (sometimes perpetrators), documents, your investigator's statement (which clarifies certain information and activities), and physical evidence. Beginning with your conclusion, the reader in a few seconds knows what the evidence leads you to believe at the time you filed your report. You support your conclusion with a section of the report I call the substantiation. Here, you identify and summarize your exhibits in the order in which you decide to have them appear, not in the order you obtain them. For example, a concise substantiation summary might appear as follows:

> A written statement was obtained from Mrs. Samantha O'Malley, who said a man wearing a red coat, black trousers, and boots, concealing his face with a red ski mask, entered her store, pointed a shotgun at her, and demanded the money.

Your reader can glance through the series of substantiation summaries and immediately determine the reasoning, based on collected information, you applied to reach the opening conclusion. If your reader has interest or a need, he or she can read the actual detailed exhibit (i.e., Mrs. O'Malley's written statement). Using a brief summation of the exhibit eliminates redundancy and makes your report as concise as the case allows. Your report is complete because the exhibits provide all the details—your report is layered, thus complete. It begins with a basis for the investigation being conducted (generally answered if forms are used); offers the reader your conclusion briefly; supports the conclusion with a brief summation of all the exhibits; and then supports all that with exhibits collected during your investigation including statements, documents, and physical evidence. It is otherwise called information management.

## FOUR CAUSES OF HEAVY WRITING IN LAW ENFORCEMENT REPORTS

Heavy writing in law enforcement reports can be traced to four common causes.

### Honestly Misguided

Most officers write in a heavy style because they honestly think they're supposed to write that way. Chances are, they're just following examples of reports on file or were told to write that way at the academy. It can be a vicious circle that is difficult to break out of or even discern. Officers also become intimately familiar with the legal system and courts, which traditionally protect their turf by using Latin and other legal terminology that only other legal technicians can understand. Law enforcement officers often develop their own heavy writing style, thinking that their writing will not only be perceived as being detached, but legalese.

### Lazy Thinking

Officers who have not thought out the information they have collected often use a heavy writing style. No direction or focus preceded the investigation, and the officers fail to recognize that their purpose is to gather information for an effective report. Writing is the end result of thinking, evaluating, and reaching logical conclusions, which must begin at the time an officer is dispatched to a scene. Obviously, the writing cannot be clearer than the thinking. Unfortunately, when law enforcement report writers use a heavy style, it is possible, even easy, to express information that is only half thought out yet written in a way that can be perceived by many as scholarly and professional. But you can't express your information simply until you've thought about it clearly.

### Trying to Impress Others

The third reason for heavy writing styles is trying to impress others. Law enforcement officers who do this are usually a little unsure of their information, or perhaps unsure of how to convey what they believe the information tells them. Their report begs, "Please notice how intelligent I am." Actually, they are conveying a far different message to a skilled reader: "I really don't know what I'm doing, but maybe I can hide it in this report."

Impress others with your writing, by all means, but do it honestly. Follow the example of professional writers—impress with the intelligence of what you write, not the scholarly way in which you write. Let the impressiveness, the scholarship, the dignity, and expertise in your profession come from the collective information you present to the reader, not the words and sentences with which you express them.

### *Concealing Weak Material*

The fourth reason law enforcement officers may use a heavy writing style is to conceal weak information. When officers know their information is weak because of their failure to perform properly on the job, they try to conceal that from readers. They hope that if the language makes the case sound complicated, nobody will understand it or recognize that the report actually reveals a flaw in professional performance.

Unfortunately, it's fairly easy for officers to get away with that kind of deception because readers normally don't have time to decode and analyze the information. In fairness, law enforcement officers who write this way on a regular basis are not contriving a scheme to hide self-willed incompetence. The incompetence is almost always traced to a lack of effective training and department leadership.

Often, thinking critically and analyzing the problems leads to finding plausible, objective solutions. Chapter 5 discusses solutions to many of the problems we've discussed in this chapter.

# FIVE

# How Structuring Provides You with the Key to High-Impact Law Enforcement Reports

A blank sheet of paper (or a blank computer screen) presents an obstacle to many writers. It seems to stare back, daring you to start writing. With traditional narrative writing techniques, the blank sheet of paper is definitely a problem, because you're forced to tell a story. It's akin to beginning a mystery novel and deciding where to begin.

With expository-style report writing, you won't have that problem. What you write is already decided by the circumstances of the event and information you collected. You allow the information to tell the story, and all you do is manage the structure.

## THINK FIRST ABOUT YOUR READERS

Earlier, I discussed the importance of your readers. You collect information and write a report for others to read and base their decisions on. Before I discuss the structuring steps, a quick review is a good idea.

Law enforcement reports have two parts. The first part is normally fill-in-the-blanks. It is designed for efficiency and to help you remember all the details. The concept is fine, but it's a reader's nightmare. All the information may appear to be there, but that's an illusion. Your busy reader will spend a great deal of precious time decoding the information. The result can often lead to a breakdown in the criminal justice system. Next time you wonder why your case didn't make it into court, or why nothing was done about a situation or event, take a look at the report you submitted. If you look at it objectively, the answer may be apparent.

I'm aware that fill-in-the-blanks forms will continue to be used, and they should; they serve a purpose. When you write, fill in the blanks first and set that part aside or use it for an information source. Forget the idea often associated with forms, which is that you only write whatever information is not already covered in the blanks. Whenever you follow that guidance, you're forcing a reader to spend valuable time decoding the form, matching what you write and trying to make sense of it all. The result is likely to ensure that your case may not be decoded. Your readers have limited hours in which to read reports and make decisions. Every day, more reports with fresh information pour in to the readers.

I once talked to a prosecutor who had a large staff of young attorneys and paralegals. The case load in this particular large city was heavy, and stacks of reports entered that office daily. The prosecutor told me that the reports are so poorly written and reading the information placed in the blanks is so difficult to read, a system of selection had to be devised for making decisions. The readers look first at the offense and set aside anything that is not considered a serious crime, like most burglaries. Next, they look at those in the priority stack to see if anyone was arrested, and if not, those cases are placed in a file stack. Then, with what's left, the decoding process begins. To do that effectively, the prosecutor created another form designed to answer all the questions, such as, Are all the essential elements of proof somewhere in the maze? If that's present, is there a solid mix of evidence to give them a fighting chance in court? And so the process goes until it's ready for a decision. Then it goes to a senior attorney for a decision and assignment. The prosecutor related that obviously he can't tie up an entire staff all day doing just that, so about 50 percent of the incoming cases that should be prosecuted are not—only because the reports are so complicated and poorly written.

The point is, fill in the blanks, set them aside, and write a report that is dynamic and results oriented.

*The scenario*: As we discuss structuring, the following scenario will be the basis for report examples shown. Developing a report example on one uncomplicated situation provides continuity. Other scenarios on different crimes and events will be provided later.

## ARMED ROBBERY

About 8:00 P.M., Saturday, December 10, 1989, three men wearing black jumpsuits, black military-style boots, and black ski masks entered Smith's Drug Store at 23 Cantrell Road, Any Town, Any State. Two men carried handguns, and a third man had a sawed-off shotgun. All three threatened employees and customers, announcing that it was a robbery and telling them to lie on the floor in an area behind a large service counter.

When the employees and customers were collected and controlled, the man with a shotgun went to the front of the store and hid behind a counter to control the door and confront anyone entering. One man guarded those on the floor while the third forced the manager to open the safe in the office and place the money in a cloth bag he provided. Next, he told the manager to empty the cash register drawers and place that money in the same bag. When completed, the manager was forced to lie on the floor with the others, and each of the men were told to take off watches and rings, empty their pockets, and place all of it, along with their wallets, on the floor alongside their head. Women were instructed to remove all jewelry from their person and place it, along with handbags, in front of them. The man standing guard then put all the items into a cloth bag he took from under his belt.

When finished, the three men slipped quietly out of the store, warning the people to remain in place and not to get up for ten minutes. No one was injured during the robbery, and no shots were fired. A couple of minutes after the men left, the manager cautiously stood up, looked around the store, and announced that the men had left. He called the police to report the event.

You are dispatched to investigate the crime while other law enforcement units converge to assist by searching the area for suspects and talking with neighboring store employees and others to determine if additional information may develop.

On arrival at Smith's Drug Store, several people are leaving the store. You require them to return inside after determining that they were present during the robbery.

Once inside, you ask the manager to lock the door and move all the people to the rear of the store to an employees lounge, and you go about conducting your investigation. When it's complete, you return to the department and write your report.

You complete the fill-in-the-blanks form and set it aside. Using the preceding scenario, you begin to write your conclusion, as follows:

About 8:00 P.M., Saturday, December 10, 1989, at Smith's Drug Store, 23 Cantrell Road, Any Town, Any State, three unidentified males, wearing ski masks, entered the store and, using handguns and one shotgun, forced store employees and customers to give them money, jewelry, and other items valued at about $12,000, the collective property of the store and other victims.

You've provided your reader with a fast glimpse of what happened. Your reader knows the time and date of the crime:

About 8:00 P.M., Saturday, December 10, 1989.

You've told the reader who is responsible for the crime:

. . . three unidentified males . . .

You're also telling your reader that you have good reason to believe a crime did occur, by noting the essential elements of proof for armed robbery:

. . . using handguns and one shotgun . . .

. . . forced employees and customers . . .

. . . to give them money and jewelry . . .

. . . valued at about $12,000 . . .

Your conclusion answers the basic questions a reader wants to know fast:

When was the crime committed?

Where was the crime committed?

What crime was committed?

Who committed the crime?

Who were the victims?

What was the motive?

Ask yourself, Are the essential elements present to support the conclusion that a crime did occur?

1. Did the perpetrators use force which would cause the average person to be in fear of his or her personal safety? Did they use weapons of any sort to threaten life?

2. For fear of their personal safety, did the victims hand over something of value to the assailants which they would not have relinquished under normal conditions?

A prosecutor doesn't need to waste time decoding what you have written. Your supervisor and others also have an immediate sense of the situation. However, one or more readers might be interested in all the information you collected at the scene. Depending on the size of your department and how it operates, your report may be referred to detectives, who will continue the investigation in an effort to identify the perpetrators and take appropriate action that leads to a trial.

Even when there are no detectives involved, you'll want a detailed report filed so at some future time the information you compile may be used effectively. Often, perpetrators are arrested in connection with the crime you investigated, and because of detailed, accurate information on file, they are identified as having committed other crimes. Detailed information presented clearly and simply can further not only your career but the criminal justice system as well.

## SUBSTANTIATE YOUR CONCLUSION

Structuring the substantiation section of your report is important. This section summarizes all the exhibits which you are attaching to the report, or have in an evidence room or at a laboratory for examination. You list the supporting information in this section in the same order as you arrange and attach your exhibits. Since expository writing starts with a conclusion, the substantiation section is concerned with a concise, item-by-item listing of information which leads you to that conclusion. Using the previous scenario and making assumptions about information your investigation disclosed, your substantiation may appear as follows:

Mrs. Joanne Robinson, manager of Smith's Drug Store, in a written statement provided details about the robbery from her viewpoint.

Copies of the Manager's Cash Ledger showing the store income and cash on hand for December 10, 1989 support in part the amount of money stolen by the perpetrators.

Mr. Samuel Smith, a customer in the store when the robbery occurred, in a written statement provided details about the robbery from his viewpoint along with a list of items taken from him coupled with approximate values.

Mrs. Joanne Overby, a customer in the store when the robbery occurred, in a written statement described the perpetrators and the rings and necklace taken from her during the robbery.

Mr. Robert Swenson, a retired police officer and customer in the store when the robbery occurred, in a written statement described the perpetrators, their method of operation, and provided a list of contents in a wallet taken from him during the robbery.

Mr. Ralph Johnson, a clerk at a liquor store adjacent Smith's Drug store, in a written statement described his observations of three men running from the drug store after exiting a rear door and the dark blue van they entered and used to leave the area.

Also included are the following:

Photographs of the store interior in general and specific areas described in the exhibits.

A sketch corresponding with attached photographs.

An investigator's statement I prepared describing my observations and activities at the crime scene, along with information not discussed elsewhere in statements and other documents.

A consolidated list of stolen money amounts, other items, and respective identification of victims.

Why bother with a substantiation section? To answer this, consider a question what the substantiation tells your reader.

a.  Your reader can scan your substantiation and immediately discern that the conclusion developed from your perception of the crime is supported by written statements. In other words, obtaining a written statement (it doesn't have to be elaborate) causes a victim or witness to make a commitment which is difficult to change later. It also removes you from the position of doubt when a detective or prosecutor reinterviews the person and receives a different story or denial of the information provided to you at the scene. Your conclusion and actions are based on the best evidence available to you at the time and based in part on written statements. In some states and jurisdictions, a law enforcement officer is empowered by law to swear the interviewee to a written statement he or she gives and signs. If you have that authority, by all means use it. Having a statement under oath of its accuracy strengthens your position and provides prosecutors with a credible document.

b. Other documents, such as the manager's cash ledger (which you copy in most cases, or when necessary obtain against receipt if justified), are attached to support or substantiate the amount of money the store claims was taken. This can be important, since we know all people aren't completely honest when it comes to money. A quick-thinking store manager might inflate the amount of a loss for a couple of reasons: one, to cover his or her own pilferage of products and funds; two, to inflate the amount of claims, supported by a police report, the store files with its insurance company. Whatever the reason, document the loss with all possible means to substantiate your report.

c. You've attached an itemized list of stolen money and other items which is derived from statements and other documents. This will provide easier reading and eliminate having to go through the exhibits later to make this determination.

d. You've noted that photographs and a sketch support and clarify information found in exhibits and other areas in your report. This will make a busy reader happy because often other information, such as that in written statements, can confuse a reader especially about who did what and where. Photographs and a sketch make it easier for a reader unfamiliar with the scene to understand what happened.

e. Your investigator's statement is designed to tie up any loose ends—it's a catch-all. For example, in a written statement, Mr. Swenson commented that one of the assailants acted like Sam Jones's boy. That might be a lead. However, where do you put that in your report? The investigator's statement is created to explain who Sam Jones is and why Swenson thinks there is a relationship. Since it's based purely on a feeling, this kind of information should not be made prominent but should be included in your statement with an explanation.

The substantiation section of your report tells your reader briefly the circumstances surrounding your conclusion. As much as possible, it's based on statements and other documents, which makes it reliable and accurate.

When you write your substantiation summaries, think about the reader. Does the substantiation clearly support your conclusion? Does it allow the reader to spend a minimum amount of time deciding if action is needed and/or deciding to continue reading further? In the previous example, a prosecutor could glance at your conclusion and discern that no suspects were arrested, so he or she need not waste valuable time reading further.

A detective, however, receiving your report through the departmental system, does have an interest. With your concise conclusion followed by a brief substantiation, he or she is able quickly to find direction and focus coupled with an idea of the exhibits' content. With that information, he or she may relate it to suspects or, at the least, have a solid starting point to continue the investigation. Let your documentation tell the story.

So far, you've filled out the blanks in the form, which amounts to the basis for your investigation, written your conclusion or concise description of what circumstances you found during the preliminary investigation, and you've supported all that with a substantiation section providing a brief summary of each exhibit attached.

Although it's important to obtain a written statement at the scene from victims and witnesses, sometimes that's not feasible. Sometimes all you have time for is to interview each victim or witness and take notes. Always include those interviews in your substantiation. They're clearly not as reliable, but at times there will be no other choice. Simply list your interviews in the same way you list written statements. For example:

> Mr. George Brown, a customer in the store and an avid gun collector, said that two perpetrators were using stainless steel, 9 mm semiautomatic handguns, manufactured by Smith and Wesson. The third perpetrator, according to Brown, was using a Winchester pump-action 12 gauge shotgun, blue finish, and modified with a sawed-off butt and shortened barrel.

Note that the information is more detailed than when a written statement is obtained. An interview listed in the substantiation must tell a story since no other documentation is obtained. If the interview is long, summarize it as shown and place the other details in your investigator's statement. The same interview, resulting in a written statement, might appear as follows:

> Mr. George Brown, an avid gun collector, described the kinds of firearms the perpetrators used during the robbery at Smith's Drug Store.

That brief summary alerts readers that the written statement of Brown may contain valuable detail and would be of interest, especially to a detective assigned to continue the investigation.

You should not, however, become a story-teller by substituting interviews for written statements and then going into lengthy summaries in the substantiation section of your report. If you do, the narrative style of writing takes over and, albeit slightly different, the same drawn-out reading process is back. When an interview takes place and the person does provide a quantity of information which you believe to be relevant to the situation, highlight the key elements in your substantiation, and write the full text of an interview in your investigator's statement. There you can tell the story. (The way to structure an investigator's statement is discussed later.)

A written statement, including your investigator's statement, should always be focused on relevancy. For example, we are not interested that George Brown traveled from Ohio the day before and walked down Elm Street to reach the store. We are interested in those things which are narrowly focused on the specific robbery. If personal expertise is pertinent, talk about that: for example, a firearms expert or gun collector, present at an armed robbery, will normally provide exacting information. If, on the other hand, knives were the weapons used at the crime, Mr. Brown the firearms expert would have little relevance aside from his perception of the event, just as other witnesses would provide. Other examples might include a security guard or an off-duty or retired law enforcement officer, who will likely provide better information because of training and experience about observation and recollection. That kind of skill should always be called to your reader's attention since it is normally relevant even from the standpoint of ensuring a credible witness.

## LIST VICTIMS AND WITNESSES IN YOUR REPORT

Following your substantiation section is a complete list of each victim and witness, which you develop during your investigation. The victims and witnesses should be listed in the same order as they appear in your written report. This consistency enables your readers to find the full identification of a person mentioned; they know where to look and do not have to search through a long list which is in no particular order. Label the list as follows: "WIT-NESS SECTION (listed in the order of appearance in the report)." Obviously, a victim is a witness to the crime, and as a result, you need not title the section "Victims and Witnesses."

The best way to make your list is to do it last. When your entire report is written and exhibits are attached, start at the beginning (your conclusions or, in some cases, the basis for investigation) and as a name appears, list it and provide full identification. Use that procedure all the way to the end of the entire report. If a person appears more than once, only list them once, the first time they appear in the report.

### How to Determine the Information Needed to Identify a Witness

Always think about your reader when writing reports. Ask yourself what information you would want to know about a witness who will undoubtedly have to be located if the case comes to trial. Detectives as well as prosecutors are likely to have an interest in a witness's credibility and capability. For example, a witness who is ninety years old and has poor eyesight and hearing might not be credible if the case coming to trial requires good eyesight, good hearing, and an overall contemporary perception of things. Although there are people of advanced age who are excellent witnesses, in many cases they aren't. The same applies to a variety of other categories, and it's important not to use valuable time locating a person who is probably not a credible witness.

As a minimum, collect the following information from each witness:

1. Full name: Include middle name or indicate no middle name.

2. Is the person a victim or witness?

3. Full address: Include temporary and permanent. Also indicate a post office box if used for mailing address, but be sure to get actual residence address.

4. Telephone number: Obtain phone number and, if no phone, obtain a number at which they can be contacted.

5. Occupation: This may be helpful, especially if their expertise is of value in the case. If retired or unemployed, also note their former occupation.

6. Age: This may affect credibility. Although a person of ninety may have an exceptional mind, he or she is not likely to be as perceptive as a witness who is fifty-two.

### EXAMPLES OF WITNESS LISTINGS IN YOUR REPORT

Mr. George Robert Brown, Witness, 3984 Merrimac Avenue, Jackson, New Hampshire 03846. Telephone: (home) (603) 383-0000; (office) (603) 383-0000; neighbor (contact) (603) 383-0000 [Sam Smith]. Occupation: Insurance Broker. Age: 63

Ms. Joanna Roberta Samuelson, Witness, 6723 Johnson Street, Allentown, Pennsylvania 18195. Currently residing at Sylvan Pines Motel, 5933 Elm Street, Jacksonville, Florida 32210 (six months during temporary corporate assignment in that area—will depart June 15, 1991). Telephone: (home) (000) 000-0000; office: (000) 000-0000; motel: (000) 000-0000; parents: (000) 000-0000. Occupation: Computer programmer. Age: 26

## LIST EXHIBITS IN YOUR REPORT _____

An exhibit is any document or item which supports your conclusions, including elements commonly referred to as physical evidence, sketches, photographs, documents (including statements), and other items which may pertain to your case.

The order in which you should list your exhibits is, once again, in the order they appear or are mentioned in your report. In other words, if your report first mentions George Smith and a written statement was obtained from him, or any other item was included as evidence, that statement or item would be Exhibit (1) or (A).

### How to Identify Exhibits

Identifying exhibits is important, just as numbering the pages of a report is important, especially if it's more than three or four pages.

If you use letters of the alphabet to number exhibits, you're limited to 26 single letters. In complex cases you may have hundreds of exhibits, which requires you to double, triple, and quadtriple letters. This becomes confusing and difficult to manage.

Using numbers is more practical in most cases, and it's my preference. You don't have a long line of letters for each item. It's much harder to correct a mistake when using letters.

Remember, any exhibit you list should have been noted and summarized in the substantiation section. This rule applies even in cases of physical evidence. For example, your substantiation might show the following:

Three casts of tire prints taken from the rear yard of 6940 Elm Street, Any Town, Any State, which did not compare with any tire on vehicles used by family or friends.

The exhibits section would list the items as follows:

(10) Three casts of tire prints taken from 6940 Elm Street, Any Town, Any State, marked JIL, 10 June 1989, Case 89-8374. (Retained in department evidence room)

Always note the current location of the evidence when applicable. Obviously, you can't attach three tire print casts to your report, although you can and should attach photographs of them. However, tell your reader their location (i.e., "Retained in department evidence room" or "Submitted to the State Crime Laboratory for examination" or whatever the situation may require). If, at a later date, they are needed for trial, for examination, or just to observe, your reader will be able to track down the item without a major waste of time.

Since all items which are considered evidence must have a strict chain of custody control, a receipt with a chain of custody becomes important the moment the evidence is found or seized. It is always necessary to have an original and several copies for each item or group of items depending on the item and situation. The original should remain with the item, and if it goes to the crime lab, so does the receipt. Copies are used for other segments of the control and verification of custody. You should also attach a copy to your report as an exhibit showing that you obtained the item and what you did with it. Statements of witnesses and suspects alike are not evidence per se which requires receipts and custody, although they are listed as an exhibit.

## HOW TO WRITE AND ATTACH YOUR INVESTIGATOR'S STATEMENT _____

Any law enforcement officer is an investigator, even if his or her title is patrol officer. Investigating events occurs in stages. Normally, a patrol officer will conduct a preliminary investigation and detectives will do the follow-up and in-depth probes. However, in many small departments each officer conducts all the investigative levels. Whatever your job title may be, you are, in concept, an investigator.

Your investigator's statement is a catch-all for tying loose ends, explaining certain aspects not discussed elsewhere in your report, and noting certain information which doesn't fit anywhere else. It's not a narrative report and shouldn't be used as such. The best way to view the investigator's statement is as a collection of explanations. The following example should clear up any confusion.

### EXAMPLE OF AN INVESTIGATOR'S STATEMENT

Investigator's statement of officer John Smith, Blank City Police Department, Any State. Date: June 10, 1989. Case Number: 89-8495 (Armed robbery)

The location of Smith's Drug Store was formerly Hanson's Drug Store. The name change occurred on Friday, October 21, 1988.

Mrs. Eleanor Johnson, a victim and witness in the robbery said she believes the perpetrators are former employees of the store. She declined to include that information in her written statement and is likely to deny making that statement if pressed. She said the reason for her feeling is that they acted uncomfortable around her, probably because she has been a regular customer at that store for the past thirty years. She declined to provide names.

Areas of the store believed to be touched by the perpetrators were dusted for latent fingerprints; however, only smudges were found. It appears the areas were wiped. No latent fingerprints or other physical evidence was found at the scene.

The foregoing is the kind of information you may use the investigator's statement to explain or convey. As you write your report, watch for any possible question that may come to your reader's mind. The name of the store, for instance, might confuse a reader who knows the area from the past and recalls Hanson's Drug Store but is unfamiliar with the new name of Smith's Drug Store.

Mrs. Johnson's comment might be an important lead, or it may be of no value. As you note in your witness section, she is elderly and may just be imagining that the perpetrators are former employees. On the other hand, she may in fact have knowledge which she's unwilling to commit herself to, but just the same is telling you where to look.

Mrs. Johnson's comment should not be mentioned in the substantiation, since only the information in the exhibit, the written statement, is summarized. Had she been willing to identify the suspects by name and further clarify her suspicions, then you would mention that in the substantiation. Always be cautious of information people are unwilling to commit themselves to. In the case of the preceding example, you note that she is likely to deny it if pressed. That simple precaution protects your integrity if indeed she is asked later and denies it.

Let your reader know that you processed the scene and nothing was found. That eliminates the question, "Did the officer process the scene or just talk to people?" Use your investigator's statement to eliminate reader questions and to help others who may have to take the investigation further.

## A QUICK REVIEW

First:      Write your conclusion.

Second:  Write your substantiation.

Third:     List witnesses.

Fourth:   List exhibits.

Fifth:      Write your investigator's statement.

## AN IMPORTANT TIP ON WRITING YOUR REPORT QUICKLY

Now that you have an idea of the report structure, it's time to discuss how to go about the organization and writing process.

Always assemble your exhibits first. Put them in the order you want them to appear—which is not always the same order you acquired them. This is especially true if your investigation is conducted over a period of time and you're finally getting around to the report or, of course, if you're a full-time investigator and work a case over a period of time. You might take a statement on June 10, and another on July 5, but the one on July 5 needs to appear first. Remember, your exhibits are telling the story. The information each exhibit conveys is important, not the date it is obtained.

When you have all the exhibits organized in the order in which they will be listed, decide what they tell you and write the conclusion. Then, in the same order they will appear in the exhibits section, begin writing the substantiation.

Place the report, now containing the conclusion, substantiation, and exhibits, and start at the beginning, listing the witnesses as they appear in the report. When that's finished, insert the witness section between the substantiation and exhibits, and you're almost finished.

Finally, go through the entire report, beginning to end, look for any question readers might ask, and make note of it. When that's finished, write your investigator's statement and attach it to the last of the exhibits. The report is finished.

All this may sound complicated now; however, as you continue reading and examining the example reports, you'll grasp how easy expository reports are to write and to read. They save time and organize information so that action can be taken.

## THE MYTHS AND TRUTH ABOUT WRITTEN STATEMENTS

There's a general idea within the law enforcement ranks that taking written statements is the exclusive domain of detectives. Perhaps that's why so many crimes are never solved. I'm aware that it's breaking with negative tradition to suggest that any law enforcement officer who is involved in collecting information at the scene of a crime or event should record witnesses' testimony in writing and have them sign and date it, but it's time to take a stand.

Mention written statements and officers think of an interrogation room and a typewriter. A written statement can be handwritten, printed, typed, or compiled on a computer and printed. It can be dictated and typed, but in whatever form, it records what a witness has to say about a specific situation, and by signing the statement, and in some cases giving an oath of its validity, the witness attests to its credibility.

If you're at a crime scene and no other means are available, use a legal pad and pen. Most form supply houses have preprinted written statement forms; other departments design their own; but whatever you use, take signed statements with you. For more years than I like to remember, I've taken written statements from those who say they know nothing. Ironically, most people like attention, and especially when they are victims, or what they know is important, they'll be willing to make statements and sign them. If you just ask them if they have any information, the answer is often no.

## THE ART OF TAKING WRITTEN STATEMENTS

If you've been a law enforcement officer for a while and have interviewed a lot of people, you'll agree that it's hard to keep an interview on course. People seem to have an inherent desire to ramble on about a variety of things when they're talking about an event or other person. The average attention span of most people you'll talk to is limited, perhaps because we all have a lot to think about and remember. In addition, the average person is not trained in law enforcement or the legal system. What is relevant to our process often does not fit their perception about the way things work. A great deal of this problem stems from an inundation of television police and lawyer shows, which often depict a Hollywood version of the criminal justice system instead of the way it is in reality.

When you begin investigating a specific situation or crime, it's critical to keep your interviewee focused. If you don't, you will waste valuable time listening to a great deal of useless information. To help keep focus, you'll have to control the conversation: First, tell the interviewee what you are interested in hearing—often, exactly what applies to him or her, no one else. Never give a sheet of paper to interviewees and ask them to write down what they know about the event. That's the first indication that the officer is either (1) a rookie, (2) incompetent, or (3) lazy. You must always control the situation and move it along quickly. An effective technique I've used for hundreds of statements is as follows:

1. I ask the interviewee to give a brief explanation of what happened to him or her specifically and about the overall event. If they begin straying into something else, bring them back on line and explain there isn't much time.

2. I write the opening statement, which is basically a summary of what the interviewee told me, and follow that with specific questions and answers. If the person indicates they know little or nothing, or I'm really pressed for time and I have twenty people to interview or the person is too hard to control and keep focused, I start out with questions and answers. Often, if you're conducting a preliminary investigation, it's the best approach.

3. When I believe the interviewee has provided all the relevant information he or she has to offer, I close out the statement and have them read it. It's a good idea to make a mistake here and there, and tell them to look for any mistakes. When they find them, correct it with one line through so it can still be read, write in the correction, and have them initial it. Later, the interviewee can never say they didn't read the statement before signing it. Another tip: Make sure the person can read English—especially if they're foreign, but it's a good idea in any case. Some people are illiterate and do an excellent job of concealing it. Ask them to read something they wouldn't have seen before; you'll find out quickly.

4. Have the interviewee sign and date the statement.

5. Sign the statement as "officer taking statement."

6. Note the location and time of day the statement is taken.

7. Number the pages as "page ___ of ___ pages."

8. Include case number, or if one is not yet issued, fill in as soon as it is.

9. Move on to the next interviewee.

The examples shown in Exhibits 5-1 and 5-2 are statements which can be made at a scene with a portable typewriter, a typewriter you are authorized to use at the scene, a portable computer system (lap-top) with a portable or built-in printer, a portable word processing system with built-in printer (I often use this); or they can be handwritten. A handwritten format is shown in Exhibit 5-5, and an example of departmental statement forms with continuation sheets which can be either typed or handwritten is shown in Exhibits 5-3 and 5-4.

An important tip that saves time and ensures accuracy: If you're handwriting statements at the scene and your department doesn't have preprinted statement forms, prepare a master of the statement on lined paper and make copies. That saves time at the scene and prevents leaving out something important on the statement. You can also adapt lined forms as shown in Exhibit 5-5. Always keep the format tight so no one can claim later that you added something after the statement was taken, read, signed, and dated. Finally, try to use black ink at all times. It looks more professional and makes better copies.

## HOW TO USE WRITTEN STATEMENTS AS YOUR INVESTIGATIVE NOTES ⎯⎯⎯⎯⎯

Your written statements can be as detailed as you want. Those shown in Exhibits 5-1 and 5-2 are guidelines and not intended to be instructional.

Beyond the advantages I already pointed out about written statements, there is yet another. You can save valuable time and develop information management accuracy using the statements as part of your on-scene notes. The result is a stronger report, case, and greater accuracy of information. Additional information about a witness can be added on another sheet of paper, or you can save more time at the scene by developing a simple worksheet. This one-page worksheet, shown in Exhibit 5-4, is copied from your master. When you arrive at the scene and have your witnesses collected, hand each a worksheet and let them fill in the information. When you interview them separately, taking a written statement, you can attach the worksheet to the statement. This provides all the information you'll need on each person, and your statements will serve as notes normally associated with on-scene interviews. The procedure is as follows:

1. Make a worksheet you'll hand out to witnesses at the scene, and make copies (or use the one shown in Exhibit 5-6).

2. Hand out the worksheet to witnesses (and victims) when you arrive at the scene.

3. Collect the worksheets from each person at the time you interview them and take written statements.

4. Attach the worksheet to the statement and use both as a substitute for notes normally associated with crime scene interviews.

A useful tip: If conditions or circumstances only allow for interviews, not written statements, the worksheet will provide valuable information and a starting point for talking to witnesses. In addition, using this worksheet will save time.

# NARRATIVE FOLLOWED BY QUESTIONS AND ANSWERS

## STATEMENT

**DATE AND TIME:**    October, 21, 1989, 9:00 P.M.

**LOCATION:**    Smith's Drug Store, Any Town, Any State

**NAME OF PERSON MAKING STATEMENT:**    George Overby

**ADDRESS:**    1549 North Traffic Circle, Apt. 10, Any Town, Any State

I, George Overby, make the following statement voluntarily, without fear, threat, or coercion, and without any promises of reward, personal gain, or benefit. (NOTE: Have your interviewee initial this opening statement.)

About 8:15 P.M., October 21, 1989, I entered Smith's Drug Store to purchase a newspaper. After I entered the store, a man with a ski mask hiding his face and wearing black clothing stood up from behind a counter and pointed a short shotgun at me and told me to keep my hands down and walk to the rear of the store. Another man, also wearing a ski mask and black clothing and pointing a handgun at me, appeared at the end of the aisle and motioned for me to come toward him. I obeyed and was in great fear of being shot and killed. When I reached the rear of the store, the man with a handgun told me to go behind a counter he pointed to and lie down on the floor, on my stomach, and not to talk to anyone. I moved around the counter and then noticed several other men and women lying on the floor. I lay down alongside another man. About five minutes later, the same man told us to empty our pockets, take off our watches and rings, and lay all of it on the floor in front of us. He moved around through us, picking up all the money and items and placed them in a cloth sack he was carrying.

**Q:**  Do you know the identities of the men?

**A:**  No.

**Q:**  Is there any way you can identify them if you see them again?

**A:**  I might recognize their voices, but I doubt it.

**Q:**  Did the men take anything from you?

**A:**  Yes, my wallet containing several credit cards, about $200 in cash, my gold retirement watch, and my gold wedding band.

**Q:**  What is your estimate of value on the items other than the money taken?

**A:**  Probably about a thousand dollars.

**Q:**  Do you have any photographs, serial number of the watch, or other marks that can identify the items as yours if found?

**A:**  The watch is engraved on the back with my name, 1976, and "In appreciation of your loyal service to the Acme Corporation." The ring is engraved with the initials of my wife and me: L.S.O. and G.R.O.

EXHIBIT 5-1

## NARRATIVE FOLLOWED BY QUESTIONS AND ANSWERS

**Q:** Can you identify the kinds of guns used other than a short shotgun and handgun?

**A:** No, I really don't know much about guns.

**Q:** How many men were there that you know about?

**A:** I saw two men, but also heard a third voice behind me, so I'm assuming there were three men, maybe more that I didn't see or hear.

**Q:** Were you in fear of your life?

**A:** Yes.

**Q:** Did you think you would be shot?

**A:** I think if any of us started a problem for the men, one or maybe all of us would have been shot. I thought they may kill us all before they left.

**Q:** Is there anything you would like to add to this statement now?

**A:** No.

### END OF STATEMENT

**SIGNATURE OF PERSON MAKING STATEMENT:** (George Overby)

**OFFICER TAKING STATEMENT:** John Doe

**PAGE _____ OF _____ PAGES**          **CASE NUMBER:** _____

Exhibit 5-1

# QUESTIONS AND ANSWERS ONLY

## STATEMENT

**DATE AND TIME:**    October 21, 1989, 9:00 P.M.

**LOCATION:**    Smith's Drug Store, Any Town, Any State

**NAME OF PERSON MAKING STATEMENT:**    George Overby

**ADDRESS:**    1549 North Traffic Circle, Any Town, Any State


I, George Overby, make the following statement voluntarily, without fear, threat, or coercion, without any promises of reward, personal gain, or benefit. (Initials)

**Q:**  What time did you enter Smith's Drug Store today?

**A:**  About 8:15 P.M.

**Q:**  Why did you enter the store?

**A:**  To buy a newspaper.

**Q:**  What happened after you entered?

**A:**  A man dressed in black clothing and concealing his face with a ski mask stood up from behind a counter and pointed a short shotgun at me. He told me to walk to the rear of the store, keeping my hands down at my side. Another man, dressed the same, appeared at the rear of the store and motioned for me to approach him. When I did, he told me to go behind the counter and lie on the floor on my stomach, and I did. There were several other men and women already lying on the floor, so I positioned myself alongside another man.

**Q:**  What happened after you were lying on the floor?

**A:**  After a few minutes, the same man told everyone to empty their pockets, putting wallets and handbags in front of them, and to put all their watches, rings, and jewelry there as well. When everyone had done that, the man moved around and collected everything in a cloth bag.

**Q:**  Did you see or hear any other people besides those already mentioned?

**A:**  Yes, I heard another man talking to the man who took our possessions, but I didn't see him.

**Q:**  Would you remember their voices if you heard them again?

**A:**  Maybe, but I'm not sure.

**Q:**  Do you have any knowledge of the men's identities?

**A:**  No.

**Q:**  What is the value of your losses?

**A:**  I had about $200 in my wallet along with credit cards and my gold retirement watch, worth about $500 or more; and my gold wedding band, worth about $500.

EXHIBIT 5-2

# QUESTIONS AND ANSWERS ONLY

**Q:** Does your watch have a serial number, or do the watch and ring have any way to be identifiable to you should they be located?

**A:** Yes, my watch is engraved on the back with my name and the year, 1976; and the ring has both my wife's and my initials inside the band: L.S.O. and G.R.O.

**Q:** At any time were you in fear of your safety or life?

**A:** Yes, I think the men would have shot anyone who didn't do as they said. And hearing all the news these days, I was concerned that before they left the store, all of us would be killed so there would be no witnesses.

**Q:** Can you describe the guns the men were using?

**A:** I don't know much about guns, just that one man had a short shotgun, double barrel, and the other man had a silver-colored pistol. I think it was one of those automatic kind.

**Q:** Do you have anything to add to this statement?

**A:** No.

## END OF STATEMENT

**SIGNATURE AND DATE OF PERSON MAKING STATEMENT:** _____

**NAME AND SIGNATURE OF OFFICER:** _____

**PAGE** _____ **OF** _____ **PAGES**     **CASE NUMBER:** _____

Exhibit 5-2

# ARKANSAS HIGHWAY POLICE

Arkansas State Highway and Transportation Department

## — WITNESS STATEMENT —

| Date/Time | Location |
|---|---|
| Name of Person Making Statement | Address |

I, _____ make the following statement voluntarily, without fear, threat or coercion, without any promises of reward, personal gain or benefit.

_____     _____
**EXHIBIT NUMBER**                                                              **REPORT NUMBER**

_____     _____
**DATE & SIGNATURE OF PERSON MAKING STATEMENT**        **SIGNATURE OF INVESTIGATOR**

A.H.P. FM 9                           — FOR OFFICIAL USE ONLY —

Exhibit 5-3

118

STATEMENT OF _____ CONTINUED:

_____     _____     _____

REPORT NUMBER         INVESTIGATOR'S INITIALS        SIGNATURE OF PERSON MAKING STATEMENT

— FOR OFFICIAL USE ONLY —

EXHIBIT 5-3

# ARKANSAS HIGHWAY POLICE

Arkansas State Highway and Transportation Department

## – VOLUNTARY STATEMENT –

DATE _____ TIME _____ LOCATION _____

NAME _____ ADDRESS _____

I, _____, hereby state that I was born on _____,

at _____ , and that I presently reside at _____;

that I am making this statement to _____, who I believe to be a state law enforcement officer of the Arkansas Highway Police.

I am freely and voluntarily making the following written statement after first being advised that I have the right to remain silent; that anything I say can be used against me in Court; that I have the right to a lawyer for advice, and to have a lawyer with me during questioning and during the making of this or any statement; that if I cannot afford a lawyer, one will be appointed for me before I make any statement; that if I start a statement without a lawyer present, I have the right to stop the statement at any time and request a lawyer. I further state that I am making this statement without threat, offer of benefit, coercion, favor, leniency or offer of leniency by any person and I certify that the statement is true and correct to the best of my knowledge.

Signature of Person making statement/Date _____

_____     _____
Signature of Investigator                Witness

### –STATEMENT–

_____     _____
EXHIBIT NUMBER                           REPORT NUMBER

_____     _____
DATE & SIGNATURE OF PERSON MAKING STATEMENT     SIGNATURE OF INVESTIGATOR

A.H.P. FM 4

– FOR OFFICIAL USE ONLY –

EXHIBIT 5-4

**120**

STATEMENT OF _____ CONTINUED:

_____  _____  _____
REPORT NUMBER       INVESTIGATOR'S INITIALS       SIGNATURE OF PERSON MAKING STATEMENT

— FOR OFFICIAL USE ONLY —

Exhibit 5-4

DATE _____ PAGE NO. _____

## STATEMENT

**DATE AND TIME:** _____

**LOCATION:** _____

**NAME OF PERSON MAKING STATEMENT:** _____

**ADDRESS:** _____

I, _____ , make the following statement voluntarily, without fear, threat, or coercion, and without any promises of reward, personal gain, or benefit.

_____

_____

_____

_____

_____

_____

_____

_____

_____

_____

_____

_____

_____

## END OF STATEMENT

**SIGNATURE OF PERSON MAKING STATEMENT:** _____

**OFFICER NAME AND SIGNATURE:** _____

**TOTAL PAGES IN STATEMENT:** _____ **CASE NO:** _____

EXHIBIT 5-5

# HANDOUT WORKSHEET FOR ON-SCENE INTERVIEWS AND STATEMENTS

## IDENTIFICATION WORKSHEET

This worksheet is provided to save time and ensure accuracy of information. Please give all information requested. This helps the investigating officer accomplish the task at hand with the least inconvenience to you. This worksheet will be collected from you when an officer calls on you for an interview in a few minutes. Thank you for your cooperation.

FULL NAME: _____

ADDRESS: _____

CITY AND STATE: _____

TELEPHONE NO.: _____

DATE OF BIRTH: _____

PLACE OF BIRTH: _____

OCCUPATION: (if retired, your preretirement occupation) _____

_____

LIST INJURIES SUSTAINED IN THIS INCIDENT: _____

_____

_____

LIST PROPERTY STOLEN DURING THIS INCIDENT AND ESTIMATED VALUE
(Include money and credit cards): _____

_____

_____

_____

DATE: _____ CASE NO.: _____

INVESTIGATING OFFICER: _____

Exhibit 5-6

## LISTEN TO WHAT PEOPLE SAY: A CRITICAL STEP IN STATEMENT TAKING AND REPORT WRITING EXCELLENCE

With all the information we are bombarded with from a variety of sources each day, most people tend to shut out some of it. The result is that we become poor listeners, even when we really want or need to hear something.

Information management excellence, culminating in a well-written report, demands effective listening skills. Successful law enforcement officers must place a high priority on being an effective listener. An average law enforcement officer spends about 75 percent of his or her duty time listening to people (perhaps more, depending on the jurisdiction). Most of our listening involves police radios, complainants, people with problems, information providers, and our fellow officers. A majority of our listening is connected with the task of gathering and assimilating information used in some way to satisfy our job requirements.

At a crime or vehicle collision scene or other situation which requires focused information collection, we record not only what we observe and discover but, most importantly, what we hear from witnesses. This is especially true when taking written statements, which are totally dependent on what people are willing to say and on what we hear them say. In general, we listen a great deal and actually hear and assimilate little. We can increase our skill of listening and assimilating the task at hand by practicing the following basic skills:

1. Hearing
2. Understanding
3. Remembering
4. Interpreting
5. Evaluating.

These five skill categories make a big difference in your communication ability, resulting in better written statements and reports. Each of the skills is achieved by practicing the following techniques.

### Essential Actions to Increased Hearing

To listen effectively, you must (1) concentrate on what the speaker is saying; and (2) allow the entire message to be delivered without interruption.

The primary problem encountered in developing this category is distractions, which prevent us from focusing and maintaining our attention on the person who is speaking. We also must make every effort to provide the interviewee the same distraction-free environment whenever possible.

Controlling the scene environment is the key to eliminating external distractions. The solution to this problem is to anticipate distractions, which results in a way to avoid them. For example, if you are at Smith's Drug Store investigating a robbery and you have fourteen victims and witnesses to interview and take written statements from, distractions are the last thing you'll need. Since the perpetrators were masked and no one seems to know who they are, the information you'll collect from witnesses is the highest priority if the case is to be concluded successfully. That will depend on your report and how much you can put in it. To control that environment, you've asked the manager to lock the door and stand by. Only law enforcement officers are to enter, and you have a backup officer with the manager to handle any information needed. You've collected all the witnesses into a rear employee lounge, which is quiet and far from any distractions in the store. You've provided each witness with a worksheet and asked them to fill them out, giving them a chance to settle down and concentrate on something. You've decided to use the manager's office as a private, quiet place to conduct interviews and take statements. In doing this, you have taken control of the environment and eliminated external distractions. Now your objective is to draw out every shred of information each witness can provide. Somewhere within all the testimony you'll receive may be the one important clue which will ultimately bring a successful prosecution, but obtaining information requires keen listening and showing a genuine interest in the person being interviewed and what he or she says.

Anything you can do to keep yourself actively involved in the talk will help you concentrate. Take notes, ask questions, or check your perceptions by restating the interviewee's main points. Behave the way you think a good listener should behave—sit forward, nod your head, and provide other nonverbal cues that show the person you're listening and think it's important. This will help you keep your mind on the subject at hand and will encourage the interviewee to continue speaking. As noted before, you'll have to control the interview and keep the interviewee on track with regard to relevance. The techniques noted here will help you accomplish that task as well.

One problem with maintaining our concentration is that we can listen about three times faster than most people can talk. We end up with a great deal of unused mental time. It's tempting to use this bonus time to think about other things, particularly when there's a compelling event pulling at your attention span, like the end of your shift. But it's necessary to concentrate specifically on the interviewee and shut out other thoughts.

### Interruption: A Major Cause of Missed Information

Officers usually feel that they must hurry when investigating a crime or vehicle collision scene or other situation. This is caused either by being in a jurisdiction where a great deal is happening which calls for law enforcement attention; or being in a jurisdiction where little happens but there's only a couple of officers on duty to handle it.

The result is a natural tendency to encourage an interviewee to get on with it, especially when the person is not inclined to relate information quickly. You interrupt, not allowing the interviewee to finish. You jump to a conclusion and interrupt, sometimes finishing the interviewee's sentence. When this happens, you are going to miss some information which may be vital; and you'll certainly discourage and distract the interviewee and discount what they're about to say.

### Understand What You Hear

Good listening involves a thinking process that is different from reading comprehension or memory. Perhaps the biggest obstacle you'll encounter in understanding an interviewee is differences among individuals' way of perceiving events. Each person's unique background, immediate needs and interests, and attitudes determine what meaning words and experiences will have for that person. The idea of what is and is not a crime, for example, is far different depending on what the event is and where it is. Learn from your conversations with people of different backgrounds, and during interviews consider that your interviewee may have knowledge of some important fact which he or she doesn't perceive as being a part of a crime or important to the matter at hand.

### Remember What You Hear

Although your memory is not a part of the listening process itself, it's essential to listening comprehension. When you are an effective listener, you must do more than just hear and understand; you must also be able to connect the new information to information already stored in your memory. Information not retained for later retrieval is not useful. You must be able to perceive the relationships among the ideas and pieces of information—both those you are hearing and those already in your memory—before you can take appropriate action on what you hear.

### Interpret What You Hear

Interpretation involves many of the skills that apply to understanding. To interpret an interviewee's information successfully, you must look at the situation from their point of view as well as your own. It's particularly helpful to know the context behind the interviewee's remarks.

### Paralanguage

Law enforcement officers quickly learn that words carry only a small portion of a total message. The rest comes through tone of voice, stance, eye contact, and the like. During an arrest, you're looking carefully at the suspect to detect trouble brewing. Direct the same alert attention to interviewees. As an effective, attentive listener, you'll observe several facets of an interviewee's communication beyond his or her spoken words. Meaning communicated in this way is generally termed *paralanguage*. The interviewee's voice communicates important information about attitudes and feelings. Combinations of vocal characteristics such as pitch, rate, and volume convey different meanings. All are areas you'll be wise to listen for when determining key areas of exaggeration, deception, truthfulness, and sincerity.

### Evaluate What is Said to You

Evaluation is a natural human behavior and becomes increasingly a part of a veteran law enforcement officer's life. We are so much a product of our past experience that our instant evaluations, before any words are spoken, may block effective communication. Developing listening skills requires you to suspend judgment during interviews and again when you write your report. Suspending your judgment involves two rules: (1) Don't let your emotions influence your judgment; and (2) Practice objective thinking.

Several mental habits can help you suspend judgment and listen with an open mind. First, remember that you never have all the facts. Whenever you interview or even talk with anyone, consider the possibility that the person might be presenting new information. Officers who act as though they know it all will ultimately back themselves into a corner and find it difficult or impossible to revise their position as circumstances change.

### Avoid Labels

Finally, to be an effective listener, you'll have to recognize shades of gray. Things are not either/or, as they often sound. Often, when we speak of other people, for example, we label them careful or careless, competent or incompetent. In many cases there are points in between. If we think of performance or behavior on a continuum, instead of as a choice between polar opposites, we can think more reasonably about the problems we encounter and listen more openly to the opinions and information we hear. Keep in mind that your interviewee may not be either/or, and look for a middle ground that can enable you to gain information successfully.

## QUICK REFERENCE GUIDE

Ask yourself these questions when you're faced with investigating an event which requires interviewing people.

1. Do I control the environment so that I can concentrate?
2. Do I use my extra thinking time to consider the interviewee's points?
3. Do I listen to the interviewee's entire message before formulating my response?
4. Do I understand what the words an interviewee uses mean to him or her?
5. Do I restate the interviewee's main points for clarification?
6. Am I sensitive to the interviewee's voice, as well as his or her words?
7. Do I recognize and consider important nonverbal cues?
8. Can I maintain my objectivity when listening and not become emotionally involved?
9. Do I maintain a flexible, open-minded orientation?

## SEVEN TELLTALE BODY LANGUAGE SIGNS TO WATCH FOR WHEN INTERVIEWING

Voice tone is important when you're talking to someone, especially taking written statements or conducting an investigation. The following seven areas are important to your information management process during interviews:

1. *Eyes.* No matter what their mouth says, their eyes will tell you what interviewees are thinking. If the pupils widen, they have heard something pleasant. You've made them feel good by what you've said. If pupils contract, the opposite is true. If eyes narrow, you've said something they don't believe, and a feeling of distrust is setting in.

2. *Eyebrows.* If one eyebrow is lifted, you've told them something they don't believe or which they perceive to be impossible. Lifting both eyebrows indicates surprise.

3. *Nose and ears.* If they rub their nose or tug at an ear while saying they understand you, it generally means they're puzzled by what you're saying and probably don't know at all what you want them to do.

4. *Forehead.* If they wrinkle their forehead downward in a frown, it means they're puzzled or don't like what you've said. If the forehead is wrinkled upward, it indicates surprise.

5. *Shoulders.* When they shrug their shoulders, it usually means they're completely indifferent. They have no interest in what you're telling them.

6. *Fingers.* Drumming or tapping fingers on the arm of a chair or top of a desk indicates either nervousness or impatience.

7. *Arms.* If they clasp their arms across their chest, it usually means they're trying to isolate themselves from you, or they're actually afraid of you, trying unconsciously to protect themselves.

Obtaining effective written statements which provide credible information for your reports is enhanced by applying the foregoing information. The diversity of contemporary law enforcement responsibilities and community obligation demands every possible advantage. Structuring your reports, knowing how to pack them with information, with written statements, and other documents leads us to an additional technique of investigation which will enhance all your information management: sketching and photographing the scene.

## HOW TO SKETCH AND PHOTOGRAPH THE SCENE

Law enforcement officers normally receive some training about making crime scene sketches during basic training at an academy or during later training seminars or courses about investigative techniques. Such sketches are often roughed out with lots of measurements, location of evidence, where the officer stood while taking photographs, and other pertinent information. The idea of sketches, I was always told, is to re-create a scene. However, I've rarely heard of that happening. Vehicle collision investigation generally requires a sketch of the scene, usually drawn by an officer within a small part of a fill-in-the-blanks form.

The sketches I'm about to discuss are used to interview witnesses, enhance understanding of your report, and at some point assist you while talking to suspects who decide to confess. I call them report-oriented sketches. They are, as is your investigation, designed to enhance your report by managing information with greater accuracy—not solve the crime or reconstruct the scene.

Often, when you arrive at the scene, witnesses and victims are confused about specific information. Your sketch is not intended to coach witnesses, only to assist them in remembering or showing you what they are having difficulty explaining.

A good time to make your sketch is after witnesses are in a controlled environment and during the time they are filling out your witness identification worksheet (discussed earlier).

### How to Make a Report-Oriented Sketch of the Scene

I normally rough out my sketch by using a house furnishings template, shown in Exhibit 5-7, which is available at most office supply stores or through a variety of law enforcement equipment suppliers. An example of templates, in this case available through Criminal Research Products, Incorporated, Conshohocken, Pennsylvania, is shown in Exhibit 5-8. I start by drawing a line around the outside edge of a square template, as shown in Exhibit 5-9. Other templates useful in making your sketch are shown in Exhibit 5-10, available through Bear-Aide, Incorporated, Tempe, Arizona. Full-size drawing kits, which can be helpful if you conduct both preliminary and in-depth investigations of crimes, vehicle collisions, and other situations, are also available from Criminal Research Products, Incorporated, and examples of them are shown in Exhibit 5-11.

When you're dealing with both interior and exterior situations, or more than one room or general area within a building, it's a good idea to split your rough sketch format as shown in Exhibit 5-12, and place a legend section at the bottom for notes that will help you remember later and make the sketch clearer to a reader when attached to your report as an exhibit. Recognize that all you're trying to do at this point is creating a "working zone" for your sketch. If several rooms, or multiple exterior areas, are involved, make a comparable number of sketch working zones and label each accordingly.

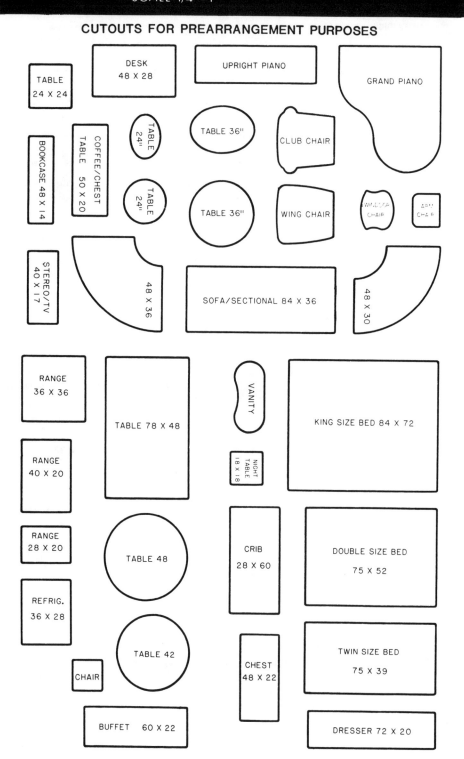

# R-714 HOUSE FURNISHINGS
## SCALE 1/4"=1'

### CUTOUTS FOR PREARRANGEMENT PURPOSES

EXHIBIT 5-7

# CRIME SCENE SKETCH TEMPLATES

### Traffic Accident Investigators Template

**PRODUCT NO. 99-733** For diagramming traffic accidents on report and investigation forms. Used by local police departments and state highway patrols. Template assures proper proportion and uniformity in description and integration of accident scene. **Template size:** 5¼" x 2½".

### Traffic Accident Diagramming Template

**PRODUCT NO. 99-734** Symbols used by state highway departments and insurance companies to delineate traffic accident scenes. **Template size:** 10¼" x 5".

### Architects Template

**PRODUCT NO. 99-735** For sketching most architectural symbols used in the profession. **Template size:** 9½" x 4½".

### House Furnishing Template

**PRODUCT NO. 99-736** To plan furniture and appliance arrangements when sketching burglaries, robberies and homicides that occur within a house or apartment. **Template size:** 8" x 5½".

### Store Layout Template

**PRODUCT NO. 99-737** Has most standard size counters and tables for use in laying out store display cases, counters, etc. **Template size:** 5¼" x 9¼".

### Office Plan Template

**PRODUCT NO. 99-738** This template contains the most often used symbols within offices with furniture and appliances. **Template size:** 5" x 8".

## QUADRILLE RULED PAD

**PRODUCT NO. 99-739** This 50 sheet quadrille ruled pad is the same as supplied with all our crime scene sketch kits. **Scale:** ¼" quadrille.

**CRP INC.**
CONSHOHOCKEN, PA. 19428-0408 U.S.A.

EXHIBIT 5-8

130

**START YOUR SKETCH BY OUTLINING THE EDGE OF A SQUARE TEMPLATE**

Exhibit 5-9

# Crime Scene Template
## Only $10.95 includes shipping & handling

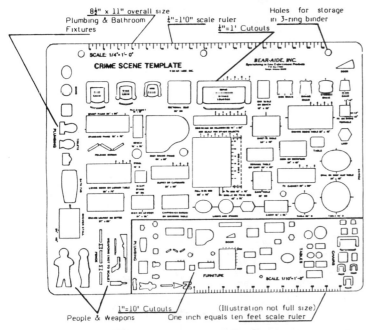

TWO USEFUL SCALES ON ONE TEMPLATE
(Scale rulers included for each scale)

NOTEBOOK SIZE — 8½" X 11"

REPLACES THREE OR FOUR OTHER TEMPLATES

FITS THREE RING BINDER

CUSTOM DESIGNED

PROFESSIONALLY MANUFACTURED

# Human Figure Template
## Only $10.95 includes shipping & handling

**DESIGNED TO COMPLIMENT THE CRIME SCENE TEMPLATE**
The Human Figure Template is designed for use with the Bear-Aide Crime Scene Template but can be used wherever the drawing of a male or female figure is required.

**UNIQUE DESIGN MAKES NUMEROUS BODY POSITIONS POSSIBLE**
By moving the template during drawing, it is possible to draw the human figure in various positions. This feature allows the drawing of realistic and informative diagrams.

**SCALE DRAWINGS POSSIBLE WITH BALLPOINT PEN**
The Human Figure Template is designed to produce figures of the size indicated on the template when drawn with a medium ball point pen.

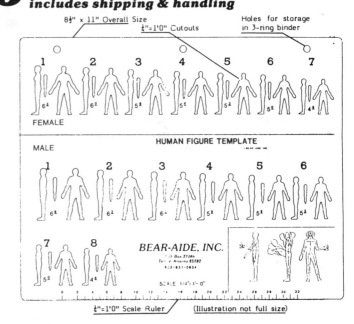

**BEAR-AIDE, INC.**
*Specializing in Law Enforcement Products*
**P.O. Box 27086**
**Tempe, Arizona 85285**
**(602) 831-0834**

EXHIBIT 5-10

# MASTER CRIME SCENE SKETCH KIT

**PRODUCT NO. 98-731** A complete kit that will enable an investigator to perform the following:

1. Rough Sketch
2. Finished Sketch
3. Finished Scale Drawing

A useful addition for the modern police department. All components are housed in a vinyl leatherette finished briefcase type carrying case for field use when necessary.

### CONTENTS OF KIT:

1—Vinyl, Leather Finish Briefcase Type Case
1—Vinyl Clipboard Type Folder
1—50 sheet Quadrille Ruled Pad
1—12 inch Transparent Rule
1—Mechanical Sketch Pencil
1—30/60° Clear Plastic Triangle
1—45/90° Clear Plastic Triangle
1—House Furnishing Template
1—Store Layout Template
1—Office Plan Template
1—Architects Template
1—Universal Lensatic Compass
1—50 Ft. Steel Tape Measure
1—Set Professional Drawing Instruments
Complete Instructions

# CRIME SCENE SKETCH KIT

**PRODUCT NO. 98-732** A complete kit for rough sketching and finished sketching. All the components fit neatly into clip board type folder.

### CONTENTS OF KIT:

1—Vinyl Clipboard Type Folder
1—50 Sheet Quadrille Ruled Pad
1—12 inch Transparent Rule
1—Mechanical Pencil
1—30/60° Clear Plastic Triangle
1—45/90° Clear Plastic Triangle
1—House Furnishing Template
1—Store Layout Template
1—Office Plan Template
1—Architects Template
Complete Instructions

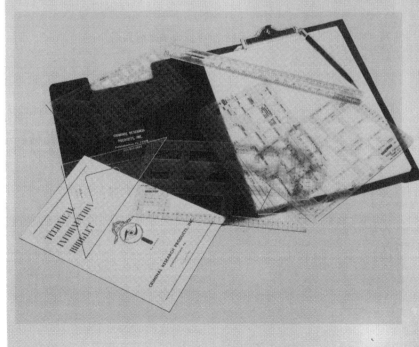

Exhibit 5-11

## CRIME SCENE SKETCH WORKSHEET

**LEGEND**

Exhibit 5-12

Using the Smith's Drug Store robbery as an example, I would use a template to rough in counters, display shelves, and other key furnishings. It's not necessary to be too detailed. In this kind of situation, I would use the House Furnishings template shown in Exhibit 5-7.

With a general layout of the scene, I would begin my interviews of the witnesses. People who are nervous during an interview feel more at ease when they can show you as well as talk about their knowledge of a situation. For example, while interviewing Mr. George Overby, I can walk through the movement he describes by using the sketch. This technique saves time when taking written statements and prevents misunderstandings. Overby can show you where he was first confronted and where the second man was standing. He can show you where others lay on the floor, where he lay during the robbery, and where he believes the third, unseen perpetrator was when he heard two of them talking. Not only are you able to develop a clear, relevant, and concise statement from all his information, but you are certain of its credibility as well. Some information gained with this assistance is helpful in other ways. When you're interviewing a dozen witnesses you'll be dealing with a dozen different perceptions. There's always differing information; however, in some cases, perceptions should be the same, especially when two or more people have experienced exactly the same situation. However, using the sketch as a guide, you'll be able to detect exaggerations and information gained through imagination or listening to others rather than first-hand knowledge. It's important to detect this immediately rather than wait until it comes out in court at some future time.

I can't say enough about being certain your information in a report, including all the exhibits, is as accurate and credible as possible. If, for example, someone is called into court as a witness based on a written statement and a revelation is made that he or she actually didn't hear or see or know the information contained in the written statement, you'll ultimately be scorned for reporting inaccurate information. You reported what the witness told you, but his or her excuse will be confusion, or any number of other circumstances. Law enforcement officers are rarely offered the luxury of excuses for their performance.

For example, if Mr. Smith says a perpetrator was at a specific location and five other witnesses disagree who should have experienced exactly the same thing as did Mr. Smith, it's likely a problem exists with Smith. Witnesses tend to go along with everyone else and don't want to appear stupid or get left out of the spotlight. So they say what others say; however, the problem is, since they really didn't have the experience, it's likely some important point will be left out or different. For instance, Mr. Smith came into Smith's Drug Store two minutes after the perpetrators left. He observed what others had who entered the store during the robbery, and walking to the rear discovered people lying on the floor. Others presumed that Smith was in the store during the robbery and also that his standing there indicated the perpetrators had left. When you arrive, Smith, who knows some of the victims, is talking with them. You ask him to go into the employee's lounge with the others and hand him an identification worksheet. As far as you're concerned, he is one of the witnesses of the robbery. Smith isn't really sure of his position either, whether he is or isn't supposed to be a witness. However, as he talks with the others and gets the details, he begins to think it would be better to just go along with it than tell you he really doesn't know anything first hand. In many cases, a person in Smith's situation gets involved in an investigation by accident and after a time becomes afraid to say anything. They often think that if they tell the truth, the investigating officer will be upset for wasting time on them, or they'll appear to be sneaking out of involvement, or they'll be left out of the excitement surrounding the incident. People are inherently curious and want to participate in some way, even as onlookers: Just notice the crowds which gather at the scene of a serious vehicle collision or some other situation.

Let's assume Smith tells you his story but portrays himself as not remembering too much. He even tells you his watch and wallet were stolen. Since he's elderly, it's late, and there's more to do, you take his statement and assume a great deal. Smith's story is nearly the same as the seven witnesses before him. Six months later in court, after the perpetrators are arrested and linked to the Smith's Drug Store robbery, all the witnesses you listed and took statements from are considered credible. Of the twelve, only five are available now for appearing in court. Some are in the hospital, others moved away, two are dead. But, reading statements you took at the scene, five will be sufficient in the eyes of the prosecutors. One of the five is Mr. Smith, and it's a jury trial.

Can you envision the elderly Mr. Smith making his way to the witnesses stand, taking his oath, and sitting down? He's distinguished, with short, gray combed hair, a blue suit that fits loosely (probably from earlier days when he was heavier), and he adjusts his hearing aid, looking intently at the prosecutor. He's asked to tell the court what he experienced during the robbery. Then comes a bombshell, a revelation that he came in the store after the robbery, not during it. The prosecutor is aghast, the defense lawyer's eyes light up, and the judge frowns. The jury is now glued on the drama unfolding. In an effort to salvage his image in the courtroom, the prosecutor holds up a written statement you took and is signed by Smith. He's asked about that. The prosecutor hopes Smith will confess he just didn't hear the question correctly. But Smith explains that the officer asked him what he knew about the robbery, and he told him all he knew. Smith says he didn't recall saying anything about his wallet and watch being stolen; that he was referring to the others who had told him their experience. Enraged, the prosecutor asks him why he signed the statement, and Smith, grinning sheepishly, tells the court that he doesn't see very well without his glasses and he didn't have them with him that night. He adds that he didn't want to make the officer's job harder by telling him he couldn't actually read what he was signing.

Smith's denial probably won't lose the case, but you can be sure the defense lawyer will raise the question now about the accuracy of all the witnesses—perhaps they were coached by you, and their recollection of what happened might be more or less what you told them happened. Depending on the weight of the total evidence, a case might be lost, and guess who's going to be at fault in the mind of a prosecutor and others.

That can be avoided easily by first asking the right questions, and second by using the sketch to learn if the person really experienced a situation or is conveying to you what he or she heard from others. For example, Smith could be asked to show you where the perpetrators were when he entered the store. It's highly unlikely he would be able to show you as those who did experience the event are able to show you. When that happens, be skeptical and spend the time to pursue the matter further. If the person persists, start checking with other witnesses and be *sure* before you assume the person is telling the truth. It's happened to me, and probably happened to you, but lessons learned prevent it from happening again.

### More Advantages of a Report-Oriented Sketch

Sometimes a case you worked on may come to court months or even years after the event and your investigation. You may even be retired or working at a different department 2,000 miles away. For instance, you're called to testify four years after the Smith's Drug Store robbery. All you have is a faded memory, your report, and perhaps a few notes taken that night to refresh your recollection.

Your sketch might well be vital, since Smith's Drug Store burned down three years earlier and a condominium development now occupies that location. During the past three-and-a-half years, you've worked as an officer in a city 2,000 miles away and investigated hundreds of robberies and other crimes. Again, your sketch may be the one item in your report and notes that will bring your focus back to that night four years earlier, allowing you to envision the layout and what you were told or where you may have found a key item of evidence.

Your report reader will appreciate sketches as well. Not only do they orient him or her to the scene and correlate the witnesses' statements, but they show that you went to considerable effort to ensure that all the information in your report is accurate. A defense attorney will also recognize your efforts and is less likely to challenge your investigation or try to embarrass you in court trying to create a credibility question in the juror's minds.

### Crime Scene Sketches Opposed to Report-Oriented Sketches

To be sure you're not confused with my explanation of report-oriented sketches and crime scene sketches, I point out the following key difference: A crime scene sketch is made to stand as evidence in a criminal trial. It is made by an officer and specifically for an officer who processed a crime scene in considerable detail, developing each step as potential evidence. A report-oriented sketch, on the other hand, is designed to provide you with a tool for interviewing witnesses, providing your reader with a means of collating other information with the sketch to permit better understanding.

Making a report-oriented sketch is for clarifying information contained in your report, while your crime scene sketch is best compiled after interviewing witnesses and serves to identify evidence collected and in many cases serves as evidence itself.

### A Few Quick Tips on Sketching

If you're an artist, the task of sketching a crime scene is easy for you. If you're like me, you'll need a template. Although you can adapt one template made for a specific purpose to another use, it's a good idea to have a selection of the various templates. They don't cost much, don't require much room in your briefcase, can make your sketch easier to do, save time, and cause you to look professional.

## A PICTURE IS WORTH A THOUSAND WORDS

We hear the adage "A picture is worth a thousand words" from an early age. That statement is true anytime a crime or other situation is investigated, especially months or years later.

I once investigated a homicide resulting from an armed robbery at a cafeteria. The manager and two employees fell victim to the perpetrators after the establishment closed for the night. The three victims were taken from the cafeteria and were found in a wooded area the following morning by hunters. All three were lying on the ground, and each was shot twice through the head. Since the crime occurred on a weekend evening and the cafeteria wasn't to open on the following day, the discovery of the crime resulted from discovery of the bodies. An intense investigation followed; however, no arrests were made until nearly five years later.

Identification of the perpetrators resulted from an unrelated arrest of one person who, finding himself in a lot of trouble, decided to make the best deal he could. He told the prosecutor that he would identify the perpetrators of the robbery, kidnapping, and homicide if he would be granted immunity and tried on a lesser charge for the trouble he was in at the time. The suspect related that his knowledge came from being a driver; he had not entered the cafeteria and did not have any control over the others when the men were kidnapped and murdered. From information and evidence gained through the investigation, his story proved credible, and a deal was struck. The result was that the two men who planned the crime and actually carried it out, including shooting the three victims, were arrested and brought to trial. The case was strong because once they were identified the third suspect's testimony and details he provided were corroborated with evidence gained throughout the investigation.

As a key member of the investigating team, I was called to testify about a few crucial items of evidence found when I processed the crime scene. When the trial began, nearly six years had passed since the crime had occurred. It had been five years since I had worked in that area. I returned a couple of days before I was scheduled to testify to refresh my memory by reading reports, notes, and other information and to return to the scene and look at it once more. Unfortunately, some years earlier the cafeteria closed and the building was torn down and replaced with an office center.

Fortunately, I'm a compulsive photographer at crime scenes, and I found a thick file of photographs I'd taken during the scene investigation. They alone helped me to testify with confidence and accuracy about the evidence I collected that cold autumn day nearly six years earlier.

Some crimes may not seem important in the scheme of things. However, especially when there are victims of any kind, it's our job to ensure the most complete investigation possible. That responsibility and obligation always should include a lot of systematic photographs. It is the only possible way to preserve the scene as it was at the time you arrived. Photographs record not only the general scene from different angles and positions, but closeup photos of evidence can be vital to a successful prosecution.

Photographs at a crime or vehicle collision scene or other situation also provide your reader with a clear picture of what you observed. Photos take your reader to the scene, clarify much of what you say in your report, and often corroborate your exhibits. The best way I've found to include photographs in your report is shown in Exhibit 5-13. Throwing a handful of pictures in an envelope and stapling the envelope to a sheet of paper (as I've too often observed in report files) detracts from their importance and certainly detracts from the credibility of your report.

---

### QUICK REFERENCE CHECKLIST

1. Write your conclusion first, based on your investigative findings.
2. Support your conclusion with a substantiation section.
3. Instead of taking copious notes of witness and victim interviews during preliminary investigations, take written statements.
4. Save time by having witnesses fill out identification worksheets.
5. While witnesses are filling out worksheets, make a report-oriented sketch of the scene.
6. Use the report-oriented sketch as an accuracy guide and checkpoint during your statement taking.
7. Watch for paralanguage and body language during witness interviews.
8. Take photographs of the scene and preserve it as you first observed the location.
9. Limit notes to information not discussed in statements, thus saving valuable time.
10. Convert your notes into an investigator's statement when information needs to be clarified or included.
11. Structure your case file and report logically using Exhibit 5-14 as a guide.

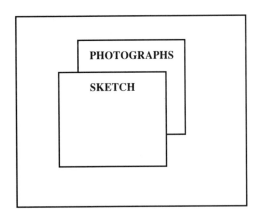

When you set up exhibits, always place the crime scene worksheet before the crime scene photos.

This procedure allows the reader to orient the scene and gain a comprehensive point of view for the photographs that follow.

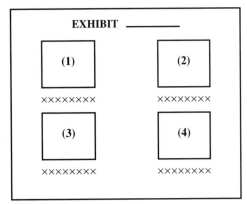

Each sheet used for photographs should have the exhibit number.

(1) Establishing photo [exterior]
(2) Establishing photo [exterior]
(3) Establishing photo [interior]
(4) Establishing photo [interior]

Use heavy paper (35#) and attach photos with rubber glue, which allows removal without damaging the photographs. When film is used, place film in small envelope and staple to the exhibit.

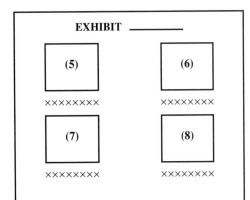

(5) Establishing photo of scene
(6) Establishing photo of scene
(7) Closeup of physical evidence that appears in establishing photograph (5)
(8) Closeup of physical evidence that appears in establishing photograph (6)

××××××× Denotes your label or identification of photo

Use as many pages as required for mounting photographs; however, limit the number to four per page. Space and labeling aids the reader to develop quickly an understanding of the information. When showing physical evidence, place the establishing photo directly above the closeup of the item and include the explanation in your label.

Exhibit 5-13

The crime scene sketch and crime scene photographs are the last items in your report exhibit list.

Although law enforcement departments often have generalized reporting procedures, most are focused on fill-in-the-blanks forms.

This example demonstrates a logical arrangement of your report and supporting documents. Note that the photographs are last, preceded by the crime scene sketch.

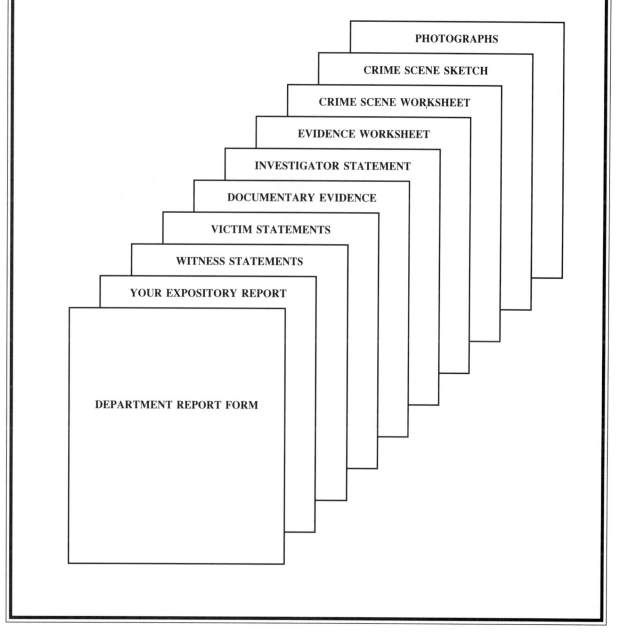

Exhibit 5-14

# Investigative Report Techniques for Law Enforcement Detectives

Becoming a detective is not only an important move up the career ladder; it strikes terror in the heart of a law enforcement officer used to wearing a uniform. It is without question an entirely different way of life.

Recalling my first week as a criminal investigator some twenty-five years ago brings back fond memories of how confused a veteran uniformed officer can become. After long months of impatient waiting, I was accepted to the position of special agent—criminal investigator with a Federal agency. The normal procedure involved an orientation period for a few weeks, followed with an apprenticeship nurtured by seasoned detectives. That process, which lasted a few months, was theoretically an evaluation period designed to find out if an experienced uniformed officer could adjust to the civilian-clad investigative world. Areas such as attitude, demeanor, and potential were carefully observed by those who jealously protected the sought-after positions. With their stamp of approval, the new detective apprentice was sent off to a few months of specialized training. With that ordeal successfully completed, we had the privilege of working alone, although we were still considered a rookie.

In the few years following that initiation into the world of investigating high crimes, my successes brought considerable attention. It came to a point where cases believed to be unsolvable were assigned to me, and all but a few turned out successfully. Then one Monday morning the special agent in charge called me to his office and introduced me to a young man, impeccably dressed, with a fresh haircut, shined shoes, and eyes that reflected what we all experienced that first day: fear. It's one thing to be in uniform for years and another to be faced with complex, in-depth criminal investigations. In uniform, a complaint often sends us running. We investigated the scene, interviewed witnesses, took statements, and did all the things I've talked about thus far in this book. But as a criminal investigator, we pick up the case and carry it forward, often wondering where to begin and how to go about finding perpetrators when no one seemed to have any idea about their identities. Even if we could identify them, how do we go about collecting enough circumstantial, physical, and other evidence to get them to trial and hope for conviction?

During the first few days working with my apprentice, he was clearly apprehensive about saying or doing anything that might interfere or upset me. Finally, as he relaxed and began asking questions, one came up which I've never forgotten and is probably the seed that led to this book over two decades later. The question came enroute to arrest a suspect in a robbery and homicide case. The young detective prefaced his question with some conversation about my reputation and then asked, "Will you teach me to solve cases the way you do?" After thinking about it a minute, I assured him that I would—as soon as I could figure out how I did it. I really didn't know and hadn't thought much about how I was able to be successful when others were not. I was in a different league; it seemed natural, and being a criminal investigator was fulfilling an aspiration harbored since childhood. I always supposed whatever I did to solve cases was something natural or inherent.

To this day I can envision that young man asking that question. For several days I thought about it, going through old case files and reports, many of which were transferred to me from other detectives that often worked months on a case as they had time without any progress. Finally, it dawned on me what was happening: I wasn't solving the cases; the information I collected was solving the cases. The difference which set me apart was that I collected more information, likely because I put greater effort into the task, and over the years learned to manage the information well. So there it was—I didn't feel so privileged after all; actually anyone, knowing that secret, could enjoy the success I experienced and have continued to experience through all the years since, working throughout the U.S., Europe, the Far East and Southeast Asia, Central and South America, and anywhere else assignments or cases sent me. The secret, then, is no secret; it is a system coupled with management and understanding. I can vouch that the systems, procedures, and information imparted here work for detectives. It all has to do with information management, which culminates in your reports. Detectives write many reports on the same case, or should, along with keeping investigative activity journals and managing voluminous case files. They normally begin where uniformed officers complete their responsibility. Keep in mind as you read this chapter: It's much easier to achieve your goals if you know precisely where you're going, the steps that will get you there, and how long it will take you to achieve your goals.

What does the professional term *criminal investigation* really mean? In the law enforcement profession, we use a number of terms that identify positions, duties, responsibilities, and obligations, but most of us rarely think about what they really mean. It's important for understanding this text to define the terms I use frequently. I'll start with my definition of criminal investigation, and as new terms are presented I'll provide my definition of them whenever their definition is important to implementing a system or procedure.

A criminal investigation is extremely specific in intent and limited in objective. It is always based on an allegation or information that a law or laws have been violated and an offense committed. This information or allegation may also point to an individual or individuals as either probably or possibly responsible for the commission of the alleged offense. The objectives of a criminal investigation are to establish whether a crime has been committed; to determine the identity of the individual(s) responsible for the commission of the offense; and to collect evidence for prosecution.

## THE COMPLEX CRIMINAL INVESTIGATION REPORT WRITING FORMATS AND TECHNIQUES SYSTEM OF INFORMATION MANAGEMENT

Your law enforcement report of investigation concerning a criminal offense must include all information relevant to prove or disprove allegation of that alleged offense.

Your ability to write effective law enforcement investigative reports makes you a valuable asset to both your department or agency and the profession as a whole. The key word is *effective*; anyone can place words on paper. The difference is how your words are organized, what they say, and where they lead.

Thus far in this book, we've discussed response reports, normally first to be written, most often by uniformed officers. Often, these reports are sufficient for prosecution, especially in misdemeanor cases when an arrest is made at the time or soon after the crime. Serious crimes (felonies) and those requiring weeks, months, or years of investigation are another matter.

It's important to note here that a great number of departments across the country are small, and the luxury of employing detectives is not possible. Patrol officers not only make a response investigation but continue with criminal investigations even though they have not had the benefit of specialized training and have a difficult time fitting criminal investigations into their already busy daily response obligations. Either way, your success depends entirely on information management. Let the information you collect solve the case, and manage that information effectively through writing dynamic reports.

Determining what information is relevant begins with analyzing your objective as a criminal investigator as defined earlier in this chapter.

*1. A criminal investigation is extremely specific in intent and limited in objective.* This idea refers to the response or preliminary investigation and report. This information management function is contained within three steps: (a) responding, (b) preliminary investigation, and (c) writing a report. With that concept, the complaint is contained with only relevant information collected, making the investigation extremely specific. For example, while conducting a preliminary investigation of armed robbery, a witness tells you about her husband, who is a professional burglar. She offers to ask you into their home and will show you the fruits of his several crimes. Of course you're not going to ignore her information; however, at that moment, you're investigating an armed robbery and her information has no relevancy to that case. Her information is obtained separately and is a different complaint. You should never take a statement about the armed robbery from her and include the information about her allegation about her husband's crimes, which are unrelated.

A strong guide to use is your recollection of what goes on in court—always focused on a specific event. You must do the same with your information management to ensure that your report is effective and dynamic. A rule of thumb I have used for years during interviews is: Does this piece of information support or substantiate my report conclusion?

*2. Criminal investigation is always based on an allegation or information that a law has been violated and an offense committed.* This comes back to earlier advice about beginning to write your report on the way to a crime scene by reviewing in your mind the essential elements of proof. The same applies with the follow-up investigation and prevents a problem that has existed for a long time, often referred to as witch-hunting. This concept doesn't prevent developing new information, such as identifying the man committing an armed robbery and along the way discovering he has committed several armed robberies, a few burglaries, and sells drugs. However, keep in mind that each offense which is unrelated to another specific offense is also a separate case and investigation. An exception could be one or more persons who commit multiple crimes stemming from one crime: for example, in an armed robbery a clerk is shot; a female customer is kidnapped and forced to accompany the perpetrators; she is raped and beaten by the perpetrators. In this case, the crimes may be merged because all are a chain of events stemming from one initial event. On the other hand, perhaps the same armed robbery occurred without injury; the next day the same perpetrators kidnap a woman, beat and rape her; and a few days later they shoot a person. All of the crimes are unrelated and must be investigated separately with separate reports if the results are to be successful. Merging the first example is not only plausible but makes your case against the perpetrators stronger by showing constructive criminal conduct. In the second example, however, lumping three unrelated crimes together in a report weakens all three events because, although the perpetrators are shown as having constructive criminal minds, one case may be strong, one may be weak, and the other questionable. Consolidating the three, simply because they are committed by the same men, may well cause all to be weak and result in unsuccessful prosecution or no prosecution.

*3. This information or allegation may also point to an individual or individuals as either probably or possibly responsible for the commission of the alleged offense.* Remember, your report is based on the investigative conclusion and developed from the essential elements of proof (not the complaint, which resulted in an investigation). A complainant is not expected to know the essential elements of proof. What he or she perceives to be a crime may not be, depending on the circumstances. For example, a complainant says that John Doe entered her home by forcing open a rear door and stole her television set. On the face of it, a burglary and theft occurred. During your follow-up investigation, however, you learn that a son living there broke the door and took the television set to a repair shop. Being too quick to implicate someone for committing a serious crime is a responsibility you'll have to guard carefully. A mistake because of poor information management can have serious repercussions on you and your department. Don't listen to a complainant's assurance that a crime was committed and who committed the crime. You develop the information based on the complaint and make your own conclusions.

*4. The objectives of a criminal investigation are to establish whether a crime has been committed; to determine the identity of the individual(s) responsible for the commission of the offense; and to collect evidence for prosecution.* This statement sums up the purpose of your investigation, preliminary and follow-up. Establishing your objective (purpose) clearly enables effective information management, which leads to a dynamic report. Purpose is the cornerstone of your report and provides a specific direction to focus your writing skill.

### Setting up Your Criminal Investigation Report Writing Systems and Formats

Chances are, your criminal investigation reports are written on plain paper or forms significantly different from the preliminary report fill-in-the blanks forms common in most departments. Since most criminal investigations require time, perhaps weeks, months, or years to resolve, the greatest problem you are confronted with is how to report information as it develops without confusing readers. One of the problems I've encountered over the years is impatient readers who fail to understand how difficult and slow-moving certain investigations can be. If you're like most of us, you have more to do than resources to do it. I can recall times when criminal investigators worked on twenty to thirty complex cases at the same time, obviously doing something on each whenever the opportunity came along. Assembling a completed investigative report can in itself take days, especially when it involves hundreds of exhibits. Your written sections may be 200 pages or more, and all that takes time. There is, however, a way of quenching your readers' thirst for information, and it's very effective.

### Progress Report System

You can solve your problem of reader impatience and increase your efficiency of information management at the same time. This system has an added benefit: You'll experience a higher success percentage—you will solve more cases and save time.

When the preliminary investigation comes to you through your department system, or if you conducted a preliminary investigation and are continuing with a criminal investigation, begin satisfying your readers with a first progress report.

Your first progress report satisfies several effective information management requirements: (1) It notifies readers that you have the case, who's working it, and what its status is at that time—it brings everyone concerned up to date; (2) it helps you establish a point of departure for your investigation; (3) it is the first step in setting up your case file; and (4) it helps you envision a plan of investigation.

Thereafter, until the investigation is complete, write a sequential progress report every thirty days or immediately on developing a significant, key element of information, such as identifying the perpetrator. That process of writing a progress report every thirty days also serves a variety of purposes: (1) Your readers are kept informed of the investigative progress or the reason it may be in abeyance; (2) each progress report renews your focus and helps you analyze your investigative plan and make any revisions necessary to bring the case to a successful conclusion. Examples of each progress report and a final report are shown later in this book. With a reporting system established (a first progress, followed by thirty-day progress reports such as second, third, fourth progress reports and a completed report), it's time to discuss your case information management system.

There are a number of pros and cons about the use of progress reports. Most detractors believe it makes the administrative load excessive, and the whole investigative effort slows down because of time spent on paperwork. If you're not familiar with how to write effective reports, that might be true (for example, trying to tell an entire story over and over, adding some information each time). However, that isn't expository writing. The minutes required for effective expository writing are always available.

Other reasons for resisting progress reports include laziness and incompetence. My experience over three decades has revealed those reasons to be prevalent each time a criminal investigator resists the opportunity to tell readers about what he or she is doing on a specific case. In reality, progress reports keep you attuned to the case load and each case within it. It's easy to let cases slide, especially when nothing much is developing. But it's a lot easier to close out a case that's a dead end if your readers are aware that you've done a competent job of investigating and information isn't available. However, I always find it hard to accept that crimes are so well executed that there isn't information which will bring the investigation to a successful conclusion. Much of the failure rate today, which is not often discussed because it's very high nationwide, is traced directly to information management, and that includes writing regular progress reports. It's tough to send in three, four, or five progress reports telling your reader nothing is being developed. It can raise some questions you'll have to answer. It's much easier to let a case lie dormant for a few months, build up a case load, do the easy ones, and then periodically close out a case that isn't exciting any longer. I know the routine, and I've never agreed with it. However, you don't have to do that; and as you continue this book, it'll become apparent how professionally valuable my solutions are to your career and the criminal justice system.

## *Visual Network Planning for Criminal Investigations*

This kind of planning is essential for managing complex investigative information, including providing your objective direction. Without careful planning you'll waste valuable time doing tasks that are not relevant or not material. The term *material* is very important to understand and apply to criminal investigations. Information may be relevant but not material to your case.

Material evidence or information is that quality of evidence or information which tends to influence the trier of fact because of its logical connection with the issue. Evidence which has an effective influence or bearing on questions in issue is material.

If, for instance, you have a witness who is able to recognize a perpetrator, it's both relevant and material to your case and prosecution. On the other hand, a witness who observed an event but is unable to describe or identify the perpetrator for reasons such as bad eyesight or incapacitation may have evidence that is relevant but not material because he or she is unable to provide any evidence.

## ORGANIZE YOUR CRIMINAL INVESTIGATION WITH VISUAL NETWORK PLANNING: AN EIGHT-STEP PLANNING PROCESS _____

A network is a group of interrelated, linked activities. For example, rather than interview and take statements here and there, now and then, try to schedule a day or a few days, whatever necessary for the case, to do them all. There are several benefits to doing this. Besides saving valuable time, you'll have the advantage of continuity, drawing out every shred of information that may otherwise be overlooked. Often, *witnesses* will tell you only what they remember, or even just answer your questions or follow your guidance. I've had witnesses come up with a key piece of information, and when asked why they didn't tell me earlier when we talked or tell the responding officer at the scene, they answer, "He [or you] didn't ask me."

*Step 1*: Write your objective. Specify what you want to accomplish and when you want to accomplish it. You don't have to put it in the case file officially; however, it's a good idea to have your plan in the jacket especially if you're working several cases simultaneously. At least keep it in a private file.

*Step 2*: Break your objective into major steps or activities. I like to set priorities. For example, if I have a few pieces of physical evidence which must be sent to a laboratory but have no possibility of deteriorating, and I have several key witnesses that can provide crucial information, I'll consider the witnesses a higher priority and do that first. The items going to the laboratory can be assigned another priority.

*Step 3*: Organize your investigative activities in logical order. I've observed detectives run themselves silly, working hard instead of working smart. None of them has much success in getting their cases to a court room. Assigning priorities is one way to organize your activities. In addition, try to organize your investigations collectively, based on geographical locations. If you have to drive an hour, interview, take statements, or conduct some other activity for two or three hours, and drive an hour back, by the time you bring your journal up to date and handle any other administrative work, the day is over and all you gained is one element of one investigation. Sometimes it's unavoidable, but most of the time you can organize your investigations collectively. In other words, if you are working seven cases, and if you have the case file organized, each case containing a planning process sheet, it's likely you can combine your activities in geographical areas. For example, if I have to drive for an hour to reach an area for one item on one case, then I try to find other work that can be accomplished on the way, in the vicinity, or on the way back on other cases I'm working.

*Step 5*: Estimate how long each activity will take to complete. This is really important, considering that you will have eight hours a day, unless you're able to put in a few more hours each week for compensation or overtime and your family or personal life will permit it. I once worked for a state agency conducting white-collar crime investigations statewide. I was based in the state capital, but besides having an office there, I never had a case there. Most of them ranged from 100 to 400 miles from home. Although I had the option of staying away over weekends, sitting in hotel rooms watching television isn't my idea of a good time. I was able to estimate how long each interview, written statement, affidavit, meeting, or other activity would take. On Monday morning I would file all the reports, normally written in hotel rooms on a portable system, make necessary calls and receive new case assignments (just what I needed), and get ready to travel. While doing all that I planned my itinerary, mostly by calling every place and everyone I needed to see at the distant location. I would set times and central locations to save time, normally renting a meeting room at the hotel, which allowed the people to come to me and kept me from wasting time traveling. I packed an eight- or 10-hour day, and on Friday afternoon I was enroute home with everything accomplished and up to date.

*Step 6*: Determine your critical factors. Regardless of how familiar you are with a law, it's a good idea to look it up and note the annotations and any recent court decisions that might have an effect on the weight and kind of evidence (information) you collect. This practice is helpful to set your direction and refresh your memory about specific crimes. I also like to make a copy of the statute and put it in the case file. That can save time later if I am seeking a search or arrest warrant or getting ready to testify before a grand jury or in court. Always know exactly what your critical factors are before you begin a criminal investigation. That practice will benefit you throughout, and when writing a report you'll be certain that what you're saying is accurate.

*Step 7*: Assign calendar dates to each activity. When you set goals it's hard to forget something. For example, if you have to attain information prior to a meeting with the chief or prosecutor about the case, having it will save an embarrassing excuse about not having it. It's also helpful in setting priorities.

*Step 8*: Review the case file regularly, and make a note in the activity log that you did review it. Even if you're waiting for information or a laboratory report or you're too busy on other cases to work on this one, take a few minutes and look over your file. It seems to help keep your finger on the pulse of the investigation and prevents you from letting an investigation lie dormant too long. After a time, it's hard to regain continuity.

## WHAT A FIRST PROGRESS REPORT LOOKS LIKE

I'm sure you already use a form or format that includes your department identification, a case number, and all the other administrative details necessary to keep control and records of departmental documents. I won't get into all that, which is routine in any report format. Here, you're concerned with what you write beyond all that.

Remember that regardless of the kind or level of report you write, the format is always the same; whether it's a first progress, eighth progress, or completed report, the parts of it don't change.

Using the Smith's Drug Store robbery example, here is what your first progress report should look like:

### BASIS OF INVESTIGATION

Report number 00-0000 written by Patrol Officer George Bell, dated October 22, 1990.

*Note*: All you need to tell your reader is *why* you're investigating. In most cases, criminal investigators pick up cases from reports filed by patrol officers. If, however, you are doing both, you simply replace officer Bell's name as shown in the example with your own, because you will be writing and filing a preliminary report just as he would. You would still refer to that report in your basis.

### OFFENSE(S)

Armed robbery, RSA 000000000, 1989 edition

*Note*: In this section you tell your reader *what* you're investigating; in this case one item. If, however, there is more than one offense, or if more develop for the next progress report, the offense section would appear as follows:

1. Armed robbery, RSA 000000000, 1989 edition
2. Kidnapping, RSA 000000000, 1989 edition
3. Rape, RSA 000000000, 1989 edition

*Note*: As shown, when there are multiple criminal offenses, number them. This is based on an earlier scenario of a woman being abducted by force from the scene of an armed robbery, taken to the countryside and raped. All by the same perpetrators and each offense stemming from the first.

## SUSPECTS

Unknown

*Note*: If no arrests have been made, you have no suspects. I once read an investigator's report in which he listed three suspects. Reading the reports, I found no basis for naming anyone, and I asked him why. He replied that one of the witnesses thought it was the three. *Never* list suspects until you have solid evidence against them. Someone thinking they know who a perpetrator might be is not evidence. If, however, suspects are credibly identified or arrested, list them as follows:

## SUSPECTS

John Robert Doe, Sr., 1894 South Elm Street, Any City, Any State (1, 2, 3)

John Robert Doe, Jr., 1320 East Maple Avenue, Any City, Any State (1, 2, 3)

John Robert Doe, III, 2855 North Plaza Drive, Any City, Any State (1)

*Note*: In the preceding example, the whole family was involved and arrested or credibly identified as the perpetrators. List their name and address, and follow that information with (1, 2, 3) or applicable numbers according to which of the multiple offense they are linked to. If there is only one offense, there is no need of numbering either the offense or including it beside the name. There is no need to identify the suspects further, since all that information should be contained on a suspect identification worksheet or in your investigator's statement. A worksheet is best and will be discussed and shown later.

You may have already noticed I haven't used the traditional law enforcement word *subject*. That's because it's a negative tradition and a misnomer. I admit, for many years I joined the pack and used the word *subject* when referring to anyone: suspects, victims, witnesses, or whoever. Then one day I thought about the word and came to a conclusion it really was not saying what I intended to say. The word *subject* doesn't apply to people, and saying *subject of investigation*, as is commonly done, doesn't mean what it's perceived to say. For example, the subject of investigation in an armed robbery case is armed robbery. When perpetrators of the crime are identified or arrested, they become suspects; prior to that, unidentified, they are perpetrators. Subjects are *what* you're investigating, not *who*. It's the old problem of doing it because everyone has always done it—not a reason, but an excuse.

So far, you've told your reader *why* (basis) you're using time investigating; *what* (offense) the crime is that you're investigating; *who* (suspect), if known, is responsible for committing the crime and is credibly linked to the crime. Now it's time for your conclusion, always appearing first, under the heading "Summary."

## SUMMARY OF INVESTIGATION

About 8:15 P.M., October 21, 1989, at Smith's Drug Store, 5560 Cantrell Road, Any City, Any State, three unidentified men entered the store and, threatening with firearms, forced the store manager and several customers to hand over monies, jewelry, and other items valued at about $24,000.

The investigation is continuing.

*Note*: Here you've told your reader in concise terms about the crime and closed your summary with a statement that an investigation is in progress. Criminal investigations may have longer summaries than preliminary reports; however, a good rule is to say as much as possible in as few words as possible. Remember, your conclusion is based on your information, which is attached as exhibits. If the amount on the original report said the value of stolen items was $12,000, and since that time you've found it's $24,000, change it to that amount. If an address is corrected, different from the original report, put the correct address in your first or subsequent progress report. *Don't* explain it in the summary; instead include that and other information in your investigator's statement.

Now you're ready to substantiate or support your summary. It should appear as follows:

## SUBSTANTIATION

In a preliminary investigation report, Officer George Bell provides information including written statements taken soon after the event.

*Note*: This is your first progress report. You've just received the case, and the report's purpose is to tell your readers you're working on it. Then you begin your case file. You could, of course, break officer Bell's report into sections, listing the report and each of his exhibits. However, he's already done that in his substantiation and exhibits section, along with listing all the witnesses and how to contact them and an investigator's statement explaining other information. Doing all the writing would waste valuable time and accomplish nothing.

There is another important reason for keeping officer Bell's report intact. Depending on the procedures in your jurisdiction, reports referred to detectives for further investigation normally are not forwarded outside the department (i.e., the prosecutor's office). Criminal investigations should always be forwarded to the prosecutor even if there's nothing new or no activity. It's a courtesy, alerting the office that a prosecution may be needed if the case concludes successfully. It allows that office to begin its own file with that eventuality in mind.

## WITNESS SECTION

Shown in the attached report written by officer Bell.

*Note*: Again, there's no need to waste time here relisting all the witnesses when it's already been done. This is only a first progress report.

## EXHIBITS SECTION

For this first progress report, your only exhibit is officer Bell's complete preliminary report, which is listed as follows:

Report number 00-0000, written by officer George Bell, dated October 22, 1989. (cy)

*Note*: After the exhibit, always indicate whether it's a copy (cy) or (original). Originals of documents, reports, or any other item should only be attached to the completed report of investigation. Until that report is forwarded, attach copies and maintain originals in the case file. Prosecutors taking a case to court will need the originals; however, until the case reaches that stage, don't risk losing them by attaching them to a progress report.

# MAKE AN INVESTIGATIVE ACTIVITY LOG _____

The next step in developing your case file is setting up your investigative activity log. This can be done with a legal pad, plain paper, or a form you have or design. It's purpose is to record all activity you perform on the case. An example follows:

October 25, 1989   Received case assignments from the chief of detectives.

October 26, 1989   Reviewed officer Bell's Report and submitted first progress report.

October 27, 1989   Prepared investigative plan. Contacted material witnesses and set up a collective reinterview date of November 5, 1989 at the sheriff's substation in Garden View section. Scheduled the interviews for one hour ten minutes each, which includes taking typewriter statements.

October 28, 1989   Contacted Mrs. Ralph Jones, Jones is the daughter of Mr. and Mrs. Sam Hanson, previous owners of the store now called Smith's Drug Store. Mr. Hanson is dead, and Mrs. Hanson, having had a stroke, is at a nursing home and doesn't remember much of the past. Mrs. Jones ran the store until it was sold during August 1989 to Robert and Nancy Smith. Mrs. Jones has all the old records from the store, which operated for thirty-five years under the Hanson ownership. Want to examine the employee records for the past five years and run record checks. Will interview Mrs. Jones and determine if I'll take a written statement from her.

*Note*: Your activity file lists not only activity, but some planning and arrangements, details of what you know, and in some cases suspicions. Be careful, however, that you don't taint the prosecutor's case by putting in items that make you appear prejudicial against a person. Your activity file can be subpoenaed by the defense and introduced into the court record. Another reason for the activity file is that when a case is transferred to another detective, that investigator will know what you've done, what you have arranged, and other details that are vital. If, for example, the case goes on for two years and next year you retire, transfer, take a different job, or become ill, another detective can assume the case and not waste time by trying to figure out what you've accomplished or planned. The activity log also provides an excellent record of items going to and coming from a laboratory and making your investigator's statements. It's a valuable tool.

## SECOND AND SUBSEQUENT PROGRESS REPORTS

Your second and subsequent progress reports will be in the same format; however, the context will be different. In the first progress report, your goal is to notify readers that you're investigating the case and to provide yourself with a committed point of departure. Once you've written the first progress report, you are committed to producing effective results or, as a minimum, making a strong effort to do so. Your second and subsequent progress reports are updates for both your reader and you. They tell the reader what has happened in the case during the last month and provide a constructive building process for your case. It's embarrassing to submit a progress report when there's no progress to report. The purpose of progress reports, other than what we've already discussed, is that they keep you from becoming lazy and complacent and procrastinating. A former supervisor would tell us, "Work the cases or close 'em out. But if you close 'em—I better not find you didn't work 'em."

### SECOND PROGRESS REPORT—BASIS FOR INVESTIGATION

See first progress report dated October 25, 1989.

*Note*: When you're writing the second and subsequent progress reports, there's no requirement of repeating the same information already in previous reports. You do have to inform your reader where to look for the original basis if they're interested.

## OFFENSE(S)

Armed robbery, RSA 000000000, 1989 edition

*Note*: It's a good idea to restate the offense, because in some cases new offenses or lesser included offenses might develop during your investigation. It's also a good reminder to busy readers who aren't closely involved and don't recall what happened months ago at Smith's Drug Store. If multiple offenses are listed, number each—for example, (1) Armed robbery, (2) Burglary, (3) Assault.

## SUSPECT(S)

John Appleton, former residence at 298 Maple Lane, Any City, Any State

Saumuel Johnson, former residence at 298 Maple Lane, Any City, Any State

George Samson, former residence at 298 Maple Lane, Any City, Any State

*Note*: When suspects are juveniles (under age eighteen), their age should be noted at the end of their address. Additional identification, such as Social Security number and physical description, should be included in your investigative activity file and identification worksheets, but not shown in the report. It is of no interest to your reader, with the exception of age. Adults are simply listed without showing age. If there are multiple offenses, place the applicable number(s) in parentheses after the address. In cases where only one offense is listed, you need not list offense numbers.

## SECOND PROGRESS REPORT—SUMMARY OF INVESTIGATION

Investigation disclosed identities of three suspects in the Smith's Drug Store robbery. The three men are believed to be in another state.

The investigation is continuing.

*Note*: Here you've apprised your reader of how the suspects came to be listed and why they haven't been arrested or action hasn't been taken leading to indictment.

## SUBSTANTIATION

In a written statement, Mrs. Susan Quincy, a victim of the Smith's Drug Store robbery, said she is certain the three perpetrators were former employees. Quincy was also a former employee of the store when it was doing business as Hanson's Drug Store. She identified the men listed as suspects in this report.

Store personnel records were obtained from Mrs. Joan Jones, daughter of the former store owners (Hanson), and all three men identified by Quincy were verified to be former employees.

Information developed from personnel records coupled with criminal records searches revealed that all three men have juvenile criminal records.

In a written statement, Mr. Clyde Goodman, apartment manager where suspects formerly lived, stated that he is a casual friend of the three suspects, and each told him about the robbery and said they were leaving the city until things cooled off. He said they purchased a new van.

A bill of sale (cy) from Cal Overton Ford dealership revealed suspect Appleton purchased a new van on October 28, 1989 and paid cash.

*Note*: Your substantiation is an overview summary of what exhibits demonstrate in detail. You're providing your reader with a quick explanation about how you arrived at your conclusion and identified suspects.

## WITNESSES

Mrs. Susan Quincy, 4289 South Hampton Drive, Any City, Any State

Mrs. Joan Jones, 740 North Oak Street, Any City, Any State

Mr. Clyde Goodman, 299 Maple Avenue, Any City, Any State

Mr. Cal Overton, 78 Commercial Way, Any City, Any State

*Note*: List witnesses in the same order they first appear in your report—in this case, beginning with your substantiation section.

## EXHIBITS

A written statement, dated November 18, 1989, taken from Mrs. Susan Quincy (cy)

A written statement, dated November 21, 1989, taken from Mrs. Joan Jones (cy)

Hanson's Drug Store personnel records pertaining to suspects Appleton, Johnson, and Samson (cy)

Juvenile Criminal Records report, dated November 23, 1989

A written statement, dated November 23, 1989, taken from Mr. Clyde Goodman (cy)

A certified copy of a Bill of Sale from Cal Overton Ford dealership to John Appleton, 298 Maple Avenue, Any City, Any State

*Note*: Exhibits are listed in the same order as discussed in your substantiation. You don't need a lot of detail about your exhibits, since they are attached to your progress report.

## THIRD PROGRESS REPORT

Your third progress report will not contain any of the information shown in the second progress report, and that rule continues through to the completed report of investigation. Each progress report tells your reader only information collected since the last progress report.

## COMPLETED REPORT OF INVESTIGATION

In your completed report of investigation, merge all the progress reports along with all additional information collected since the last progress report.

When writing a completed report of investigation, you are recounting the entire case, beginning to end. You'll need to write it with completeness so a reader who never heard of the case will obtain all relevant and material facts. However, continue to use the same format as discussed throughout this book.

Exhibit 6-1 demonstrates an actual completed report of investigation; however, names, dates, places, and some circumstances have been changed to protect the privacy of those involved.

# COMPLETED REPORT OF INVESTIGATION: EXAMPLE

Your department heading, case number, and other pertinent administrative information, which is routine on all reports, is not included in this example.

## BASIS OF INVESTIGATION

On October 10, 1989, Mr. George Smith, Chief of Internal Audit Section, Department of Highways and Transportation, Any State, reported that analysis of a recent audit coupled with other information at the District 21 Headquarters revealed theft of state property valued at about $3.5 million during a period from October 1986 to October 1989.

## OFFENSE(S)

1. Theft of property, RSA 000000 (class C felony), 1986–1989 editions

   *Summary of offense*: "(1) A person commits theft of property if he knowingly takes or exercises unauthorized control over, or makes an unauthorized transfer of interest in, the property of another person with the purpose of depriving the owner thereof."

2. Criminal solicitation, RSA 000000 (class D felony), 1986–1989 editions

   *Summary of offense*: "(1) A person solicits the commission of an offense if, with the purpose of promoting or facilitating the commission of a specific offense, he commands, urges, or requests another person to engage in specific conduct which would: (a) constitute that offense; (b) constitute an attempt to commit that offense; (c) cause the result specified by the definition of that offense; or (d) establish the other person's complicity in the commission or attempted commission of that offense."

3. Criminal conspiracy, RSA 000000 (class D felony), 1986–1989 editions

   *Summary of offense*: "A person conspires to commit an offense if with the purpose of promoting or facilitating the commission of any criminal offense he: (1) agrees with another person or other persons: (a) that one or more of them will engage in conduct that constitutes that offense; or (b) that he will aid in the planning or commission of that criminal offense; and (2) he or another person with whom he conspires does any overt act in pursuance of the conspiracy."

4. Aiding consummation of offense, RSA 000000 (class D felony), 1986–1989 editions

   *Summary of offense*: "(1) A person commits an offense under this section if he knowingly aids another by safeguarding or securing the proceeds of an offense or by converting the proceeds of an offense into negotiable funds."

Exhibit 6-1

# COMPLETED REPORT OF INVESTIGATION: EXAMPLE

5. Forgery, RSA 000000 (class C felony), 1986–1989 editions

   *Summary of offense*: "(1) A person forges a written instrument if, with purpose to defraud, he draws, makes, completes, alters, counterfeits, possesses, or utters any written instrument that purports to be or is calculated to become, or to represent if completed, the act of a person who did not authorize that act.... (3) a person commits forgery in the second degree if he forges a written instrument that is: (a) a deed, will, codicil; contract, assignment, check, commercial instrument, credit card, or other written instrument that does not or may evidence, create, transfer, terminate, or otherwise affect a legal right, interest, obligation, or status."

6. Tampering with a public record, RSA 000000 (class B misdemeanor), 1986–1989 editions

   *Summary of Offense*: "(1) A person commits the offense of tampering with a public record, if with purpose of impairing the verity, legibility, or availability of a public record, he: (a) makes a false entry in or falsely alters a public record; or (b) erases, obliterates, removes, destroys, or conceals a public record." "Commentary: Statute 000000 is primarily designed to ensure the integrity and efficiency of governmental operations."

## SUSPECT(S)

Thomas Sanders, 3742 East 34th Street, Any City, Any State (1 through 6)

Charles Boyd, 1435 Maple Drive, Any City, Any State (1 through 6)

Garland Mayfield, 76 Milford Lane, Any City, Any State (1 through 6)

Ira McGuire, 1840 South Highland Drive, Any City, Any State (1 through 6)

John Moore, 9823 Broad Street, Any City, Any State (1 through 6)

James Eggleston, 22 South Way, Any City, Any State (1 through 6)

Ruben Kinslow, 1458 South 72d Avenue, Any City, Any State (1 through 6)

Charles Sutherford, 2481 South Elm Street, Any City, Any State (1 through 6)

David Blalock, 3618 East Oak Lane, Any City, Any State (1 through 6)

Brian Cauldfield, 7384 Central Blvd., Any City, Any State (1 through 6)

Robert Jones, 5472 Central Blvd., Any City, Any State (1 through 6)

Garland Suffield, 1829 East Pine Blvd., Any City, Any State (1 through 6)

Jules Simpson, 2218 South River Road, Any City, Any State (1 through 6)

Edith Crenshaw, 42 Skyview Drive, Any City, Any State (1 through 6)

Diane Smith, 4567 South 24th Street, Apartment 5, Any City, Any State (1 through 6)

Roberta Klein, 341 County Road South, Any City, Any State (1 through 6)

Exhibit 6-1

# COMPLETED REPORT OF INVESTIGATION: EXAMPLE

## SUMMARY OF INVESTIGATION

Investigation disclosed that during the period October 1, 1986 through October 1, 1989, steel commodities, the property of the State of Blank, were sold without authorization to Steel Buyers, Inc., Any City, Any State, by employees of the Blank State Department of Highways and Transportation, District 21 Headquarters. The proceeds, totaling $3.5 million gained from the illegal sales, were converted to the personal use of those listed as suspects.

The conversion of State property to money for personal use was accomplished through a system of "paper corporations" and four bank accounts (corporations which were formed by suspect Thomas Sanders). [List all the suspects as officers and/or on the board of directors.] The purpose of the companies is listed as "consulting services." Each corporation maintained a commercial bank account coinciding with the corporate names designed also to accommodate checks appearing to be payable to the state:

1. State Roads and Highway Services, Incorporated. Steel Buyers, Inc. was asked to make checks payable to State Roads and Highway Services.

2. Statewide Consultants, Incorporated. Checks were made from State Roads and Highways Services, Inc. to this corporation for "services rendered."

3. The Administrative Support Corporation, Inc. Checks were made from Statewide Consultants, Inc. to this corporation for "goods and services."

Corporations 2 and 3 carried all of the suspects as "contract consultants" and made payments to each, thus avoiding a requirement of submitting payroll deductions and other employee-required records and taxes.

A fourth bank account was discovered in the name of Sanders Associates and was used to conceal personal funds rather than deposit them in a personal account. Sanders would obtain cash from this account, which was traced back to the other accounts.

Each suspect was found to cash the corporate checks made payable to them, and each was discovered to have a safe deposit box at various banks where the personal cash, proceeds from the illegal activities, was maintained.

On December 10, 1989, all the suspects were indicted by the Statewide Grand Jury and arraigned. Bond was set at $100,000 each. All suspects posted bond and are pending trial at a later date.

## SUBSTANTIATION

An internal audit report and analysis indicating an unexplained shortage of steel commodities, questioned documents, missing documents, and irregularities of required recordkeeping procedures was found during an unannounced audit of District 21 Headquarters, Blank State Highway and Transportation Department.

In a written statement, Mr. John Smith, Blank State auditor, explained the audit procedures and unexplained discoveries resulting from his work at District 21.

Exhibit 6-1

# COMPLETED REPORT OF INVESTIGATION: EXAMPLE

Segments of applicable books and records containing questioned documents and procedures were obtained with a search warrant issued by Blank District Court Judge Walter O'Reilly.

In a written statement, Mr. George Thompson, night security guard at District 21 Headquarters, said that Sanders and other suspects regularly would have late-night meetings in the conference room and periodically would be in the open storage yards. He assumed they were working on projects. On several occasions, Thompson said he observed some of the suspects operating equipment in the storage yards, loading tractor trailer trucks with steel beams and other steel items.

In a written statement, Mrs. Grace Overby said she retired from District 21 during April 1987. She explained that during the last few years of service, her job was as book-keeper for expendable but accountable items, such as gasoline, oil, and wood. Although not directly involved with steel commodities, she heard that unusual amounts of steel shipments were coming in and going out, but she assumed they were being used on construction jobs. Overby said that around July 1986, the legislature approved a massive construction effort in that district which included interstate highways, bridges, and other projects, all requiring massive amounts of materials, including steel. Under the circumstances, she concluded that it would be easy to conceal the theft of nearly any commodity, because so much was being used throughout the area.

Records and cancelled checks obtained from Steel Buyers, Inc. revealed that $3.5 million was paid to State Roads and Highways in return for steel purchases.

In a written statement, Mr. John Hilton, owner of Steel Buyers, Inc., said that all the steel hauled into his yard was on State trucks, and since he had purchased steel surplus and scraps for years, he didn't think anything of it, especially with all the construction projects going on in the area. Hilton said Sanders contacted him around September 1986 and told him he received authorization to sell large quantities of steel rather than transport it to the State Capitol disposal yard 150 miles away. Hilton said his demand for steel was up, and he was able to buy it for a good price, so agreed to take all Sanders sent to him. Hilton said that around 1988 he began to have suspicions, but it was a feeling rather than any evidence that the commodities were stolen. He said that was based on an assumption that the State had tight controls on all its property.

Complete microfilm copies of bank records were obtained from various banks for the three corporate accounts, the business account maintained by Sanders, and personal accounts of each suspect.

Search warrants were obtained for each safe deposit box located in the names of each suspect, and the contents were seized as evidence. Contents included a total of $1.8 million in cash and a variety of documents recording the cash income.

Documents obtained from State Motor Vehicle Records disclosed motor vehicles purchased by each of the suspects during the period October 1, 1986 through October 1, 1989. The records were used to trace purchases to dealerships.

Exhibit 6-1

# COMPLETED REPORT OF INVESTIGATION: EXAMPLE

Records from eight new motor vehicle dealerships were obtained showing that each of the suspects purchased three automobiles or pickup trucks during the period October 1, 1986 through October 1, 1989, and they paid cash for each.

Records obtained from the County Courthouse disclosed that several suspects made purchases of new homes, paying cash, within the period of October 1, 1986 through October 1, 1989. Other suspects paid their mortgages in full during the same period, and others made significant improvements to their homes, in each case paying cash.

Records of the corporations established by Sanders were seized by search warrants authorizing a search of Sanders's home, along with notebooks and other documents showing the sales of the steel, the amounts paid, and corporate bookkeeping and bank records. Cancelled checks paying money to all suspects involved were also obtained.

In a written statement (with counsel present), Garland Mayfield, Steel Commodities Stock Supervisor, District 21, admitted the conspiracy and implicated all other suspects and the various roles, with common intent, each played in the theft and conversion of State property. Mayfield said he received about $200,000 from the sale of stolen steel commodities, and he surrendered a diary which he used to record payments.

In a written statement (with counsel present), Ira McQuire, Bookkeeping Supervisor, District 21, admitted the conspiracy and implicated all other suspects and the various roles, with common intent, each played in the theft and conversion of State property.

In a written statement (counsel waived), Charles Sutherford, Vehicle Control Supervisor, District 21, admitted the crimes and his role of providing vehicles coupled with altering usage records. Sutherford implicated all other suspects and relinquished notebooks and other records used to keep control of the vehicles used for the illegal enterprise.

In a written statement (counsel waived), Robert Jones, Construction Supervisor, District 21, admitted the crimes, implicated all other suspects, and explained the procedures used to increase legitimate orders of steel commodities for each approved project.

In a written statement (counsel present), Jules Simpson, Steel Commodities Control bookkeeper, District 21, explained how he attempted to conceal and adjust records to hide the steel which was stolen and sold. Simpson said that all the suspects played a role in the bookkeeping in one way or another, some forging signatures, making false work orders and commodity use sheets, and other devices designed to conceal the thefts.

In a written statement (counsel present), Charles Boyd, Deputy District Director, District 21, said that during October 1986, Sanders approached him with the scheme of stealing and selling steel commodities to Steel Buyers, Inc. Boyd said that together, Sanders and he went over all the people who would need to be involved, and over the next two weeks they talked to each one privately and obtained their consent. He said they were afraid that one or more of them might get cold feet and report their plans before they were involved. He said they also feared that someone might tell after being involved. But when the money flowed, everyone was happy and each became trusted. Boyd turned over notebooks and other information he had written over the years to keep track of the enterprise.

Exhibit 6-1

## COMPLETED REPORT OF INVESTIGATION: EXAMPLE

In a written statement (counsel waived), David Blalock, Administrative Supervisor, District 21, implicated himself and all the suspects, saying that all of them helped in one way or another in all the areas involved. Blalock said that Sanders and Boyd masterminded the enterprise and controlled it and the money. He said that insofar as he knew, each of the suspects received an equal share of the money raised through the theft and conversion sale to Steel Buyers, Inc. He said that if any cheating was suspected someone would have leaked the enterprise, so Sanders was careful in making sure that everyone saw all the records, sale invoices, and checks from the buyer. Blalock said each of the suspects received about $200,000 over the three years, and most bought cars, houses, and paid bills. He thinks many kept a lot of their money in safe deposit boxes, suggested by Sanders, as it was the best way to prevent tracing the money or having to pay tax on it.

Invoices of all steel purchases made by District 21 were obtained from various steel suppliers.

Actual usage of steel compared to completed and ongoing projects during the period of October 1, 1986 through October 1, 1989 was determined by independent engineers from the firm Johnson and Hanson, Any City, Any State.

A comparison between steel purchased, steel used, and steel on hand during the period October 1, 1986 through October 1, 1989 was provided by Johnson and Hanson and reviewed and verified by the Internal Audit Section.

A comparison of steel shortages was made with records provided by Steel Buyers, Inc., which revealed only a 1,000-pound difference.

A comparison analysis of all bank records obtained and seized, coupled with records and cancelled checks provided by Steel Buyers, Inc., revealed that all money derived from the illegal enterprise was accounted for with regard to being deposited and transferred among the accounts and paid to the suspects.

An investigator's statement discusses all relevant and material information not discussed elsewhere in this report.

### WITNESSES

Mr. George Smith, Chief of Internal Audit Section, Any State Department of Highways and Transportation, 8374 South Highway 10, Any City, Any State

Mr. John Smith, Blank State Auditor, Internal Audit Section, Any State Department of Highways and Transportation, 8374 South Highway 10, Any City, Any State

Judge Walter O'Reilly, Blank District Court, Any City, Any State

Mr. George Thompson, Security Guard at District 21, 7834 Highway 45, Another City, Any State

Mrs. Grace Overby, Retired Bookkeeper, 2394 South 35th Street, Any City, Any State

Mr. John Hilton, Owner, Steel Buyers, Inc., 1710 Commercial Blvd., Another City, Any State

Exhibit 6-1

# COMPLETED REPORT OF INVESTIGATION: EXAMPLE

## EXHIBITS

1. Internal Audit Report, Blank State Department of Highways and Transportation, dated October 8, 1989 (cy)

2. Written statement taken from Mr. John Smith, dated October 10, 1989 (original)

3. Search warrant signed by District Court Judge Walter O'Reilly dated November 5, 1989 (cy)

4. Written statement taken from Mr. George Thompson, dated October 14, 1989 (original)

5. Written statement taken from Mrs. Grace Overby, dated October 15, 1989 (original)

6. Printed microfilm records for the period October 1, 1986 through October 1, 1989, supplied by the First National Bank of Downtown, Any City, Any State, pertaining to a checking account in the name of State Roads and Highways, Inc. (cy)

7. Printed microfilm records for the period October 1, 1986 through October 1, 1989, supplied by the Prescott State Bank, Any City, Any State, pertaining to a checking account in the name of Statewide Consultants, Inc. (cy)

8. Printed microfilm records for the period October 1, 1986 through October 1, 1989, supplied by the New Bank, Any City, Any State, pertaining to a checking account in the name of The Administrative Support Corporation, Inc. (cy)

9. Printed microfilm records for the period October 1, 1986 through October 1, 1989, supplied by the Hampton Village National Bank, Any City, Any State, pertaining to a checking account in the name of Sanders Associates, Inc. (cy)

10. Sixteen search warrants, one each for search of each suspect's safe deposit boxes at various banks and seizure of contents; Issued by Judge Walter O'Reilly, Any City District Court (cy)

11. Printed record from the Department of Motor Vehicles, Any State, showing vehicles registered to each suspect during the period October 1, 1986 through October 1, 1989 (original)

12. Twenty-one copies of bills of sale from eight automobile dealers within Any County, which match with the vehicle information provided in Exhibit 11

13. Eleven real estate transaction documents recorded at the Any County courthouse pertaining to the suspects

14. Copies of sixteen real estate transaction and mortgage payoffs obtained from seven banks in the Any County area, pertaining to real estate transactions and or mortgage payoffs by the suspects during the period October 1, 1986 through October 1, 1989 (cy)

15. Written statement taken from Garland Mayfield, dated October 20, 1989 (original)

16. Written statement taken from Ira McQuire, dated October 20, 1989 (original)

Exhibit 6-1

# COMPLETED REPORT OF INVESTIGATION: EXAMPLE

17. Written statement taken from Charles Sutherford, dated October 21, 1989 (original)

18. Written statement taken from Robert Jones, dated October 25, 1989 (original)

19. Written statement taken from Jules Simpson, dated October 23, 1989 (original)

20. Written statement taken from Charles Boyd, dated October 26, 1989 (original)

21. Written statement taken from David Blaylock, dated October 26, 1989 (original)

22. Seventy-two invoices provided by eleven steel commodity suppliers pertaining to sales delivered to District 21 during the period October 1, 1986 through October 1, 1989 (cy)

23. Actual project usage analysis prepared by Johnson and Hanson Engineers, pertaining to steel usage at District 21 during the period October 1, 1986 through October 1, 1989 (original)

24. A comparison worksheet between steel purchased, used, and on hand during the period October 1, 1986 through October 1, 1989 provided by Johnson and Hanson Engineers (original)

25. Consolidated list of purchases made by Steel Buyers, Inc. from the illegal enterprise operated by the suspects, dated November 1, 1989 (original)

26. Comparison worksheet of purchases made by Steel Buyers, Inc. and Audit detected shortages, dated November 2, 1989 (original)

27. Comparison analysis of corporation bank records and cancelled checks obtained from Steel Buyers, Inc. (original)

28. Investigator's statement, dated November 21, 1989 (original)

*Note*: This example of a completed report is provided as a guide. Although based on an actual case, the case itself was far more complex, with all exhibits listed separately. It is your choice to consolidate or list separately each exhibit. In a real situation, I prefer to list each separately. In the actual case in which this example is based, the entire report, including exhibits, numbered 326 pages, far too many to show here.

Exhibit 6-1

# A QUICK REFERENCE QUIDE
# FOR CRIMINAL INVESTIGATION REPORTS

After your routine heading, including department identification, case number, and other department requirements, do the following:

1. Write your *basis for investigation. Why* are you using time and resources to do this?
2. Write your *offense section. What* is the direction and focus of your investigation?
3. Write your *suspects section. Who* are the persons responsible for committing the offenses?
4. Write your *summary of investigation. What* information has your investigation disclosed?
5. Write your *substantiation section. How* are you supporting your conclusions?
6. Write your *witness section. Who* are credible witnesses that can provide relevant and material information?
7. Write your *exhibits section. What* is your hard evidence to prove or disprove the allegations and your conclusions?

# SEVEN

## Information Management Systems for Complex Criminal Investigation Reports

Once your report format is clear and your case file is organized to include an investigative activity log, an investigative plan, and other sections we've already discussed, you're ready to develop additional information management systems that compliment those discussed in chapter 6.

## UNDEVELOPED LEADS REPORT

Our society today is mobility oriented—in other words, people travel without much thought of distance. Criminals travel to avoid identification or arrest; witnesses travel to take new jobs, for health reasons, or just to have a change of scenery. Information you may need can often be scattered throughout the country, even in other countries. A traditional way of obtaining information is by telephone, writing letters, or not bothering with it at all. However, the correct way of obtaining assistance from other law enforcement agencies is making use of an Undeveloped Leads (UDL) Report. There are several benefits from using a UDL report:

1. You can use the same fast-reading, specific report format we've been talking about since the beginning of this book.

2. Receiving an easy-to-understand report which is an official request for assistance provides the receiving department with solid justification for expending resources. With a UDL, you're providing the receiving department with a reason to take an interest, and you're not trying to keep the reason a secret. Far too often, requests for assistance are regarded as favors when actually they are a professional responsibility and courtesy.

3. You'll have a credible record of your investigative effort.

4. Often, when you send a UDL report, you'll get an official report back, along with statements or whatever you requested.

5. Sending UDL reports helps you to manage your case file and information systems.

### What is a UDL Report?

Suppose you're investigating a burglary (or any crime), and you discover that a witness to the crime provided the officer responding with a short written statement. You also note that the officer made a comment in his investigator's statement that he believed this witness has more information but seemed to be afraid at that time to become further involved. When you go to the witness's address, a landlord tells you she moved a couple weeks ago and gives you her forwarding address, a thousand miles away.

Now you have a choice—forget it, or get help from the local law enforcement department at her new address. In most cases investigators drop the effort, because traditionally, if you don't know someone at that department, it's a lost cause. That's because people are too attached to telephones and not typewriters. Envision yourself, loaded with cases, not enough hours in a day, the chief or prosecutor or media turning up the heat. Amid all that, some detective a thousand miles away calls and wants you to go out and find some woman, interview her, and take a statement. You don't want to be discourteous to a fellow officer, so you scratch down what he is able to explain over the phone, and you tell him you'll see what you can do. Let's face it, you won't do anything because in the first place that's not the way to do business.

However, if your chief gets a UDL report in the mail, chances are he'll route it through operations to the detectives, and it'll receive a control number just like any other case. It'll be assigned and worked into your busy schedule and case load management. Maybe a week later you'll be in the area where the witness lives or works, and you can stop by and fulfill the request. A couple days later when you sit down to do report updates, you'll type out a UDL reply report and drop it in the mail.

### How to Write a UDL Report and Reply

Basically, a UDL report is not a lot different from a progress report (with some exceptions, of course) because you're either asking or answering a question or request for assistance. Exhibits 7-1 and 7-2 show common examples of UDLs and replies.

Your standard report heading information is routine, along with your case number, prefixed as UDL-0000000000. Your heading, instead of "Report of Investigation" should say, "Request for Assistance—Undeveloped Leads" or "Undeveloped Leads Reply," whichever the situation may be.

The UDL shown in Exhibit 7-1 tells the receiving department sufficient information to conduct a comprehensive interview of O'Malley, including a copy of the preliminary investigation made by the responding officer.

Exhibit 7-2 shows a possible reply to the UDL.

## SUPPLEMENTAL REPORTS OF INVESTIGATION _____

Next in your information management system is another valuable tool, the supplemental report. This report is used for two key purposes: (1) to update a progress report when an important item develops but this is not sufficient for another progress report. For example, you submit a third progress report on a case, and two days after you forward that report, a suspect is identified. It is the only addition to the progress report you just forwarded. You can apprise your readers of this new information with the least amount of confusion by writing a supplemental report. (2) The report is also used for reporting information after a completed report of investigation is written and forwarded. For example, you write a long,

# UNDEVELOPED LEADS REQUEST

*Your department heading or form, case number, date, and other routine information, followed by your UDL report.*

## BASIS FOR INVESTIGATION

Between May 5 and May 7, 1990, at 1620 Commercial Way, Any City, Any State, persons unknown forced entry into a warehouse and stole computers and software valued at $42,000.

## OFFENSES

1. Burglary
2. Theft

## SUSPECTS

Unknown

## SUMMARY OF INVESTIGATION

Investigation disclosed that a female secretary was working in an adjacent building at the time of the burglary, believed to be on May 6, 1990. The secretary, identified as Heather O'Malley, was interviewed by a responding officer and provided a written statement. The interviewing officer believed O'Malley has more information than provided at the time and should be reinterviewed. O'Malley may provide key information in this case.

## REQUEST FOR ASSISTANCE

Locate Ms. Heather O'Malley, believed to be residing in your city at 88 Park Avenue, Apartment 25, according to a forwarding address left with a former landlord and a change of address card filed with the Postal Service.

Request that your department representative reinterview O'Malley at the earliest opportunity and obtain a written statement if additional information is provided. Also ascertain if O'Malley is willing to testify in court should that be necessary.

## ATTACHED

Copy of Preliminary Investigation report written by Officer Paul O'Neill including O'Malley's statement dated May 8, 1990.

Exhibit 7-1

# UNDEVELOPED LEADS REPLY

## BASIS FOR INVESTIGATION

On June 4, 1990, a request for assistance was received from Any City Police Department, in reference to case number 000000. The request included locating Ms. Heather O'Malley, 88 Park Avenue, Apartment 25, This City, This State; interviewing her about identifying burglary suspects; and obtaining a written statement.

## SUMMARY OF INVESTIGATION

On June 7, 1990, at 88 Park Avenue, Apartment 25, This City, This State, O'Malley was located and agreed to cooperate regarding her knowledge of the burglary. O'Malley stated that when first interviewed she was planning to move to this city, accepting a better job. She believed at the time that if she became an important witness, police may prevent her from moving. She is willing now to testify in court should that be necessary, pending payment of expenses and approval of her current employer. She agreed to provide a statement about her observations, including descriptions of the men involved and the license number of a van used to transport the stolen goods. O'Malley does not believe she was observed by the burglars, since her car was parked inside another warehouse in which she was working at that time.

## ATTACHED

Returning a copy of your department's Police Report and Preliminary Investigation written by officer Paul O'Neill.

Original of Ms. Heather O'Malley's written statement obtained and given to Detective Sergeant Herbert Goodman.

Exhibit 7-2

complex completed report of investigation, and two days after it's forwarded to your readers, another item of evidence or another witness is identified. You can write a supplemental report which adds that new information.

Supplemental reports should always be numbered—for example, first supplemental (first progress report); second supplemental (first progress report); first supplemental (completed report), and so forth. The idea is to tell your reader that this is a supplemental report and what report it is supplementing. Always place the report designation in parentheses. Remember, when numbering your supplemental report, it is the first, second, or third supplemental to a specific report (i.e., the first progress report). If you forward supplemental reports in reference to the second progress report, begin numbering again with first supplemental (second progress report), and follow that procedure with each progress report. When you forward supplemental reports for a completed report, begin with first supplemental (completed report) and continue in sequence as often as necessary for that report. Often, a supplemental might be written a year after a completed report is sent.

### Reopening a Closed Investigation with a Supplemental Report

Depending on your work load and department policy, a case which is not developing may be closed. You would write a completed report; however, explain that there are no suspects or that insufficient evidence developed to prove or disprove that the suspects committed the offense.

A year later, new evidence surfaces—perhaps a gun is found which traces to the crime and the suspect, or a new witness comes forward. Whatever the situation, you need to re-open the investigation. I've been in departments which give the case a new control number and start all over. That's using valuable time and is confusing to your reader.

A closed case is best reopened with a supplemental report, or several depending on the situation. For example, if you start over, progress reports and a new case file are necessary, and the result is wasted administrative time and confusion. Just use the same case number, same case file, and instead of progress reports announcing you're now working on a case previously closed, use a first supplemental report. Instead of a second progress report, use a second supplemental report, and so forth. If the reopened case brings a successful conclusion which is sufficient for prosecution, you can close the case a second time with a supplemental completed report of investigation.

A supplemental report of any kind is designed to convey new information, not rehash old information. A supplemental completed report should contain only the aggregate information collected from the point of reopening the case, not rehash and include all the information contained in the original completed report of investigation.

Examples of the various uses of supplemental reports are shown in Exhibits 7-3 through 7-5.

## THE IMPORTANCE AND BENEFITS OF WRITTEN STATEMENTS _____

Throughout this book I frequently discuss written statements and their value. That emphasis is due to both personal experience and observation of other officers who relied on interviews only to have a witness disclaim certain parts of testimony or deny having said anything about the matter at all. When a witness backs out of a case, it can often destroy weeks, months, or years of investigative effort. All that can be avoided in most situations with written statements. First, a witness can hardly make you appear foolish or cause a credibility gap with your superiors and readers if, after signing a statement, they change their story. Second,

# EXAMPLE OF A FIRST SUPPLEMENTAL REPORT (FIRST PROGRESS)

## BASIS OF INVESTIGATION

See first progress report, dated October 3, 1989.

## OFFENSES

See first progress report, dated October 3, 1989.

## SUSPECTS

3. George Robert Stevenson, 589 Vista Road, Any City, Any State

## SUMMARY OF INVESTIGATION

About 5:20 P.M., October 5, 1989, at the Blank County Sheriff's Substation, Any City, Any State, Stevenson, accompanied by his attorney, Mr. Sam Slick, surrendered and signed a confession which implicated suspects 1 and 2 shown in the first progress report.

## SUBSTANTIATION

In a written statement, George Stevenson confessed to being one of the men involved in the armed robbery at Smith's Drug Store on September 30, 1989.

## WITNESSES

Deputy Sheriff Miles Pryor, Blank County Sheriff's Department, Any City, Any State
Deputy Sheriff Linda Johnson, Blank County Sheriff's Department, Any City, Any State
Deputy Sheriff Robert Kinslow, Blank County Sheriff's Department, Any City, Any State

## EXHIBITS

Written statement of George Stevenson, dated October 5, 1989 (cy)

*Note*: Remember, you have submitted your first progress report only two days before writing this first supplemental report. You are apprising your readers *only* of new information, not rehashing what has already been written in previous reports. Note that the copy of the statement was attached rather than the original. Always attach copies for progress reports and supplementals to progress reports.

Exhibit 7-3

# EXAMPLE OF FIRST SUPPLEMENTAL REPORT (COMPLETED REPORT)

## BASIS OF INVESTIGATION

See completed report, dated July 9, 1989.

## OFFENSES

See completed report, dated July 9, 1989.

## SUSPECTS

3.    George Michael Seabrook, 2894 South Way Blvd., Any City, Any State

## SUMMARY OF INVESTIGATION

About 4:20 P.M., July 12, 1989, at the Any City Police Department, Seabrook surrendered and confessed to being involved in the armed robbery at Smith's Drug Store on May 15, 1989.

## SUBSTANTIATION

In a written statement, George Seabrook confessed to being one of the men involved in the robbery at Smith's Drug Store and implicated suspects 1 and 2 as shown in the completed report of investigation. Seabrook stated that he just returned from California, and on hearing of the warrant for his arrest decided to surrender.

## WITNESSES

Desk Sergeant Samuel Smith, Any City Police Department, Any City, Any State
Detective Lieutenant Mark Johnson, Any City Police Department, Any City, Any State
Detective Sergeant Roger Jones, Any City Police Department, Any City, Any State

## EXHIBITS

Written statement of George Seabrook, dated July 12, 1989 (original)

*Note*: This is a supplemental report to add new information to a completed report already forwarded to your readers. You need only include new information, such as the surrender of Seabrook, who may have been identified in the completed report but was at large. The same reporting procedure would apply if a third suspect is known or even not known to be involved but is identified after the case is closed and goes forward.

EXHIBIT 7-4

# EXAMPLE OF A SUPPLEMENTAL REPORT
# REOPENING A CLOSED REPORT OF INVESTIGATION

## BASIS OF INVESTIGATION

See completed report, dated December 10, 1987.

## OFFENSES

2. Conspiracy

## SUSPECTS

2. Johnathan Rafferty, 3894 East Elm Street, Any City, Any State

## SUMMARY OF INVESTIGATION

On July 4, 1988, at the Any City Police Department, Any City, Any State, Johnathan Rafferty, accompanied by counsel Attorney Sam Slick, surrendered stating that he was involved with suspect 1 in the planning and execution of the armed robbery at O'Malley's All-Night Market. Previous investigation did not disclose a second person being involved in the robbery. Investigation is continuing.

## SUBSTANTIATION

In a written statement (with counsel present), Rafferty stated that Robert Smith (suspect 1) and he planned the armed robbery at O'Malley's Market for several days prior to actually doing it. During the robbery, according to Rafferty, he remained outside the store as a lookout; however, he received an equal split of the money taken during the robbery.

In a written statement, Robert Smith, now serving a twenty-year sentence for the O'Malley armed robbery, said that Rafferty did help plan and did participate in the robbery. Smith said no one seemed to know about a second man after he was identified and arrested, so he decided to remain silent about Rafferty. However, since Rafferty is willing to admit the crime, Smith said he corroborates the information.

## WITNESSES

Desk Sergeant Roy O'Neill, Any City Police Department, Any City, Any State
Detective Stan Stafford, Any City Police Department, Any City, Any State
Patrol Officer George Simpson, Any City Police Department, Any State

## EXHIBITS

Written statement of Johnathan Rafferty, dated July 4, 1988 (original)
Written statement of Robert Smith, dated July 6, 1988 (original)

EXHIBIT 7-5

## EXAMPLE OF A SUPPLEMENTAL REPORT
## REOPENING A CLOSED REPORT OF INVESTIGATION

*Note*: In this report, you're apprising readers about a new development in an old case long ago closed, in which the suspect Smith was prosecuted and convicted for an armed robbery. For whatever reason, accomplices who were not even known to be involved will sometimes come forward, or a witness or other suspect may implicate them months or even years later. In this supplemental report to a completed report, you're letting the reader know also that you intend to do additional investigative work (i.e., the investigation is continuing). In such cases, you would likely have to do more than just take a corroborating statement from Smith, who may deny rather than implicate Rafferty. Rafferty's confession is certainly not sufficient to prosecute, even if Smith does corroborate it. Additional investigation will take place and tie the two together prior to, during, and after the robbery. The best way to proceed is to use the old information as a base and add new information with a first supplemental reopening the case, followed by a second and subsequent supplemental reports until the case is resolved. The case is closed or completed once more simply by noting on the applicable supplemental report (the one that brings the case to a close), "No Further Investigation Required—Completed Supplemental" at the end of your investigative summary.

Exhibit 7-5

in my experience, a witness who signs a written statement has never changed their testimony except to add to it, making it even stronger.

Criminal investigations require credible, relevant, and material information. A great deal depends on witnesses corroborating physical and circumstantial evidence. For example, witnesses who observed a crime have firsthand knowledge about the suspects before, during, and/or after a crime; this, coupled with the smoking gun and circumstances which place the suspects where they would have to be if their involvement is to be proven, builds a strong case. Actually, without these three areas of evidence, cases are rarely successful, especially when going through the appeal processes.

Earlier in this book I discussed preliminary investigations normally conducted by officers who respond to the scene of a crime. Even if detectives go to the scene and conduct the investigation, it's difficult to obtain statements which are well thought out, typewritten, and in a standard format. However, as I suggested, obtain a written statement, handwritten if need be. A criminal investigation, however, is under controlled, planned, and quieter conditions. In an emergency, a handwritten statement is still better than your summary of an interview, but detectives should always find a way to take typewritten statements.

There are actually three kinds of statements you'll be concerned with: (1) witness statements, (2) suspect statements, and (3) investigator's statements.

A witness statement includes victims of a crime. A suspect is anyone who you believe at the time of the interview and statement is in some way implicated in a crime. Always advise a suspect or probable suspect of their rights before interviewing and taking a statement, and have them sign all that as well. Miranda warnings are required only when you arrest a person; however, even when a suspect or probable suspect consents to talk with you and/or make a written statement, when it comes time for court that person will try to get the statement thrown out of court, claiming that no one said anything about his or her rights at the time of arrest. It's better to have the suspect remain silent than be caught in that situation. If he or she chooses to remain silent, you'll at least know you're on the right track.

Your investigator's statement is a valuable tool because it provides a place to put important or clarifying information that would clutter your report. I'll discuss each of the three statements in greater detail on following pages along with examples of each.

Before that, however, there are a number of tips involving the art of taking effective, efficient, and dynamic written statements.

## Twelve Tips About Taking Statements

1. *Don't clutter your statements with information that isn't relevant and material to the case.* Although the statement is another person's testimony, you control the input. Don't expect interviewees to know what's important or what isn't; they expect you to provide that guidance. The idea of sitting down and taking a statement from someone verbatim will cause you a great deal of problems. If you've been in law enforcement for a while, you probably know how difficult it is to maintain attention span, focus, and direction and obtain succinct answers from those you interview. As noted earlier in this book, when you interview and take statements you're dealing with a variety of perceptions. What one person considers a terrible injustice another views as a routine matter.

2. *Ask questions and insist on specific answers.* Don't accept opinions and ideas. Either the person giving a statement is certain about a fact or isn't. You can, however, note elsewhere opinions and ideas simply because sometimes people are reluctant to say what they do know. Instead, they'll offer information as an opinion, idea, or guess. Don't put such information in the statement, but make a note; they may be trying to tell you something important they're not willing to put in writing.

3. *Don't ever hand a piece of paper to anyone, even another law enforcement officer, and ask him or her to write a statement.* Doing that is a sure sign of inexperience or lack of competence. When you ask someone to write a statement, you'll receive an incredible collection of useless information. You're the investigator working a specific case, following a plan, and the only person who knows what information you need, what's relevant, and what's not.

4. *Don't be lazy.* If a solid, informative, valuable statement requires ten pages or more, take the time to do it. Being brief has certain attributes, but it could also be detrimental. The idea is to obtain and record accurate, relevant, and material information. The length of a statement is not a factor.

5. *Use clear language.* The statement is information provided by another person. Don't use your distinctive language or jargon; use the common language the interviewee is providing. Remember that we don't write the way we talk. The same applies to the interviewee, who may be poorly educated or use slang or profanity. Adjust your writing to the person and always keep the language clear and easy to understand. Remember, the statement you write is information coming from the other person who will have to read, understand, and agree with the information you have written.

6. *Try to do your own work.* I've watched detectives who delegate their work, and it is clearly an ego boost to have someone do your work for you. However, show me someone who uses stenographers and dictates or records a statement and hands it to a typist to transcribe, and I'll also show you a mediocre law enforcement investigator. Having someone else do the work removes you from the "feel" of an investigation. It's not different from having lab workers process a crime scene, and you just look at the results. You're not only far removed, but you can't be sure they really did all that could have been done. Do it yourself and you'll know. Take your own statements and you'll have a solid, successful case. If you don't know how to type, learn; it's not difficult.

7. *Focus the witness/victim prior to taking their statement.* One of the key problems I've observed throughout the country when working with law enforcement officers and detectives is their lack of focus on the matter at hand. If you aren't focused, don't expect your interviewee to be focused. Sometimes during an interview, information emerges which leads to an expansion of what you intended the witness to provide. That's fine—but you'll need a clear picture of what information you hope to gain from the interviewee and before you start talking explain what you are seeking. For example, "Tell me what you know about the robbery" isn't going to bring the interviewee into focus. Explain the crime from an investigative point of view; bring the interviewee's perspective into line with what's relevant and material to the case. Be careful not to coach witnesses or put words in their mouth; often witnesses will say whatever they think you want to hear.

8. *Make sure the interviewee is literate.* Whenever you interview and take a written statement from a person with a heavy foreign accent, beware. Part of the statement taking process is having the person read and agree with what you have written (typed), noting any errors, initialing errors, and perhaps making a change here and there. If a person cannot read the statement, you have a problem. In some cases, illiterate people can hide their situation well, since it causes them some embarrassment. However, if you have a signed statement and later learn the person is unable to read, you'll be embarrassed or worse. I normally have an interviewee read something, not as an obvious test, but in a routine way. If the interviewee is not able to read, then find a credible witness and read the statement with the witness and interviewee present. Note on the bottom of the statement that you did so and that the interviewee agreed it was an accurate portrayal of the information they provided. Have the witness to the reading sign the statement. In cases of foreign persons who are unable to speak fluent English, you'll have to locate a certified interpreter and translator. I've taken dozens of statements through an interpreter, having the statement written in the interview-

ee's native language and then translated. If you control the conversation and apply the other rules cited here, it will be a good statement.

9. *Remember the essential elements of proof.* The written statement should always try to satisfy one or more of the elements of proof when the investigation involves a crime. As a general rule, involved or direct witnesses who are unable to satisfy one or more of the elements are not material witnesses. Taking a statement filled with useless information during a criminal investigation is wasting valuable time. For example, if a person witnessed a robbery but is blind and deaf, there is no witnessing that could be material to your investigation and in a court of law. The person couldn't see the assailants or hear their voices. That may sound like an unlikely situation, but it's happened in two of my investigations in past years. You'll have to determine the credibility of a witness's testimony, based on a number of factors but surrounding their ability to provide one or more essential elements or other material information.

10. *Line up your witnesses.* This technique pays off when you're working with witnesses. When a preliminary investigation is conducted correctly by a responding officer, you have the edge of reviewing statements he or she took at the scene. Those statements will give you valuable clues about which witness liked to talk most and which seemed to have a vivid memory of the event. Perhaps you'll have an idea about which witness is most credible. Interviewing and obtaining statements is a building process, since you'll often obtain bits and pieces of information you didn't anticipate, a kind of bonus in the case. For this process to work effectively, you have to line up your interviews with the strongest witness first. That witness will, if you figured correctly, tell you a great deal of important information. If, for example, a strong witness tells you all about the crime and covers all the elements of proof, weaker witnesses can collectively corroborate parts of the strong witness's testimony. Remember, you're not coaching a witness here, but you can ask specific questions. Let's say your strong witness says the assailant was wearing a black jumpsuit. Your weak witness doesn't mention clothing when you're taking the statement, but you can ask the witness to describe the assailant's clothing. The weak witness says: "Oh yes, he was wearing a black outfit of some kind." You've just corroborated your strong witness's statement, and vice versa. You can do this throughout your statements by asking specific questions based on information gained from the strongest witness, who seems to remember every detail of the event.

11. *Start with the weakest suspect.* Interviewing and obtaining statements from suspects requires a shift in your technique, actually a reversal. The suspect, after hearing his or her rights, consents to an interview and further consents to making a written statement. In this case, you also want the suspect who will say the most as your starting point, providing you have multiple suspects. In my experience, if there are two or more suspects, one will be the toughest, one will be the weakest, and the others will be somewhere in the middle. The weakest will probably tell you far more information than he or she intended to say and often more than you ever expected to receive. With that statement complete, select the next suspect in the group who is weaker than the rest and build your way toward the strongest. When the tough interviewee finally has his or her turn, you will be able to tell him or her exactly what happened. This is unnerving, and normally even the tough one will decide it's no use to deceive you, and coming clean might work in his or her favor.

12. *Leave the suspects until last.* Over the years I've tried all kinds of approaches to criminal investigations, and I've learned a great deal of my successful techniques from both experience and observation of other investigators who aren't successful but work hard. One of the more prevalent reasons for failure seems to be the urgency of interviewing suspects. Going after the all-important confession requires application of carefully crafted strategy, and although all investigations are different in one way or another, leaving the suspects until last seems to remain a consistently successful technique. I once worked in an agency where

the chief would tell all new investigators that the best way to get information was to ask the suspect. I recently heard that he is managing a landfill. The best technique is to collect every shred of evidence and information and thus be in a position where the suspect's story or confession doesn't matter; your case is ready to go with or without the suspect. When you finally confront your suspect or suspects individually, give them the opportunity to tell their side of the story. I normally preface my interview with a little speech that goes something like this: "Before I advise you of your rights and you decide either to talk about the offense, remain silent, or talk to a lawyer, I want you to remain silent and let me tell you what happened. I also want you to understand that if you choose to make a statement or remain silent, it makes no difference to me, because I don't need your information to go forward with a prosecution. However, it's only fair that you have the opportunity to tell your side of the story if you choose to do that." Then I explain the charges, advise the suspect of his or her rights, and let him or her make the choice. In the hundreds of serious criminal investigations I've conducted, I can't recall any suspects that didn't make a full confession in a written statement. Even suspects want to tell what they know, and I'm always ready to write it out. However, don't tell a suspect it will help him or her to talk unless it will. Don't coach or put words in his or her mouth. You can get specific by asking specific questions.

Exhibits 7-6 through 7-8 show examples of statements discussed in the twelve technique tips, beginning with a strong witness, followed by weaker witnesses, and then an example of a statement given by the weaker of two suspects. Note that the statement of the weaker suspect, coupled with the arrest and physical evidence, leaves only tying up loose circumstantial facts like verifying the suspects were at Joe's, met a man named Luke, pawned items at a pawn shop, and bought items at the surplus store. With their residence verification, police reports, employment verification, and other loose ends, your case is completed. The strong witness, on hearing all the facts, is likely to corroborate all of it.

## EXAMPLE OF A STRONG WITNESS STATEMENT TEXT

I came into Smith's Drug store to buy a few things needed and noticed no one seemed to be around inside the store. That was unusual, because evenings are normally busy at that store. Soon after I entered the store, a man dressed in black clothing and wearing a black ski mask popped up from behind the cosmetic counter. He had a short gun in his hands, the kind with two barrels; I think they're called a shotgun. He pointed it at me and said, "Just keep walking to the back of the store and you won't get hurt." That man had an average voice, but I could tell he was trying to make it deeper than it is; I suppose he hoped he would sound sinister. I considered turning and running out the door (it was only about 10 feet away), but I remembered television shows where people were shot trying to get away, and I was afraid this man would do the same to me. So I did as he said, and just before reaching the back of the store, near the pharmacy section, another man, dressed the same way, popped out from behind the aisle display shelves and pointed a small silver pistol at me. I noticed he was kind of shaking and figured it was either fear or drugs. He told me to go over behind the counter and lie on the floor. The counter he motioned to runs adjacent the pharmacy section across the back of the store, and that's where the cash register is. To get behind that counter, I had to walk along it to the far end and around. It's a long store, but narrow. When I walked around the end of the counter, I was shocked; people were lying on the floor; must have been ten or twelve men and women. Everyone was on their stomachs, sort of cradling their heads in their arms. It was terrible to see that kind of thing. At first I thought they were dead and thought, "Oh no, he's going to kill me now," but then I realized they were alive. That man told me to get down on the floor and lie on my stomach and keep my mouth shut. He was still shaky, and young I think, judging from his build, voice, and actions. I did as he said and wondered what would happen next. I thought maybe they would just come over and shoot us all, lying there helpless. After a while, which seemed like hours but actually was only about ten minutes or less, I heard the man with the pistol talking to another man, but I couldn't see him; his voice sounded young, too. They talked about getting everyone's money and jewelry. Then the second man spoke to all of us lying on the floor, telling us to put our purses, wallets, rings, watches, and any money we had in our pockets on the floor near our heads. Everyone did that, and he moved through us picking it up and stuffing everything in a bag. One of the people must have looked up, and the man yelled, "Keep your heads down, don't look up." I had a glimpse of what he was doing; he had a large cloth bag, like a shopping bag, and was stuffing everything in it. I recognized the bag because the store sells them. They keep them over near the end of the counter on a rack. When he finished picking up all the things, I heard him say "Okay," and I could hear them moving around and then silence. After a couple minutes or so, I heard Gloria, she's the manager, say "They're gone, is everyone okay?" Everyone just lay there for a while. Then I could hear people getting up from the floor, and a lot of talking at first in whispers and then out loud. A man helped me up, and I just leaned against the counter looking around. Gloria appeared from the pharmacy section, that's where her office is located, and told us the police were on the way. She walked around and asked each of us if we were okay. In a few minutes, four or five police officers appeared, some coming in the back way and some from the front. Then one young officer told us that he must talk to each of us and asked us to go into the employee's room over on the back side of the store, near the back door. It's a room with soft drink machines, some tables, chairs, and lockers. After everyone

Exhibit 7-6

# EXAMPLE OF A STRONG WITNESS STATEMENT TEXT

was in the room, most of us sitting down, the officer passed out sheets of paper, forms to fill out about who we are and what was taken from us, and Gloria passed out some ballpoint pens. The officer asked us to fill them out, and in a few minutes he would talk to each of us separately in Gloria's office. In a few minutes, Gloria came in and started sending us to her office so the officer could talk to each of us and take a statement, which he wrote out and we signed. After we signed the statement, he told us we were free to leave the store, and detectives would be contacting us soon. I asked him about the chances of getting our jewelry back; my wedding ring was handed down from my grandmother. He said everything possible would be done to recover the items stolen from us.

**Q:** Mrs. Rafferty, would you have given your jewelry, money, purse, and other items taken from you if the men didn't force you to do so?

**A:** Absolutely not. They had guns, and I was certain they would have shot us, maybe everyone if anyone of us crossed them.

**Q:** Are you a regular customer at Smith's Drug Store?

**A:** Oh yes, I live just a block away and have come here for thirty-five years. The Hansons used to have the store and then sold it to Smiths a few months ago.

**Q:** Has the store changed much, regarding the interior arrangement?

**A:** It's looked this way for thirty-five years; nothing has been changed. That's why I like to come here.

**Q:** Can you describe the first man who confronted you after entering the store?

**A:** As I said, he was wearing black clothing, they looked like coveralls, and a black mask, the kind they use for keeping warm when skiing. I've seen them on sale over at the mall during the winter. It was black, too. He was wearing black gloves, leather, I think, and tight fitting. The gun was black, what I could see of it, and there were two barrels, like the one my husband used to go duck hunting. He called it a double-barreled shotgun. But this one was short, like on television, sawed off I think they're called. Criminals use them. He had a silver-colored watch, too; I remember seeing that. Otherwise, nothing showed. He was Caucasian; I could tell that from the holes in the ski mask and around the sleeves of the coveralls between that and the gloves. He was about 5'10" tall, and about 150 pounds. He wasn't a big man, and from his build, voice, and actions, I perceived him to be a young man, early twenties is my estimation.

**Q:** Can you describe the second man who confronted you?

**A:** He was dressed the same way as the first man, but I could see he was wearing black sneakers. The coveralls were too large for him, fitting baggy. He had a black belt, looked like heavy canvas around his waist. He had gloves on, too, leather and tight. I didn't notice a watch or other things. He was Caucasian; I'm certain about that. And his gun was silver colored, and from what I've seen on television, I think it was an automatic. He was about 5'10" too, slight build, maybe 130 pounds. From the way he acted, I estimate he was in his early twenties, too, maybe younger. The gun was shaking, making me believe he was nervous, maybe very afraid, or was on drugs or something.

Exhibit 7-6

# EXAMPLE OF A STRONG WITNESS STATEMENT TEXT

**Q:** Anything you can tell me about the third man?

**A:** As I said, he stayed out of my sight, but his voice sounded young, twenties maybe, and sort of consoling. It seemed he was assuring the other man that everything would be okay. He seemed to be in charge and giving orders.

**Q:** Do you know the identities of the men who committed the robbery?

**A:** I believe they used to work for the Hansons when they ran the store.

**Q:** Why do you believe that?

**A:** Their voices. I remember hearing them before, and their appearance, actions, builds. I sensed a familiarity about them, and they kind of acted toward me like they knew who I am. You know I've been shopping at that store a couple times a week for thirty-five years. I've known everyone who worked there during those years; some became old friends. I'm just interested in people and young people, too. Maybe that's why the one man was so nervous; he probably felt like he was robbing a friend. I always treat people nice, and I know these young men, but I can't name them specifically. Maybe in time I'll think of their names. If I heard them, it might come back.

**Q:** You're sure you didn't hear the voices elsewhere or may be mistaken?

**A:** No. Thinking about it now, I know they have worked in that store at one time or another. You know, Mr. Hanson used to hire young people to give them a chance, and many times Mrs. Hanson was worried because some of them had been in trouble. He was that kind of man. But, when the Smiths took over they changed all that, fired everyone and brought in their own people from the other store on East 5th Street, the one that burned down a year or so ago. It was okay I suppose; everyone here now is a good person; but I did feel sorry for all those who lost their jobs.

**Q:** Do you know anyone who drives an old blue van?

**A:** Yes. Mike Appleton, one of the boys who used to work here. Yes, he had an old blue van. He made deliveries for Mr. Hanson, but that was about three years ago, when I was laid up after a hip operation. I would call over, and Mike would deliver my things to the house. Now that we are talking about it, I think Mike's voice is the third man I couldn't see. He was always a take-charge kind of young man and told me once he would like to be the manager, but then things changed. I think he was working part time before Mr. Hanson died, going to City college. He used to work full time in summers during high school and part time when school started. He got kind of a raw deal I guess, when the Hansons sold out.

**Q:** Do you believe Mike Appleton was one of the men?

**A:** Yes, I do. What a shame. I hate to say it, but I do think he was one of them.

**Q:** You base that only on a voice you heard?

**A:** Yes, but I've heard it so many times, it's hard to mistake.

EXHIBIT 7-6

# EXAMPLE OF A STRONG WITNESS STATEMENT TEXT

**Q:** Why didn't you tell the officer about that after the robbery?

**A:** I told him the men and voices sounded familiar, that I thought they might be former employees. He didn't put that in my statement but said he would note it until I was sure. Now that time has passed and I've had time to rethink it all, and talking with you today, I'm certain about that.

**Q:** What was taken from you during the robbery?

**A:** My purse; it wasn't worth much, an old thing actually. But I had some pictures of my late husband, my children, and grandchildren. They were in one of those small albums that can be stuck in a purse. And a small wallet with a Master Card, Visa, and American Express card. I think I had about a hundred dollars cash, in small bills, and a couple check cashing cards, one for the supermarket and another from the drug store over in the mall. And some cosmetics, comb, and other odds and ends. The biggest loss is my wedding ring, which belonged to my grandmother and was handed down in the family. It was to go to my daughter when I pass away. It was handmade in England 150 years ago. And my watch, old and not worth much, but it was an anniversary present from my husband thirty years ago. That meant a lot.

**Q:** Do you have the watch serial number, and were any of the items engraved or marked so you can positively identify them?

**A:** Yes, the ring was engraved with the name Ruth Fleming—that was my maternal grand-mother—and the watch was inscribed on the back. It was worn but readable, "For the love of my life," a message from my husband. He used it a lot. It was a Waltham brand with Roman numerals on the face, and 18 carat gold.

**Q:** Is there anything you want to add to this statement at this time?

**A:** No, I can't think of anything now.

## END OF STATEMENT

EXHIBIT 7-6

# EXAMPLE OF A WEAKER WITNESS STATEMENT TEXT

When I came into the drug store to pick up a prescription, a man jumped up from behind a counter near the door and pointed a gun at me, telling me to go to the back of the store. At the back of the store another man pointed a gun at me and said to lie on the floor along with the others, and I did. Later, he took our wallets, watches, and money, and they left. That's about all there is to tell.

**Q:** Can you describe the men, what they were wearing, mannerisms, guns, and other things?

**A:** I really didn't pay much attention; I think they wore black clothes, masks, gloves, and had guns, which I don't know much about.

**Q:** What about their voices?

**A:** Men's voices, maybe young.

**Q:** What do you mean by young?

**A:** Well, the way they acted; they weren't big, average build but slender, and the texture of their voices just struck me as young rather than mature men.

**Q:** What age group are you talking about?

**A:** Early twenties, I think.

**Q:** Were you afraid during the robbery?

**A:** Sure, I hear all the news stories about these people killing all the people in a robbery. I was scared.

**Q:** Is fear the reason you handed over your wallet and other things?

**A:** That's the only way I would do that.

**Q:** Did you see anything about the men that would help identify them?

**A:** No. They said to keep my head down and mouth shut, and that's what I did.

**Q:** Do you know the identities of the men?

**A:** No.

**Q:** Have you ever seen or heard their voices before?

**A:** Well, I couldn't see them because of the masks, but the voices did sound familiar, but that may be my imagination.

**Q:** Do you shop at Smith's Drug Store often?

**A:** In and out periodically. Maybe once a week to get a paper, magazines, or medication.

**Q:** How long have you shopped at Smith's Drug Store?

**A:** About five years, after we moved into the neighborhood. It was Hanson's Drug Store then.

Exhibit 7-7

# EXAMPLE OF A WEAKER WITNESS STATEMENT TEXT

**Q:** Do you think any of the men were at one time employees at the store?

**A:** I don't know. I've never paid that much attention to who worked at the store.

**Q:** What was stolen from you during the robbery?

**A:** My wallet, and several credit cards; I gave the other officer a list and cancelled them the next morning. About fifty dollars in cash, that's about all in the wallet. My watch, a gold Boliva, worth about $1,200. And my wedding ring, a band worth about $500.

**Q:** Do you have a serial number of the watch, or was the watch or ring engraved?

**A:** No. Nothing like that.

**Q:** Is there anything you wish to add to this statement at this time?

**A:** No.

## END OF STATEMENT

Exhibit 7-7

# EXAMPLE OF A WEAK SUSPECT STATEMENT TEXT

Sam Smith and I met at his place about noon and had a few beers. We talked a lot about needing money, and going to California. He has a sister living there. About 4 P.M. we went to Joe's Pool Hall, just to hang out, and met a guy there who was trying to sell some guns. Joe vouched for him, so we figured he was okay. I guess he used to live around here and was just passing through. It gave Sam and me an idea, maybe robbing a few places so we would have enough money to go to California and live good. After a while, we asked Luke about the guns he was selling, and he took us to his car in the alley and opened the trunk. He had a bunch, selling them for $100 each. We picked out a couple and paid him the last money we had between us. Sam got a .357 snub nose revolver, and I picked a 9 mm semiautomatic. Luke threw in a box of shells for each since we were old friends of Joe. Later, I guess about six, we went to a pawn shop and pawned our watches, a couple cameras, and a gold ring Sam had. It brought us enough money to fill up my van with gas, and we went over to the Army Navy Surplus store and bought some black jumpsuits, ski masks, sneakers, and gloves. After that we drove around town looking for someplace that we could rob, get a lot of money, and not get caught. We drove around until about midnight and went back to Sam's place to sleep. The next morning, we got serious about knocking over two or three places the same night and then getting out of town, going to California. We packed his stuff and went to where I had a room and packed my stuff and put it all in the van. We went over to Joe's Pool Hall and hung out until about eight when it was dark; then drove over to Elm Street Park and changed clothes in the van. That night we hit Snead's All Night Market and picked up $500 and the 42nd Street Liquor store and picked up $750 from the cash register, but the safe was open and it had $1,500. And then some jerk half drunk came in and we took him for $2,500 he was carrying in his pocket. We started out of town and decided to hit one more place and stopped at George's Quick Shopper and hit that place for another $800. On the way out of town, some old woman drove out in front of me and I hit her with the van, smashed it bad, and a cop happened to be passing by, looked us over in those black outfits, and put us under arrest.

**Q:** Who is Joe?

**A:** Joe Dunnington; he owns Joe's Pool Hall.

**Q:** Was he involved in your plans?

**A:** No. We just hang out there; he don't know anything about what we do.

**Q:** Who is Luke?

**A:** That's all I know about him. I think Joe could tell you more.

**Q:** Where did you live?

**A:** 1839 South Broad Street. It's kind of a rooming house; I had a room there for $20 a week.

Exhibit 7-8

---

## EXAMPLE OF A WEAK SUSPECT STATEMENT TEXT

---

**Q:** Where did Sam live?

**A:** He had an efficiency at the Sleepy Time Motel over on Elm Street, kind of a run-down place.

**Q:** Where did you work?

**A:** I've been unemployed about six months, collecting unemployment checks, but they run out. Used to work at the Highland Bowling Lanes as a maintenance man.

**Q:** What about Sam, where did he work?

**A:** Sam worked at the City Salvage Yard for about three years until it closed; then just did odd jobs, here and there.

**Q:** How many other robberies have you done?

**A:** None, that was it, for both Sam and me.

**Q:** How did you and Sam plan to split the money from the robberies?

**A:** We figured we'd pool the money until we got to California, and then split what was left. I planned to sell the van and get rid of that, maybe go up to Montana or someplace and start over. California is to expensive to stay. Sam planned to stay on with his sister.

**Q:** Is there anything you wish to add to this statement?

**A:** No.

### END OF STATEMENT

Exhibit 7-8

### The Investigator's Statement

The best rule of thumb for writing an investigator's statement in a criminal investigation is to discuss anything relevant and material to the case which is not discussed elsewhere in your report.

Throughout this book I've referred to an investigator's statement as a catch-all, but don't misunderstand that definition. Nor is the investigator's statement like witness or suspect statements, which tell an individual's story or perception about an event.

The investigator's statement clarifies specific facts, which includes identifying people who are not witnesses but are mentioned in a statement provided by a witness or suspect. For example, who are Luke and Joe mentioned in the suspect statement in Exhibit 7-8? Your investigation revealed that they are not part of the robbery; however, they are mentioned and need to be explained.

Another benefit of your investigator's statement is to note information you should have included in your report but didn't for whatever reason. For example, you've written a 200-page report, and it's ready to go. But going through it, you find you omitted an address or some other fact that is not critical but needs to be in the report. Explain it and put it in the investigator's statement.

In the case of the robberies discussed in the suspect statement in Exhibit 7-8, you have three separate cases until they are found to be linked. Each robbery was planned and executed by the same people, the same night, and with a common purpose. Although three cases opened, they can and should be merged. However, although your report explains the facts as one case, you should note in your investigator's statement that originally three cases were opened and merged and explain why. The investigator's statement is a place to explain things that don't fit elsewhere in the report.

You can use your statement to discuss what kind of equipment was used, investigative techniques if applicable, weather conditions, and anything that your reader might wonder about. A good rule is to include answers to any question you can envision your reader having as he or she reads your report.

You can also add supplemental information in lieu of taking another written statement when a minor but still important fact is brought up after you have obtained a written statement. For example, after taking a statement from a witness, he or she remembers that in a robbery a diamond cocktail ring was also stolen. It's not mentioned in the witness's statement.

Perhaps a suspect contacts you after a confession and written statement and tells you he remembers that Luke's name is Luke O'Leary, a fact he was unable to remember when you took his statement. Since it has nothing directly to do with the crime of armed robbery but should be clarified as the source of the firearms used in the robberies, put it in your statement. An example of an investigator's statement is shown in Exhibit 7-9.

## EXAMPLE OF AN INVESTIGATOR'S STATEMENT TEXT

George's Bar and Grill, mentioned in the statement of Robert Johnson (Exhibit 21), is located at 3465 Sunset Boulevard, Any City, Any State.

The blue van mentioned in the statement of Grace Simpson (Exhibit 34) is identified as a 1980 Ford Econoline Van, serial number 000000000000000, registered to Sam Jones, 8394 Commercial Way, Any City, Any State.

Merging of cases 00000, 000000, and 000000 into this case number 00000000 was necessary. The suspects in all three cases were disclosed to be the perpetrators, and the crimes were all committed in sequence beginning with case number 000000.

Efforts to contact Zeke Roberts, identified in Exhibit 38, met with negative results. Roberts is believed to have left the state with no forwarding address.

The name Jim Brown, mentioned in the statement of Clyde Dudley (Exhibit 39), is fully identified as James Browne, 2948 Georgetown Lane, Any City, Any State.

The camera used to photograph the crime scene is identified as Canon, 35 mm, with F4 settings.

Tool marks on a door removed from the crime scene were later found to be marks caused by a maintenance man and verified to have no connection to the burglary. Statements obtained from the suspects disclosed that they entered through a window, and that information was verified by other evidence. The door was returned to owners.

Latent fingerprints developed at the crime scene were identified belonging to a security guard, who was cleared of any involvement in the crime.

The watch reported stolen during the burglary by Ralph Englewood, identified in a written statement (Exhibit 41) as being a Rolex, was corrected by Englewood and should read Rolaflex.

One computer reported stolen during the burglary shown as Bell XT, serial number 000000000, was discovered in a storage room and deleted from the stolen property list.

**END OF STATEMENT**

Exhibit 7-9

# Criminal Intelligence Report Writing Systems

Criminal intelligence has in recent years come of age in the law enforcement profession. In past years, intelligence played a role dominated by using personally developed and closely guarded informants on the streets. Informants are still used extensively; however, their motives are generally clear: information in exchange for money or favors. The result is, of course, questionable reliability.

Personally developed informants also present another problem. The information they give to only certain officers remains within a secrecy pact and does little or no good to the criminal intelligence effort overall.

In some states, criminal intelligence organizations comprised of law enforcement departments and agencies within the state hold periodic meetings, exchange information, and attempt to further the idea of information collection and management about criminal activities. National organizations are much the same; however, another factor is now becoming the key to sharing information—the computer.

As this new phenomenon grows and law enforcement departments become more sophisticated, criminal intelligence will become a valuable asset in preventing crime and in bringing those responsible for crime into the criminal justice system.

All this emphasis on criminal intelligence operations is of little value unless effective, efficient, and dynamic criminal intelligence reporting systems emerge as well. This chapter shows the options and procedures of implementing reporting information that evolves into credible criminal intelligence.

## INTELLIGENCE VERSUS INFORMATION

Information is unevaluated material of every description including that derived from observations, communications, reports, rumors, and other sources from which intelligence is produced. Information itself may be true or false, accurate or inaccurate, confirmed or unconfirmed, pertinent or impertinent, positive or negative. Intelligence is the product resulting from the collection, evaluation, and interpretation of information which concerns one or more aspects of criminal activity.

Just as investigation of a crime requires essential elements of proof, criminal intelligence operations and reports concentrate on essential elements of information (EEI). If the EEI is sufficient, information becomes credible intelligence.

## THE CRIMINAL INTELLIGENCE CYCLE

The activities connected with criminal intelligence operations generally follow a four-phase cycle oriented on the department's policy. Supervising and planning are inherent functions involved in all phases of the intelligence cycle. The phases are as follows:

1. Directing the collection effort
2. Collecting the information
3. Processing the collected information
4. Writing reports, disseminating, and using the resulting intelligence.

The intelligence cycle is continuous, and all four phases may take place concurrently. At the same time that new information is being collected, other information previously collected is analyzed, processed into a comprehensive report, and disseminated.

Directing the collection effort begins with determining requirements and establishing priorities. A continuously updated collection plan keyed to the departmental policy on intelligence must be developed. Based on this plan, an effective criminal intelligence program develops within your department.

A key element is your intelligence report. Just as conducting a criminal investigation in itself doesn't have any impact without organizing the information into a useable report, criminal intelligence doesn't serve any purpose until it is organized into a useable report.

However, the negative tradition of each officer having a personal string of informants and keeping his or her information secret serves no purpose beyond perhaps massaging personal ego (i.e., knowing something no one else knows and keeping it that way). An effective criminal intelligence program requires that pertinent information concerning criminal activities affecting your community or jurisdiction and, in some circumstances other jurisdictions, be collected from available sources and recorded, processed, and disseminated as appropriate. Information having a purely local application will be recorded, processed, and disseminated to applicable local law enforcement officers and agencies.

## DISSEMINATION OF CRIMINAL INTELLIGENCE DATA

Due to the nature of criminal intelligence, it's important that strict control over its dissemination be maintained. For example, handing out information in the form of flyers to each officer would surely not protect either the information or the sources. On the other hand, in many cases you need each officer to be alert for certain activities and report their observations. The best rule of thumb is that before releasing criminal intelligence, establish who needs to know. A way of releasing information to gain assistance is to isolate or create "cells" within your intelligence file. For example, there is no requirement, even when help is needed to collect information, to give officers the entire case. On the other hand, you can isolate a requirement, such as recording all the license plate numbers of automobiles observed during a shift at a specific address. There is no requirement to tell the officers why; explaining that it is to assist with a discreet inquiry is sufficient. Judgment is a key factor in determining which information should be released and to whom it should be distributed. Keeping secrets is obviously an ineffective way to operate; however, revealing total information isn't effective, either. Create cells of information which don't relate to another cell or make your sources obvious.

## TERMINOLOGY IS IMPORTANT TO YOUR CRIMINAL INFORMATION AND INTELLIGENCE REPORT SYSTEMS

Developing a system of reporting criminal information and intelligence relies first on terminology applied to the categories of reports within your system.

1. *Information report.* This is a summary of information provided by one or more sources who may or may not suspect criminal activity. That information and your training and experience as a law enforcement officer arouse suspicion based on known indicators of crimes. For example, an informant discloses that Joe's Pancake House is a meeting place for traffickers of drugs. During the late evening hours each Thursday, you notice two late-model expensive automobiles with out-of-state license plates parked in the rear of the pancake house parking lot. Driving past the location later, you observe local automobiles parked alongside the out-of-state cars and a group of people standing outside talking. Deciding to park and observe, you notice periodically two of the members of the group go to the expensive cars and open and close the trunk lids, but it's too dark and you're too far away to see if anything is taken out or put into the trunk compartments. Based on an informant's tip and your observation over a period of two weeks, there appears to be drug trafficking in progress. You don't have sufficient credible information to be certain; perhaps it's some other scheme in operation or perhaps it's legal. However, you're obligated to write a report with the information which can be evaluated, perhaps collated with other information you're not aware of or used to alert other officers to observe the area. Criminal information is possible activity which is not verified.

2. *Criminal intelligence report.* This report is leading to a criminal investigation; however, insufficient evidence prevents that action. For example, information is developed from three or four informants that the out-of-state automobiles you observed in the rear of the pancake house parking lot each Thursday evening are in fact drug traffickers, and the local cars are dealers coming to pick up their shipment of drugs. Since the information is coming from several sources unrelated to each other, the observations you've made indicate validity of their allegations, and a check of license plate numbers links the participants to past drug offenses, it's credible that the illegal operation is occurring. However, until better evidence is obtained, a criminal investigation is not feasible. As a general rule, criminal intelligence identifies the following:

a. Alleged criminal activity in which probable cause is yet insufficient to initiate a criminal investigation

b. The existence of organized crime, its strength, structure, activities, and support

c. The current and emerging criminal leaders and their associates

d. The areas, legal and illegal, which are most vulnerable to organized crime and which have been active in the past

e. The existing and potential high crime areas and the basic causative factors

f. The trends and patterns in crime rates to establish a basis for special enforcement operations, the reallocation of existing resources, and the relocation of normal law enforcement operations.

1. Includes information pertaining to the background on persons, places, and organizations, as well as information on past criminal acts and planned occurrences.

Criminal intelligence applies to acts of crime committed within your jurisdiction, throughout the country, and internationally by individuals or organized criminal groups, if the acts have some impact on your area of jurisdiction.

2. Includes development of collection, processing, and dissemination phases, along with utilization of intelligence in the conduct of law enforcement operations.

3. *Command intelligence.* The total intelligence available to the chief, sheriff, or other command authority, which is used to develop resources and courses of action.

4. *Operational intelligence.* A category of intelligence required for planning and executing law enforcement activity focused on a specific element of criminal activity.

5. *Reciprocal intelligence.* Intelligence that is exchanged between law enforcement departments and agencies on a required or continuing basis. Normally, this intelligence or information is of mutual interest.

6. *Essential elements of information and criminal intelligence.* These elements are critical items of information pertaining to the individual criminal, criminal activities, and crime areas that, when related with other available information, provide the law enforcement officer or department with the intelligence for reaching conclusions and making decisions. Essential elements of criminal intelligence provide guidelines for collection of information to assure that critical items of information are collected, processed, and disseminated to the appropriate user.

7. *Source.* Sources are traditionally referred to as informants. Using the word *informant* is both inadequate and a misnomer. Often, sources of information are law enforcement officers and departments; banks, other businesses, and business persons; prominent citizens or officials; and persons who trade information for money or favor. Even those persons who are paid to provide or collect information should be referred to in your reports as sources, which encompasses all levels of persons or agencies providing you with information about criminal activity.

## HOW INFORMATION AND INTELLIGENCE REPORTS DIFFER FROM PRELIMINARY AND CRIMINAL INVESTIGATIVE REPORTS

Although similarities do exist, information and intelligence reports differ from one another, and both differ from preliminary and criminal investigative reports.

### *Information Reports*

Information reports contain raw data from one or more sources which indicate possible criminal activity. For instance, your intelligence system has revealed that a real estate fraud group operated recently in several nearby states. Although law enforcement departments learned about the crime and started action, the group already moved on, leaving only fictitious names and other misinformation that prevented successful investigation. A few days after reading the bulletins received by your department warning of this criminal activity, you're talking with a local printer. He tells you that two well-dressed men came to his business a few days ago and placed a large order for brochures, business forms, letterheads, and other documents. The men provided the printer with examples of each, with the previous names marked out. The printer tells you this in passing, while you're having a general conversation about all the new businesses coming into town. The printer comments that he really needs the business, and these men paid in cash, in advance. While he is thinking about business, you're thinking about crime and the bulletins which recently arrived at the department. Since you know that printers keep records and samples of work they do, at some later time more information can be obtained. However, pressing the printer now might cause him to become defensive, even tell the customer you're interested, and nothing will be gained. On the other hand, it's always possible that the men are completely legitimate, but it's time to begin some discreet, creative collection activities and to begin writing criminal information reports.

### Intelligence Reports

Criminal intelligence is processed information concerning known crimes and criminals; or information gained from credible sources alleging that a crime or offense is about to happen, is happening, or has happened. For example, the printer in the previous example calls you and says that while going through the materials the two men left as examples to follow, he discovered a newspaper clipping. It indicates that the two men are under investigation in another state for conducting criminal real estate schemes. He says that the names in the clipping are different, but the documents they want printed, along with information in the article, cause him to believe they are the same people. The printer says he needs the business, but certainly not enough to conceal the information found.

The clipping in itself is an indicator, and all the information at this point satisfies the essential elements of information required to write a criminal intelligence report. A phone call to the out-of-state law enforcement agency reveals that no indictments or outstanding arrest warrants are issued for the two men. Since no crime has yet occurred in your jurisdiction and the men, to the best of your knowledge, are not wanted by other jurisdictions, you'll need to develop the case through an intelligence process rather than a criminal investigation.

## THE CRAFT OF WRITING INTELLIGENCE REPORTS

Your first responsibility in writing intelligence reports is to avoid the idea that you are conducting a witch hunt. In other words, don't write a report until you can determine what crime the information implies may have occurred or may occur in the future, or both. This is often a difficult task, especially when you're dealing with white-collar or economic crimes. There's also a jurisdiction problem you'll have to think through. For example, does the scheme you're uncovering have to do with an existing law which your department is obligated to enforce? Does the information fall within jurisdiction of another agency? Often, with white-collar crimes, economic crimes, drug trafficking, and stolen automobile operations fall into multiple jurisdiction enforcement. Perhaps state and federal tax laws apply to the crime, and the IRS and state tax enforcement have jurisdiction. Perhaps the perpetrators are operating across state lines or county and/or city lines. If your jurisdiction is on the border of another country, that becomes a factor if the suspects are operating over those lines. In other words, criminal intelligence can become complicated with regard to disseminating the information and making sure you're talking about probable criminal activity.

If you receive information which is clearly not within your department's area of responsibility, write a report and forward it to the applicable agency. For example, a while back I received some credible information and documentary evidence that a criminal fraud was planned in our jurisdiction but would be carried out in a city 2,000 miles away. I sent a detailed criminal intelligence report to the appropriate department, which enabled them to move in and bring the perpetrators into the criminal justice system quickly before a long list of victims could develop. The fast move also recovered most of the money the few victims already preyed upon had lost.

## Which Writing Style Should You Use— Expository or Narrative?

Deciding whether to write your information or intelligence report in either an expository or narrative style can be a tough call. Remember, expository places your conclusion first, and the remainder of your report is used to support that conclusion. A narrative style is used to tell a story exactly as it unfolded to you.

While expository is always a preferred style for law enforcement reports, information and intelligence reports don't always permit you to do that because, more often than not, you have no conclusion. You have fragmented information in the beginning and eventually may have more information that is credible and sufficient to justify an intelligence report. The question is, Can you say what happened? For example, earlier I used an example of drug traffickers operating from a pancake house parking lot on Thursday evenings. If you made an arrest, you apprise your busy reader exactly what happened up front, as follows:

> About 9:40 P.M., at Joe's Pancake House, 9384 East 87th Street, Any City, Any State, Robert and Linda Purcell sold 15 ounces of cocaine to Detective Robert Smith, Any City Police Department, Any City, Any State.

You have in the example a specific event to tell your reader about. Later, in your substantiation which summarizes your exhibits, you'll support the conclusion by showing arrest reports, witness statements leading to the arrest, and so forth.

Criminal information and intelligence is not narrowly focused. Despite what appears to be happening, regardless of how credible the information or careful the analysis, a crime may not have occurred, be occurring, or ever occur at all. In many cases what is perceived as a crime can't be found in the statute books, either federal, state, or local. The event may be morally wrong, but that doesn't make a crime. When you're writing information or intelligence reports, you don't know for certain if criminal activity is involved, so it is irresponsible to state this.

Another problem arises when you're writing information or intelligence reports. With rare exceptions, you won't review the identity of your sources, and rarely will you have physical evidence or even credible circumstantial evidence. In other words, you'll have nothing tangible to support a conclusion.

The result is a compromise or a mix of expository and narrative. Since narrative is a story-like description of an event, using that exclusively in your information or intelligence reports isn't appropriate. Since no specific event can be pinpointed and supported yet, expository writing doesn't work exclusively, either. What you wind up with in this kind of report is a mix, conveying information succinctly, not an endless story.

Exhibits 8-1 and 8-3 show actual intelligence reports (with changes of names, places, and some details to protect confidentiality of the origin) which represent *how not to write* intelligence reports. Exhibits 8-2 and 8-4 demonstrate *how to write* effective intelligence reports using the same information as shown in Exhibits 8-1 and 8-3. A critique follows each set of examples.

# AN INCORRECTLY WRITTEN INTELLIGENCE REPORT

Subject: Stolen checks, forgeries, and narcotics

The following intelligence is being conducted by the Blank Police Department and the Blank Sheriff's Department. The preliminary information has already revealed multiple jurisdiction involvement, as well as interstate ramifications.

In summary, the information has revealed that an organized group is obtaining stolen checks, commercial and private. As of this date, states in which stolen checks have been passed are California, Iowa, Wisconsin, and Texas. In addition to obtaining stolen checks, this organized group is also obtaining facsimile signatures and account numbers relevant to the stolen checks.

The organization is utilizing females, white and black, to pass the stolen checks at small branch bank locations, using falsely obtained drivers licenses and also stolen identification. The white female subject captioned, Linda Smith, has used fictitious voters identifications and Social Security numbers to obtain multiple Blank State driver's licenses. The captioned female subject, Linda Smith, is currently in custody in Blank County for failure to appear on Blank County counts of forged prescriptions and for solicitation for prostitution. The captioned subject, Linda Smith, is also awaiting extradition to Blank County for forged prescriptions. An association has been identified between the captioned female, Linda Smith, and the captioned male, Robert Johnson. The captioned subject, Robert Johnson, was arrested by the Blank Police Department in December of 1981 for a check forging scam that used the names and accounts numbers of some forty bank customers at ten banks.

The organization, operating in 1981, would obtain checks stolen in business or residential burglaries, purse snatches, or mail theft and then use members to acquire the numbers of bank accounts of legitimate unrelated individuals. In 1981, over a period of six months, ten local banks received losses totaling approximately $50,000. This organization, currently operating since the release of captioned subject Robert Johnson from Blank Correctional Facility, has passed forged and stolen checks in the Blank County area totaling approximately $20,000.

It should be noted that several of the uninvolved individuals whose accounts were used to legitimize the stolen checks have no involvement or understanding as to how the suspects obtained the account number information as well as a facsimile signature. The Blank County Sheriff's Department has contacted credit bureaus in the state to identify possible similar credit checks on the uninvolved individuals, and then show any inquiries other than normal legitimate banking being conducted by the uninvolved individuals. It is possible that the group involved in this organization has unauthorized access to credit bureau information and might possibly have the ability to obtain facsimiles signatures from major credit bureaus.

Information involving similar operations or involvement of the captioned subjects should be directed to Detective Blank, Blank City Police Department.

Detective Blank

*Note*: This actual intelligence report was written by a detective and disseminated to several law enforcement departments and agencies. After thirty years of law enforcement experience, I have a difficult time decoding this intelligence report. In Exhibit 8-2, I'll decode the report, writing the information as you should in your intelligence reports.

EXHIBIT 8-1

# A CORRECTLY WRITTEN INTELLIGENCE REPORT

Subject: Stolen checks, forgeries, credit card fraud, and drug trafficking

Information developed from multiple sources discloses that an interstate organization believed to be operating in California, Iowa, Wisconsin, and Texas is involved in the following criminal activities:

1. Obtaining blank checks from commercial and residential burglaries, and in some cases purse snatching and mail thefts

2. Cashing stolen checks using false identification which corresponds with the names shown on the checks

3. Obtaining false identification through legitimate agencies, such as driver's licenses, using forged and stolen documents including voter's registration cards and Social Security cards. The fraudulent identification matches the names shown on stolen blank checks.

4. Obtaining prescription drugs using false identification and/or forged physician authorizations

5. Acquiring bank account numbers and other information enabling organization members to appear legitimate when passing forged checks at banks.

The organization normally employs both white and black females, who carry out the fraudulent criminal activities.

The organization is believed to be controlled by Robert Jones, previously convicted for check fraud, serving three years at the Blank Correctional Facility. An associate also controlling the criminal enterprise is believed to be Linda Smith, also with a criminal record involving fraudulent prescription drug purchases, prostitution, and suspicion of other offenses. (Full identification, including photographs, is attached to this report.)

Jones, Smith, and/or other members of the organization may have unauthorized access to credit bureau information, which aids them to select victims and obtain key background information about credit cards, bank accounts, and other personal information.

Contributing to the organization's success is their ability to sign checks and other instruments with a signature that duplicates the victim's. Although examples of signatures can be obtained in burglaries and purse snatching where other documents are obtained, sources believe they also are able to obtain victim signature examples illegally.

Information regarding Jones, Smith, other members of the organization, and the organization's criminal enterprises may be sent to Detective Sam Spade, Blank Police Department.

Exhibit 8-2

## CRITIQUE OF EXHIBITS 8-1 AND 8-2 _____

Exhibit 8-1 is copied from an actual police intelligence report (names, places, dates changed) and is typical, if not above average, for most intelligence reports I've encountered over the years. The following problems are noted:

1. The report is confusing and contains lots of useless information, such as the following:

   a. Criminal records of the suspects Jones and Smith. Avoid the clutter and attach criminal record sheets, full identification sheets, and photographs to your report.

   b. Lots of words that say nothing. Be as brief as possible. You're not writing a story, only recording intelligence that is credible and/or verified information received from confidential sources.

   c. Where did all this information come from? Always indicate where the information you write in an intelligence report comes from (i.e., multiple confidential sources). It's important to a reader.

   d. Rehashing old cases which involved one or more members of this organization serves little purpose and should be noted on the identification sheet, not cluttering this report. This report must be studied and decoded. One almost has to take notes reading it to make sense of what information is current, what's old, and where it is leading. Are these people still around, or is this just passing gossip?

   e. There is a serious lack of homework and coordination regarding the credit bureaus. Credit bureaus are often envisioned as Big Brother, with computers filled with all kinds of things about people, and file rooms filled with volumes of personal information. In reality, credit bureaus are highly regionalized, and a few of the major bureaus have fragments of credit information. It all has to do with who is a member of a particular bureau and regularly submits financial transaction information. Some credit bureaus also provide information to affiliated credit bureaus. Accessing that information is governed by laws; however, anyone with a few hundred dollars can be affiliated with information brokers licensed to access about 1,500 credit bureaus across the country. There are nine areas authorizing access; however, nothing must be documented. The only time a problem would come up is if the person whose credit was checked discovered it, made a complaint; and even then, a civil remedy is most likely. A personal computer with a modem and membership in one of the broker connections are all that's needed, and all legal, and anyone's credit can be searched out. However, one key item credit bureaus don't have is signatures. The officer writing the intelligence report shown in Exhibit 8-1 believes incorrectly that the organization is accessing credit bureaus to obtain facsimiles of victims' signatures. When another officer familiar with credit bureaus reads that report, he or she will wonder how much other information is tainted. Always know what you're talking about—until you do, it's only information, not intelligence.

   f. In the next-to-last paragraph of the report shown in Exhibit 8-1, the writer makes another error. The writer says the victims of stolen checks aren't involved in the criminal enterprise and do not understand how the criminals are obtaining their account numbers. Obviously, if a check is stolen, the account number is on the check. When a burglary occurs in this case, we presume its primary purpose is to obtain blank checks and other background information such as account passbooks, receipts, credit cards, bills, and bank statements with canceled checks (bearing signatures).

g. Terminology such as "captioned subject," "subject," and other jargon traditionally found in poorly written law enforcement reports is confusing and meaningless. What is a "captioned subject"? What "subject" is being identified? Does this mean "suspect"? Or does it refer to the crime? Call a person involved in a crime a suspect, not a subject.

Exhibit 8-2 is an example of a comprehensive well-written intelligence report.

1. This report tells the reader up front that the intelligence is processed from multiple sources. This can include people, documents, observations, and other law enforcement departments and agencies. Generally, unless a source gives permission to reveal his or her identity, or it's important for the reader to know about nonpersonal sources of information, the statement used in this example is sufficient.

2. Exhibit 8-2 itemizes, rather than complicates, the offenses and briefly tells your reader who is likely to be controlling the enterprises.

3. You're telling a reader that more information about each person identified in the report is attached along with photographs (if available). Going into detail within your report only clutters and confuses.

4. A busy reader can scan the report shown in Exhibit 8-2 and quickly determine if he or she has any other similar information on file and/or if the information pertains to his or her jurisdiction. In other words, the information is quickly discerned and put to use.

5. Nothing absurd is mentioned, like the credit bureaus being the source of victim signatures, so your reader believes that what you're reporting is credible, not a story a street informant provided for twenty bucks.

6. No confusing language, like "captioned subject," is used. Most readers have no idea what that means. It sounds like a writer trying to impress a reader with catchy terminology.

Criminal intelligence reports must be brief and get to the point fast if they are to be anything except fodder for the filing cabinet. Exhibit 8-3 shows an example from a different jurisdiction and is followed by a corrected version in Exhibit 8-4. A critique of both is also provided to clarify the correct way to write intelligence reports.

## CRITIQUE OF EXHIBIT 8-3

This report, as the one shown in Exhibit 8-1, requires decoding before the reader can make any sense of what the writer is saying.

The first consideration is how many organizations the report is talking about. It seems at the onset that there's one; however, tucked away in the text we find one absorbing another; and later a comment is made about another organization. Is John Paul Doe still the boss? We really aren't sure, only that he's a fugitive. For what? Parking tickets, murder, tax evasion? We can't be sure, although at the beginning the writer says, "The alleged head...is presently a federal fugitive." It seems that Doe is still considered the moving force behind all this confusion.

There is all kinds of conflicting information about how much smuggling has taken place. The writer says "more than twenty" and then in the next sentence mentions fourteen "ventures," which I assume refers to shipments, from another organization which arrived at the same place. Again, we're confused. What is this other organization; is it the one that absorbed the other? Or is it something new?

# AN INCORRECTLY WRITTEN INTELLIGENCE REPORT

Subject: Drug trafficking

The undersigned officer is submitting the following criminal intelligence report:

The Blank Police Department is involved in an ongoing intelligence operation of an organization involved in drug smuggling activities in Any State and four additional states. More than twenty members have been identified and it has been determined that this group has operated since 1979 and continues to operate today. The alleged head of this organization is presently a federal fugitive.

The existence of this organization has been documented as far back as 1974, and it is believed to have been operating prior to that time. This organization absorbed and expanded an organization run by John Paul Doe, who was incarcerated in early 1972, through a common interest—the North County Airport. The primary crime in this operation is the illegal importation of marijuana and cocaine. Additional crimes include, but are not limited to, illegal gun exporting and the laundering of monies, both foreign and domestic, through several organizations, businesses, and corporations. State and federal violations are involved.

Through the use of a developed confidential informant, more than twenty smuggling ventures can be documented occurring from 1974 through the present. Additionally, fourteen ventures have been documented coming into the North County Airport from another organization for a present total of thirty-four plus. These loads include the air smuggling of 1,000 to 5,000 pound loads of marijuana and from 1 to 5 kilos of cocaine. More than twenty individuals with direct involvement have been identified with various levels of responsibility throughout the organization. These include pilots, financiers, wholesalers, off-loaders, and distributors. Importation is from Colombia, Ecuador, Belize, and the Bahamas. Points of destination include several states. No estimated economic value has been determined at this time; however, it is thought to be in the multimillion dollar category. The illegal proceeds are allegedly laundered through many identified Blank State businesses and corporations as well as several identified alien corporations.

The goal of this intelligence operation is to further corroborate present information and to develop and continue to use present confidential informants for a successful case and prosecution of this case. In addition, it is expected that there will be numerous and large seizures under racketeering laws.

It is anticipated that this intelligence operation will be concluded in November. Further action anticipated in this case includes identification of addition criminal ventures, members, and assets and successful prosecution of these members. Through the use of Blank State statutes, attempts will be made to seize a considerable number of aircraft, vessels, vehicles, and real property, including at least one airport and several businesses.

All information regarding this organization or related organizations or any members of this organization can be sent to Detective Tryhard, Blank Police Department.

EXHIBIT 8-3

# A CORRECTLY WRITTEN INTELLIGENCE REPORT

Multiple confidential sources of credible information disclose that an organized criminal enterprise is operating in this jurisdiction and several other states. Using air and sea transportation, drugs (including marihuana and cocaine) are smuggled into a central distribution point identified as North County Airport, Any City or County, Any State.

Additional criminal activity believed to be in progress by members of the organization includes (1) illegal firearms exporting and (2) money laundering, both foreign and domestic.

Reliable information indicates that the controlling person is John Paul Doe, with about twenty other unidentified persons working under Doe's direction. Among the specialists who are employed or associated with Doe in the organization are the following:

1. Aircraft pilots

2. Financiers

3. Drug wholesale suppliers

4. Off-load technicians

5. Drug distributors.

The organization is believed to be laundering money gained from its criminal enterprises through a variety of businesses and corporations, foreign and domestic, which provide a legitimate appearance.

According to sources, incoming shipments of drugs have the following country origins:

1. Colombia

2. Ecuador

3. Belize

4. Bahamas.

The organization is alleged to be operational since 1974, with about thirty-four known incoming shipments ranging from 1,000 to 5,000 pounds of marihuana and 1 to 5 kilos of cocaine per shipment.

John Paul Doe is currently a federal fugitive. Doe's identification, criminal record summary, photograph, and list of known past associates are attached.

Any information developed about Doe and/or this organization can be forwarded to the Blank Police Department, attention Detective Joe Tryhard.

EXHIBIT 8-4

Although the writer is having trouble figuring out the value, he or she is clear about the number of shipments and how much arrived on each. Multiply that times the street value, and we have a fairly good guesstimate of the economic value. However, economics isn't the point of this report, and it's best to eliminate that altogether. Talking about money and crime can have drawbacks. One reader will get excited over a mention of a million dollars, while another will find it nothing to be excited about and, as a result, do nothing. In a case like this, it's best to leave money out of it; the crimes and implications are sufficient.

Mentioning goals in a report is not only unnecessary; doing so demonstrates that the writer is trying hard to convince us he or she is competent, but actually the writer doesn't have any idea of what is going on. Is the goal for the reader or for the detective? A reader receiving this report naturally assumes the goal is to bring the criminals into the criminal justice system; you need not convince him or her.

Never set a deadline—you then have to meet it. Saying you'll have the intelligence operation wrapped up in November (what year?) really puts you on the hook, especially when a reader sees the confusion and conflict in this report. He or she would indeed ask, In what year?

Telling your reader about all the seizures that are planned, including entire airports, several businesses, aircraft, vessels, and real property, is again putting the detective far out on a weak limb. Cases this complex take a long time, and all the benefits of success will come with criminal convictions. Writing about how incredible you are and all that will be accomplished is amateurish. Write about the bare details, and leave the rest for your daydreams of greatness. It doesn't impress a reader, who knows the difference between reality and wishing wells.

## CRITIQUE OF EXHIBIT 8-4

This report demonstrates the correct way of presenting key information contained in Exhibit 8-3. Show the probable situation in the quickest way so your reader can scan through the report and discern if he or she has an interest.

Remember that although a case you're working on is exciting for you, it may not be a big deal to a reader. Just as, earlier in the book, I discussed problems of perception, the same advice applies to intelligence reports.

For example, if you're working on this case and your reader at another department receiving your report is working on a case five times bigger, your enthusiasm, goals, and dreams become a joke. However, if, as shown in Exhibit 8-4, you are simply passing on information which clearly could develop into a major case, your reader will have respect and will likely take notice. Keep it simple; put all the confusion in your notes if you must, but not in your report.

## HOW TO MANAGE INTELLIGENCE REPORT INFORMATION EFFECTIVELY

A significant problem of intelligence operations and reports is effective information management. Since most intelligence collections last several months, perhaps years, one or two detectives working on a specific case know most of the details from memory. The problem is that no one else knows all the details. To find out, a reader has to lock himself or herself in a quiet room and read for days. I've produced intelligence reports on a specific case that numbered a thousand pages or more.

There are effective ways to prevent such information overload. It's not uncommon to collect bits and pieces of information, now and then, for two or three years. In fact, a couple of years ago I participated with federal, state, county, and local law enforcement for nearly three years before we accumulated enough information to open a criminal investigation. The person in question had been a drug trafficker for years; it wasn't a big secret. However, proving it and going about collecting information that could prove it without his knowledge was tricky and painstakingly slow. Most effective criminal intelligence operations pay off in the long term if everyone concerned is able to keep up with the information. Occasionally, a new detective is assigned to a case. How does the new detective catch up with twenty ongoing intelligence operations, all ranging in age from one to three years?

### How to Manage Collective Intelligence Information Using Progress Reports

Criminal investigation reports are managed with a series of progress reports leading to a completed report. Each progress report contains only information collected since the last progress report.

Criminal intelligence and criminal information reports (reports which contain information not analyzed or determined to be credible) are best managed in the same way. Your first intelligence report should be titled "First Progress—Intelligence Report." There are two major differences between criminal intelligence and criminal investigation reports. Remember, with criminal investigations I suggested that you submit a first progress report as soon as possible to inform your readers that you assumed the investigation and will be following up on the preliminary investigation normally conducted by a patrol officer. Each thirty days thereafter a progress report should be written and forwarded to your readers.

Intelligence reports are not bound to any time periods, or shouldn't be. Perhaps the first progress report will also be the only intelligence report you'll write on a specific case. Or perhaps the second progress report will be written weeks, months, or a year later. On the other hand, you may write a progress report on an intelligence case every few days. The only purpose of using the titles first, second, and third progress reports and so on is to allow a reader to follow the information logically and easily. Like the investigation progress report, your intelligence progress report after the first will contain only new information developed since the last progress report.

For example, using Exhibit 8-4 as a model for the first intelligence progress report, let's assume that a month or two later you receive additional information identifying five of the organization's key members, along with some aircraft numbers and the names of a couple businesses used to launder money from illegal activities. You should immediately write a second progress report, summarizing only that information. In your first progress report you set up the foundation, and all subsequent progress reports build on that information.

### How to Close Out a Criminal Intelligence Case or Convert it to a Criminal Investigation

There comes a time when an intelligence case will be either closed out or enough proof has been collected to convert it to a criminal investigation, the first step toward prosecution. In either case, you'll want to manage the information properly and keep it on file as a future reference. Unlike a completed criminal investigation report, your completed or closed criminal intelligence report reflects only that you're breaking off work in the case and explains why. For example, if the suspects are known to have moved to Africa, and your department has no reason to continue the case, just summarize the reason briefly and note that the case is closed. If you're converting the case to a criminal investigation, write a brief summary of why the case is being converted, and close it out. Your basis of investigation for the criminal case would be your intelligence report. Never conceal that you've been working on an intelligence case; however, you shouldn't reveal your sources unless they are not placed in a dangerous or embarrassing position. For example, if your source is another law enforcement department, agency, or officer, or public documents you obtained legally, it's okay to note that information. If however, you obtained the information from a confidential source and legitimately promised to not reveal who the source is, then don't use the name without the source's permission, and try to avoid the direct information the source provided.

## How to Manage Information Sources

There are negative points about using persons as a source of information to develop intelligence cases, especially when the person refuses to give information unless his or her identity is never revealed. I've found over the years that most of the fear connected with human information sources is self-styled opposed to reality. Still, a promise is a promise, and there's always a chance that revealing the identity of a source could place him or her in danger.

A good rule of thumb when an information source is asking you to not reveal his or her identity is to take the information you receive and develop it in other ways. For example, a source meets you in a dark alley and tells you all about a major drug operation and who is involved. If the information is credible, you can begin to develop intelligence in other ways, such as financial intelligence, or searching courthouse real property records and other public records that can reveal far more wealth than legitimate income. That can lead to surveillance, which leads to banks and other important leads. Although your source provided the tidbit which identified people, your efforts developed the real damaging information.

I always try not to use a human source of information who refuses to be identified at some point, such as being listed as a witness in a criminal investigation and/or testifying in court. If your entire intelligence case is based solely on information provided from a human source, the case will likely never reach the criminal justice system or have little or no success if it does.

## What are Public Sources of Information?

I've talked about managing your intelligence reports and information sources and suggested that you develop information based on human-provided information, but in other legal ways. However, few detectives know about the vast number of information sources available to them, probably because they are not told how to find information beyond internal law enforcement channels. I would be remiss if I did not provide you with a list of possibilities that will enhance your intelligence collection process, make your cases strong, and enable you to move a case into the criminal justice system. Common sources which can be accessed through public records are discussed next.

*Address locators*: One of the easiest ways is through mailing list companies. There may be a fee involved, since they'll have to search their computer files. You'll be surprised how many people can be located, or their true address discovered, from mailing lists.

Another source of information about addresses is the U.S. Postal Service forwarding service. Any person filing a change of address card with the Postal Service becomes public information.

Criss-cross telephone directories also provide an address from a telephone number.

There are a number of information broker services that charge a fee but are connected to dozens, sometimes hundreds, of databases across the country. A personal computer and modem is helpful, but many, once membership is established, will take orders for information by telephone, fax, or mail. Because of the vast databases available, most brokers can search through credit bureau databases and link a name to an address anywhere in the country; provide an address from a telephone number; from an address provide several names of persons who are neighbors; provide a telephone number for a specific address; and locate persons often with just a Social Security number (all credit records are keyed to Social Security numbers).

Aircraft identification is available through the FAA in Washington, D.C., by providing the owner's name or tail number. Boats and vessels can be identified through most state agencies and through the Coast Guard in Washington, D.C.

*Commercial credit records*: Although personal credit records have some restrictions established by federal law, commercial credit records are public information. Often a wealth of information can be gained through Dun and Bradstreet, credit bureaus, Standard and Poor's, TRW, and several other sources that compile commercial credit records.

*Corporation records*: Corporate records are public information and are available through every state's Secretary of State office at the respective state capitals. This source also includes corporate officers, directors, and other offices. The same information is available about proprietorships, partnerships, and public or private companies.

*Bank accounts*: A nationwide search, and even worldwide searches, can be conducted by information brokers through various databases. Such a search is not always successful and can be expensive.

*Canadian federal corporations and directors*. This is helpful if your case extends into Canada.

*Commercial subsidiaries*: You can uncover business relationships by linking one company to another. This is normally best achieved through database providers.

*Federal tax liens*: These are a good source for developing information when tax is owed by a person or company.

*Insurance casualty claims*: Most insurance companies will cooperate and have access to this information. An alternative is a commercial information broker with access to national databases.

*Judgment searches*: These are available through county and state database providers for individuals or companies. Although each county courthouse in the country can be checked, a database search can provide this information quickly.

*Litigation searches*: Searches are available through some database providers which record all lawsuits filed nationwide.

*Motor vehicle records and criminal records*: These are available through law enforcement channels.

*Probate court searches*: Database providers can search nationwide in minutes.

*Real estate ownership nationwide*: Database suppliers can search nationwide in minutes and provide hard copies in days.

*Uniform commercial code (UCC)*: There is a record at every courthouse for the county of residence or business regarding any property or items purchased with a loan.

*Welfare records*: These can be searched nationwide by database providers.

*Worker's compensation claims*: This information is available in all states on request. It is managed by a state agency.

The foregoing do not comprise all the possibilities; however, considerable information is available from these sources.

## GLOSSARY OF CRIMINAL INTELLIGENCE TERMS _____

Every profession has a language of its own. I often discourage the use of jargon and traditional law enforcement language, but the following glossary lists acceptable professional language for the world of criminal intelligence.

*Business associate*: Someone who is engaged in a legitimate occupation that provides services to an organized crime enterprise.

*Command intelligence*: Intelligence that provides an entire picture of a situation to one or more persons making decisions about policy, procedures, and/or prosecutions.

*Criminal associate*: One who interacts on a voluntary basis with a member of an organized crime enterprise to further illegal interests.

*Criminal history information*: Any arrest record information, nonconviction record information, conviction record information, and correctional and release information.

*Criminal intelligence/information*: Information associated with an identifiable individual, corporation, business, or other entity, compiled by a criminal justice agency in the course of conducting an inquiry related to suspected criminal activity.

*Information or data*: Written documents and reports telling of an event or activity.

*Intelligence*: Information that has been processed (i.e., collected, evaluated, collated, analyzed, and reported).

*Intelligence investigation*: The compilation of data wherein the immediate objective is not arrest and prosecution.

*Legitimate law enforcement purpose*: Any situation wherein a bonafide law enforcement agency's objective or intention is to develop criminal information or intelligence for either tactical or strategic purposes.

*Mass media source*: Any information obtained from sources of public communication (i.e., newspapers, television, radio, or other publications).

*Need to know*: Any intelligence, criminal history, or criminal investigative data requested by a bonafide law enforcement agency that is necessary to initiate, further, or complete a criminal investigation or criminal intelligence operation.

*Operational intelligence*: Intelligence that is useful to ongoing departmental or agency policy within a specific jurisdiction.

*Organized crime*: A group of persons structured for the purpose of engaging in a continuing course of criminal activity for financial gain.

*Organized crime intelligence system*: Any information system capable of collecting, evaluating, collating, analyzing, and disseminating data on organized criminal activity.

*Primary source of information*: An individual from whom an original, direct, or first-hand fact is obtained.

*Privacy*: The claim of individuals, groups, or institutions to determine for themselves when, how, and to what extent information about them is communicated to others.

*Professional associate*: Those whose professional services are employed by a member of organized crime on a continuing basis to further illegal activity.

*Prominent organized crime figure*: An individual who is considered a controlling factor within an organized crime group.

*Raw data*: Information that has not been put through the intelligence process.

*Relationship*: The manner in which one is dependent on or relies on another.

*Right to know*: Any agency and/or individual who, through legislative or court mandate, has been given the authority to obtain any intelligence, criminal history, or criminal investigative data.

*Secondary source of information*: Any information derived from a source other than a primary source.

*Social associate*: One who interacts on a voluntary basis with a member of an organized crime group.

*Strategic intelligence*: Intelligence that indicates significant patterns of activity that may become a major input to the planning and decision levels of the department or agency.

*Tactical intelligence*: Intelligence that is immediately useful to the enforcement element of any department or agency.

# NINE

# How to Write Effective Vehicle Collision Investigation Reports

Vehicle collisions, commonly called traffic accidents, are extremely confusing events. How they occur, who or what caused them, and why they occur are factors law enforcement officers must determine at the scene. The negative traditional term *traffic accident* adds confusion to the investigation. Collisions are much like suicides because an inexperienced or poorly trained investigator views the scene with a foregone conclusion. In the case of collisions, he or she perceives the event to be an accident, which means that no one intended for it to occur. I compare collisions to suicide investigations because many homicides are perceived to be suicides, simply because of appearance. Always approach vehicle collision investigations with the idea that there may be a crime involved, and if the facts prove that idea wrong, you've conducted a fair and impartial but complete investigation. On the other hand, if you approach a collision with the idea that it is an unintended event, chances are you'll miss any evidence that may prove otherwise. That's why I work hard to avoid using the term *traffic accident*. I do the same when approaching a death which appears to be caused by some person, avoiding a label until all the facts are collected and analyzed. If I treat it as a murder, I'll be sure to collect all the evidence and information.

Vehicle collision investigation is one of the primary subjects taught at law enforcement academies, during in-service training and special seminars. Criminal investigation schools and many colleges offer courses in vehicle collision investigations, although without exception, to the best of my knowledge, the term *traffic accident* is always used. Another problem is an inherent dependence on fill-in-the-blanks forms used for collision investigations. Like all fill-in-the-blanks forms, the intention is not to replace comprehensive writing but to provide all the identifying information, along with a rough sketch of the scene. A problem develops when the collision is more complex than a minor fender bender, and especially if a crime is involved. The form, along with the perception that the event must be an accident, regularly contributes to a failure of competent investigation.

We often hear of accidents occurring, and from the details printed in newspaper accounts and a comment that no charges were filed, we wonder if the event was indeed an accident. The accident doesn't sound like an entirely unintentional act. Although the charge of manslaughter applies to killing a person without malice aforethought, which creates the crime of murder, manslaughter is a crime. Often, a vehicle collision involves manslaughter, but if you approach it as an accident, no one will ever know if malice may have been involved, or if a total disregard for the responsibilities associated with operating a motor vehicle is present among the information at the scene. Alcohol consumption is usually determined by actions and odor; however, there are a great many other factors that cause people to create a vehicle collision deliberately.

## ESSENTIAL ELEMENTS OF A VEHICLE COLLISION INVESTIGATION

When you conduct an effective investigation, all the essential elements are answered: who, what, when, where, how, and why. Alone, or supported by diagrams, photographs, and written statements, your report must provide that information as a minimum. I should point out here that the text within this chapter does not include fender-bender events, where fill-in-the-blanks forms are normally sufficient.

The information in this chapter applies when a vehicle collision includes the following:

1. Fatal injuries

2. Incapacitating injury—an injury which prevents a person from walking, driving, or continuing normal activities, even on a temporary basis

3. When there's evidence that a serious offense was committed, such as driving under the influence of drugs or alcohol, hit-and-run collisions, and reckless driving

4. When extensive damage results from a collision, making it impossible for the vehicle to be driven away safely and normally

5. Whenever any government vehicle is involved, local, county, state, or federal. Even minor accidents involving government-owned vehicles should be thoroughly investigated because of liability problems and because ownership does involve taxpayers.

6. When there's extensive damage to private and/or government-owned property

7. When there's an environmental impact resulting from a vehicle collision—for example, toxic fumes, chemical leaks, gasoline and oil spills, and other similar problems.

8. When a vehicle collision occurs as a direct cause or proximate cause of a law enforcement vehicle being in pursuit of another vehicle

9. Other collisions of a serious nature which are not listed here.

## VEHICLE COLLISION INVESTIGATION REPORT WRITING STYLE

A vehicle collision investigation report should be written using expository style, meaning that you begin with a summary conclusion of the event. As with other reports, your collision investigation report is organized according to the following format:

1. *Basis of investigation.* Why are you investigating, and why are you reporting the information? If you're using a fill-in-the-blanks form, this requirement is normally satisfied with that information.

2. *Conclusion.* This is based on the information collected, including evidence.

3. *Substantiation.* A concise explanation of each exhibit attached to the report which led you to making the conclusion.

4. *List of witnesses*. Include victims.

5. *Exhibits*. Your proof that the collision happened in the way you concluded it happened.

## CLASSIFICATION, TERMINOLOGY, FACTORS, AND STAGES OF VEHICLE COLLISIONS

Vehicle collision investigation, although similar to criminal investigations of common crimes, has a number of different elements you must know and understand before conducting an investigation or writing a report.

Vehicle collisions are generally classified by the type of collision, as follows:

1. Overturned
2. Other noncollision
3. Collision with pedestrian
4. Collision with motor vehicle
5. Collision with motor vehicle on other roadway
6. Collision with parked motor vehicle
7. Collision with a railway train
8. Collision with a pedal cycle (two or three wheels, no engine)
9. Collision with an animal
10. Collision with any object.

Collisions are also classified according to severity, as follows:

1. Fatal (within twelve months of collision, if that is the cause or proximate cause of death)
2. Incapacitating injuries
3. Nonincapacitation injuries
4. Possible injuries
5. Disabling damage to vehicle (cannot be moved under its own power)
6. Functional damage to vehicle (can be moved under own power, but would be unsafe)
7. Other damage to vehicle (minor damage, not unsafe).

## GLOSSARY OF VEHICLE COLLISION INVESTIGATION TERMS

Using the following definitions ensures standardized analysis and reporting procedures.

*Traffic way*: The entire width between property lines, or other boundary lines, of every way or place of which any part is open to the public for purposes of vehicular travel as a matter of right or custom. All highways are traffic ways, but traffic ways also include some areas on private property, such as shopping centers.

*Highway*: The entire width between the boundary lines of every way publicly maintained when any part thereof is open to public use for purposes of vehicular travel; a street; a publicly maintained traffic way.

*Road*: The part of a traffic way which includes both the roadway, which is the traveled part, and any shoulder alongside the roadway. Where there are unmountable curbs, the road and roadway are the same. If there is a guardrail, the road is considered to extend to the guardrail.

*Roadway*: That portion of a highway improved, designed, or ordinarily used for vehicular travel, exclusive of the berm or shoulder. In the event a highway includes two or more separate roadways, the term *roadway*, as used herein, refers to any such roadway separately, but not to all such roadways collectively. If there's a curb, the roadway is considered to extend to the curb; hence *roadway* may include lanes commonly used for parking. If there is a paved shoulder, the roadway may be distinguished from the shoulder mainly by a painted line marking the edge of the roadway.

*Shoulder*: That portion of the road contiguous with the roadway for accommodation of stopped vehicles, for emergency use, and for lateral support of the roadway structure. The line between the roadway and the shoulder may be a painted edge line, a change in surface color or material, or a curb. On some modern traffic ways, there may be a surfaced shoulder on the right side and frequently a narrow shoulder on the left side of a one-way roadway.

*Motor vehicle*: Every vehicle which is self-propelled, and every vehicle which is propelled by electric power obtained from overhead trolley wires, but not operated on rails.

*Traffic*: Pedestrians, ridden or herded animals, vehicles, streetcars, and other conveyances, either singly or together, while using any highway for purposes of travel.

*Driver*: Person who drives or is in control of a vehicle.

*Motor vehicle collision*: An event involving one or more moving vehicles, occurring on, but not limited to, a traffic way, which results in property damage, personal injury, or death.

*Pedal cycle*: A vehicle operated solely by pedals, propelled by human power, such as a bicycle or tricycle.

*Collision factors*: Combinations of simultaneous and sequential (in sequence) circumstances which cause collision.

*Collision investigation*: Detailed systematic search to uncover facts (who, what, when, where, why, and how) and determine the truth of the factors.

*Collision diagram*: A plan of an intersection or section of roadway on which an accident occurred. It is drawn by means of arrows showing the manner of collision. Date, time, and road conditions are entered on one of the arrows representing each collision.

*Property damage*: A loss suffered by a person, firm, or other entity when property is marred, defaced, spoiled, ruined, or destroyed.

*Simultaneous factors*:   Factors which must be present at the same time to cause an accident.

*Sequential factors*: Factors which are apart from the crucial event of the collision; certain actions that set up situations which may increase the probability of a collision.

## FACTORS ASSOCIATED WITH VEHICLE COLLISIONS

The three primary factors involved in vehicle collisions are as follows: (1) operational, (2) condition, and (3) remote condition.

An operational factor is any unconventional or hazardous behavior or negligence by a road user which contributes directly to the collision. This can be any of the following:

1. Speed: Greater or lesser than a safe normal speed which (a) makes it impossible to follow a desired curve; (b) makes it impossible to take successful evasive action; or (c) presents an unusual surprise to other traffic units.

2. Initial behavior: This includes (a) unusual action (skidding or spinning out); (b) illegal actions (driving on wrong side of road); and (c) hazardous actions (excessive lane changing).

3. Delayed perception: This is a failure to perceive and safely respond to impending danger of a possible collision caused by inattention or distraction.

4. Faulty evasive action: Evasive action is taken when the road user reacts to a dangerous situation after the perception of the danger. This may include slowing, stopping, accelerating, or turning.

A condition factor contributes to an operational factor. There may be one or more condition factors, such as skidding on a curve (an operational factor) and slippery pavement (a conditional factor).

A remote condition factor sets up an operational factor. For example, a road with severe potholes is a remote condition factor. If a vehicle with bald tires hits a pothole and a tire blows out, that's a condition factor. If a car swerves into the opposite lane and another car collides with it, that's an operational factor.

## STAGES OF VEHICLE COLLISIONS

Each vehicle collision involves a number of stages or a chain of events. Every collision will have a key event; however, not all collisions include all stages.

1. *Point of possible perception*: Time and place at which the unusual or unexpected movement or condition could have been perceived by a normal person.

2. *Point of perception*: Time and place at which the danger of a collision is perceived or actually seen. This point comes after the point of possible perception. Perception time is the period between these two points. (This point does not exist in all cases—for example, when a driver falls asleep at the wheel while in motion).

3. *Point of no escape*: Time and place after which the vehicle collision cannot be avoided. It may occur before or after the point of perception.

4. *Key event*: The most important stage of a vehicle collision. There is only key event, determined by the first harmful event. It determines the exact time, place, and type of collision. It may be one of the following: (a) collision on the road—when vehicles have made their first contact (point of initial contact); (b) noncollision on the road—when only the vehicle is involved, and the key event occurs on the road; (c) collision or noncollision off the road—when the first harmful event occurs after the vehicle leaves the roadway.

5. *Point of maximum engagement*: The time and place in a collision when vehicles are forced together as much as they will be. It follows the point of impact.

6. *Final position*: Place where the vehicles involved in a collision finally come to rest. Any collision following this stage should be considered as another vehicle collision.

7. *Other events*: The following events or stages appear to a lesser degree in a vehicle collision: (a) encroachment—movement into the lane, path or area designated to another vehicle; (b) start of evasive action—when first action to avoid collision occurs; (c) disengagement—separation of vehicles after colliding.

## EFFECTIVE VEHICLE COLLISION REPORT WRITING REQUIRES EFFICIENT INFORMATION MANAGEMENT

Investigating a serious vehicle collision may be the most difficult kind of investigation you'll experience. Normally, in addition to confusion, a collision causes additional dangers, with other traffic moving through the area, curious onlookers, emergency vehicles, and often darkness or inclement weather. When a collision involves injuries, the immediate priority is removing the injured from the scene to a medical facility. All of the aforementioned factors cause an immediate and continuing deterioration of the collision scene. Witnesses and victims are difficult to talk with at the scene and may provide exaggerated or inaccurate information.

### *Begin Writing Your Report on the Way to the Collision Scene*

While you are enroute to a collision scene that is reported as serious, begin writing your report by collecting as much information available via radio from your dispatcher. Such information may include the following:

1. Location

2. Time of notification

3. Who notified your law enforcement department

4. Weather and visibility conditions

5. General information, such as seriousness of the collision, number and extent of injuries, whether it's a hit-and-run, amount of traffic congestion, and other information associated with that situation. Ask the dispatcher for assistance in determining an alternate route for traffic approaching the scene (dispatchers normally have detailed wall maps), and if feasible ask for supporting law enforcement units to arrange for detouring traffic.

6. Determine if wreckers, ambulances, and/or other law enforcement units are at the scene or enroute.

*An important tip*: The best tool for this and other urgent and confusing investigative situations is a hand-held, battery-operated tape recorder. As information is provided over the radio, you can record it for later reference and use it throughout your investigation. Often, collisions occur at night or during inclement weather. Those factors, coupled with confusion and a rapidly deteriorating scene, make it vital to record as much information from your immediate and continued observations as possible. Unlike a crime scene, which you can control for as long a period as necessary to conduct a methodical investigation, collision scenes may be limited. For example, if your scene is on a highway and there's no feasible detour available and it's dark, raining, and foggy, clearing the scene as soon as possible is important. Your tape recorder will be invaluable for saving time and collecting accurate information for your report.

### *Minimum Equipment Necessary to Conduct a Vehicle Collision Investigation*

You must have at least the following equipment to conduct a vehicle collision investigation.

☐ One hundred-foot metal-reinforced fabric measuring tape or plastic-coated fiberglass measuring tape

☐ Traffic accident investigator's template

☐ Required department forms

☐ Lined and unlined paper and ruler

☐ Sturdy clipboard

☐ Number 4 lead pencils

☐ Ballpoint pens with black ink

☐ File folders

☐ Hand-held electric lantern with ground stand

☐ Hand-held flashlight

☐ Hammer, nails, and stakes

☐ Yellow lumber crayon and chalk

☐ Spray paint in aerosol cans for marking roads (yellow or orange is best)

☐ Steel pins to anchor end of tape and mark its length when making long measurements

☐ Lead weights with hook to anchor end of tape when pins cannot be used

☐ Engineer's tape and long steel push-in pins (to secure scene)

☐ Practical-sized briefcase that can serve for a writing surface and safe storage of documents.

## Continue Writing Your Report at the Vehicle Collision Scene

Your situation establishes what you do immediately on arrival at the scene of a traffic collision. If you are the only officer at the scene, your beginning activities will be focused on gaining control, looking after the injured, and establishing a safe area, all of which are not directly associated with writing your report. When all those tasks are finished, you resume report writing.

## How to Collect and Manage Information at the Scene

*Step 1*: The first investigative step is to photograph the scene systematically. Always try to find reference points to include in the establishing photograph. Obtain close-up shots of important items and points you'll want to emphasize in your report. Photographs will help you clarify the confusion by attaching them as exhibits to your report.

*Step 2*: Ideally, you want to keep the scene you're investigating intact, exactly as it is immediately after the collision movement has ceased. However, in many circumstances that's not possible. Often, in the interest of the safety of other motorists, vehicles involved in the traffic accident must be moved. When moving the vehicles is necessary, mark the position(s) carefully at the wheels with orange or yellow spray paint. Also, with the paint, indicate a rough outline of the vehicle showing front and rear.

*Step 3*: After completing steps 1 and 2, you must record facts needed to complete your report and to arrive at a logical and objective conclusion. Prior to forming a conclusion, however, all facts concerning the traffic accident must be obtained. The main thrust of your investigation is to determine whether there is a violation of the law; and if so, to prove each element of the offense.

*Step 4*: Systematically collect your report exhibits. You can do that best by keeping in mind that you must reach and support a conclusion. If the conclusion includes a criminal offense, such as vehicular homicide or manslaughter, remember the essential elements of proof. When you determine if a criminal offense is involved, your traffic accident investigation includes a criminal investigation. It can be a complex situation, and you can envision from that how difficult and important your report will be to readers using information you collect, analyze, and explain.

Managing information at a vehicle collision scene involves identifying and preserving evidence. Any fragile evidence that can be damaged, altered, destroyed, or removed from the scene by any willful or negligent act must be identified and secured. Prior to the collection and removal process from the scene, document position through photographs, sketches, and location marked by spray paint or chalk. Examples of this kind of evidence are puddles of gasoline, oil, blood, or pieces of broken glass. The position of turn signal levers should be checked. Alcoholic beverage containers inside a vehicle should also be secured. Physical evidence which can be retained must he marked, tagged, and controlled.

You'll note that much of the physical evidence I've mentioned is not recoverable (i.e., puddles, broken glass, patterns of broken glass, turn signal lever positions, oil spots). Your report, supported with documentary exhibits such as photographs and sketches, becomes the evidence. It's absolutely vital that your report be accurate, comprehensive, and complete.

Managing information also involves taking statements. Questioning and taking statements of witnesses and victims should be accomplished at the scene, if possible. However, as noted earlier, traffic accident scenes are difficult, at best, unlike a burglary, robbery, or even a conventional murder scene. As noted earlier, a hand-held recorder can help you during a traffic accident investigation. When circumstances do not permit obtaining written statements at the scene, attempt to obtain a recorded statement. You can later transcribe it. Label and secure the tape for later reference. Another course of action that may work in some cases is to take a statement on a sheet of paper as part of the interview and have it signed and dated. Later, if the situation warrants, you can retake the statement, perhaps in greater detail. The important point in having statements is that your exhibits tell the story.

The formats, style, and techniques of statement taking in traffic accident investigation are unchanged from that discussed in earlier sections of this book.

After you collect all the information possible from persons involved in the accident either as victims or witnesses, begin to examine the physical condition of the scene, and carefully document your observations. The following items are among the most important:

1. *Vehicle final rest position*: Your examination should start where the vehicle came to final rest. Debris or broken parts from vehicles, with other indications, will help locate the key event and indicate the paths of the vehicles involved. Marks or traces such as skid or scrape marks help you locate pertinent points accurately. All marks, puddles, bits of metal, and contents of vehicles must be located and their positions measured and recorded in your notes, sketches, and photographs. Skid marks are very important since they show position and direction of travel, evasive action, or unlawful behavior. You should note especially things that help locate the point of first contact, such as changes in skid marks, chips in pavement, and damage to roadside objects. The description and documentation of this information in your report will be the total record of this element of the traffic accident.

2. *Path of vehicles*: Your next step in the observations part of investigating a traffic accident is retracing the paths of the vehicles involved. Note visibility, condition of signs and signals, road surface condition, traffic volume, angles of view, and possible distractions.

3. *Vehicle search and inspection*: Your careful inspection of vehicle equipment and contents is necessary, not only as a duty of skilled investigation, but also as a duty of a skilled report writer. Items affecting vehicle control should be particularly checked, such as tires, brakes, lights, steering, signals, and safety equipment. You may, depending on the circumstances, require a qualified mechanic to examine further one or more vehicles involved in a traffic accident, to verify certain conditions. For example, you may need to know whether a tire blew out as a result of the accident, or whether a tire blowout became a possible contributing factor of the acci-

dent. Often, you can find a solution by analyzing skid and scuff marks. Contents of the vehicle may also give important information concerning the identity, residence, occupation, destination, and position of vehicle occupants. All such information is important to arrange within your report, since your reader will be asking such questions. An incomplete report suggests incompetence to your reader, whether or not you have the facts. If the information isn't obtained, you lack the ingredients to write an accurate, well-supported, complete report.

4. *Sketches*: Earlier in this book, I talked about the importance of investigative sketches of a crime scene. They are important in traffic accident investigation and report writing as well. Depending on the severity of the traffic accident, your sketch may range from a simple sketch to a detailed scaled drawing. In a complicated traffic accident, you may need to do a layered sketch, which is a master drawing of the scene with a series of overlays to provide the reader with a clear, step-by step view of your findings. Your rough sketches of the traffic accident scene serve four purposes: (a) They help you explain the accident; (b) they help you reveal facts; (c) they locate any given point at the scene; and (d) they serve as the basis for accurate scale drawings.

## FIVE IMPORTANT STEPS IN MAKING A VEHICLE COLLISION SCENE SKETCH _____

1. Draw the roadway, shoulder, and other areas of the scene which are pertinent to your investigation. That includes any physical characteristics which may constitute contributing factors to the cause of the accident or which you will use as a base point.

2. Draw base points on the sketch. You can make the base points by finding the most permanent objects, such as telephone poles, mileage markers, and road sign posts. The base points you select become points from which you begin triangulation measurements, always from the place where the base point meets the ground. When you select circular objects, such as telephone poles, the exact point where your measurement departs the base point should be marked with paint or a nail.

3. The next portion of the sketch shows the final position of the vehicle, occupants, and objects involved in the traffic accident. All damage is indicated on the sketch and will correlate with your photographs.

   When you write your report, in addition to the sketch, drawing and photographs, you must write about that information. The exhibits are there to support and clarify.

4. Complete the sketch by including information on vehicle marks and debris at the scene. Vehicle marks include skid and scuff marks, scratches, scrapes, and gouges of the pavement and marks left from yaws. You can use the marks to determine the speeds of vehicles involved in the accident and to support conclusions, findings, and other exhibits contained in your report.

   Debris is useful in determining the point of first contact. Outlines of the areas in which debris has come to rest are included in your sketch. Debris is usually spread in an elongated pattern in the direction of travel. Points where debris concentration is greatest are also indicated. You should note if there appears to be two or more separate debris areas.

5. After you complete your field sketch, recheck it while still at the scene. There's nothing worse than sitting down to write your report and finding conflicting exhibits. The scene is no longer there, your exhibits conflict, and your report is not going to be accurate. Don't allow yourself to get in that position.

Examples of vehicle collision sketches are shown in Exhibits 9-1 through 9-4.

## Measurements

Your report, with all the carefully collected exhibits and a logical conclusion, will be in doubt if you cannot substantiate much of your information with accurate measurements at the scene. Accurate measurements are necessary to relocate and relate exact points in collision scenes. There are two methods you can use to obtain accurate information.

1. *Triangulation method*: This is the best method you can use on unpaved roads without clean-cut edges or on sharp curves and irregular intersections. The steps in this technique are as follows:

   a. Determine two fixed base points, such as telephone poles, edges of buildings, etc.

   b. Measure from both base points to each object, such as the accident vehicle.

   c. Write measurements as 12/6 for 12 feet, 6 inches. The normal symbols for feet ' and inches ( " ) are not used, to avoid misreading or confusion.

   d. Fixed base points should be widely spaced to provide wide angles in measuring. Narrow angles increase the probability of error.

   e. Show measurements to the wheel positions on one side of the vehicle or to the front and rear of the vehicle if undamaged. Also show measurements to large debris and to victims not in the vehicle involved.

   f. Measure skid marks from where the road surface first shows any marks of tires grabbing.

2. *Coordinate method*: This method is best used on roadways with well-defined edges and when measurements are to be made within 25 feet of the roadway edge.

   a. The edge of the roadway forms one coordinate. The distance to the object, measured at a right angle to the first coordinate, is the other.

   b. A point along the roadway edge is selected as the zero or reference point. Its exact location must be recorded. Measurements are taken from the zero point. Measurements are recorded by compass direction. Measurements may be recorded on the sketch in chart form, thus keeping the sketch from becoming overly cluttered.

## Photography

Your photographs are used to supplement the traffic accident investigation, making your report credible and supporting your conclusions. When used in court testimony, your photographs help you to indicate and explain the chain of events. Photographs, however, never take the place of your investigation as a whole or your detailed report.

You should take as many pictures as possible at the traffic accident scene. Your photographs should represent what you actually saw; thus, scale, angles of view, color, and light should be as nearly like what you saw as possible. Your photographs must be taken as follows:

- *Establishing photograph*: Show the scene, the approaches to the scene, and a fixed object in the background to establish the scene.

- *360-degree photographs*: Show all four sides of the accident scene, looking north, south, east, and west.

- *Damage photographs*: Include close-up pictures of damage to all vehicles involved, both contact and induced damage.

- *Debris, skids, marks, and other elements*: Any persons, materials, or marks not included in the original scene should not be included in your photographs. These include police, wrecker personnel, bystanders, chalk marks, measuring devices, etc.

The locations from which photographs are taken should be recorded on an overlay to the diagram (sketch and/or drawing). Each of your photograph positions should be numbered in sequence, along with a brief description of your picture scene placed on the reverse. For example, "Photo #6, collision scene, facing south." To avoid confusion with other photographs, your first exposure of a roll or series should include a data card which shows the time, date, location, and your initials. The same scene should then be photographed without the data card.

### Nighttime Photography

At night, you will experience greater difficulty establishing the scene and being able to provide details and distance relationships in your photographs. If you find it is impossible to have permanently fixed objects in the scene to establish the photograph, use a data board. Greater detail can be achieved by adjusting the f-stop of the camera to allow more light to enter (smaller f-stop). If you can, use an extension flash attachment to reveal depth at night. If none is available, take several photographs successively closer to the object. Go back and rephotograph the complete area during the day from the same positions, and couple the two as one exhibit (night and day) in your report.

### Photographs in Court

Make sure your traffic accident scene photographs not only support your report, but are admissible in court. This involves four steps:

- *Authentication*: Photographic evidence will be authenticated in court by you. It's a good idea to have with you the negatives or any other element that proves you took the photographs and that those you're viewing are not different from your negatives.

- *Marking*: Each roll of film you use must be marked with your name, Social Security number, date, time and location of the accident, type of accident, a control number, and the sequence in which the film was used. If it is desirable to point out a specific area of a photograph, an acetate overlay should be used. Never mark directly on your print.

- *Relevancy*: All your pictures must be clear, sharp, and free of distortion. The photographs must be relevant to your investigation. Your photographs not only support your report but also your testimony in court. They must not be inflammatory or provide elements of shock value, particularly photographs of injuries. Photographs of bodies in relation to the vehicles' position are not, however, considered inflammatory if relevant to support a point of testimony.

- *Supportive only*: Your photographs alone do not substantiate facts—your report and testimony based on the report do. You must be able to testify that the photos and information in your report reflect a true representation of the traffic collision scene.

### Inspection of Vehicles

After sketching, measuring, and photographing the traffic accident scene, begin an inspection of the vehicle(s) for condition and damage. The purpose is to obtain supporting information concerning statements of witnesses, victims, and other elements which will support and substantiate your report. Inspect the following:

- *Vehicle condition*: Any physical characteristic of the vehicle(s) existing prior to the accident. Some unsafe aspect may be determined to have been an intermediate or early cause of the accident, such as a bald tire.

- *Vehicle damage*: The resulting physical characteristics of the vehicle(s) caused by the traffic accident. Damage is classified as either contact or induced.

  - Contact damage occurs as a direct result of contact with or by an object. It can occur in more than one location on the vehicle.

  - Induced damage is caused to vehicle parts which did not come in contact with the object struck, but resulted from the shock of the collision.

- *Vehicle body condition*: Check locations of damage. The amount of buckling or breaking can indicate the force of the accident. Check for alteration to the frame, body, or suspension, which could have affected the driver's vision or vehicle reaction.

- *Tires and rims condition*: Check to see if the tires are fully inflated, have good tread, or show signs of a blowout. Check for tread scrape marks and sidewall scrapes or cuts, which can indicate how well the vehicle held up to braking and sideways skidding. Check rims for fresh scrapes, cuts, or scratches. The elements may indicate that a blowout occurred prior to the accident.

- *Light conditions*: Check all vehicle lights for operation and position of knobs and levers used to control lights. The checks are often necessary to verify statements obtained. Also note any lights burning when you arrived at the scene. Check for obstructions to lights such as dirt film. If lights are to be checked by a crime laboratory, the entire light structure should be sent. If the light switch is on but not operating, perhaps due to the accident, the lab can determine whether the filament is intact or broken and whether the break is new or old.

- *Glass condition*: The condition of the glass may have caused poor visibility and may indicate the manner in which injuries were caused. Check to see if glass is cracked or broken. If cracks are clouded or discolored, the cracks existed prior to the accident. Note obstruction on the glass such as dirt or frost. For side windows, note position, up or down, if relevant. Operation of side and rear view mirrors should also be noted.

- *Interior vehicle equipment*: Various items of equipment inside the vehicle should be checked for proper operation by a qualified mechanic, if necessary. Additionally, the position of equipment may indicate actions or intended actions of drivers. These include the turn signal lever, pedal operation, horn, seat belts, sun visors, ignition switch, accessory switch (especially defroster in cold weather), and gear shift lever. The speedometer may give some indication of speed.

- *Miscellaneous equipment*: Check any material inside the vehicle which may have contributed to the accident. This might include alcoholic containers, drugs, toys, etc. In doing this, remember that for other than items in plain view, further search of the vehicle will require the owner's or driver's permission or a search warrant. If safety inspection stickers are present, check their validity.

Checks of vehicle damage compared to scratches and gouges on the roadway or other damage to roadway objects may show vehicle position and direction of travel after the key event. The age of all damage should be determined to relate it to the specific accident. All accident damage and vehicle conditions should be photographed, if relevant to your investigation.

*Special Considerations*

Weather, especially snow, ice, and rain, will cause you problems with regard to using orange or yellow paint and chalk to mark positions of vehicles, debris, or other important items. In such cases, large spikes with orange plastic flags attached can be driven into ice, packed snow, or a roadway when rain is a factor. If the roadway is concrete, use whatever may be available, such as rocks, bricks, or other improvised materials.

When distances to triangulation or coordinate measuring points is too great, use premade heavy, rigid wire markers with an orange or yellow plastic flag to measure in specific increments from the primary measuring point. For example, beginning at a selected measuring point, go to the end of your tape and plant a flag. Then measure on from the flag, or flags, and the total will provide an accurate measurement.

## HOW TO WRITE A VEHICLE COLLISION INVESTIGATION REPORT

### *A Traffic Accident Form Report Versus an Effective Report*

Exhibits 9-14 through 9-16 show examples of traffic accident forms used by law enforcement departments across the country.

Envision yourself as a busy reader needing accurate, easy-to-understand information quickly. A form certainly does not fill those requirements. Even so, departments continue to use forms. That's how it is with tradition, good or bad; it's always been and always will be, until someone changes it.

However, you can use a form, in part as a checklist, thus satisfying department tradition. Then sit down and write an effective vehicle collision investigation report that's accurate, complete, easy to read and understand, and dynamic. Who knows, maybe you'll be the person that starts a new tradition—but this tradition will be beneficial.

When you have all the blanks filled in, the boxes checked, and a variety of other confusing data noted, set the form aside and begin writing. Using your department form as a cover, follow it with a report written on plain paper using headings and information organized as follows.

*Step 1*: *Begin writing with a basis for investigation.* This section should inform the reader why you are writing the report. For example:

> On April 30, 1989, Mr. George Smith reported a traffic accident occurred at the intersection of 12th Street and Elm Avenue, Blank City.

Your reader, at a glance, knows that a Mr. Smith reported the accident. No further detail is necessary.

*Note*: If your investigation discloses that an intentional criminal offense is involved with a traffic accident, step 2 should then involve listing one or more suspects in the report. That section is not prominent here, because rarely will a crime be involved. Being responsible for the accident is not a crime. However, if a situation involves reckless driving, driving under the influence of drugs or alcohol, or other cases where the traffic accident could be or become a case of filing criminal charges, this section should be used to list the suspects. This is not used, however, to list someone issued a citation for being at fault. Citations or tickets in most states are violations of motor vehicle laws and are not considered a crime (misdemeanor or felony).

*Step 2*: *Write your investigative conclusion first.* Your traffic accident (collision) report is an investigation, similar to your investigation of a crime. Although a traffic accident has unique characteristics not found in other situations you'll be investigating, the style of reporting the information you collect is most effective using expository techniques.

Your conclusion is based on the information and physical evidence you collect at the scene. It tells the reader quickly and efficiently what happened. In a traffic accident report your conclusion may be longer; however, strive to be as concise as possible. Recall that earlier we discussed clarity and concluded that if you strive for clarity, brevity will be a result.

An important factor in traffic accident investigation reports is using terminology to avoid confusion and explain what happened. In fact, using terminology and jargon has a reverse effect. The most common way of describing vehicles involved is to number them. There's nothing inherently wrong with that process except that using the numbering system to explain what happened creates confusion. It becomes a major problem when several vehicles and persons are involved. For example, consider the following excerpt form a vehicle collision report:

> Vehicle 1 was traveling south on Route 113 and attempted to negotiate a curve, losing control and colliding with Vehicle 2, which was traveling north on Route 113. Vehicle 3 was following Vehicle 1, and before Vehicle 1 and Vehicle 2 collided swerved to the left into the path of Vehicle 4, which was following Vehicle 3 and also swerved to the left and accelerated. Vehicle 4 collided with Vehicle 3, and both Vehicles 3 and 4 slid into the ongoing collision of Vehicle 1 and Vehicle 2. Vehicle 5 and Vehicle 6 were traveling south on Route 113 and, being unable to stop, Vehicle 6 collided with the rear of Vehicle 5. Together Vehicles 5 and 6 slid into Vehicles 1 and 2, and then Vehicle 6 careened to the northbound lane and collided with Vehicle 3, which had careened to the northbound lane after colliding with Vehicle 4.

Although the information is there, you would need a pencil and paper and be good at decoding to figure out what happened. An alternative is to look at sketches and continue to figure out what happened. There are several problems with this traditional explanation about a traffic accident, beyond general confusion. It becomes confusing because it depersonalizes the accident. One might believe that the vehicles, having a mind of their own, were piling into each other, ignoring those riding inside, or that no people are involved here, only vehicles.

The forms which normally serve as the completed report in most departments list witnesses, occupants, and other information, but do not elaborate. For example, a witness can be many things. What is the person a witness to? The entire accident, or parts of it? Was the witness driving, walking, sitting alongside the road, looking out a window, or what? More questions can be raised and will be raised by your reader. The same problem arises when passengers are labeled as occupants, with no other information given.

Another common comment in traffic accident reports is that speed was excessive for conditions. That's not an unreasonable statement, if we knew what the conditions are, what the speed limits is, and how fast the vehicle was traveling—but how do we know if only a form is used?

The list of problems is long when we rely on fill-in-the-blanks forms. A tiny area is sandwiched among dozens of questions to show a sketch of the entire accident scene, with another like area allotted to show damage to vehicles. However, most, if not all, forms only have room to show damage to two vehicles, and the sketch area is about the same scale. What if there are three, four, or ten vehicles involved? The forms usually indicate to use additional sheets of paper to record additional information. Thus, more confusion of numbers, vehicles, occupants, witnesses, and so forth. Finally, there is the area on the form for you to give a description of the collision, and there's not a chance of squeezing anything beyond a minor fender bender into the space allotted.

Forms are checklists—not a report of investigation. If we place the forms in their proper perspective and use them as one means of taking notes, our professional expertise grows. If we rely on the form to take the place of writing, our professional expertise diminishes.

When you conduct a thorough investigation, your exhibits tell the story. Your conclusion is a brief summary of what the reader will find if all the exhibits are examined, so you are saving him or her a lot of valuable time. Your conclusion might look like the following example:

> About 2:25 P.M., January 10, 1989, Mr. George Brown, operating a vehicle traveling south on Route 113, at mile marker 42, lost control on a curve and collided with a vehicle traveling north operated by Mrs. Samantha Smith. Four other vehicles became involved in the traffic accident. Two vehicles following Brown and two following Smith, attempting to stop and/or take evasive action, traveled into the ongoing collision.

> All vehicles involved became inoperable during the collisions. Brown, determined by information and physical evidence discovered during this investigation, is determined responsible for causing the six-vehicle traffic accident. Injuries by two vehicle operators and four persons riding in various vehicles involved were minor. All have been examined, treated, and released by the Blank City Hospital.

With the foregoing conclusion, your reader has the necessary details. He or she knows when and where the traffic accident occurred, who the primary drivers are, and a concise overview of what happened once the accident started. He or she knows about injuries, damage, and responsibilities. If the reader is interested, the exhibits are attached to support your conclusion and provide a source of detailed information.

*Step 3*: *Summarize your exhibits and support your conclusions with the substantiation section.* Your substantiation serves two primary purposes: (1) It provides your reader with a concise overview of information provided in the detailed exhibits; and (2) it provides you with an effective information management tool, allowing the exhibits to tell the story.

An effective, efficient, and comprehensive traffic accident investigative report must be written the same as any investigative report. Traditional fill-in-the-blanks forms are not time efficient, either in the filling-out or reading process. When finished reading a form, one still isn't sure of the details.

Your substantiation, on the other hand, presents the facts, which are supported by the exhibits, in a logical order, easy and fast to read, and comprehensive. An example is as follows:

> In a written statement obtained from Mr. George Brown (operator of Vehicle 1), details from Brown's point of view are presented. Brown said the vehicle (a 1989 Lincoln Town Car) was purchased earlier on the day of the traffic accident, and he was unaccustomed to its handling. When he attempted to travel around a curve, the vehicle seemed to wander, colliding with Smith, who operated a vehicle traveling in the opposite direction. Brown freely admits he caused the accident; however, does not admit negligence.

> In a written statement obtained from Mrs. Samantha Smith (operator of Vehicle 2), details of the traffic accident are provided from her view. Smith said that as she traveled around a curve on Route 113, she noticed a car coming toward her, and just prior to the point where the Smith and Brown vehicles would pass in opposite directions, the car Brown was driving wandered out into her lane. She said because of the closing speeds of the combined vehicles, the close proximity of Brown's vehicle, and the shock of the situation, little was possible to avoid a colli-

sion. Smith said she applied the brakes and thinks she attempted to swerve to the right, but isn't sure.

In a written statement, Mr. Samuel Johnson, a farmer who was working in a field adjacent to the location where the traffic accident occurred, said he observed the entire accident from a clear viewpoint about 50 yards away. Johnson said he had stopped his tractor and was lighting a pipe while watching the traffic on Route 113. He observed the Brown, Smith, and other four vehicles involved in the accident, and said that Brown clearly wandered over into the oncoming traffic lane just before the Smith vehicle passed by. Johnson said Smith did apply the brakes and did turn to the right; however, Brown's car was already colliding at the time. He said none of the vehicles, including Brown and Smith, appeared to be traveling at excessive speed. The other vehicles, according to Johnson, just didn't have time to stop, and all appeared to try to avoid a collision but could not.

The substantiation allows you to lay out the facts in a way that enables your reader to scan through the substantiation and learn how you came to the conclusion. This section also provides you with a tool to organize the exhibits in a logical order. Recall that a thorough traffic accident investigation can have many exhibits, and perhaps items of physical evidence which you must somehow present logically in a report. When you don't arrange the information logically, your report can become as confusing as the fill-in-the-blanks form and the traditional numbered vehicle report terminology.

Your substantiation is not telling the story, simply presenting key elements and concise summary of the exhibit. Collectively, your exhibits tell the story to a reader.

*Step 4: Don't forget to write an investigator's statement.* One of the greatest assets you have is an investigator's statement. In the substantiation, all you need say is that an investigator's statement discusses all information relevant to the investigation which is not discussed elsewhere.

The investigator's statement is a powerful tool for you to tie up loose ends. All the little odds and ends, bits and pieces, that are relevant and must be told go into your statement. The traditional way of writing traffic accident investigation reports (and all other reports) is either to cram this kind of information into a narrative or leave it out of the report.

The following are some items you should include in your investigator's statement.

- The weather and time of day or night often plays a significant role in traffic accidents. This information, along with your observations of the scene when you arrive, is important. You can be as detailed as you want; make certain you don't leave information out of a report because there is no place to put it.

- This is an excellent forum to express your opinion as long as you clearly show it is an opinion and currently no facts or evidence have been located or identified to support the opinion. For example, you may think that Mr. Brown is not telling you all he knows about the accident; however, you're not certain what he could be withholding. Later, some item of information may come forward which will indicate that Brown was distraught earlier and told a friend he wasn't sure if going on with life had any merit. Perhaps other information may be developed which indicates Brown intentionally caused the accident. If you omit your opinion from your report, although you felt strongly about its validity, you might appear incompetent for not conducting a thorough investigation.

- Explanations (not excuses) about why something wasn't done which may be important. For example, a traffic accident occurring during a torrential rainstorm, or even worse, a blizzard, is a good reason that photographs, exact measurements, location, and other information may be missing or scant.

- Any information relevant—or possibly relevant—to the case that is not discussed elsewhere in the report should be written in your investigator's statement.

*Step 5: Catalog the witnesses.* Witnesses (including victims) developed during your investigation should be listed in this section in the order in which they first appear in your report.

All persons listed in this section should be fully identified, and in the case of traffic accident investigations, all persons involved, even if one or more drivers are responsible for the accident.

In cases in which a driver is charged with one or more criminal offenses resulting from your investigation, a separate section should be added at the beginning of the report titled "Suspects."

Identification of each witness placed in this section should be as complete as possible, including, as a minimum, the following:

- Full name, address, and telephone number
- If the person listed was a driver during the collision, list a driver's license number and state of issue, expiration date, any restrictions, or other pertinent information.

It's important to manage this information carefully, since witnesses tend to fade away, not wanting to take sides, get involved, or use their time to testify. This is especially true with bystanders or passersby.

*Step 6: The exhibits section.* As in all investigative reports, this section is where all your evidence is listed. In a traffic accident investigation, it's often a good idea to include exhibits beyond pure investigative information to provide your reader with reference items unique to this kind of investigation. The following are examples of reference items that may be relevant:

- Formulas used to determine a fact
- Copy of a speed nomograph
- Some other item used to reach your conclusion that readers are unfamiliar with.

Evidence collected at the scene which is not documentary, such as oil samples, alcoholic beverage containers, or any other item that is sent to a laboratory or being examined by a certified mechanic (such as a car with defective brakes which has been impounded temporarily) should be listed and its present location noted.

## HOW TO WRITE A SUPPLEMENTAL VEHICLE COLLISION INVESTIGATION REPORT

If acquiring missing information will take several days or weeks, do not wait for the information to file your report. Perhaps you had to send items to a crime laboratory for analysis and the technicians tell you it will take two weeks or more. Or a witness was identified at the scene, but left before you had an opportunity to interview or obtain a written statement. In a postscene effort to contact the witness, you learn that he or she is away on a business trip or vacation and isn't expected back for about three weeks.

When the information becomes available, you can write a supplemental report, and it's a good idea to label these reports as first supplemental, second supplemental, and so forth. As items of information arrive, file a supplemental report.

Your supplemental report format is the same as the original investigation report, except that you only include additional information and note "no change" in all sections which remain the same. For example, a bottle of capsules you found on the front seat of a vehicle involved in a traffic accident went to the crime laboratory for analysis. You made a note of it in your investigator's statement and in the exhibits section of your report. You did not mention it elsewhere because the mere presence of a bottle of capsules has no relevance to the investigation.

The laboratory sends back the bottle of pills and their report, which says the capsules are a prescription drug for colds which normally causes disorientation and drowsiness.

You contact the driver of the vehicle and by appointment go to his home and reinterview him about the capsules. He admits to taking one a half hour before driving the car and that he was having difficulty staying awake just prior to the accident. The man consents to another written statement, which adds this new information. Since you've already cited him for causing the accident and the drugs are prescription (which you verify after you obtain the statement), and, since the accident resulted only in property damage and minor personal injuries (i.e., scratches, etc., which were treated), no further charges against the man are contemplated.

However, all this new information must be documented and included with your original traffic accident investigation report.

Your supplemental report would be organized as follows:

CASE CONTROL NUMBER: (same number)

DATE: (date of supplemental report)

BASIS FOR INVESTIGATION:
    No change

SUSPECTS:
    No change

INVESTIGATIVE SUMMARY: (CONCLUSIONS)
    [Briefly note new information only.]

SUBSTANTIATION:
    [Note item supporting new information only.]

EXHIBITS:
    [Note new item(s) only.]

The supplemental report only conveys additions to the original case.

# TRAFFIC ACCIDENT FIELD SKETCH

**LEGEND/NOTES**

EXHIBIT 9-1

Case No._____ Date_____ Time Reported_____ Time of Arrival_____

Location_____ Weather_____

No. of Vehicles_____ Type Vehicle(s) _____

Legend: 1. _____    6. _____

2. _____    7. _____

3. _____    8. _____

4. _____    9. _____

5. _____    10. _____

Prepared by: _____  Assisted by: _____

Sirchie Form 711AC7

# Accident Report

Exhibit 9-2

**VEHICLE DIAGRAM**

AUTO

Direction
Headed

Year _____ Color _____ Model _____ Make _____

Tag No. _____ Year _____ State _____ V.I.N. _____

Owner _____ Address _____

Driver _____ Address _____

Mileage _____ Gas Guage _____ Oil Changed _____

Mileage and Station

Doors Locked? _____ Keys in Ignition? _____ Operational? _____

Damage _____

Remarks:

Examined Where? _____ Time: _____

DATE _____ OFFICER _____ CASE _____

EXHIBIT 9-3

226

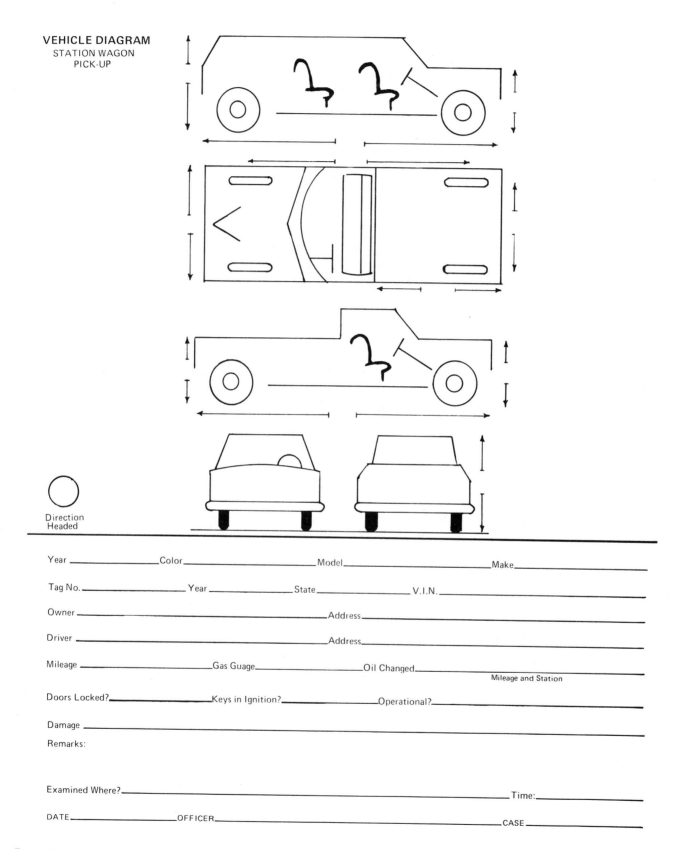

**VEHICLE DIAGRAM**
STATION WAGON
PICK-UP

Direction
Headed

Year _____ Color _____ Model _____ Make _____

Tag No. _____ Year _____ State _____ V.I.N. _____

Owner _____ Address _____

Driver _____ Address _____

Mileage _____ Gas Guage _____ Oil Changed _____
                                                    Mileage and Station

Doors Locked? _____ Keys in Ignition? _____ Operational? _____

Damage _____

Remarks:


Examined Where? _____ Time: _____

DATE _____ OFFICER _____ CASE _____

Exhibit 9-3

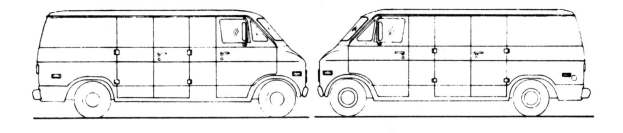

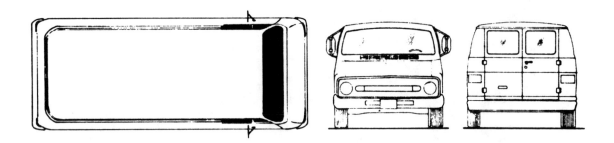

LEGEND _____

_____

_____

_____

_____

_____

Driver _____

Passenger(s) _____

_____

_____

Description of Damage _____

_____

Citation Issued _____ Charge(s) _____

Vehicle Towed To: _____ Towed By: _____

_____

Comments:

_____

_____

Make _____ Model _____ Color _____ Year _____

Sirchie Form 711AC4

EXHIBIT 9-4

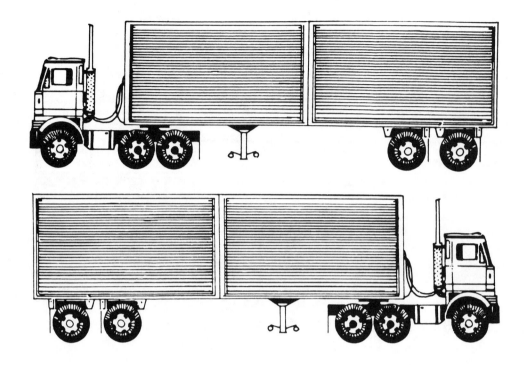

LEGEND_____

_____

_____

_____

_____

_____

Driver_____

Passenger(s) _____

_____

_____

Description of Damage _____

_____

Citation Issued_____Charge(s) _____

Vehicle Towed To:_____ Towed By: _____

_____

Comments:

_____

_____

Make _____Model_____ Color_____ Year_____

Sirchie Form 711AC6

Exhibit 9-4

TOP

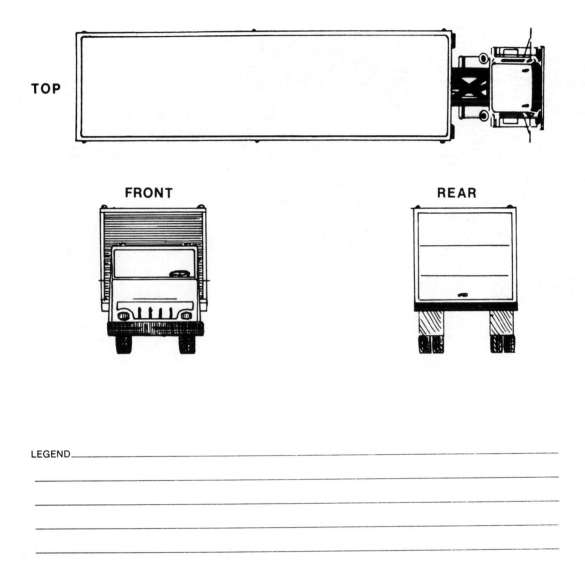

FRONT

REAR

LEGEND

EXHIBIT 9-4

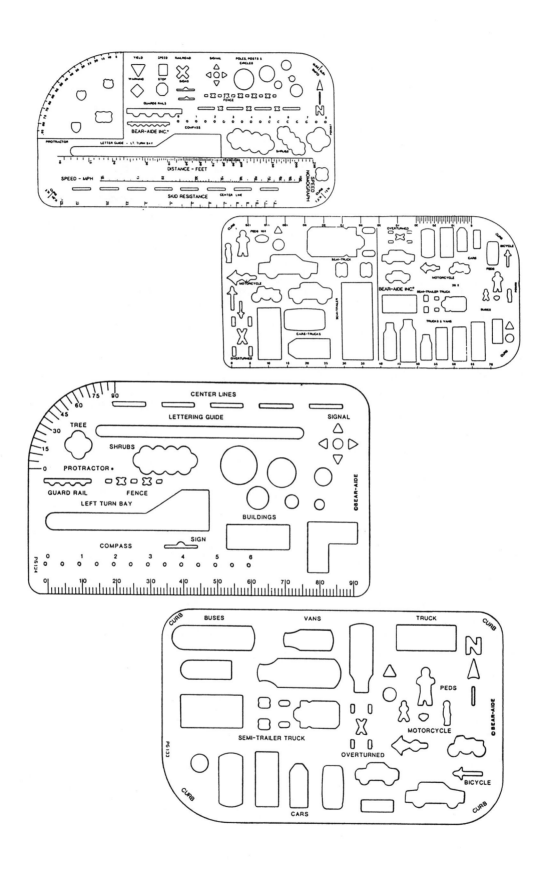

EXHIBIT 9-5

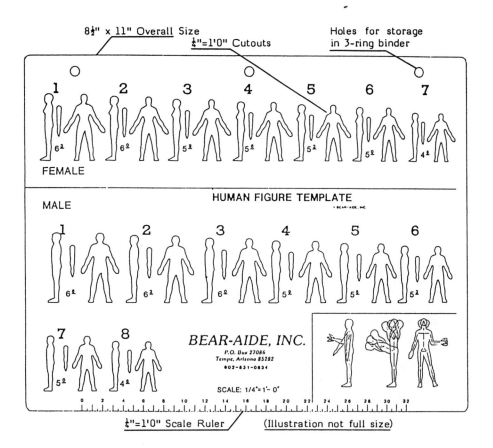

8½" x 11" Overall Size

¼"=1'0" Cutouts

Holes for storage in 3-ring binder

FEMALE

HUMAN FIGURE TEMPLATE

MALE

BEAR-AIDE, INC.
P.O. Box 27086
Tempe, Arizona 85282
602-831-0834

SCALE: 1/4"=1'- 0"

¼"=1'0" Scale Ruler        (Illustration not full size)

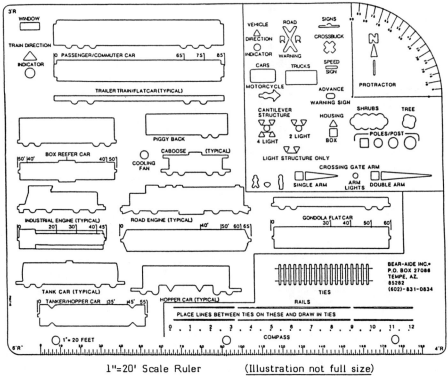

1"=20' Scale Ruler        (Illustration not full size)

Exhibit 9-6

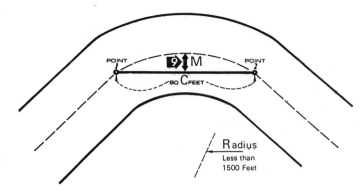

$$R = \frac{C^2}{8M} + \frac{M}{2}$$

$$R = \frac{80 \times 80}{8 \times 9} + \frac{9}{2}$$

$$R = \frac{6400}{72} + \frac{9}{2}$$

$$R = 88.88 + 4.5$$

$$R = 93.38$$

$$R = 93^{5*}$$

**Legend**

M  Middle Ordinate

🔟  Length of M (9 Feet)

C  Chord

93⁵* = 93 Feet 5 Inches

*Measuring Radius of a Sharp Curve*

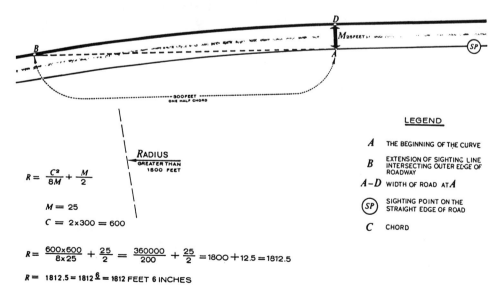

$$R = \frac{C^2}{8M} + \frac{M}{2}$$

$$M = 25$$

$$C = 2 \times 300 = 600$$

**LEGEND**

*A*  THE BEGINNING OF THE CURVE

*B*  EXTENSION OF SIGHTING LINE INTERSECTING OUTER EDGE OF ROADWAY

*A–D*  WIDTH OF ROAD AT *A*

(SP)  SIGHTING POINT ON THE STRAIGHT EDGE OF ROAD

*C*  CHORD

$$R = \frac{600 \times 600}{8 \times 25} + \frac{25}{2} = \frac{360000}{200} + \frac{25}{2} = 1800 + 12.5 = 1812.5$$

$$R = 1812.5 = 1812\tfrac{6}{} = 1812 \text{ FEET 6 INCHES}$$

*Measuring Radius of a Long Sweeping Curve*

Exhibit 9-7

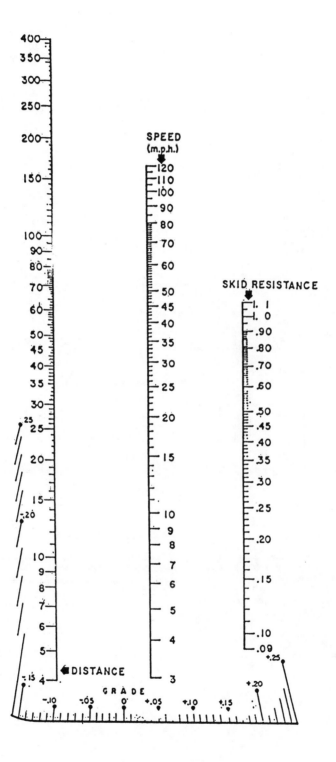

EXHIBIT 9-8

234

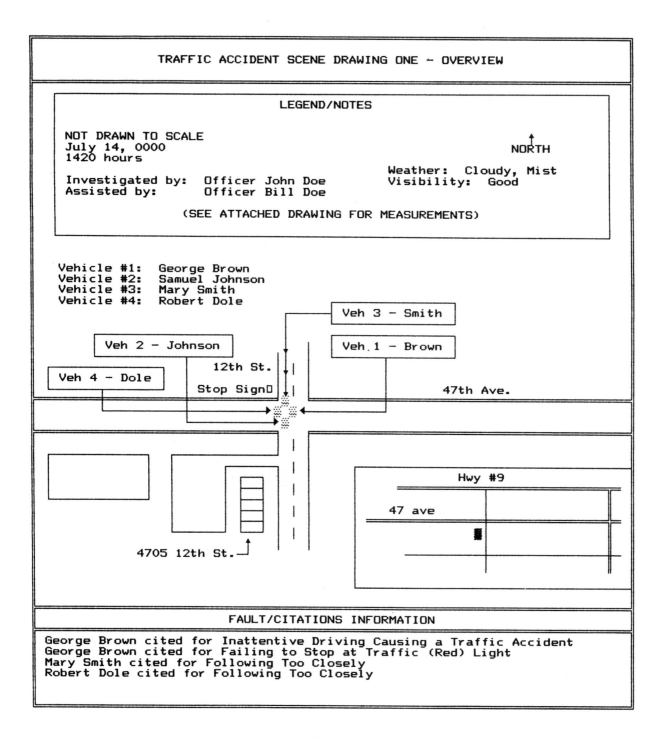

TRAFFIC ACCIDENT SCENE DRAWING ONE - OVERVIEW

LEGEND/NOTES

NOT DRAWN TO SCALE
July 14, 0000                                                    NORTH
1420 hours
                                          Weather:  Cloudy, Mist
Investigated by:  Officer John Doe        Visibility:  Good
Assisted by:      Officer Bill Doe

(SEE ATTACHED DRAWING FOR MEASUREMENTS)

Vehicle #1:  George Brown
Vehicle #2:  Samuel Johnson
Vehicle #3:  Mary Smith
Vehicle #4:  Robert Dole

Veh 3 - Smith

Veh 2 - Johnson          Veh 1 - Brown

                12th St.
Veh 4 - Dole
                Stop Sign□              47th Ave.

4705 12th St.

Hwy #9

47 ave

FAULT/CITATIONS INFORMATION

George Brown cited for Inattentive Driving Causing a Traffic Accident
George Brown cited for Failing to Stop at Traffic (Red) Light
Mary Smith cited for Following Too Closely
Robert Dole cited for Following Too Closely

Exhibit 9-9

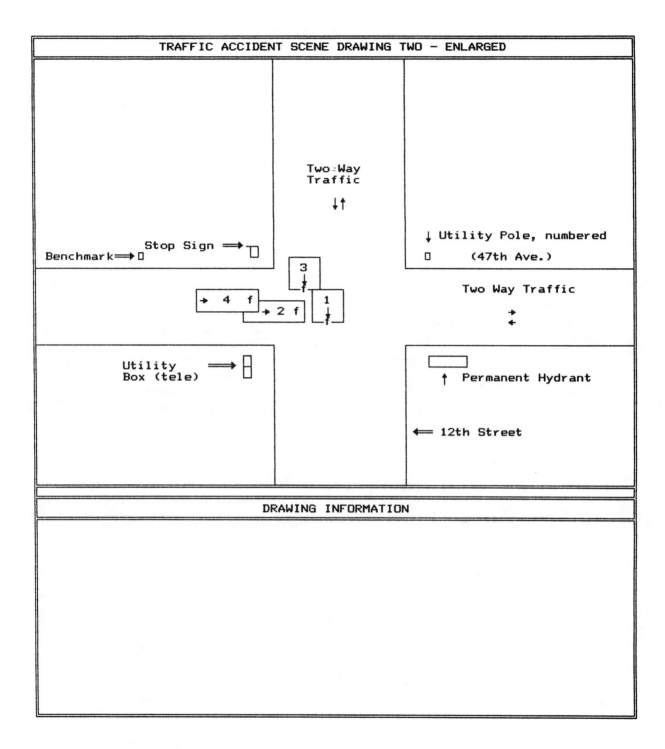

# TRAFFIC ACCIDENT SCENE DRAWING TWO - ENLARGED

Two Way
Traffic

↓↑

↓ Utility Pole, numbered
▫ (47th Ave.)

Stop Sign ⟹ ▯

Benchmark ⟹ ▫

Two Way Traffic

→
←

3
↓ f

→ 4  f

→ 2 f

1
↓ f

Utility
Box (tele) ⟹ ▯

▭
↑ Permanent Hydrant

⟸ 12th Street

# DRAWING INFORMATION

Exhibit 9-10

*State of New Hampshire*

# DEPARTMENT OF SAFETY
## DIVISION OF MOTOR VEHICLES
# MOTOR VEHICLE ACCIDENT REPORT

N.H. RSA 264:25    REPORTING REQUIREMENTS

IN THE STATE OF NEW HAMPSHIRE, ANY MOTOR VEHICLE ACCIDENT CAUSING DEATH, PERSONAL INJURY, OR COMBINED VEHICLE/PROPERTY DAMAGE IN EXCESS OF $500 MUST BE REPORTED WITHIN 5 DAYS. FAILURE TO REPORT IN THE CASE OF DEATH OR PERSONAL INJURY IS A FELONY. FAILURE TO REPORT FOLLOWING A PROPETY DAMAGE ONLY ACCIDENT IS A MISDEMEANOR.

## SECTION A : INSTRUCTIONS
### PLEASE PRINT OR TYPE ALL INFORMATION
### USE BLACK OR DARK BLUE INK
- FOLLOW THE INSTRUCTIONS IN "SECTION B" BELOW
- COMPLETE OTHER SIDE OF REPORT USING DIRECTIONS BELOW AS A GUIDE.

1. The location of the accident is very important and you should describe it as accurately and completely as possible in the space provided . When describing the location of your accident, indicate the direction and distance from the crash site to the nearest intersecting road or on Interstate Highways use Exit numbers.

2. Give your own and the owner's CURRENT name and/or address when completing the **DRIVER #1** part of the form. Report all other driver and vehicle information exactly as it appears on each license and registration.

3. If you were involved in an accident with a Pedestrian or Bicyclist enter the Pedestrian or Bicyclist information in the DRIVER block in the space provided for **OTHER DRIVER #2**, and print PEDESTRIAN or BICYCLIST in the **OWNER** block.

   If you were involved in an accident with an off-highway-recreation-vehicle, e.g. snowmobile, trail bike, all-terrain vehicle, etc., enter the driver, owner, and vehicle information as you would normally for **OTHER DRIVER #2**.

   If a vehicle is unoccupied, enter all available information. Be sure to enter the correct vehicle plate number and vehicle make in the appropriate **VEHICLE** block.

4. If you were involved in an accident in which there were more than two vehicles, an additional report form must be filled out. On that form, place the information for the third vehicle in the space marked **REPORTING DRIVER #1** and mark it No. 3. Use the space marked **OTHER DRIVER #2** for the fourth vehicle, and mark it No. 4 and so on

5. You must use the **REPORT ALL INJURIES** part of the form to give information on each person injured in the accident. TYPE OF INJURY is determined as follows:

   **K**
   Any injury that results in death.

   **A**
   Severe lacerations , broken or distorted limbs, skull fracture, crushed chest, internal injuries, unconscious when taken from the accident scene, unable to leave accident scene without assistance.

   **B**
   Lump on head, abrasions, minor lacerations

   **C**
   Momentary unconsciousness, limping, nausea, hysteria, complaint of pain (no visible injury)

   **U**
   Unknown

6. When a pedestrian is injured place a 'P' in the WHICH VEHICLE OCCUPIED box. When a Bicyclist is injured place a 'B' in this box. If there are more than three persons injured, another report form is needed. In the injury section of that report, give the required information for all additional injured persons.

7. Attach any additional report forms to page one. Each page of the report must be numbered in the upper right corner. **Sign the report(s) on the bottom line.**

Submit the report(s) to:

**DEPARTMENT OF SAFETY**
**FINANCIAL RESPONSIBILITY**
**HAZEN DRIVE**
**CONCORD, N. H. 03305**

## SECTION B

Enter the number of the item in the corresponding box provided which best describes the circumstances of the accident.

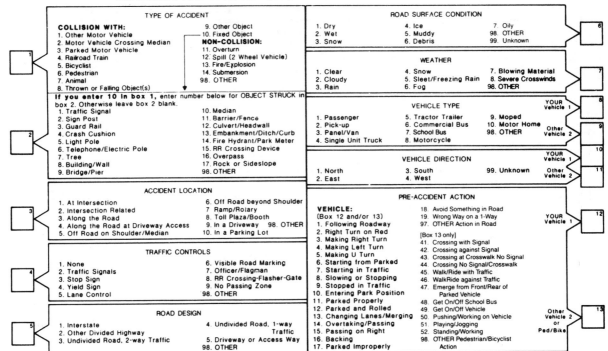

EXHIBIT 9-11

| LOCAL USE | STATE OF NEW HAMPSHIRE UNIFORM POLICE TRAFFIC ACCIDENT REPORT | | Sheet of Sheet(s) M.V. USE ONLY No. Date Rec'd |
|---|---|---|---|

Please Print or Type

Amended Report ☐  Hit and Run ☐

| DATE OF ACCIDENT | DAY OF WEEK | TOTAL KILLED ☐ | TOTAL INJURED ☐ | TOTAL VEHICLES ☐ | CITY/TOWN | COUNTY |
|---|---|---|---|---|---|---|

| TIME OF ACCIDENT (Military) | POLICE NOTIFIED | POLICE ARRIVED | AMBULANCE ARRIVED | POLICE DEPARTMENT |
|---|---|---|---|---|

ACCIDENT OCCURRED ON

MILES ☐  N ☐  E ☐  OF  INTERSECTING ROAD, BRIDGE, TOWN LINE (not telephone pole, house)
FEET ☐  S ☐  W ☐
☐ AT INTERSECTION WITH

ROUTE NO. AND/OR STREET NAME          ROUTE NO. AND/OR STREET NAME          POSTED SPEED

Complete first node for accidents at node, complete both for accidents **between** nodes.

| FIRST NODE | DISTANCE FROM FIRST NODE TOWARD SECOND | SECOND NODE | MILE-MARKER ON INTERSTATE ONLY | MILE |
|---|---|---|---|---|

___ 10 ___  ___/___    FEET  ___ 10 ___  ___/___    ___ FEET

MAP  ZONE  NODE  SUF          MAP  ZONE  NODE  SUF    N ☐  E ☐  S ☐  W ☐

| UNIT 1 | VIOLATION RSA | COURT NAME | CHEMICAL TEST ☐ NOT TAKEN ☐ TAKEN ☐ REFUSED | BAC | UNIT 2 | VIOLATION RSA | COURT NAME | CHEMICAL TEST ☐ NOT TAKEN ☐ TAKEN ☐ REFUSED | BAC |
|---|---|---|---|---|---|---|---|---|---|
| | | ☐ WARNING | | | | | ☐ WARNING | | |

| DRIVER'S NAME FIRST, MIDDLE, LAST | S.S. NO. (Optional) | DRIVER'S NAME FIRST, MIDDLE, LAST | S.S. NO. (Optional) |
|---|---|---|---|

| NUMBER AND STREET | PHONE NO. | NUMBER AND STREET | PHONE NO. |
|---|---|---|---|

| CITY/TOWN | STATE | ZIP CODE | CITY/TOWN | STATE | ZIP CODE |
|---|---|---|---|---|---|

| DRIVER LICENSE NO. | STATE | CLASSIFICATION | DRIVER LICENSE NO. | STATE | CLASSIFICATION |
|---|---|---|---|---|---|

| D.O.B. | SEX | RESTRICTIONS | RESTRICTIONS COMPLIED WITH ☐ YES ☐ NO | D.O.B. | SEX | RESTRICTIONS | RESTRICTIONS COMPLIED WITH ☐ YES ☐ NO |
|---|---|---|---|---|---|---|---|

| OWNER 1 NAME FIRST, MIDDLE, LAST | OWNER 2 NAME FIRST, MIDDLE, LAST |
|---|---|

| NUMBER AND STREET | NUMBER AND STREET |
|---|---|

| CITY/TOWN | STATE | ZIP CODE | CITY/TOWN | STATE | ZIP CODE |
|---|---|---|---|---|---|

| V.I.N. | MILEAGE | V.I.N. | MILEAGE |
|---|---|---|---|

| MAKE | GROSS WEIGHT | YEAR | INSURANCE CO. (Optional) | MAKE | GROSS WEIGHT | YEAR | INSURANCE CO. (Optional) |
|---|---|---|---|---|---|---|---|

| HAZARDOUS MATERIAL ☐ YES ☐ NO ID. # | AGENT/POLICY NO. (Optional) | HAZARDOUS MATERIAL ☐ YES ☐ NO ID. # | AGENT/POLICY NO. (Optional) |
|---|---|---|---|

| PLATE NO. | STATE | TRAILER PLATE NO. | STATE | PLATE NO. | STATE | TRAILER PLATE NO. | STATE |
|---|---|---|---|---|---|---|---|

**VEHICLE NO. 1**  Check one of the 8 diagrams if it adequately describes the accident, **or draw** your own in space on back.  VEHICLE NO. 2

☐ INDICATE PROBABLE POINT OF IMPACT

1 | 2 | 3 | 4 | 5 | 6
13 Front  14  Rear 15
12 | 11 | 10 | 9 | 8 | 7

16 Undercarriage
17 Rollover
18 Fire/Explosion
19 Total

Circle numbers indicating areas damaged.

Rear | Passing | Lt Turn | Intersection
Rt Turn | Rt Turn | Head-On | Sideswipe

Indicate Vehicle Numbers on Arrows Above

INDICATE PROBABLE POINT OF IMPACT ☐

1 | 2 | 3 | 4 | 5 | 6
13 Front  14  Rear 15
12 | 11 | 10 | 9 | 8 | 7

16 Undercarriage
17 Rollover
18 Fire/Explosion
19 Total

Circle numbers indicating areas damaged.

| 26 | 27 | 28 | 29 | 30 | 31 | NAME(S) OF **INJURED PERSON(S)** | ADDRESS/PHONE | 32 | 33 | 34 | 35 |
|---|---|---|---|---|---|---|---|---|---|---|---|
| | | | | | | | | | | | |
| | | | | | | | | | | | |
| | | | | | | | | | | | |

| RECOMMENDATIONS: UNIT 1 | ☐ M.V. DRIVER RE-EXAMINATION ☐ M.V. HEARING ☐ OTHER _____ | RECOMMENDATIONS: UNIT 2 | ☐ M.V. DRIVER RE-EXAMINATION ☐ M.V. HEARING ☐ OTHER _____ |
|---|---|---|---|

DSMV-159 (Revised 12/82)

EXHIBIT 9-12

238

| PROPERTY DAMAGE OTHER THAN VEHICLES | ACCIDENT SKETCH |
|---|---|
| DESCRIBE PROPERTY AND DAMAGE | Indicate North |

**ACCIDENT SKETCH**

Indicate North

by Arrow

APPROX. COST OF REPAIRS $

LOCATION OF PROPERTY

CITY/STATE

OWNER'S NAME

ADDRESS

CITY/STATE

ZIP CODE                    PHONE NO.

Please Print or Type

(to be supplemented with scale diagram or DSMV-161, if necessary)

**GIST OF THE ACCIDENT**

**SUMMARIZE STATEMENT OF DRIVER #1**   ☐ Check if DRIVER #1 was given a MOTORIST ACCIDENT REPORT

**SUMMARIZE STATEMENT OF DRIVER #2**   ☐ Check if DRIVER #2 was given a MOTORIST ACCIDENT REPORT.

**WITNESSES OTHER THAN PERSONS INVOLVED**

| NAME | D.O.B. | ADDRESS/PHONE |
|---|---|---|
| | | |
| | | |
| | | |

| SIGNATURE OF INVESTIGATING OFFICER | DATE OF REPORT | REVIEWED BY |
|---|---|---|
| DEPARTMENT/DIVISION/TROOP | PHOTOS TAKEN ☐ YES ☐ NO | BY _____ |

EXHIBIT 9-12

# TEN

# How to Write Crime Prevention Reports a Businessperson Can Understand

Throughout this book I've talked about crimes, vehicle collisions, criminal intelligence, and related subjects. I haven't yet talked about crime prevention.

Most progressive law enforcement departments have crime prevention programs aimed at local businesses. The program is a public service effort which serves three primary purposes: (1) It helps businesses protect their assets; (2) it decreases the department's workload by preventing crimes against businesses; and (3) it serves to bring law enforcement departments and officers into a better harmony with businesses and citizens of the community.

The scope of services vary according to the department's policy, kind of community businesses, amount of business-related crime experienced, number of officers available, and amount of specialized training participating officers have received. Normally, a crime prevention program is limited to physical security—for example, locks, keys, window and door barriers to burglars, alarm systems and similar measures. Some departments venture into environmental security, which measures the internal and external security of a business. The concept of the prevention survey is to determine the level of vulnerability of a specific business location to robberies, burglaries, shoplifting, bad check artists, fast change scams, and all the problems caused by criminals who target small businesses.

Officers normally call on businesses to offer the service or, initially, newspaper publicity announces the department's no-cost service and a number to call for information. As time permits, officers assigned either full or part time to the program will visit the business and conduct a survey. In most jurisdictions, a checklist is used, and weaknesses are noted, often leaving the solutions to the business owner. The problem is, if the owner knew how to provide effective solutions, the deficiencies would not have been present. Or, if the business owner could afford to hire professional assistance to solve the problems, he or she would already have done so. In effect, the program sounds good, appears good, but does not obtain its objective. Departments must require officers participating in crime prevention programs to write a comprehensive report that not only spells out deficiencies found during their inspection of a specific business location, but also provides viable solutions to correct the deficiencies. A business owner benefits from a comprehensive crime prevention program offered by a law enforcement department in the following ways:

1. Crimes against the business are reduced or eliminated.

2. Insurance rates will normally decrease or remain lowest if crime claims are not filed.

3. Managers and employees feel comfortable working in a safe environment.

4. The business operation is not damaged, slowed, or bankrupted by crimes such as (a) armed robberies, which cause employees to quit, make it hard to hire new employees, and make potential customers reluctant to enter the store in fear of another robbery; (b) burglaries, which can deplete inventory, causing a business to close during reorder time; and (c) damage by burglars or arsonists.

5. A business owner feels more confident and can devote energies toward the business rather than coping with crime.

These benefits are possible only if the businessperson participates in the cost-free law enforcement crime prevention effort; and the extent of benefits is determined by how extensive and broad the program is, how well trained the officers are, and, most important, a comprehensive report written and provided to the owner.

Your crime prevention survey report must fit the program, including its limitations. You should not leave a checklist of deficiencies behind at the business, since criminals may be employees or friends of them. Take your checklist or worksheet with you after completing the inspection, and hand deliver the report or send it by certified mail to an owner's private address. I always like to have a receipt with the report and have the owner sign for the report unless it's sent by certified mail, return receipt requested. All the precaution protects you, the department, and the business owner jointly. The last thing you want to do is make a business location appear vulnerable to a criminal element.

One of the key considerations for writing a crime prevention report is telling the businessperson all the vulnerabilities and how to correct the problem inexpensively or at a minimum cost. Your report must be well written; the businessperson must understand exactly what you're talking about.

In the same way you begin writing a preliminary investigation report on the way to a crime scene, vehicle collision, or other situation, carry that technique into crime prevention inspection using your report format as a guide. Prior to leaving the department, you should have a list of businesses you'll be inspecting. The list should include a brief description about the kind of business being conducted at that location and the number of crimes reported there over the past year or more. For example, if five burglaries occurred at Sam's Clothing Store, review the investigation reports before you leave the department. That information may help you find an overall flaw in the store's security environment. The owner may be trying hard but may lack the insight a law enforcement officer can provide about improving security barriers.

One way I've found to be effective before, during, and while writing my report about deficiencies found during the inspection and viable solutions, is to use a systems approach.

## USE A WORKSHEET TO DEVELOP YOUR SYSTEMS APPROACH CONCEPT FOR CRIME PREVENTION INSPECTIONS AND SURVEYS

Information management techniques apply in any situation requiring a written report; security inspections are no exception. The minimum information you'll need for both your inspection and written report includes the following:

1. Business definition

   a. *Who* owns the business? For example: Independently owned; or by a corporation, partnership, part of a franchise chain?

   b. *What* kind of business is conducted at the location? For example, is it a clothing store, grocery store, camera store?

   c. *Where* is the business located? Is it part of a mall, a minishopping area, or free-standing?

   d. *When* is the business in operation? What are its hours of operation?

   e. *How* is the business operated? By mom and pop with two part-time employees; an employee staff of twenty with one manager and two assistant managers?

2. Design of structure

   a. Is the business located in a building with other businesses, for example a mall or minimall?

   b. Is the structure wood frame, concrete block, a combination of both, or some other kind of construction?

   c. What's the interior like? How many rooms are there, and what are they used for? For example, a sales or retail area 25' × 25'; an office space 10' × 10'; a stock storage room 20' × 20'; a basement 20' × 20' containing files and a heating system.

   d. What's the exterior like? For example, seven entry/exit points, including four windows which can provide access if broken or removed; three doors including the customer entrance/exit, a rear employee entrance/exit; and a large commodity receiving door in the stock storage room.

   e. Is there a parking lot? For example, is there exterior lighting during hours of darkness? Would concealment of burglars be probable?

3. Threat estimate

   a. Is this a high crime area?

   b. How many crimes have been reported by this business?

   c. What is the potential for crime against this business?

   d. What kinds of crimes would most likely be committed against this business?

4. Security assessment

   a. What was the situation at the time of inspection/last inspection?

   b. What is the owner/management interest in security?

   c. What is the owner/management interest in improvement?

   d. What are the cost/benefit factors?

   e. What are the owner/management resources?

A detailed inspection worksheet example is shown in Exhibit 10-1. You can use it or develop your own.

I suggest that a permission form be developed and that the businessperson who invites or accepts your courtesy crime prevention inspection signs it prior to beginning your inspection. It should spell out what's taking place, who's conducting the inspection, and all other details and information applicable. An example of a permission form is shown in Exhibit 10-2.

# CRIME PREVENTION CHECKLIST FOR BUSINESS ESTABLISHMENTS

1. Does the manager/owner of the business, at the end of each business day, inspect the premises to insure that all window, doors, safes, etc. have been closed and that no person is hidden in restrooms or elsewhere?

_____

_____

_____

2. Is an intrusion detection device/system installed?

_____

_____

_____

3. Is the intrusion detection device/system operational?

_____

_____

_____

4. How does the intrusion detection device/system notify law enforcement departments that an intrusion is in progress? Does the intruder know that the intrusion detection device/system is activated?

_____

_____

_____

5. Are service entrances locked from the inside when not in use for authorized movements of materials?

_____

_____

_____

6. Is a strong light kept burning over the safe during nonoperational periods? Is the safe visible to passing law enforcement and/or private security patrols?

_____

_____

_____

EXHIBIT 10-1

## CRIME PREVENTION CHECKLIST FOR BUSINESS ESTABLISHMENTS

7. Is the business equipped with closed circuit television for surveillance of customers, stock rooms, employees, or for other purposes?

_____

_____

_____

8. Does any portion of the interior arrangement of this business lend itself to pilferage or shoplifting?

_____

_____

_____

9. Does this business employ security persons for a deterrent against crime during business hours? After business hours?

_____

_____

_____

10. Are employees briefed on handling shoplifting offenders, armed robberies, and other situations such as customer illness?

_____

_____

_____

11. Are law enforcement, fire, and paramedical assistance telephone numbers known or posted for employees?

_____

_____

_____

12. Is there a tally-in or tally-out system, as appropriate, for checking supplies received or shipped against shipping documents?

_____

_____

_____

Exhibit 10-1

# CRIME PREVENTION CHECKLIST FOR BUSINESS ESTABLISHMENTS

13. Are there any shortages in high-value items such as cameras, watches, jewelry, etc. (if applicable)?

_____

_____

_____

14. What action is taken when high-value, identifiable items are discovered missing?

_____

_____

_____

15. Do sales slips indicate serial numbers of items when applicable?

_____

_____

_____

16. Are valuable items such as watches, cameras, etc. stored in separate secured storage in stockrooms or other areas? Describe storage precautions.

_____

_____

_____

17. Are items of comparatively high value displayed in a manner in which they could be readily stolen with little chance of discovery?

_____

_____

_____

18. Are service doors supervised by competent employees when opened?

_____

_____

_____

Exhibit 10-1

# CRIME PREVENTION CHECKLIST FOR BUSINESS ESTABLISHMENTS

19. Are garbage and trash inspected before removal to assure they're not being used as a means of unauthorized removal of store merchandise?

_____

_____

_____

20. Are employees required to check with the manager/owner prior to leaving the premises of the business?

_____

_____

_____

21. Are employees required to keep purses and other items in a locker and away from store merchandise?

_____

_____

_____

22. Are employees permitted to ring up their own purchases?

_____

_____

_____

23. Are all sales recorded on cash registers?

_____

_____

_____

24. Are excessive amounts of money and large denomination currency removed from cash register drawers regularly and unannounced?

_____

_____

_____

Exhibit 10-1

## CRIME PREVENTION CHECKLIST FOR BUSINESS ESTABLISHMENTS

25. Are amounts rung up on cash registers visible to customers?

_____

_____

_____

26. Are customers desiring to cash checks, money orders, and traveler's checks required to produce identification prior to the transactions?

_____

_____

_____

27. Is a manager/owner consulted and required to approve all checks cashed regardless of the type?

_____

_____

_____

28. Is the business safe secured to prevent removal?

_____

_____

_____

29. Who has access to the safe with a combination?

_____

_____

_____

30. Is the safe combination changed regularly?

_____

_____

_____

Exhibit 10-1

# CRIME PREVENTION CHECKLIST FOR BUSINESS ESTABLISHMENTS

31. Are cash funds limited to the minimum consistent needs of the business?

 

 

 

32. Is door construction adequate from a security standpoint?

 

 

 

33. Are all floor openings, other than doors, in excess of 96 square inches barred, grilled, or covered with chain link material?

 

 

 

34. Is there a crawlway beneath the building?

 

 

 

35. Does the crawlway provide a feasible surreptitious entry into the business?

 

 

 

36. Are heating/air conditioning ducts arranged so they can be used to gain access to the building?

 

 

 

Exhibit 10-1

## CRIME PREVENTION CHECKLIST FOR BUSINESS ESTABLISHMENTS

37. Are all doors other than customer entrance/exit points kept locked other than when being used and supervised?

_____

_____

_____

38. Are door hinge pins either of the lock-pin variety or welded to prevent their removal?

_____

_____

39. Are padlock hasps installed to prevent removal when in a locked position?

_____

_____

40. Are keys to the building and internal locks controlled?

_____

_____

_____

41. Are managers or other employees provided keys to all door locks and locks within the building?

_____

_____

_____

42. Are locks changed or rekeyed when an employee resigns, retires, or is fired?

_____

_____

_____

Exhibit 10-1

# CRIME PREVENTION CHECKLIST FOR BUSINESS ESTABLISHMENTS

43. Are there feasible entrances into the building through devices on the roof? If so, are there barriers to prevent entry?

_____

_____

_____

44. Are darkened areas outside the building lighted during hours of darkness?

_____

_____

_____

45. Is exterior lighting protected to prevent easy disablement?

_____

_____

_____

46. Is there adequate lighting within the interior of the business during hours of darkness to allow passersby, law enforcement, and security patrols to view the interior easily?

_____

_____

_____

47. Is there an auxiliary or emergency power source?

_____

_____

_____

48. Are employees screened prior to hiring?

_____

_____

_____

49. Other observations and comments:

_____

_____

_____

EXHIBIT 10-1

## DEPARTMENT LETTERHEAD

## PERMISSION AND AUTHORIZATION TO CONDUCT A CRIME PREVENTION INSPECTION

Name of Business: _____

Address: _____

_____

Owner: _____

Manager: _____

I am authorizing     (officer)
_____

representing     (law enforcement department)
_____

to inspect this place of business to ascertain any and all common deficiencies of internal and external security. I understand this inspection is a public service, and its purpose is to assist me in finding ways to protect my assets, employees, and business from the threat of criminal activity. I understand that I have the right to refuse this inspection and that it is not being conducted with any intention of gathering information or collecting evidence against me, my employees, or business operations.

Signature of Manager/Owner: _____

Date: _____     Time: _____

Exhibit 10-2

## HOW TO WRITE A CRIME PREVENTION INSPECTION REPORT _____

Earlier, I mentioned that a major consideration in writing your crime prevention inspection report is that the reader (business owner or manager) understands what you're saying. All other law enforcement reports you write are intended for use within the criminal justice system. (Some exceptions are readers who generally have a clear understanding of criminal justice mechanics, or insurance adjustors in vehicle collision investigations.) Crime prevention reports, however, are provided as a service to businesspersons and must be written with that in mind.

You'll need to develop a heading that satisfies department document and file controls, probably similar to all the investigative reports. That's an administrative matter, not considered in depth here.

Begin with a conclusion. Just as with investigative reports, you should begin with a concise, to-the-point conclusion of your crime prevention inspection, as in the following example.

### SUMMARY OF CRIME PREVENTION INSPECTION

On July 15, 1990, at Sam's Clothing Store, 2834 Broadway Avenue, Any City, Any State, a crime prevention inspection revealed seven vulnerable areas. Inspection entrance and exit briefings were conducted with Mr. Sam Herringbone, owner of the business.

Your opening conclusion is summarizing for the reader that you did conduct a crime prevention inspection and talked to the owner prior to and after the inspection. The entrance and exit briefings are important to inform a businessperson about what you'll be looking for, how the program can help him or her, and for general public relations. After you complete the inspection, an exit briefing will point out major problems along with viable solutions, so the owner, if he or she chooses, can begin immediate remedial efforts. Don't leave a copy of the worksheet. Sam might lay it on a desk, allowing employee Sly Advantage to make a copy and give it to his cousin, an accomplished burglar. After you write your report, hand deliver it to Sam and apprise him that overall security includes that report. If he chooses to be sloppy and still treat the report lightly, there's nothing more you can do. I suggest you use a report receipt form like the one shown in Exhibit 10-3.

When you've written the conclusion, actually a declaration, you're ready to support it, but in a different way than investigative reports. Remember, your reader is a businessperson. In addition, department records are a factor. An effective crime prevention program is dependent not on only one inspection, but repetitive inspections, in most cases annually. As your program develops, you'll have a record of the last inspection or several inspections, coupled with an update of any crime reported from that business since your last visit. All the information will help you to formulate better ways to help a businessperson, or in some cases determine that the owner isn't interested in improving.

For both reasons, you'll need to structure your report so the businessperson can understand it, and provide a credible department record for yourself or another officer who will make the next inspection.

## DEPARTMENT LETTERHEAD

## RECORD OF RELEASING CRIME PREVENTION INSPECTION REPORT

Name of Business: _____

Address: _____

_____

Manager/Owner: _____

Date and Time of Inspection: _____

Crime Prevention Inspection Report Number: _____

Dated _____ , written by _____

is released to _____

at (time and date) _____

This information is provided to the owner or his or her designee as a public service. All information contained in this report, and safeguarding the report, is the sole responsibility of the person now receiving it. The undersigned forever waives all rights or desires to hold this department or the officers shown liable for the release of any information in this report which is proved to be unauthorized.

Received By: _____

Time and Date: _____

Exhibit 10-3

Support your opening declaration with a systems approach. Explain your findings and solutions within the following format:

## BUSINESS DEFINITION

Sam's Clothing Store is owned and operated by Mr. Sam Herringbone. The store is incorporated as Sam's Clothing, Inc., with Sam Herringbone the sole corporate person.

The business sells a full line of mid-priced men's clothing exclusively and has been in business for thirty-five years at the same location.

The business is located within a building which is divided into twelve stores. Sam's Clothing is located in the center with other unrelated businesses on either side. The location is on a well-traveled street near the center of the downtown section of Any City.

Sam's Clothing Store is open six days a week, closed on Sunday. Hours of operation are 9:00 A.M. to 7:00 P.M. during the summer months, and 9:00 A.M. to 5:00 P.M. during the winter months.

The business is operated with five full-time floor salesmen, two part-time stock employees, with Sam Herringbone normally supervising at the store. There are no managers; however each floor salesman, all long-time employees (twenty years or longer), has full charge and responsibility for an assigned section of the store and its inventory.

## DESIGN OF THE STRUCTURE

The building in which Sam's Clothing Store is located is about sixty years old and well maintained. It is a mix of concrete, wood, and steel construction, one story, and structurally sound.

The store interior consists of an open sales floor divided into departments. The sales floor is about 40' × 40', and adjoined with a 40' × 30' stockroom. A small office is located off the stockroom where all business records are maintained; it's about 10' × 25'. A customer restroom is off the sales floor, with an employee's restroom located off the stockroom adjacent the office.

The heating and cooling is provided by a centralized system providing services to the entire building, including the neighboring stores.

The store is abutted on two sides by other stores, and the front has one centrally placed customer door and two large plate glass windows which have platforms for displaying mannikins, shoes, and other clothing items in full view to passersby. The rear of the store has a loading dock that spans the entire building. The rear doors at Sam's Clothing Store are a large double door that accommodates off-loading incoming shipments, and a regular rear door for employees and other business. Both doors are constructed of steel and secured with two deadbolt locks and top and bottom fasteners.

## THREAT ESTIMATE

During the past five years, Sam's Clothing Store has experienced two armed robberies, three burglaries, and several incidents of shoplifting, some resulting in arrests, others escaping the store.

## SECURITY ASSESSMENT

A crime prevention inspection revealed the following vulnerable areas:

*Front of store*: Currently, the window display areas consist of two large plate glass windows facing the street with two plate glass windows on both sides of a 10-foot entranceway with the front entry door at the end. This configuration forms a display area for dressed mannikins and other assorted clothing. The window display areas are partitioned at the ends next to the store with small access doors allowing entry to arrange displays. Although the configuration increases interior display space (opposite the partitions), viewing the store interior from the street side is prevented. The front door is solid wood and has no windows. Passersby, law enforcement, or security patrols have no view of the interior day or night, allowing armed robberies, burglaries, or other crimes to occur unnoticed from the outside.

*Suggested solution*: Remove the partitions from the window display area and arrange mannikins and clothing displays so passersby, law enforcement, and security patrols have a clear view of the store interior day or night. Enhance this advantage by leaving ample interior lights on even when closed. During closed hours, leave lights in the display area off or dimmed to allow passing law enforcement or security units to view the interior. Cost is minimal and armed robbery, burglary, and other criminal activity opportunities are significantly reduced.

*Rear doors*: Although the doors are steel and well-secured with lock capability, at the time of inspection Mr. Herringbone said the doors are normally left unlocked during the business day. He admitted that two armed robberies occurred with perpetrators entering through the back door, and three burglaries are believed to have been enabled by persons hiding within the store until after closing. On at least five occasions, shoplifters have exited the store through the rear doors, unnoticed until too late to catch up with them.

*Suggested solution*: Keep rear doors locked at all times, except when in use and supervised.

*Roof area*: Inspection of the roof disclosed a heat and air conditioning ventilation duct large enough for a small or slender person to gain direct access into the store. The duct is bolted together but can easily be unbolted, pulled apart, and used to enter the store.

*Suggested solution*: Remove the duct at the first vulnerable section and install a steel grate, welded in place. Replace the duct and bolt into place, then spot weld the bolt heads and nuts to prevent easy removal.

*Summary*: Correcting the vulnerable areas noted is believed to have a significant benefit on overall crime prevention at this location. The cost is minimal.

## EXHIBITS

Photographs of vulnerable areas provided to Mr. Sam Herringbone (negatives on file)

Sketch of business location showing vulnerable locations noted during inspection

Waiver form allowing crime prevention inspection, signed by Mr. Sam Herringbone

Exhibits 10-4 through 10-6 merge the previous report into a model report for crime prevention inspection reports.

# DEPARTMENT HEADINGS

## SUMMARY OF CRIME PREVENTION INSPECTION

On July 15, 1990, at Sam's Clothing Store, 2834 Broadway Avenue, Any City, Any State, a crime prevention inspection revealed seven vulnerable areas. Inspection entrance and exit briefings were conducted with Mr. Sam Herringbone, owner of the business.

## BUSINESS DEFINITION

Sam's Clothing Store is owned and operated by Mr. Sam Herringbone. The store is incorporated as Sam's Clothing, Inc., with Sam Herringbone the sole corporate person.

The business sells a full line of mid-priced men's clothing exclusively and has been in business for thirty-five years at the same location.

The business is located within a building which is divided into twelve stores. Sam's clothing is located in the center with other unrelated businesses on either side. The location is on a well-traveled street near the center of the downtown section of Any City.

Sam's Clothing Store is open six days a week, closed on Sunday. Hours of operation are 9:00 A.M. to 7:00 P.M. during the summer months, and 9:00 A.M. to 5:00 P.M. during the winter months.

The business is operated with five full-time floor salesmen, two part-time stock employees, with Sam Herringbone normally supervising at the store. There are no managers; however, each floor salesman, all long-time employees (twenty years or longer), has full charge and responsibility for an assigned section of the store and its inventory.

## DESIGN OF STRUCTURE

The building in which Sam's Clothing Store is located is about sixty years old and well maintained. It is a mix of concrete, wood, and steel construction, one story, and structurally sound.

The store interior consists of an open sales floor although divided into departments. The sales floor is about $40' \times 40'$, and adjoined with a $40' \times 30'$ stockroom. A small office is located off the stockroom where all business records are maintained, it's about $10' \times 25'$. A customer restroom is off the sales floor, with an employee's restroom located off the stockroom adjacent the office.

The heating and cooling is provided by a centralized system providing services to the entire building, including the neighboring stores.

The store is abutted on two sides by other stores, and the front has one centrally placed customer door and two large plate glass windows which have platforms for displaying mannikins, shoes, and other clothing items in full view to passersby. The rear of the store has a loading dock that spans the entire building. The rear doors at Sam's Clothing Store are a large double door that accommodates off-loading incoming shipments, and a regular rear door for employees and other business. Both doors are constructed of steel and secured with two deadbolt locks and top and bottom fasteners.

EXHIBIT 10-4

# DEPARTMENT HEADINGS

## THREAT ESTIMATE

During the past five years, Sam's Clothing Store has experienced two armed robberies, three burglaries, and several incidents of shoplifting, some resulting in arrests, others escaping the store.

## SECURITY ASSESSMENT

A crime prevention inspection revealed the following vulnerable areas:

*Front of store*: Currently, the window display areas consist of two large plate glass windows facing the street with two plate glass windows on both sides of a 10-foot entranceway with the front entry door at the end. This configuration forms a display area for dressed mannikins and other assorted clothing. The window display areas are partitioned at the ends next to the store with small access doors allowing entry to arrange displays. Although the configuration increases interior display space (opposite the partitions), viewing the store interior from the street side is prevented. The front door is solid wood and has no windows. Passersby, law enforcement, or security patrols have no view of the interior day or night, allowing armed robberies, burglaries, or other crimes to occur unnoticed from the outside.

*Suggested solution*: Remove the partitions from the window display area and arrange mannikins and clothing displays so passersby, law enforcement, and security patrols have a clear view of the store interior day or night. Enhance this advantage by leaving ample interior lights on even when closed. During closed hours, leave lights in the display area off or dimmed to allow passing law enforcement or security units to view the interior. Cost is minimal, and armed robbery, burglary, and other criminal activity opportunities are significantly reduced.

*Rear doors*: Although the doors are steel and well-secured with lock capability, at the time of inspection Mr. Herringbone said the doors are normally left unlocked during the business day. He admitted that two armed robberies occurred with perpetrators entering through the back door, and three burglaries are believed to have been enabled by persons hiding within the store until after closing. On at least five occasions, shoplifters have exited the store through the rear doors, unnoticed until too late to catch up with them.

*Suggested solution*: Keep rear doors locked at all times, except when in use and supervised.

*Roof area*: Inspection of the roof disclosed a heat and air conditioning ventilation duct large enough for a small or slender person to gain direct access into the store. The duct is bolted together but can easily be unbolted, pulled apart, and used to enter the store.

*Suggested solution*: Remove the duct at the first vulnerable section and install a steel grate, welded in place. Replace the duct and bolt into place, then spot weld the bolt heads and nuts to prevent easy removal.

*Summary*: Correcting the vulnerable areas noted is believed to have a significant benefit on overall crime prevention at this location. The cost is minimal.

## EXHIBITS

Photographs of vulnerable areas provided to Mr. Sam Herringbone (negatives on file)
Sketch of business location showing vulnerable locations noted during inspection (original)
Waiver form allowing crime prevention inspection, signed by Mr. Sam Herringbone (copy)

Exhibit 10-4

# PHOTOGRAPHS OF VULNERABLE POINTS AT SAM'S CLOTHING STORE

Crime Prevention Inspection
Case #CP90-1928

Det. R. B. Smith
Det. G. L. Smart

Sam's Clothing Store
2834 Broadway Avenue
Any City, Any State

July 15, 1990

Photograph of Left Display Window

Photograph of Right Display Window

Photograph of Duct from Roof

Photograph of Duct from Stockroom

Author's Note: This exhibit is provided as a guide. Since Sam's Clothing Store is portrayed in this Model Report, actual photographs are not furnished.

Exhibit 10-4

**258**

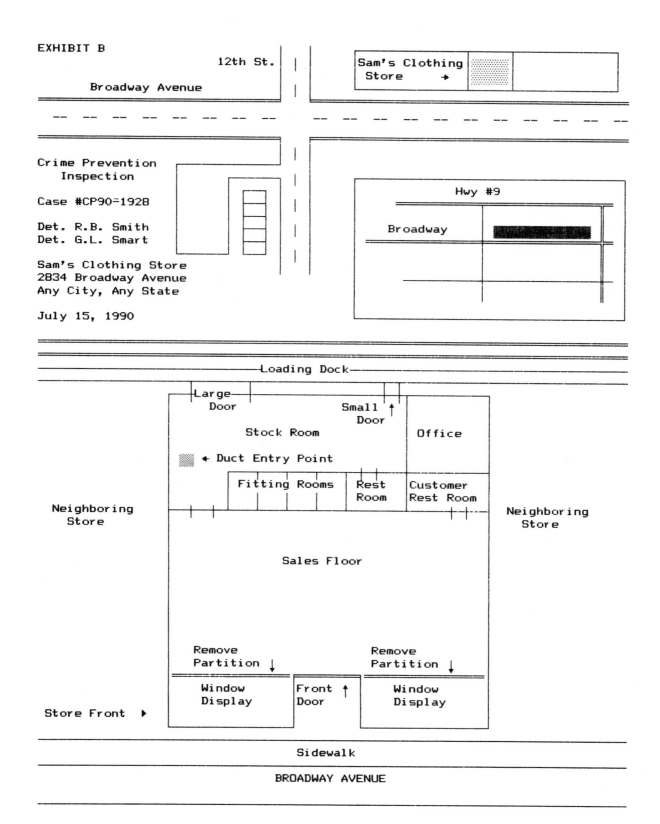

EXHIBIT B

12th St.

Broadway Avenue

Sam's Clothing
Store

Crime Prevention
Inspection

Case #CP90=1928

Det. R.B. Smith
Det. G.L. Smart

Sam's Clothing Store
2834 Broadway Avenue
Any City, Any State

July 15, 1990

Hwy #9

Broadway

Loading Dock

Large
Door

Small
Door

Stock Room

Office

Duct Entry Point

Fitting Rooms

Rest
Room

Customer
Rest Room

Neighboring
Store

Neighboring
Store

Sales Floor

Remove
Partition ↓

Remove
Partition ↓

Store Front ▶

Window
Display

Front ↑
Door

Window
Display

Sidewalk

BROADWAY AVENUE

EXHIBIT 10-5

# DEPARTMENT LETTERHEAD

## PERMISSION AND AUTHORIZATION TO CONDUCT A CRIME PREVENTION INSPECTION

Name of Business: _____

Address: _____

_____

Owner: _____

Manager: _____

I am authorizing      (officer) _____

_____

representing      (law enforcement department) _____

to inspect this place of business to ascertain any and all common deficiencies of internal and external security. I understand this inspection is a public service, and its purpose is to assist me in finding ways to protect my assets, employees, and business from the threat of criminal activity. I understand that I have the right to refuse this inspection and that it is not being conducted with any intention of gathering information or collecting evidence against me, my employees, or business operations.

Signature of Manager/Owner: _____

Date: _____      Time: _____

Exhibit 10-6

## Guidelines on Outlining, Grammar, Spelling, and Writing Style

**BENEFITS OF OUTLINING** _____

Outlining your report before you begin writing can be a valuable asset, saving you time, enhancing your image as a professional, and saving a good deal of embarrassment.

Talking and writing are both forms of thinking, and in a professional sense, both are enhanced by making outlines, both detailed and rough, depending on the complexity of the work. For example, you complete a field investigation on a complex crime or traffic accident. Your briefcase is bulging with statements, documents, photographs, and you have a load of physical evidence. As you arrive at the department, a supervisor tells you to be in the chief's office in thirty minutes. It seems the chief, mayor, prosecutor, and other high-level officials have an interest in this case and want to know everything you have collected—they're giving you ten minutes out of their busy schedules to tell them.

You certainly don't have time to even think about writing a report, and you'll be talking off the top of your head. Ten minutes isn't enough time to talk about everything. If you stammer and can't state your point clearly and succinctly, this high-level group, with the power to enhance your career or put it on a back burner, will be glaring at you with undivided attention. It's a problem we all have to cope with during our careers on occasion, but it can be solved by making what I call a scratch outline. The scratch outline works when you're making a speech, giving a briefing, or writing a report. It provides you with a tool of organizing and managing information that you have to present to others in one form or another.

In the preceding scenario, you'll have thirty minutes to organize the information, but only ten minutes to present the briefing. First, think about your report format. You begin with a concise conclusion, based on your analysis of the evidence and information collected. So that's your starting place with the outline—tell the chief and others your conclusion.

You follow the conclusion with a substantiation section, listing in concise terms all the information that led you to the conclusion. Your outline, then, will serve you in the same way that your report will serve a reader. It will provide you with a fast, organized way of presenting the facts.

In your scratch outline, list the key elements and what they tell you about the crime. You may, in your briefing, preface them with a statement such as, "That conclusion is based on collective information and evidence. Information from written statements obtained from twelve witnesses and victims of the crime indicates..." Then from your outline, run through the key elements without naming each person as you would in your report.

When that part of your briefing is complete, think again about your report format—normally in a report you would list all the witnesses and victims in the order they appear in the report. The officials you are briefing, like the busy reader, aren't interested in all that right now, so skip that and focus on your exhibits section—what is important in the exhibits that you haven't already covered in the substantiation. However, perhaps certain items must be sent to a crime laboratory for analysis, and make that point clear in your briefing. Tell the officials the items (and name them) believed to be important physical evidence collected at the scene, such as latent fingerprints developed. Explain that the burglary, robbery, or whatever crime you're presenting was conducted similar to others in the past, which were committed by a suspect who was convicted for the previous crimes and is now on probation. The laboratory is examining the suspect's fingerprints from files with those collected at the scene, and a match will identify at least one of the perpetrators. You may discuss that the tool marks and footprints found at the scene are preserved with casts and molds and held in the evidence room pending development of a suspect. A subsequent search of a suspect's residence, car, and other belongings may reveal items a laboratory can match to the casts and molds. Your briefing should be a success, moving along smoothly and logically, using your report format as a guide to develop a scratch outline.

With the briefing complete, you can now use the scratch outline to develop your report of investigation. You may need to use the scratch outline to develop a more detailed outline prior to writing your report, depending on the circumstances.

## ADVANTAGES OF MAKING AN OUTLINE BEFORE WRITING YOUR REPORT _____

An outline forces you to think, just as writing a report or discussing a case forces you to think. However, using an outline, you can make mistakes and not waste time having to re-write a report or, in the case of a briefing, stammering about the facts.

Many of us shudder at the mention of outlining, remembering the days of high school and college when we had to learn the precise rules that someone made up about how an outline should be structured. Your scratch and detailed outline, however, is not for a teacher to review and tell you all that's wrong with it. Your report outline is for you to use, and you should structure it first to conform with the format of your report, and second, in a way that works best for you. You can use numbers, letters, or whatever you want. The key of your report outline is a way or tool to save you time, force you to think, and organize the information.

I often find that jotting down information on paper works as a starting point. For example, I go through my exhibits, loosely arranging them in an order that seems logical, and then start writing them down on a sheet of paper. You don't have to be thorough about that listing; all the detailed information can come from the document itself as you write the report. What you're interested in now is organizing and testing the order. In doing so you may also discover a loophole in your case.

When all the items are listed loosely, go through the outline and see if you agree with the order of appearance. Remember, your entire report, starting with the conclusion, moving into the substantiation, depends on your organization and completeness of the exhibits. The advantage of this technique is that you can number the order of their appearance in your report here, rather than having to rewrite your report because of one item being slightly out of place.

When that's complete, then you can outline your conclusion, based on the now well-organized exhibits. You can note or outline the important elements of each exhibit, analyze it, and arrive at a logical conclusion. Remember, the idea of your conclusion is to provide the reader with a fast overview of what happened, and, to provide yourself with a declaration to support. By doing a rough outline in which you place all the exhibits in the logical order of appearance in your report, and then doing a rough outline of key elements in each exhibit, you can accurately analyze the information and write a concise, effective, and comprehensive conclusion that you are certain is supported by the exhibits.

Without an outline, the structure of your writing suffers because you tend to report the information in the order you lived it—or worse, in no order at all. Your words and sentences also suffer because you are too busy untangling the information to pay much attention to expressing them in the clearest possible way. Remember, brevity is best obtained through clarity. You are wasting time correcting mistakes on your reports instead of making and correcting them on outlines.

### Grammar is Important in Your Reports: How to Manage It

The term *grammar* is much like *outlining*, because it brings back memories of high school and college English classes. However, when we write, grammar is important.

Using the report structures I talk about throughout this book eliminates a great deal of the problem. First, using the expository style of writing your investigative reports prevents the traditional narrative style, which leads to all sorts of grammar troubles. Second, you are a professional law enforcement officer, with ever-growing requirements for skills, knowledge, and wisdom. Becoming an English composition genius is going too far; or is it? Perhaps becoming a genius is, but writing correctly is an often hidden career enhancement. Earlier in this book we talked about your image—how others view your professional competence. No matter how skilled you are, how excellent your judgment, or how developed your wisdom, appearance, and demeanor on the job, your writing is where you are judged. If you conduct the finest investigation of all times but are unable to communicate your work by writing correctly, your competence will be questioned.

We also talked about writing like you talk, only better. You have far more experience talking that writing; however, the law enforcement profession, in addition to increased skill requirements, now has increased information processing needs.

Literally everything you do is written in some form.

### THE SEVEN DEADLY SINS GRAMMAR RULE

1. Don't use a double negative, like "I can't hardly hear you."

2. Don't use a double comparison, like "That copier is more faster than the other one we used."

3. Don't use extra words, like "Where do you want me to put this here printout."

4. Use the right verb in the right tense, like "The horse has drunk," not, "The horse has drank."

5. Keep adverbs and adjectives straight. Say "I feel bad," not "I feel badly," unless you mean that something is wrong with your nerve endings. Then you could say, "I feel badly," because you wouldn't have much sense of touch in your fingertips.

6. Use appropriate pronouns: Subject pronouns for subjects (*I*, *he*, *she*, *we*, *they*, *who*) and object pronouns for objects (*me*, *him*, *her*, *us*, *them*, *whom*). Say "between you and me," not "between you and I."

7. Be sure the verb and subject agree. Say, "We were ready," not "We was ready." Watch a singular subject which is followed by a long string of words before you get to the verb; you can easily forget that you need a singular verb. For example, "Now and then, a man like Columbus, Galileo, and others has [not *have*] risked the unknown."

## Bend the Rules of Grammar

The following grammar rules are still on the books, but very few people obey them. These rules are listed here only as areas about which you'll have to make a personal choice—to break or not to break.

1. Don't end a sentence with a preposition.

2. Don't split an infinitive.

3. Make a distinction between *who* and *whom*.

4. Don't start a sentence with *and*, *but*, and *because*.

5. Make a distinction between *shall* and *will*, *may* and *can*, *among* and *between*.

## Grammar Rules for Avoiding Readers' Wrath

The following rules will help you to avoid offending your readers and will make what you've written easier to read.

1. Don't use *like* when you should use *as*.

2. Don't use *hopefully* to modify an entire sentence, but to modify a specific action by a person named in the sentence.

3. Don't say *most perfect* or *deadest* or *most unique*.

4. Don't use words with *-ize*.

5. Don't use words with *-wise* on the end.

6. Use masculine and feminine pronouns when you are talking about both men and women.

## Frequently Confounded Words

Don't confuse words that are similar in spelling or pronunciation, but not in meaning. Distinguish carefully between the words in each of the following sets:

| | |
|---|---|
| accept (to take) | except (to leave out) |
| affect (to influence) | effect (to bring about) |
| all ready (completely ready) | already (by this time) |
| all together (in unison) | altogether (entirely) |
| allusion (reference) | illusion (deception) |
| appraise (to evaluate) | apprise (to inform) |
| assistance (help) | assistants (helpers) |
| baring (uncovering) | barring (excluding) |
| bearing (carrying) | |

beside (close to)                         besides (in addition to)

biannual (twice a year)                   biennial (every two years)

breath (air inhaled/exhaled)             breathe (to respire)

calendar (tabulation of days)            calender (a smoothing machine)

capital (chief city/money)               Capitol (state house)

cloth (fabric)                            clothe (to dress)

clothes (apparel)                         cloths (fabrics)

complement (completes/fills)             compliment (commendation)

continually (recurrently)                continuously (without stopping)

correspondence (letters)                 correspondents (letter writers)

costumer (costume maker)                 customer (patron)

councilor (member of council)            counselor (adviser)

credible (believable)                    creditable (praiseworthy)

desert (dry area)                         dessert (final course of meal)

device (contrivance)                      devise (to contrive)

discomfit (to foil)                       discomfort (to make uneasy)

dual (pertaining to two)                 duel (combat)

eminent (distinguished)                  immanent (inherent)

imminent (impending)

flaunt (display boastfully)              flout (treat with contempt)

forth (forward)                           fourth (next after third)

formally (in a formal manner)            formerly (at some former time)

healthful (promoting health)             healthy (having health)

holy (sacred)                             wholly (fully)

ingenious (clever)                        ingenuous (frank)

its (possessive case of it)              it's (contraction of it is or it has)

later (tardier)                           latter (the second of two)

lead (metal)                              led (showed the way)

loose (not tight)                         lose (to suffer loss)

material (substance)                      matériel (supplies)

moral (right and proper)                 morale (sound spirit)

passed (went by)                          past (beyond)

personal (private)                        personnel (working force)

practice (to perform)                     practise (to perform)

precedence (priority)                     precedents (examples)

presence (being present)                 presents (gifts)

principal (head of school)               principle (fundamental truth)

prophecy (prediction)                     prophesy (to predict)

receipt (acknowledgment)                 recipe (formula)

reign (to rule)                           rein (part of a harness)

respectfully (with respect)              respectively (each in order)

stationary (standing still)              stationery (writing materials)

their (possessive case—they)             there (in that place)

they're (they are)
too (also)                                    to (in the direction of)
                                              two (next after one)

waive (to forgo)                              wave (to flutter)
who's (who has)                               whose (who)
your (you)                                    you're (you are)

## ELIMINATE WORDINESS IN YOUR REPORTS

| **Instead of This** | **Use This** |
| --- | --- |
| a certain length of time | a certain time |
| advance planning | planning |
| after the conclusion of | after |
| am (is, are) going to | shall, will |
| are (am) of the opinion | believe |
| as a result of | because |
| at the present time | now |
| before long | soon |
| both alike | alike |
| by means of | by |
| by the time | when |
| come in contact with | meet |
| destroyed by fire | burned |
| due to the fact that | due to, since |
| during the time that | while |
| for the amount of | for |
| in accordance with | by |
| inasmuch as | since |
| in case | if |
| in connection with | with |
| in lieu of | instead |
| in order to | to |
| in regard to | about |
| insofar as | because, since, as |
| in the event that | if |
| in the month of May | in May |
| in this day and age | today |
| in view of the fact that | since |
| it has come to our attention that | (begin with the word following "that") |
| it is interesting to note that | (begin with the word following "that") |
| I would appreciate it if | please |
| long in size | long |
| of an indefinite nature | indefinite |

| | |
|---|---|
| of great importance | important |
| on a timely basis | fast |
| on condition that | if |
| one of the purposes | one purpose |
| one of the reasons | one reason |
| prior to | before |
| provided that | if |
| the length of 10 feet | 10 feet |
| the necessary funds | money |
| with the exception of | except |

## WORDY EXPRESSIONS

| | |
|---|---|
| absolutely essential | aggregate total |
| around about that time | audible to the ear |
| back up | close scrutiny |
| combine together | connect up with |
| cooperate together | cover over |
| descend down | each and every one |
| endorse on the back | entirely eliminated |
| few in number | final end |
| first beginnings | important essentials |
| individual person | join together |
| long length | many in number |
| meet up with | more better |
| more older | necessary essential |
| necessary need | passing phase |
| reduce down | repeat again |
| resume again | return back |
| revert back to | rise up |
| small in size | blue in color |
| sworn affidavit | this afternoon at 4 P.M. |

## GUIDELINES FOR SPELLING

Accurate spelling is synonymous with using words correctly. However, spelling is one of the most difficult areas of report writing. Just as report writing skill is the only lasting demonstration of your competence as a law enforcement officer, spelling within the report has either a positive or negative impact on your reader. Words which are misspelled catch the eye and leave your readers questioning your competence. Write an accurate and dynamic report, making certain your grammar, spelling, and other elements are accurate. In the following pages, I've included the most important and easy to recall rules that will help you develop wordsmith skills. This isn't intended as an English rules book; however, writing reports, or writing of any kind, requires constant attention and effort to improve. This section can in several ways help you become an excellent law enforcement report writer.

Word building blocks (word elements) include roots, prefixes, and suffixes. A knowledge of how these elements work to create words will help you to build a better vocabulary and become a better speller.

*Roots*: The root, or the foundation of a word, can come from a variety of languages (such as Latin, Greek, French, or German). The root gives the word its basic meaning. This element can be combined with other elements (prefixes, suffixes, or other roots) to form a variety of words. These building blocks can be syllables or complete words.

*Prefixes*: Prefixes are word elements that come at the beginning of a word and modify the meaning of the word. For example, a common Latin root is *-cede*, meaning "to go." You can get new but related words by adding prefixes such as *re-* (recede) or *pro-* (proceed). *Note*: The English spelling can sometimes be different from the root.

*Suffixes*: Suffixes are word elements that appear at the end of a word and often change the part of speech of the word. For example, the suffix *-ward* changes the noun *wind* to the noun, adjective, or adverb *windward*.

By understanding the basic word elements and their effect on the meaning of words, you can learn many new words from a few and determine how some words are spelled.

Three important additional ways of determining how to spell words are (1) seeing the word correctly, (2) pronouncing the word correctly, and (3) writing the word correctly.

### See the Word Correctly

An effective way to remember correct spelling is to pay attention to the structure of individual words. Visualize each word and remember its peculiarities. For example, the word *bookkeeper* consists of the two words *book* and *keeper* and therefore has a double *k*. The word *argument* has no *e* after the *u* although the word *argue* does. The word *piece* has a *pie* in it. A great number of words lend themselves to similar observation and visualization.

### Pronounce the Word Correctly

Often, misspelling is due to incorrect pronunciation. If we mispronounce *attacked* as *attackted*, *mischievous* and *mischevious*, and *athletic* as *athaletic*, misspelling during writing is almost certain.

### Write the Word Correctly

Even though we may know how to spell a word, it's possible to misspell it during report writing. As with visualizing a word correctly and pronouncing it accurately, writing a word correctly requires practice. When you have difficulty with a word or words, a good way of solving the problem is to write the word correctly several times. It's also a good idea to make a list of words you have difficulty spelling.

### Basic Spelling Rules

In addition to the ways already mentioned, self-help techniques are also useful. Knowing only a half-dozen rules of spelling can help you with hundreds of words.

*Silent e*: In adding a suffix to a word ending in a silent *e*, drop the *e* if the suffix begins with a vowel; retain the *e* if the suffix begins with a consonant. The following words demonstrate the rule:

advise + able = advisable          like + ness = likeness

come + ing = coming                achieve + ment = achievement

imagine + ary = imaginary          concise + ly = concisely

If a word ends in *ce* or *ge*, the silent *e* is retained before a suffix beginning with *a* or *o*. Examples are *changeable*, *noticeable*, *courageous*. Other exceptions to the rule are made whenever the silent *e* is needed to aid pronunciation or to prevent confusion with other terms. Examples are *mileage*, *eyeing*, *hoeing*, *dyeing* (compare with *dying*), *lineage* (compare with *linage*).

*Final y*: When a word ends in *y* preceded by a consonant, change the *y* to *i* before adding any suffix except one beginning with *i*; when the final *y* is preceded by a vowel, retain the *y*.

| | | | | | |
|---|---|---|---|---|---|
| deny | denied | denying | delay | delayed | delaying |
| pity | pitiful | pitying | attorney | attorneys | |
| petty | pettiness | | buy | buys | |
| baby | babies | | | | |

*Final consonant*: The rule of the final consonant applies to a single-syllable word or a word in which the last syllable is accented. In either of these cases, when the final consonant follows a single vowel, double the consonant before adding a suffix beginning with a vowel. Do not double the consonant before a suffix beginning with a consonant.

| | | | | |
|---|---|---|---|---|
| begin | beginning | | benefit | benefited |
| occur | occurred | | prefer | preference (accent shifted) |
| commit | committed | commitment | | |
| allot | allotted | allotment | | |

*ei and ie*: In words spelled with *ei* or *ie*, pronounced *ee*, use *i* before *e* except immediately after *c*.

| | | | | |
|---|---|---|---|---|
| achieve | believe | field | relieve | siege |
| ceiling | deceive | receipt | conceit | perceive |

Exceptions to the rule are the words *either*, *neither*, *species*, *leisure*, and *seize*.

*Plurals*: The plural of nouns ending in *y* follows the rule for final *y*; for example, *lady*, *ladies*. The plural of words ending in *o* or *f* varies (*memos*, *tabaccos*, *heroes*, *briefs*, *leaves*). Other irregular plurals are evident in such words as *children*, *feet*, and *athletics* (same form in singular and plural). Compound nouns generally form their plurals by adding *s* to the last word of the group (*vice presidents*, *assistant managers*, *cross-examinations*); when, however, the first word in the compound noun is the important one, the plural ending is given to it (*passersby*, *brothers-in-law*, *chairmen of the board*).

*Suffixes*: It's often difficult to decide whether the first consonant of a suffix is doubled when added to the end of a word. Here, remember that the consonant appears twice only if the word ends in the same consonant. For example, *formally*, *actually*, *wanness*; *formerly*, *entirely*, *obviously*, *uselessness*.

Other word endings are troublesome because certain suffixes sound alike but are not spelled alike. For instance, words ending in *-able* (*advisable*, *suitable*, *probable*, *returnable*) are much more numerous than words ending in *-ible* (*permissible*, *audible*, *eligible*) with which they are sometimes confused. Words ending in *-ent* and *-ant* (*persistent*, *resistant*) and *-ence* and *-ance* (*conference*, *attendance*) are also confounded and must be watched carefully.

### Division of Words

The hyphen is used to divide the syllables of a word at the end of a line; do not place the hyphen at the beginning of the following line. It is correct to divide a compound word between its main parts (policy-holder, copy-writer, counselor-at-law, well-being, double-spaced copy, five-pound sacks). It is also correct to divide a word after a prefix of two or more letters and before a suffix of three or more letters (un-limited, sur-round, post-pone; surround-ing, comfort-able, interpreta-tion).

Divide as few words as possible. This will help you to avoid the pitfalls or hyphenation.

*Proper names*: Do not hyphenate a proper name at the end of a line.

*Monosyllables*: Do not attempt to divide words of one syllable—e.g., ei-ghth, phra-se, cau-ght, help-ed, pass-ed.

*One-letter divisions*: Do not split a word after or before a single letter—e.g., e-licit, e-nough, a-gainst, alread-y, residuar-y.

*Hyphenated words*: Do not divide a word that is already hypenated—e.g., post-op-erative, re-or-der, well-be-ing, deep-root-ed.

*Misreading*: Avoid any division that would result in misreading of the word—e.g., vehi-cle, intrave-nous, reor-ganize, ope-ra.

## ABBREVIATIONS

Abbreviations can be a problem in your reports if not handled correctly. Normally, a rule of thumb is to keep abbreviations to a minimum in law enforcement reports unless the word abbreviated is commonly known within and outside of law enforcement channels. Keep in mind the following guidelines.

*Periods with abbreviations*: The period is the standard mark of punctuation after abbreviations. It has become common, however, to omit periods after abbreviations of government agencies, radio stations, and other organizations usually referred to by their abbreviated titles. Some examples of abbreviations with and without the period are as follows:

CA   Calif.   etc.   Av.   Ave.   mph   m.p.h.   S.W.   SW
s.w.   NLRB   HOLC   WCBS   WNBC   WABC

*Spacing*: Put a single space between the initials of a person's name or of the name of a state. In other abbreviations, the space is usually omitted. For example, Mr. S. M. Field, N. J., S. D., F.O.B.

*Titles*: The titles Mr. and Mrs. are always abbreviated. The title Dr. is usually abbreviated when used with a name. Titles such as President, Senator, and Professor are never abbreviated in formal communications; they may be abbreviated in other correspondence only when they are used with initials or given names, but not with the last name alone.

| Incorrect | Correct |
|---|---|
| Mister Jones | Mr. Jones |
|  | Dr. Jones |
| Sen. Gray | Senator Gray |
|  | Sen. George A. Gray |
| Prof. Black | Professor Black |
|  | Prof. E. L. Black |
|  | Professor E. L. Black |

The abbreviated title Rev. and the title Honorable, whether abbreviated or not, are used only with the full name or with the last name and initials.

| Incorrect | Correct |
|-----------|---------|
| Hon. Plunkett | Hon. George E. Plunkett |
| Rev. Jones | Rev. Archer S. Jones |

*Expression of time*: Certain conventional expressions of time are commonly abbreviated. For example, a.m. p.m. or A.M. P.M.

*Names of persons*: Initials are usually used for middle names, but do not use initials or other abbreviated forms that do not conform to the style customarily employed by the person. If, for example, a person signs his name Charles H. Burke, he should not be addressed or written about as Chas. H. Burke. If he signs his name T. Frank McNeary, he should be so addressed, not as Thomas F. McNeary or T. F. McNeary.

*Titles before names of persons*: These are abbreviated as follows:

| Mr. | Messrs. | Mrs. | |
|-----|---------|------|------|
| Ms. | Miss | Dr. | Prof. |

*Company names*: When you're writing a company name, use any abbreviations or signs that appear in the spelling of the name on the company's letterhead.

*Names of months*: It's better not to abbreviate the name of the month. For example, Dec. 14, 1989, should be written as December 14, 1989.

*State names*: The following abbreviations are recommended by the U.S. Postal Service for use with zip codes. Otherwise, spell out the state name.

| AL | Alabama | AK | Alaska |
|----|---------|----|--------|
| AZ | Arizona | AR | Arkansas |
| CA | California | CO | Colorado |
| CT | Connecticut | DE | Delaware |
| DC | District of Columbia | FL | Florida |
| GA | Georgia | GU | Guam |
| HI | Hawaii | ID | Idaho |
| IL | Illinois | IN | Indiana |
| IA | Iowa | KS | Kansas |
| KY | Kentucky | LA | Louisiana |
| ME | Maine | MD | Maryland |
| MA | Massachusetts | MI | Michigan |
| MN | Minnesota | MS | Mississippi |
| MO | Missouri | MT | Montana |
| NE | Nebraska | NV | Nevada |
| NH | New Hampshire | NJ | New Jersey |
| NM | New Mexico | NY | New York |
| NC | North Carolina | ND | North Dakota |
| OH | Ohio | OK | Oklahoma |
| OR | Oregon | PA | Pennsylvania |
| PR | Puerto Rico | RI | Rhode Island |

| SC | South Carolina | SD | South Dakota |
|----|----------------|----|--------------|
| TN | Tennessee | TX | Texas |
| UT | Utah | VT | Vermont |
| VA | Virginia | VI | Virgin Islands |
| WA | Washington | WV | West Virginia |
| WI | Wisconsin | WY | Wyoming |

*Slang abbreviations:* Avoid *s*lang abbreviations and clipped words.

*Common abbreviations*: All standard dictionaries list abbreviations either in the main vocabulary or in an appendix.

# NUMBERS

Since numbers are common to almost all law enforcement reports, you may have questions about how to write their correct representation. The following guidelines are provided for your reference.

*Exact numbers*: Exact numbers and amounts are generally expressed in figures unless they appear at the beginning of the sentence, in which case they should be spelled out. For example:

> The perpetrators stole 12 diamond rings during the jewelry store robbery.
> Twelve diamond rings were stolen from the jewelry store.

If spelling out the number at the beginning of a sentence proves cumbersome, rewrite the sentence so that the number is placed in some other position.

*Round numbers*: Round numbers are commonly expressed in words or, in the case of numbers in the millions and higher, in both words and figures.

| ten thousand dollars | the first hundred dollars |
|----------------------|---------------------------|
| $170 million | $3.2 million |

*Contiguous numbers*: Except in a series, two figures should not be placed together. Use figures for one number and spell out the other, or rewrite the sentence to avoid placing the two numbers together.

| **POOR** | **BETTER** |
|----------|------------|
| In 1988, 21,000 burglaries took place in Blank City. | In 1988, twenty-one thousand burglaries took place in Blank City. |

*References to time and dates*: Use figures to express time with A.M. or P.M. and to represent dates. Spell out expressions of time followed by *o'clock*.

| 10 P.M. | 11:30 A.M. |
|---------|------------|
| 5:15 P.M. | one o'clock |

*Military and law enforcement time*: Most departments use time designations in what is normally referred to as military time. A conversion chart follows:

| 0001 = 12:01 A.M. | 1300 = 1:00 P.M. |
|-------------------|------------------|
| 0100 = 1:00 A.M. | 1400 = 2:00 P.M. |
| 0200 = 2:00 A.M. | 1500 = 3:00 P.M. |
| 0300 = 3:00 A.M. | 1600 = 4:00 P.M. |

| | |
|---|---|
| 0400 = 4:00 A.M. | 1700 = 5:00 P.M. |
| 0500 = 5:00 A.M. | 1800 = 6:00 P.M. |
| 0600 = 6:00 A.M. | 1900 = 7:00 P.M. |
| 0700 = 7:00 A.M. | 2000 = 8:00 P.M. |
| 0800 = 8:00 A.M. | 2100 = 9:00 P.M. |
| 0900 = 9:00 A.M. | 2200 = 10:00 P.M. |
| 1000 = 10:00 A.M. | 2300 = 11:00 P.M. |
| 1100 = 11:00 A.M. | 2400 = 12:00 P.M. |
| 1200 = 12:00 A.M. | |

Minutes are added as applicable (i.e., 1203, 1008, 2342, etc.).

*References to places and dimensions*: Use figures to indicate room numbers, page numbers, street numbers, serial numbers, etc.

| | | | |
|---|---|---|---|
| Room 332 | Page 46 | 670 Thames Street | Invoice No. 4359 |
| 12 by 15 feet | a .38 caliber revolver | a .45 caliber pistol | |

*Even-dollar figures*: Do not use the decimal point without the ciphers. For example, $3.00, $7.00, $12, $35, $493.

*Mixed amounts*: Always use figures to express mixed amounts. For example, $41.98, $35.26, $539.04.

When both mixed amounts and even-dollar amounts are used in a series, add the decimal point and two ciphers to even-dollar figures. For example, The checks were for $9.23, $17.30, and $19.00 respectively.

*Double representation*: A good idea in your reports is to express amounts in both words and figures to assure accuracy. For example, $139.50 (one hundred thirty-nine dollars and fifty cents).

*Amounts under $1.00*: To avoid error in understanding, use the number and word combination as follows: 48 cents, 32 cents.

*Comma with figures*: Place a comma between each group of three digits, counting from the right, except in dates, street numbers, serial numbers, and the like.

| | |
|---|---|
| 1,600 rounds of ammunition | 22,394 people |
| 5634 Broadway Street | Room 1537 |
| No. 493847563 | $1,339,293 |

*Fractions*: It is a good practice to write out fractions that can be expressed in a single compound word; other fractions and those appended to the whole figure should be written as figures. For example, one-half, two-thirds, 4/32, 35 3/4.

# PUNCTUATION

Accurate punctuation makes reading your report easier and clearer. The modern trend is to use as few marks of punctuation as is consistent with your purpose. Punctuation is as necessary to report writing as pauses are when you speak. On the other hand, punctuation can not compensate for shoddy writing. If an idea is not expressed clearly in the first place, a comma or semicolon will not make it clear. The following guidelines for punctuation are provided for your reference.

*Period*(.): A period marks the end of a complete sentence or unit.

1. Ends of sentences. Place a period at the end of a sentence that is not a direct question or an exclamation.

2. Abbreviations. Place a period at the end of every abbreviation, except as discussed earlier. If the abbreviation comes at the end of a sentence, use only one period.

3. Decimals. Place a decimal point (period) between dollars and cents in figures expressing sums of money, and before a decimal fraction and between a whole number and the decimal. For example, $15.67, $5,143.93, $.89, .384, .04.

4. Numerical and alphabetical symbols. Place a period following the symbols denoting the parts of an outline or list.

   A. Types of crimes
      1. Burglary
      2. Robbery
      3. Murder

5. After indirect questions. An indirect question is followed by a period, not a question mark.

   | **Incorrect** | **Correct** |
   |---|---|
   | The chief asked if the officers had reached a decision? | The chief asked if the officers had reached a decision. |

6. Following requests. A request put in the form of a question usually is followed by a period, not a question mark. For example, Will you please prepare a report on the Blank City crime problem.

*Question mark* (?): The question mark denotes a query or a doubt.

1. Direct questions. Use a question mark after a direct question. The question mark is usually placed at the end of the sentence, where it takes the place of the period. The question mark may, however, be placed in the middle of the sentence.

   What does the chief advise us to do?

   But shall we do it? is a question that will require much thought.

2. Suggestions of doubt. Use a question mark within parentheses to indicate that a date or other statement is questionable.

   The suspect in the murder case is John Doe, born 1952 (?).

   I thought the investigation revealed evidence (?) of the crime.

*Exclamation mark* (!): The exclamation mark is used where special emphasis is desired.

1. Indicating emphasis. Use the exclamation mark at the end of a vigorously expressed statement.

   It is necessary that our department update equipment now!

   In a written statement, Smith said Jones told him he would kill the Mayor next Tuesday night!

2. Avoiding misuse. The exclamation mark should be used with discretion.

*Comma* (,): A comma is used to indicate a short pause within the sentence or to separate sentence elements which are not closely connected in the sentence.

1. Preventing confusion. Use a comma to separate sentence elements that might be misread if the punctuation were omitted.

| Incorrect | Correct |
|---|---|
| To begin with the police car is badly in need of repairs. | To begin with, the police car is badly in need of repairs. |
| Behind a cloud of dust shrouded the vehicle. | Behind, a cloud of dust shrouded the vehicle. |

2. Placement in series. Place commas between members of a series of words or groups of words. The comma before the conjunction is advisable when the last two members of the series are joined by *and* or *or*.

   The store was decorated with red, white, and blue banners. We visited the department, talked with the officers, made a careful study of the procedures, and still failed to discover the reason for low morale.

   You can have your favorite flashlight style in large, medium, or small sizes.

   The finishes are polished stainless steel, enamel, plastic.

3. Joining coordinate clauses. Put a comma before *and*, *but*, *for*, *or*, and *nor* (coordinating conjunctions) when they join two independent clauses. However, when the coordinate clauses are short, no comma is necessary.

   Never in our history have we had so many applications for police officer positions, but never have we had so few positions to fill.

   We liked his work performance and commended him for it. (two short clauses; no punctuation)

   I made an exhaustive study of the crime problem but could find no evidence of either poor enforcement or lack of interest. (no punctuation because *but* connects a compound verb—*made* and *could find*—not two clauses)

4. Separating coordinate consecutive adjectives. Use commas between adjectives in a series when each adjective separately qualifies the noun; do not use a comma when an adjective seems to qualify the next adjective or the whole phrase that follows. When adjectives are coordinate (and require a comma), you should be able to connect them by *and* without changing their sense.

   Officers seem to prefer the slim, unpleated, self-belted trousers. (coordinate)

   Officers seem to prefer the new slim, unpleated, self-belted trousers. (partly coordinate)

   Have you seen our better lightweight cotton jump suits? (not coordinate)

5. Following introductory clauses. When, in a complex sentence, the subordinate clause precedes the main clause, separate the two clauses with a comma. A comma is not ordinarily used when the subordinate clause follows the main clause.

   Before you leave for the day, please file your reports and close your locker. (Subordinate clause precedes main clause.)

   Please file your reports and close your locker before you leave for the day. (Subordinate clause follows main clause.)

6. Writing dates. In a date consisting of the month, day, and year, set off the year by commas. In a date consisting only of the month and year, omit the commas.

Frank Jones was appointed to the bench on April 14, 1988, for a term of two years.

Frank Jones was appointed to the bench in April 1988 for a term of two years.

*Semicolon* (;): The semicolon is used to indicate a long pause within a sentence or to separate independent sentence elements.

1. Separating independent clauses. In the absence of a conjunction, use a semicolon to separate the clauses of a compound sentence.

This has been a department policy for the past two years; it will continue to be a department policy.

You do not have to take our word for it; you can check the records yourself.

You do not have to take our word for it. You can check the records yourself.

*Colon* (:): The colon is used to direct the reader's attention to a statement that follows. It also has certain conventional uses, as in expressions of time.

All his efforts point to one motive: hate.

Question: or Q: / Answer: or A: (as used in a statement)

*Hypen* (-): Use the hyphen to divide a word at the end of a line. The word is broken between syllables. Also use the hyphen to show relationship between two or more modifiers, or with certain prefixes and compounds.

John hated any overt show of emotion, especially frustration or anger.

a red-haired man

all-purpose

a slow-moving line

mayor-elect

## PUNCTUATION REVIEW

| | |
|---|---|
| ENDING SENTENCES | period (.) |
| | question mark (?) |
| | exclamation point (!) |
| MARKING BREAKS WITHIN SENTENCES | comma (,) |
| | semicolon (;) |
| | colon (:) |
| | dash (—) |
| | parentheses ( ) |
| | brackets [ ] |
| LINKING WORDS TOGETHER | hyphen (-) |
| MARKING MATERIAL OMITTED | ellipsis … |
| SHOWING DIRECT SPEECH OR THE EXACT WRITTEN WORDS OF SOMEONE ELSE | quotation marks " " |
| | single quotation marks ' ' |
| SHOWING OWNERSHIP OR MARKING CONTRACTION | apostrophe (') |

# TWELVE

# Model Reports

## MODEL 1: CRIMES AGAINST PERSONS—A MISDEMEANOR REPORT

### ASSAULT

#### The Scenario

*Definition of the crime*: Any willful attempt or threat to inflict injury on the person of another, when coupled with an apparent present ability to do so, and any intentional display of force such as would give the victim reason to fear or expect immediate bodily harm, constitutes an assault. An assault may be committed without actually touching, striking, or doing bodily harm to the person of another. (*State v. Murphy*, 7 Wash. App. 505, 500 P.2d 1276, 1281)

The term *assault* is frequently used to describe illegal force which is technically a battery. For crime of assault, the victim need not be apprehensive of fear if the outward gesture is menacing and defendant intends to harm; though for tort of assault, the element of the victim's apprehension is required. (*Com. v. Slaney*, 345 Mass. 135, 185 N.E.2d 919)

In some jurisdictions, degrees of the offense are established as first-, second- and even third-degree assault.

*Simple assault.* An assault unaccompanied by any circumstances of aggravation. A person is guilty of simple assault if he or she (a) attempts to cause or purposely, knowingly, or recklessly causes bodily injury to another; (b) negligently causes bodily injury to another with a deadly weapon; or (c) attempts by physical menace to put another in fear of imminent serious bodily injury. (Model Penal Code, § 211.1)

*Minimum investigative technique*

1. Substantiate the allegation.
2. Question the victim and obtain facts.
3. Conduct a careful, detailed search of the crime scene.
4. Consult medical authorities to determine if the sustained injuries could have been inflicted as indicated by the victim.

5. Photograph the victim's injuries.

6. Seek, locate, and question witnesses as soon after the assault as possible.

7. Try to establish a motive for the assault.

8. Develop and identify suspects, if possible.

9. Warn all suspects of their rights against self-incrimination.

10. Interview all suspects.

*Essential elements of proof*

1. A threat, attempt, or overt action to inflict injury on the victim occurred.

2. The assailant had the ability to inflict injury on the victim.

3. A touching occurred if battery is involved, or a threat if no battery is involved.

4. The assault was illegal (i.e., not self-defense or other mitigating circumstances).

# MODEL 2: CRIMES AGAINST PERSONS—A FELONY REPORT

## MURDER

### The Scenario

*Definition of the crime*: The unlawful killing of a human being by another with malice afore-thought, either express or implied. (*State v. Hutter*, 145 Neb. 798, 18 N.W. 2d 203, 206.)

Criminal homicide constitutes murder when (a) it is committed purposely or knowingly, or (b) it is committed recklessly under circumstances manifesting extreme indifference to the value of human life. Such recklessness and indifference are presumed if the actor is engaged in or is an accomplice in the commission of, or an attempt to commit, or flight after committing or attempting to commit, robbery, rape, or deviant sexual intercourse by force or threat of force, arson, burglary, kidnapping, or felonious escape. (Model Penal Code, § 210.2)

*Minimum investigative technique* (review points)

The following review points may be used to ensure that your investigation has covered all necessary points in any type of circumstance involving death.

*Initial notes*:

☐ Time police notified and by whom

☐ Temperature, humidity, and weather conditions at the scene

☐ Who found victim and the exact time and place

*Scene*:

☐ Indoors, outdoors, or both

☐ Properly protected

☐ Black-and-white photographs

☐ Color photographs

☐ Aerial photographs (if applicable)

☐ Measurements taken

☐ Humidity/temperature noted

☐ Artifacts noted

☐ Diagram—interior and exterior

☐ Street plan (if applicable)

☐ Prints (latent)

☐ Evidence collected (location):

    ☐ Weapons

    ☐ Blood

    ☐ Hairs

    ☐ Fibers

    ☐ Soil

    ☐ Tool Marks

    ☐ Other

*Victim*:

Body

☐ Note position

☐ Presence or absence of rigor mortis in following muscles

    ☐ Jaws

    ☐ Neck and fingers

    ☐ Wrists

    ☐ Elbows

    ☐ Shoulders and knees

    ☐ Hips

    ☐ Abdomen

☐ Mucous membrane dryness

☐ Condition of blood at scene (liquid, clotted, dry)

☐ Cloudy cornea (pupil)

☐ Liver mortis (Does liver blanche [turn white] when finger pressure is applied to skin?)

☐ Venereal discoloration (genitals)

☐ Blisters of the skin

☐ Factors indicative of time of death (such as snow above but not below body, run-down timepieces, spoiled food, or insect invasion of the body)

☐ Area underneath the body when moved

Victim's clothing

☐ Dishevelled

☐ Penetrated or opened

☐ Stained (blood; semen)

☐ Torn, cut, punctured

☐ Fastened

☐ Do defects in the clothing correspond to wounds on body?

☐ Laboratory tests

☐ Secured from

☐ Is clothing appropriate for circumstances

Hair (head, body, and pubic)

☐ Samples

☐ Foreign hairs—location

Blood

☐ Location

Victim's hands

☐ Bagged at scene

☐ Evidence found in hand of victim

☐ Nail scrappings taken

☐ Elimination points

☐ Wounds photographed, measurement reference

Victim's history

☐ Identity of person(s) who saw victim last (time, date, and place seen)

☐ Known enemies

☐ Motives indicated

        ☐ Large insurance policies

        ☐ Substantial estate

        ☐ Known threats

☐ Police record

☐ Association with known or suspected criminals

☐ Recent change in marital status

☐ Trouble in relationship with family or loved one

☐ Recent change in victim's behavior

☐ Did victim do anything differently on the day of his/her death (than he/she usually did on that day or that hour)?

Victim's medical history

☐ Recent complaints regarding health (time, date, and place of complaint, also name of physician and treatment)

☐ History or suspicion of alcoholism, drug abuse, or addiction

☐ Access to/possession of poisons, drugs, or medication

☐ History of nervous disorder or previous mental illness or nervous breakdown

☐ Victim's recent mental state (unhappy, upset, or depressed)

☐ History of any condition or illness to suggest fatal outcome

*Autopsy (investigator's duties):*

☐ Presence at autopsy

☐ Copies of all reports

☐ Notes and sketches

☐ Photographs

☐ Communicate to pathologists relevant circumstances

Gunshot wounds

☐ Was wound treated prior to death? How?

☐ Description of wound

☐ Photographed

☐ Intermediate targets documented (doors, walls, windows, clothing, etc.)

☐ Muzzle impression

☐ Sooty material

☐ Powder embedded

☐ Shape of wound (star shaped, round, etc.)

☐ Presence of abraded area around wound

☐ Autopsy procedures

    ☐ Were X-rays taken to locate the projectile(s)?

    ☐ Was the angle of the path of the projectile(s) detected?

    ☐ Was a full autopsy conducted?

    ☐ Was a toxicology study done?

Cutting and stabbing

☐ Body position

☐ Wound type and location (stab, cut, laceration)

☐ Wound characteristics

    ☐ Hesitation marks    ☐ Defense wounds

    ☐ Scrimmage wounds    ☐ Fatal wound

☐ Artifacts noted

    ☐ Post-mortem injuries

    ☐ Embalmer's wounds

    ☐ Prosecutor's incisions

Drug overdose (scene investigation)

☐ Signs of poisoning (vomit, chills and fever, intense thirst, etc.)

☐ Paraphernalia (tourniquets, syringe, cooker, etc.)

☐ Capsules, decks, pill bottles

☐ Prescription items, antacid, etc.

Body

☐ Position

☐ Rigor

☐ Lividity

☐ Froth at nose or mouth

☐ Needle marks

Autopsy points

☐ Tissues for microscopic examination

    ☐ Skin—subcutaneous tissues and vessels, injection sites

☐ Lung

    ☐ Granulomata, edema, congestion, pneumonia, fibrosis

☐ Lymph nodes—axillary portal

☐ Liver

☐ Heart

☐ Spinal cord

☐ Toxicological investigation

☐ Bile—presence of opiates

☐ Subcutaneous tissue and vessels—fresh injection site

☐ Urine—opiates

☐ Blood

☐ Gastric contents—capsules or tablets

☐ Liver, kidney, lung, and brain tissue

*Suspect:*

☐ Photographed when arrested

    ☐ Wounds/cuts/scratches noted

    ☐ Photographed clothed

    ☐ Photographed nude (sex offense cases)

☐ Searched

☐ Suspect's clothes and shoes obtained

☐ Fingernails scraped

☐ Body hairs obtained

☐ Head hairs obtained

☐ Blood type determined

☐ Hands swabbed (neutron activation analysis)

*Essential elements of proof* (murder; minimum)

1. Killing is unlawful.

2. Committed by one or more persons (not the victim).

3. It is committed purposely or knowingly (death intended; malice aforethought).

You are assigned to investigate a report of a dead body found in a warehouse in a commercial district of your city. On arrival, you find the body of a middle-aged man lying on the floor within the warehouse office. Paramedical personnel are at the scene and tell you the man is dead and has four gunshot wounds in the chest and head. You call for the coroner and then conduct your investigation of an implied murder. (Even if the death involved different circumstances and appeared to be a suicide, you would imply murder until your investigation proved otherwise.)

**YOUR LAW ENFORCEMENT DEPARTMENT**
**YOUR CITY/TOWN**

# REPORT OF INVESTIGATION

## FOR OFFICIAL USE ONLY

Exhibit 12-1

# REPORT OF INVESTIGATION

## ADMINISTRATIVE INFORMATION

Case Number:      89-0000
Investigated By:  Officer John Doe
Date:             July 7, 0000

## CRIME/OFFENSE

Assault (Minor Personal Injury)

## SUSPECT(S)

Unknown

## BASIS FOR INVESTIGATION

Sam Jones, bartender, Joe's Bar and Grill, 617 East 4th Street, Your City, called to report a fight in progress in an adjacent parking lot.

## SUMMARY OF INVESTIGATION

About 2145 hours, July 7, 0000, at a parking lot at 620 East 4th Street, Your City, two unidentified men assaulted George Smithers causing minor physical injury. Both offenders ran from the scene as I approached the scene.

## SUBSTANTIATION

In a written statement, George Smithers said two men followed him from Joe's Bar and Grill and into the parking lot. As Smithers reached his automobile, which was parked there, the two men came up to him and accused Smithers of dating one of the men's wives. Smithers said he had no idea what the men were talking about and told them he wasn't the man they were looking for. Then, according to Smithers, they started to hit him with fists, and he fought back. When one of the men saw the approaching police car, he told the other man to run, and they both fled into the dark. Smithers provided a detailed description of the two men with regard to approximate age, clothing, and other information.

In a written statement, Sam Jones, a bartender at Joe's Bar and Grill, said he remembered both Smithers and the two men in the bar earlier and doesn't recall seeing Smithers or the two assailants before. Jones said Smithers was having a sandwich and a beer at the bar, while the other two men sat at a table and had about three drinks of bourbon and water. Jones said that he noticed the men followed Smithers out of the bar but thought nothing of it. He stated that a few minutes later, a young couple came into the bar and reported three men were fighting in the parking lot next door. The couple then left, and he doesn't know their identity, but provided a detailed description. Jones also provided a detailed description of the two assailants.

EXHIBIT 12-1

# REPORT OF INVESTIGATION

A General Hospital report documents abrasions and contusions to the head and body of Smithers. He was treated and released.

In an Investigator's Statement, I provide relevant information not discussed elsewhere in this report.

## WITNESSES/VICTIMS

Mr. George Wilhelm Smithers, 3549 South Maple Street, Your City. Tele: 000-0000. Employed: Johnson Electronics, as a wiring technician. DOB: 8/3/39

Mr. Sam Jones, 762 2nd Avenue, Apt 1004, Your City. Tele: 000-0000. Employed: Joe's Bar and Grill, as a bartender and assistant manager. DOB: 4/2/45

## EXHIBITS

1. A written statement by George Smithers, dated July 7, 0000 (original)
2. A written statement by Sam Jones, dated July 7, 0000 (original)
3. A crime scene sketch by Officer John Doe, dated July 7, 0000 (original)
4. General Hospital Treatment Report on Smithers, dated July 7, 0000 (cy)
5. An Investigator's Statement by Officer John Doe, dated July 7, 0000 (original)

Exhibit 12-1

# INVESTIGATOR'S STATEMENT

Case Number: 00-0000
Date:         July 7, 0000
Officer:      John Doe

My observation of George Smithers did not cause me to believe he was intoxicated at the time of the assault.

Upon arrival at the scene, I observed two persons running from the scene into the dark; however, did not attempt pursuit. I could not see any identifiable features or clothing.

The weather was cloudy, and there was a light mist at the time of the offense.

George Smithers was transported to General Hospital by paramedical Unit 8 and released after treatment. He took a cab from the hospital, indicating he would pick up his car later.

The assault appears to be a case of mistaken identity; however, further problems may be encountered since the assailants probably continue to believe Smithers is the man they were looking for.

Smithers was instructed to contact this department if any further contact is made with the assailants, or if he observes one or both at a future date.

Jones was instructed to contact this department if any further contact is made with the assailants, or if he observes one or both at a future date.

## END OF STATEMENT

---

**OFFICER JOHN DOE**

Exhibit 12-1

**YOUR LAW ENFORCEMENT DEPARTMENT**
**YOUR CITY/TOWN**

# REPORT OF INVESTIGATION

FOR OFFICIAL USE ONLY

EXHIBIT 12-2

# REPORT OF INVESTIGATION

# (FIRST PROGRESS)

## ADMINISTRATIVE INFORMATION

Case Number:     00-0000
Investigated By:  Det. Sgt. Sam Jones
Date:            August 5, 0000

## CRIME/OFFENSE

Homicide (Here you would cite your statute and offense according to it.)

## SUSPECT

Unknown

## BASIS FOR INVESTIGATION

At 0900 hours, August 5, 0000, Mr. Robert Smith, janitor at Sanford Mills, Inc., reported he discovered the body of a man in a warehouse at 140 Commercial Way, Your City. Smith reported the man had been shot and believed killed.

## SUMMARY OF INVESTIGATION

Investigation disclosed that at the Sanford Mills, Inc. warehouse, 140 Commercial Way, Your City, between 2100 hours, August 4 and 0900 hours, August 5, 0000, person(s) unknown killed Mr. George Overby, a bookkeeper employed by Sanford Mills, Inc., by firing four small-caliber shots into Overby's head and chest area.

## SUBSTANTIATION

A written statement obtained from Mr. Robert Smith indicates that he arrived at the warehouse as scheduled to perform janitorial duties. Smith explained that the warehouse is normally used between the hours of 1300 to 2100 hours daily to store items manufactured by Sanford Mills, Inc. at another location. Smith said that he found Overby on his arrival, did not touch anything in the office, but went to another telephone in the warehouse area and called paramedics and the police.

A written statement obtained from the warehouse foreman, Mr. Ralph Bickers, who was called to the scene by Smith, indicates that Overby was working in the office when Bickers and a crew of five workers left the warehouse at 2100 hours, August 4. Bickers said he locked all the doors and Overby, who appeared nervous and tired, told him that he would be working on the warehouse books until about midnight.

A written statement obtained from Mr. Stephen Sanford Jr., owner/president of Sanford Mills, Inc., stated that Overby was employed ten years earlier by his company and had always performed tirelessly and with competence. Sanford also said that in recent weeks, Overby seemed preoccupied, and Sanford assumed he was experiencing some kind of personal problem, although he was unaware of what it is.

EXHIBIT 12-2

# REPORT OF INVESTIGATION

# (FIRST PROGRESS)

A paramedical response report indicates that team was notified of a man with gunshot wounds at the warehouse about 0904 hours, and arrived at 0917 hours, August 5, 0000. The report indicates Overby was dead when the paramedical team arrived and estimated death had occurred several hours prior to their arrival.

A preliminary report by Dr. John Strong, Your County Coroner, indicates time of death estimated at 0100 hours, August 4, 0000. Cause of death estimated as any one or combination of bullet wounds to the head and heart of Overby. An autopsy is scheduled for August 6, 0000.

A crime scene search revealed no physical evidence. Several latent fingerprints were developed and are on file pending identification of suspect(s). Sketches and photographs record the scene as discovered.

An Investigator's Statement discusses all relevant information not discussed elsewhere in this report.

## WITNESSES

Mr. Robert Smith, 4539 South Elm Street, Your City. Telephone: 000-0000.
Employed as a janitor by Sanford Mills, Inc. SSN: 000-00-0000. Age 53

Mr. Ralph Bickers, 8394 East 46th Street, Your City. Telephone: 000-0000.
Employed as a warehouse foreman by Sanford Mills, Inc. SSN: 000-00-0000. Age 49

Mr. Stephen Sanford, Jr., 45 Tiffany Way, Your City. Telephone: 000-0000.
Owner/president of Sanford Mills, Inc. SSN: 000-00-0000. Age 56

Mr. John Billingsley, 8459 West 105th Street, Your City. Telephone: 000-0000.
Paramedical technician for Municipal Medical Response, Inc. SSN: 000-00-0000. Age 32

Mr. Michael Buford, 932 North Park Boulevard, Your City. Telephone: 000-0000.
Paramedical technician for Municipal Medical Response, Inc. SSN: 000-00-0000. Age 27

Dr. John Strong, 4392 82d Avenue, East, Your City. Telephone: 000-0000.
Your County Coroner. SSN: 000-00-0000. Age 39

## EXHIBITS

Written statement of Mr. Robert Smith, dated Aug 5, 0000 (original)

Written statement of Mr. Ralph Bickers, dated Aug 5, 0000 (original)

Written statement of Mr. Stephen Sanford, Jr., dated Aug 5, 0000 (original)

Investigator's statement of Det. Sgt. Sam Jones, dated Aug 5, 0000 (original)

Paramedical report, dated Aug 5, 0000 (cy)

Coroner's report, dated Aug 5, 0000 (cy)

Crime scene sketch, dated Aug 5, 0000 (original)

Crime scene photographs (12 each), exposed Aug 5, 0000 (originals w/neg)

Exhibit 12-2

**YOUR LAW ENFORCEMENT DEPARTMENT**
**YOUR CITY/TOWN**

# REPORT OF INVESTIGATION

## FOR OFFICIAL USE ONLY

Exhibit 12-3

# REPORT OF INVESTIGATION

## (Second Progress)

## ADMINISTRATIVE INFORMATION

Case Number:     00-0000
Investigated By:  Det. Sgt. Sam Jones
Date:                 September 5, 0000

## CRIME/OFFENSE

Homicide

## SUSPECT

Unknown

## BASIS FOR INVESTIGATION

No change

## SUMMARY OF INVESTIGATION

During the period Aug. 5 through Sep. 5, 0000, investigation disclosed: Mr. George Overby stole $250,000 in U.S. currency from Sanford Mills, Inc. during the period Apr. 10 through Aug. 4, 0000. Overby is believed to have an accomplice, identity unknown.

## SUBSTANTIATION

An auditor's report from the firm Smith, Smith and Jones, CPAs, revealed Sanford Mills, Inc. funds in the amount of $250,000 were transferred to a bank account in the name of George Overby, during the period Apr 10 through Aug 4, 0000.

In a written statement, Mrs. Robert McNamara, chief teller, Lincoln Bank, Your Town, said that George Overby was known at the bank and had made multiple large cash deposits during the period Apr 10 through Aug 4, 0000 totalling $250,000.

In a written statement, Mr. Jerome Hillman, president of First National Bank, Your Town, said that Sanford Mills, Inc. maintained several accounts at the bank, and George Overby was a signatory in several accounts. Hillman said Overby often made deposits personally, and starting Apr 10 through Aug 4, 0000, made large withdrawals. When questioned by Hillman about authorization, Overby presented a letter from Mr. Stephen Sanford, Jr., and the signature matched the one on file. On May 25, Hillman called Sanford and learned he was on vacation, and business activities prevented a verification later, although Hillman said that Ms. Pamela Swenson, a loan officer at the bank, told Hillman she had indeed talked with Sanford and he verified the authorization.

In a written statement, Ms. Pamela Swenson said a person who identified himself as Stephen Sanford, Jr. called her on May 10 and verified the authorization that Overby had presented to the bank. Swenson said she had no reason to doubt the authorization.

EXHIBIT 12-3

# REPORT OF INVESTIGATION

## (Second Progress)

In a written statement, Stephen Sanford, Jr. said he had never called the First National Bank, nor Ms. Pamela Swenson. Sanford said he did not sign an authorization for George Overby to make withdrawals, and approved his signatory only to enable issuing certain payroll and vendor payments.

## WITNESSES

Mr. Troy Smith III, 92 West 55th Street, Your Town. Telephone: 000-0000.
Partner, Smith, Smith and Jones, CPAs. SSN 000-00-0000. Age 57

Mrs. Robert McNamara, 2938 East Lexington Avenue, Your Town. Telephone: 000-0000.
Employed by Lincoln Bank, 33 Central Ave., Your Town. SSN: 000-00-0000

Mr. Jerome Hillman, 219 Cambridge Way, Your town. Telephone: 000-0000.
President, First National Bank, 22 Central Avenue, Your Town. SSN: 000-00-0000

Ms. Pamela Swenson, 8793 South Hampton Street, Your Town. Telephone: 000-0000.
Loan officer, First National Bank, Your Town. SSN: 000-00-0000

Mr. Stephen Sanford, Jr. (same as first progress report)

## EXHIBITS

Auditor report, made by Mr. Troy Smith, dated Aug 25, 0000 (cy)
Written statement of Mrs. Robert McNamara, dated Aug 26, 0000 (cy)
Written statement of Mr. Jerome Hillman, dated Aug 26, 0000 (cy)
Written statement of Ms. Pamela Swenson, dated Aug 27, 0000 (cy)
Written statement of Mr. Stephen Sanford Jr., dated Aug 27, 0000 (cy)

Exhibit 12-3

**YOUR LAW ENFORCEMENT DEPARTMENT
YOUR CITY/TOWN**

# REPORT OF INVESTIGATION

## FOR OFFICIAL USE ONLY

EXHIBIT 12-4

# REPORT OF INVESTIGATION

## (Completed)

## ADMINISTRATIVE INFORMATION

Case Number: 00-0000
Investigated By: Det. Sgt. Sam Jones
Date: October 2, 0000

## CRIME/OFFENSE

Homicide (1)
Theft (2) (This section should be detailed with your respective statutes)
Conspiracy (3)
Obstruction of Justice (4)

## SUSPECT(S)

James Albert Rangley (1) (3), 345 Sinbad Court, Another City

Pamela Swenson (2) (3) (4), 8793 South Hampton Street, Your Town

Jerome Hillman (2) (3) (4), 219 Cambridge Way, Your Town

Stephen Sanford Jr. (1) (2) (3) (4), 45 Tiffany Way, Your Town

## BASIS FOR INVESTIGATION

At 0900 hours, August 5, 0000, Mr. Robert Smith, janitor at Sanford Mills, Inc., reported he discovered the body of a man in a warehouse at 140 Commercial Way, Your City. Smith reported the man had been shot and believed killed.

## SUMMARY OF INVESTIGATION

Investigation revealed that about 0100 hours, August 5, 0000, at the Sanford Mills Warehouse, 140 Commercial Way, Your City, James Albert Rangley shot and killed George Overby. Rangley was hired by Stephen Sanford, Jr. for a paid fee of $20,000 cash.

Stephen Sanford, Jr., Pamela Swenson, and James Hillman conspired to steal $30 million from Sanford Mills, Inc. over a period of two years and then flee to a South Pacific island where Sanford owned a large plantation under an obscure corporation which he formed with an alias.

George Overby discovered the plot and at the time of his death was assisting the FBI and other law enforcement agencies in their investigation based on information provided by Overby. Sanford, unaware that Overby had contacted federal authorities, approached Overby and asked him to participate in a scheme to embezzle $250,000, which would be payment for Overby's silence. At the direction of the FBI, Overby participated in the scheme.

Sanford, Hillman, and Swenson conspired to reveal the embezzlement through an audit process to focus attention on Overby and cover their own embezzlement scheme and process.

Exhibit 12-4

# REPORT OF INVESTIGATION

## (Completed)

Without the knowledge of Hillman and Swenson, Sanford hired Rangley to kill Overby, believing that his death would assure silence and prompt discovery of the Overby embezzlement.

After Overby's death, Sanford convinced Hillman and Swenson that certain bank records and company records should be destroyed to prevent auditors or law enforcement officers investigating the death of Overby, discovering any incriminating information. Hillman and Swenson destroyed some records, forged others, and, without the knowledge of Sanford, placed copies in a safe deposit box, believing Sanford may be planning to expose them to authorities and then disappear with the money.

Sanford placed Rangley on a $15,000 retainer so he would be available on notice to kill Swenson and Hillman for an additional $20,000 each.

Sanford was planning to depart the United States on October 21, 0000 after making a wire transfer of about $30 million to a foreign bank. The money was being moved from account to account, with additional accounts being opened in other local banks to confuse the transfer trail and conceal Sanford's intentions and actions until he was in hiding.

## SUBSTANTIATION

Written statement of Mr. Robert Smith indicates that he arrived at the warehouse as scheduled to perform janitorial duties. Smith explained that the warehouse is normally used between the hours of 1300 to 2100 hours daily to store items manufactured by Sanford Mills, Inc. at another location. Smith said he found Overby on arrival, did not touch anything in the office, but went to another telephone in the warehouse to call paramedics and police.

Written statement of Mr. Ralph Bickers, warehouse foreman, said Smith called him at home and he proceeded to the warehouse. According to Bickers, five warehouse workers and he left the warehouse about 2100 hours, Aug 4, 0000 and locked the doors. He said Overby was working in the office on books and records and told him he would be there until about midnight.

Written statement of Mr. Stephen Sanford, Jr. owner/president of Sanford Mills, Inc., said that Overby was employed ten years earlier by his company and had always performed tirelessly and with competence. Sanford also said that in recent weeks, Overby seemed preoccupied, and he assumed it was a personal problem of some kind.

A paramedical response report indicates that team was notified of a man with gunshot wounds at the warehouse about 0904 hours, and arrived at 0917 hours, August 5, 0000. The report indicates Overby was dead when the paramedical team arrived and estimated death had occurred several hours prior to their arrival.

A preliminary report by Dr. John Strong, Your County Coroner, indicates time of death estimated at 0100 hours, August 5, 0000. Cause of death estimated as any one or combination of bullet wounds to the head and heart of Overby.

Exhibit 12-4

# REPORT OF INVESTIGATION

## (Completed)

An autopsy report by Dr. John Strong, concerning George Overby, reveals the deceased was shot with a 9 mm handgun at about 5 feet distance. Three rounds entered the head through the face, and one round entered the heart. Four rounds were recovered from the body at the time of autopsy. Strong confirmed the gunshot wounds as cause of death, singularly or a combination of them. No disease, drug addiction, or other causes or contributing factors were disclosed.

An auditor's report of Mr. Troy Smith, of Smith, Smith and Jones, CPAs, disclosed that Sanford Mills, Inc. funds in the amount of $250,000 were transferred to bank accounts in the name of George Overby, during the period Apr 10 through Aug 4, 0000 and confirmed a shortage in company accounts equal to that amount is confirmed. Smith said additional shortages and irregularities are noted, however, more records and information will be required to determine the cause.

Written statement of Mrs. Robert McNamara, chief teller, Lincoln Bank, Your Town, said that George Overby was known at the bank and made multiple large cash deposits during the period Apr 10 through Aug 4, 0000, totalling $250,000.

Written statement of Mr. Jerome Hillman, president of First National Bank, Your Town, said that Sanford Mills, Inc. maintained several accounts at the bank, and George Overby was a signatory in several accounts. Hillman said Overby often made deposits personally, and starting Apr 1 through Aug 4, 0000, made large withdrawals. When questioned by Hillman about authorization, Overby presented a letter from Mr. Stephen Sanford, Jr., and the signature matched the one on file. On May 25, Hillman called Sanford and learned he was on vacation, and business activities prevented a verification later, although Hillman said that Ms. Pamela Swenson, a loan officer at the bank, told him she had indeed talked with Sanford and he verified the authorization.

A written statement of Ms. Pamela Swenson disclosed that a person who identified himself as Stephen Sanford, Jr. called her on May 10 and verified the authorization which Overby had presented to the bank. Swenson said she had no reason to doubt the authorization.

A written statement of Mr. Stephen Sanford, Jr. said he never called the First National Bank, nor Ms. Pamela Swenson. Sanford said he did not sign an authorization for Overby to remove cash from company accounts, and approved his signatory only to enable issuing certain payroll and vendor payments.

A letter from the FBI confirms that Overby was assisting them in an investigation of Hillman, Swenson, and Sanford after he voluntarily notified them of information discovered in the books. Overby accepted the offer from Sanford and followed through with the activities under full authority and control of the Bureau and other federal agencies with an interest in the case. Overby had contacted the FBI on Aug 4, 0000 and told them he found additional evidence in the warehouse books and would recover the information that evening, which would enable them to obtain a search warrant. The FBI warned him about the risk, and he declined an offer for protection.

EXHIBIT 12-4

# REPORT OF INVESTIGATION

## (Completed)

A written statement of Mr. Jerome Hillman reveals admission of involvement with Swenson and Sanford in a systematic embezzlement of company funds. He said the company was nearing bankruptcy, and Sanford was concerned the IRS would discover he had for years used company funds for personal gain over and above salary and benefits. Hillman said Sanford and he were old friends socially, and that Swenson was involved romantically with Sanford, who is divorced. Hillman planned on deserting his wife and children when the three moved to Sanford's plantation under aliases, saying their marriage was nearing an end. Hillman admits planning to make Overby appear to be the main player and had plans for framing a teller at the bank as his accomplice. The plan was to cover all other activities until the three could slip away and vanish. Hillman denies any knowledge or involvement in the death of Overby.

A statement of rights signed by Ms. Pamela Swenson confirms her desire to remain silent and not make any statements concerning the crimes.

A statement of rights signed by Mr. Stephen Sanford, Jr. confirms his desire to remain silent and not make any statements concerning the crimes.

Telephone toll call records for Stephen Sanford, Jr. obtained for the month of July and August 0000 revealed four calls made to a number which was identified as belonging to Mr. James Albert Rangley, Another Town.

A criminal history, NCIC, and criminal intelligence check revealed that James Albert Rangley is believed to be a contract killer, suspected in multiple deaths and wanted for murder in three states. Photographs obtained.

A car rental agency at City Airport identified Rangley from photographs, indicating he rented a car on Aug 3 under an alias and converted the rental agreement to long-term rental on Sep 18. Their records revealed the car to be paid in full through Nov 1 and provided an address of a local motel.

A warrant arrest of Rangley at the Shady Rest Motel, Your Town, and search of the room revealed a 9 mm Beretta handgun, and ammunition. Twenty thousand dollars in $100 bills and Sanford's telephone number were found in a briefcase, along with several drivers licenses and other forms of identification in aliases.

A State Crime Laboratory Report discloses that the 9 mm handgun found in the motel room of Rangley is the gun that was used to fire the bullets into the body of Overby. The ammunition box and loaded clips are missing four rounds. The ammunition is verified as being the same kind as the slugs removed from Overby's body. Rangley's fingerprints were verified on the handgun, the briefcase interior and exterior, and on the sheet of paper showing Sanford's name, address, and telephone number.

A State Crime Laboratory Report discloses that some of the currency found in Rangley's briefcase has Sanford's fingerprints on it.

Exhibit 12-4

# REPORT OF INVESTIGATION

## (Completed)

The briefcase was traced to an office supply store, Your Town, from a business card found in one of the interior pockets. Records of the store indicate a briefcase was purchased on July 30, by Sanford Mills, Inc., charged to the company account and signed for by Stephen Sanford, Jr.

A written statement of Mr. James Albert Rangley admits he shot and killed George Overby resulting from a contract provided by Stephen Sanford, Jr. and received $20,000 cash, which he relinquished to law enforcement officers at the time of arrest. Rangley admitted ownership of the handgun and ammunition and said that Sanford provided the cash and briefcase.

A State Crime Laboratory Report confirms that the sheet of paper bearing Sanford's name, address, and telephone number has Sanford's fingerprints, and a handwriting analysis confirms the writing to be that of Sanford.

A bank examiner's report discloses the complex shifting and withdrawal of funds by Sanford Mills, Inc. during the period Jan 5 through Sep 30, 0000, and multiple wire transfers of funds to other banks in the U.S. and three foreign countries.

An audit report by Smith, Smith and Jones, in cooperation with federal and local law enforcement agencies and requested by Sanford Mills, Inc. stockholders and Board of Directors, revealed over $3 million missing from normal accounts and about $2 million located in various accounts, some in names not associated with the company. An additional $2 million is generally unaccounted for, but shown in records as authorized payments which are now known to be false. This audit is continuing.

An investigator's statement discusses all relevant information not discussed elsewhere in this report.

## WITNESSES

Mr. Robert Smith, 4539 South Elm Street, Your City. Telephone: 000-0000.
Employed as a janitor by Sanford Mills, Inc. SSN: 000-00-0000. Age 53

Mr. Ralph Bickers, 8394 East 46th Street, Your City. Telephone: 000-0000.
Employed as a warehouse foreman by Sanford Mills, Inc. SSN: 000-00-0000. Age 49

Mr. John Billingsley, 8459 West 105th Street, Your City. Telephone: 000-0000.
Paramedical technician for Municipal Medical Response, Inc. SSN: 000-00-0000. Age 32

Mr. Michael Buford, 932 North Park Boulevard, Your City. Telephone: 000-0000.
Paramedical technician for Municipal Medical Response, Inc. SSN: 000-00-0000. Age 27

Dr. John Strong, 4392 82d Avenue, East, Your City. Telephone: 000-0000.
Your County Coroner. SSN: 000-00-0000. Age 39

Mr. Troy Smith III, 92 West 55th Street, Your Town. Telephone: 000-0000.
Partner, Smith, Smith and Jones, CPAs. SSN: 000-00-0000. Age 57

Exhibit 12-4

# REPORT OF INVESTIGATION

## (Completed)

Mrs. Robert McNamara, 2938 East Lexington Avenue, Your Town. Telephone: 000-0000. Employed by Lincoln Bank, 33 Central Avenue, Your Town. SSN: 000-00-0000. Age 42

Federal Bureau of Investigation, Washington, DC

Mr. Joseph P. Cleveland, State Crime Laboratory, State Capital. Firearms and Ballistics Section

Mr. Steven C. Englewood, State Crime Laboratory, State Capital, Fingerprint and Questioned Documents Section

Mrs. Rachael Stone, 4938 West Oak Street, Your Town. Telephone: 000-0000. Bookkeeper, South Park Office Supply Center, Your Town. SSN: 0000-00-0000. Age 61

Mr. Mark Robertson, 9201 South Portland Boulevard, Your City. Telephone: 000-0000. Bank Examiner for FDIC, Washington, DC

## EXHIBITS (ATTACHED UNLESS OTHERWISE INDICATED)

Written statement of Mr. Robert Smith, dated Aug 5, 0000 (original)

Written statement of Mr. Ralph Bickers, dated Aug 5, 0000 (original)

Written statement of Mr. Stephen Sanford, Jr., dated Aug 5, 0000 (original)

Paramedical report, dated Aug 5, 0000 (cy)

Preliminary coroner's report, dated Aug 5, 0000 (cy)

Coroner's autopsy report, dated Aug 10, 0000 (cy)

Audit report, dated Aug 25, 0000 (cy)

Written statement of Mrs. Robert McNamara, dated Aug 26, 0000 (original)

Written statement of Mr. Jerome Hillman, dated Aug 26, 0000 (original)

Written statement of Ms. Pamela Swenson, dated Aug 27, 0000 (original)

Written statement of Mr. Stephen Sanford, Jr., dated Aug 27, 0000 (original)

Letter from the Federal Bureau of Investigation, dated Sep 5, 0000 (original)

Written statement of Mr. Jerome Hillman, dated Sep 31, 0000 (original)

A statement of rights pertaining to Ms. Pamela Swenson, dated Sep 31, 0000 (original)

A statement of rights pertaining to Mr. Stephen Sanford, Jr., dated Sep 31, 0000 (original)

Telephone company toll call records for Jul/Aug 0000, pertaining to Mr. Stephen Sanford, Jr. (cy)

Criminal history, NCIC, and Criminal intelligence documents pertaining to Mr. James Albert Rangley (cy)

Automobile Rental Agreement Forms, dated Aug 3 and Sep 18, 0000 pertaining to Rangley (cy) (original in evidence room)

Arrest warrant/search warrant for James A. Rangley, dated Sep 25, 0000 (cy)

EXHIBIT 12-4

# REPORT OF INVESTIGATION

## (Completed)

Property receipt for items seized from Rangley, dated Sep 25, 0000 (cy) (original in evidence room with items)

One 9 mm Beretta pistol, serial number 9938857329, in evidence room

Two 9 mm ammunition clips for Beretta pistol, in evidence room

Forty-six rounds 9 mm ammunition, in evidence room

One briefcase, containing $20,000 in U.S. currency, in evidence room

One sheet of paper, containing handwritten name, address, and telephone number of Stephen Sanford, Jr., in evidence room

Two state crime laboratory reports, dated Sep 31, 0000 (originals)

Written statement of James A. Rangley, dated Sep 26, 0000 (original)

FDIC Bank Examiner's Report, dated Sep 19, 0000 (cy)

Audit report, dated Sep 18, 0000 (cy)

Crime scene sketch, dated Aug 5, 0000 (original)

Twelve crime scene photographs, exposed Aug 5, 0000 (original w/negatives)

Clothing removed from body of Overby in evidence room

Investigator's statement, dated Aug 5, 0000 (original)

Investigator's statement, dated Oct 1, 0000 (original)

Case file with notes, checklists, misc. information (on file)

EXHIBIT 12-4

## MODEL 5: DRUG TRAFFICKING _____

*Note*: This model report is an actual case, with names, dates, and places altered. The person discussed throughout this model as Walter R. Seabrook III (fictitious name) pleaded guilty in Federal Court during 1988 and was sentenced to twenty years in a Federal prison. In addition, Seabrook voluntarily forfeited all the property and funds the investigation proved to be derived from the sale of drugs. The forfeiture, including real estate, aircraft, vehicles and other property, totalled $8.6 million. Seabrook agreed to plead guilty and forfeit his holdings in return for a twenty-year prison term. If the case were tried, Seabrook would have been charged as a career criminal in addition to drug trafficking. In the New England state, the prison term, on conviction, would have resulted in a life sentence. Property seizure under those terms would have been under RICO laws. A three-year investigation, beginning with an information report, moving into an intelligence collection process and reports, and finally a criminal investigation, is represented here in a series of report models that follow the case from beginning to end.

The actual case, including dossiers, telephone call analysis, wire tap information, and exhibits, numbered over one thousand pages.

This model is provided as a guide to complex cases which begin with an item of information alerting you to one or more crimes that have not been previously reported. Unlike cases where clearly defined victims or complainants are identifiable and there is a crime scene to begin the case, some criminal activity, especially drug trafficking, is discovered through unconfirmed information.

The model shows a progressive process from information from a confidential source, through a major intelligence collection operation and, at a point where evidence is conclusive, a criminal investigation, the first step toward a prosecution.

Collecting information during intelligence operations, unlike a systematic criminal investigation, is normally fragmented and comes in no particular order. Although a general direction plan is beneficial during intelligence operations, the narrow objective of criminal investigations is replaced with a broad overview, attempting to define what the crime, if any, actually is, and if there's evidence to support those crimes that appear to be identified.

Here, we'll move through the often murky process and notice that patterns, motives, and clear evidence sources begin to emerge. As noted before, this model is abbreviated since it does not serve as a critique of the actual case which served as its pattern, nor an investigative training device. It is intended only as an example of managing information as it develops on a crime not previously identified.

Headings and other administrative information are omitted from the model to allow concentration structure and process of development in a complex case.

*Note*: Subsequent progress reports include all new information since the previous progress report. When all available information and evidence is obtained and verified, write the completed report.

In the actual case, the report and exhibits, which included documents supporting testimony of witnesses, exceeded one thousand pages.

Your completed report in such cases as demonstrated here is the first time you'll actually break down and present the case in its entirety, in a logical, systematic order. Remember, your exhibits continue to tell the story to a reader, and the substantiation will give readers a fast one- or two-sentence summary of what each exhibit demonstrates, all of which supports your concise investigative summary.

## CRIMINAL INFORMATION REPORT 1: DRUG TRAFFICKING

### 1985, Northern New England

On June 4, 1985, Confidential Source 498 reported a major drug trafficker (cocaine, heroin, marihuana), identified as Walter R. Seabrook III, is operating in the Any Town, Any State area.

Seabrook is alleged to be using a development corporation identified as Sea King, Inc. as a front for the trafficking activities.

The source of drugs is believed to be Colombia and other South American countries through Blank State, into Blank State, and finally to a warehousing system in Blank State.

Seabrook is alleged to be living at 45 Benton Place, Any Town, Any State, with a woman identified as Diane Doe. He reportedly has other homes in Blank State and Blank State.

Confidential Source claims personal knowledge, having watched an incoming shipment of cocaine and marihuana unloaded at a barn located in a remote area of Blank State, about 20 miles south of Any Town. Source said the shipment was brought to Blank State by Seabrook's elderly father and mother, who reside in Blank State and make several trips a year in a motor home used for smuggling drugs.

Exhibit 12-5

## CRIMINAL INFORMATION REPORT 2: DRUG TRAFFICKING

### 1985, New England, Re: Walter R. Seabrook, III

On June 24, 1985, Confidential Source 295 reported that he witnessed a meeting at the Coffee and Donuts Shop, 3942 South 54th Street, Any Town, Any State, about 2:00 A.M., June 23, 1985. Source said Walter R. Seabrook III met with four unidentified men, who arrived about 2:10 A.M. in a new Mercedes sedan with Blank State license plates.

Source said Seabrook asked him to be at the Donut shop but wait in a different area until Seabrook invited him to the table where the meeting was taking place. About 2:45 A.M., Seabrook motioned Source to come to the table, and he was introduced to the four men. No last names were used, and he can only recall two first names, Vinny and Mike. He was not asked to sit down, only introduced by Seabrook, saying, "I want you to meet my main man." None of the men offered to shake hands, just nodded at the Source. After a couple of uncomfortable minutes, Seabrook told the Source he would see him the following day, and Source left the shop.

Source reported the license number of the Mercedes as Any State 59683.

Source says he was approached by Seabrook about two weeks ago asking him to become his bookkeeper at Sea King Development, Inc. He accepted the position and will begin work at the warehouse on 12th Street, Any Town, which Seabrook uses for an office. Source agreed to report any new information.

EXHIBIT 12-5

## CRIMINAL INFORMATION REPORT 3: DRUG TRAFFICKING

### 1985, New England, Re: Walter R. Seabrook III

On August 2, 1985, Confidential Source 745 reported she has been to Walter R. Seabrook's home on Pelican Lake and describes it as an estate. She says the house is plush and surrounded by about 50 acres fenced with a high chainlink fence and an electrically controlled gate about a block from the house, which is the entrance to the estate.

Source says Seabrook keeps a single engine seaplane and a couple of boats moored at the docks near the house and brags about his skills as a pilot. He told Source two other planes, which he uses for flights around the country, are kept at St. George Municipal Airport, nearby.

She said Seabrook has offered her cocaine and is trying to convince her to sell cocaine, marihuana, and heroin locally, telling her there's big money to be made. His comment, according to the Source, is, "I'm making millions, you can too, you've got the looks. I can bring you in as a dealer and move you up. My organization is growing and I've got lots of connections."

Source agreed to continue contact and to delay becoming involved until instructed to do so under department control.

EXHIBIT 12-5

# CRIMINAL INTELLIGENCE REPORT—FIRST PROGRESS: DRUG TRAFFICKING

## 1985, Re: Walter R. Seabrook III

Information developed during the period June 4 through September 1, 1985, from Confidential Sources 498, 295, and 745, along with surreptitious financial background searches regarding Walter R. Seabrook III, revealed the following information:

### REAL PROPERTY OWNED WITH NO MORTGAGE OR LOANS

| | |
|---|---|
| Residential: | 89 Colonial Drive<br>Any City, Any State |
| | 18 Northern Blvd.<br>Any City, Any State |
| | 2265 24th Street<br>Any City, Any State |
| | 67 Mason Street<br>Any City, Any State |
| | 2 Regency Court<br>Any City, Any State |
| | Briar Wood Estate<br>Pelican Lake<br>Any City, Any State |
| | 45 Benton Place<br>Any City, Any State |
| Commercial: | Dream Beauty Salon<br>Any City, Any State |
| | Haircuts, Inc.<br>Any City, Any State |
| | Sea King Development, Inc.<br>Any City, Any State |
| | Warehouse<br>39 South 34th Street<br>Any City, Any State |
| | Farm on State Route 7<br>20 miles south of Any City, Any State |

Exhibit 12-5

# CRIMINAL INTELLIGENCE REPORT—FIRST PROGRESS: DRUG TRAFFICKING

## 1985, Re: Walter R. Seabrook III

**CORPORATIONS SET UP BY SEABROOK:**

1978    Caribbean Southern Trading Company
Southern City, Any State

1978    Caribbean Split, Inc.
Southern City, Any State

1979    Southern Development Corporation
Southern City, Any State

1981    Investments Worldwide, Inc.
Any City, Any State

1983    Sea King Development, Inc.
New England City, Any State

1984    Mountain Region Development, Inc.
New England City, Any State

**AIRCRAFT AND MOTOR VEHICLES REGISTERED TO SEABROOK AND/OR A CORPORATION OWNED BY SEABROOK:**

1983    Cessna, twin-engine aircraft
Tail number N73842
Maintained at St. George Airport
Any City, Any State

1984    Cessna, twin-engine aircraft
Tail number N84759
Maintained at St. George Airport

1984    Seaplane, single engine
Tail number N84738
Maintained at Pelican Lake and
St. George Airport

1984    Cadillac Fleetwood sedan

1983    Mercedes sedan

1984    Ford pickup truck

1985    Chevrolet Blazer

1930    Packard (restored)

Exhibit 12-5

# CRIMINAL INTELLIGENCE REPORT—FIRST PROGRESS: DRUG TRAFFICKING

## 1985, Re: Walter R. Seabrook III

### FINANCIAL INFORMATION—ACCOUNTS:

First National Bank
Any City, Any State

Third National Bank
Any City, Any State

City Savings and Loan
Any City, Any State

Information developed through Confidential Source 593 indicates that Seabrook has a safe deposit box at Third National Bank. Each Tuesday and Thursday, Seabrook exchanges exactly $9,000 in tens and twenties, into $100 bills. He goes to the safe deposit box with the currency and returns soon after without the currency.

Information developed through Confidential Source 295 indicates that Sea King Development, Inc. is reporting an annual income of $50,000.

Information developed through Confidential Source 295 indicates that Seabrook is filing income tax, reporting an annual personal income of $35,000, which is paid to him as a salary from Sea King Development, Inc.

Other corporations formed by Seabrook have no apparent active business, and research is currently being conducted.

Undeveloped criminal intelligence leads are pending at Southern City Police Department, Any State; and Southern County Sheriff's Department, Any State.

Coordination with Drug Enforcement Administration (DEA); United States Customs (New England Branch); Internal Revenue Service; Any State Drug Task Force; and the Other State and Another State Police; along with This State's Police. Other agencies as needed.

Currently, an ad hoc task force chaired by Any City Police Department will begin meeting on the Seabrook intelligence collection project on November 29, 1985.

EXHIBIT 12-5

# CRIMINAL INTELLIGENCE REPORT—SECOND PROGRESS: DRUG TRAFFICKING

## 1986, Re: Walter R. Seabrook III

On November 29, 1985, multiple federal, state, county, and local law enforcement agencies, chaired and coordinated by Any City Police Department, met and agreed to proceed with criminal intelligence collection regarding Seabrook on an integrated enforcement basis.

The ad hoc task force will meet at Any City Police Department on the third Tuesday of each month, beginning during January 1986. Each participating agency will provide written update reports on information collected since the previous meeting.

Any City Police Department, Criminal Intelligence Bureau, will compile all information and disseminate a consolidated monthly update to each member of the ad hoc task force.

### INFORMATION UPDATE: JANUARY 1986

According to information provided by United States Customs, Seabrook is known to make frequent trips to Canada from St. George's Airport and return. Each trip lasts only flight time plus five hours. Destination on flight plans provided by FAA indicate that Seabrook is traveling to and from Montreal.

The ad hoc task force members agreed to invite a representative of the Royal Canadian Mounted Police (RCMP) to be a member of the Seabrook Project.

An inquiry to the RCMP received a positive reply, and a representative will attend each meeting.

According to information provided by the DEA, Seabrook was arrested in Southern State during 1982 when a search of his aircraft on arrival from Jamaica revealed 20 kilos of cocaine. The aircraft was registered to Caribbean Split, Inc., one of the companies solely owned by Seabrook. Also arrested with Seabrook was another pilot identified as Merrill Johnson, who had previous drug trafficking arrests but no convictions.

One week before the trial, Johnson was reported killed in a plane crash near Bogotá, Colombia, when the plane he was piloting developed engine trouble during a final approach to a remote dirt runway.

Charges were dropped against Seabrook in the Southern State case after Johnson's death because the U.S. customs agent exercised a probable cause search of Seabrook's aircraft based on recognition of Johnson. The agent was unable to identify Seabrook positively since he was concentrating on remembering Johnson.

State Drug Task Force reported that an undercover officer would be sent into the area during February for a period of two weeks in an effort to develop more information about Seabrook's local operation.

Exhibit 12-5

## CRIMINAL INTELLIGENCE REPORT—THIRD PROGRESS: DRUG TRAFFICKING

## 1986, Re: Walter R. Seabrook III

Records research on Seabrook revealed additional information as listed:

**VEHICLES OWNED:**

1985 Cadillac four-door sedan
Fleetwood—Dark Blue
Blank State Lic. 84732A

1973 Ford F600 Stake Truck
White
Blank State Lic. UR3985

1976 Lincoln four-door sedan
Green
Blank State Lic. 83748B

1977 Chevrolet four-door sedan
Black and tan
Blank State Lic. 84759D

1983 Chevrolet Stake Truck
Blue
Blank State Lic. 8374658

1983 Mercedes 280SL Conv.
Blue
Blank State Lic. 27643A

1977 Buick Electra four-door sedan
Black
Blank State Lic. 28394B

1973 Jaguar XJ6 four-door sedan
White
Blank State Lic. 82294E

1983 Shore Boat Trailer
Gray
Blank State Lic. 82743T

1983 Shore Boat Trailer
Gray
Blank State Lic. 28747T

EXHIBIT 12-5

# CRIMINAL INTELLIGENCE REPORT—THIRD PROGRESS: DRUG TRAFFICKING

## 1986, Re: Walter R. Seabrook III

### ARREST RECORD (TRAFFIC):

March 4, 1974
Possession of drugs
DL suspended 60 days
Blank City, Any State

March 4, 1974
Unregistered vehicle
$100 fine
Blank City, Any State

August 27, 1982
Noninspection
$50 fine
Blank City, Any State

November 19, 1982
Speeding
$150 fine
Blank City, Any State

May 22, 1985
Speeding
$120 fine
Blank City, Any State

August 29, 1985
Traffic signal
$50 fine
Blank City, Any State

September 5, 1985
Speeding
$180 fine
Blank City, Any State

### CRIMINAL ARREST RECORD:

April 14, 1982
Possession of cocaine
Southern City, Any State
Case dismissed

Exhibit 12-5

# CRIMINAL INTELLIGENCE REPORT—THIRD PROGRESS: DRUG TRAFFICKING

## 1986, Re: Walter R. Seabrook III

On March 14, 1979, Seabrook was detained in Jamaica by Jamaican authorities. Intelligence sources report Seabrook was piloting an aircraft containing about 600 kilos of cocaine originating in Colombia. In custody for about ten hours, Seabrook was suddenly released and allowed to fly to Miami, Florida. On arrival in Miami, his aircraft was searched and found to be empty.

On March 3, 1980, an aircraft believed to be piloted to County Road Airport, Any City, Any State, by Seabrook was inspected, and 500 pounds of cocaine were discovered. The aircraft ownership was a defunct corporation whose owner is deceased. Seabrook did not return to the airport, and the aircraft was never claimed.

On August 6, 1985, at the New Credit Union, 394 Southland Avenue, Any City, Any State, Seabrook cashed a check in the amount of $12,202 drawn on the Downtown City Bank, Any City, Any State. Payor is unknown.

On December 28, 1985, at the North National Bank, 8394 51st Street, Any City, Any State, Seabrook cashed a check drawn on a commercial account of Sea King Development, Inc. in the amount of $37,000. The check was payable to Seabrook and signed by Seabrook.

On January 14, 1986, at the Blank National Bank, 9340 23rd Avenue, Southern City, Any State, Seabrook deposited $67,500 in cash into a commercial account in the name of Caribbean Split, Inc.

On January 16, 1986, at the Southern National Bank, 2938 East Palm Blvd., Any City, Any State, Seabrook deposited a check in the amount of $67,500 drawn on an account in the name of Caribbean Split, Inc. and payable to Investments World Wide, Inc., signed by Seabrook.

On January 18, 1986, at the Northern National Bank, 283 Main Street, Any City, Any State, Seabrook deposited a check in the amount of $67,500, drawn on an account in the name of Investments World Wide, Inc. and payable to Mountain Region Development Corporation, signed by Seabrook.

(All corporations, all accounts are solely controlled by Seabrook.)

All toll call telephone records for the past six months for telephones listed or unlisted in the name of Seabrook, or any company he solely controls, are under subpoena issued by the U.S. Attorney.

Exhibit 12-5

## CRIMINAL INTELLIGENCE REPORT—FOURTH PROGRESS: DRUG TRAFFICKING

### 1987, Re: Walter R. Seabrook III

U.S. Customs (PAIRS) reports the following aircraft flights with Seabrook registered as pilot:

| | |
|---|---|
| April 28, 1984 | Southern Airport to Montego Bay, Jamaica |
| May 1, 1984 | Montego Bay, Jamaica to a Southern State |
| June 3, 1984 | Montego Bay, Jamaica to a Southern State |
| June 5, 1984 | Southern State to Great Inagua, Bahamas |
| August 18, 1985 | Southern State to Georgetown, Bahamas |
| August 19, 1985 | Jamaica to Southern State |
| August 28, 1985 | New England State to Montreal, Canada |
| August 29, 1985 | Montreal, Canada to New England State |
| October 1, 1985 | Southern State to Great Inagua, Bahamas |
| October 2, 1985 | Great Inagua, Bahamas to Southern State |
| February 9, 1986 | New England State to Montreal, Canada |
| February 11, 1986 | Montreal, Canada to New England State |
| April 26, 1986 | Southern State to Great Inagua, Bahamas |
| April 30, 1986 | Great Inagua, Bahamas to Southern State |
| September 18, 1986 | New England State to Montreal, Canada |
| September 20, 1986 | Montreal, Canada to New England State |

### ANALYSIS OF TELEPHONE CALLS:

All telephone toll calls made by Seabrook for the period November 1985 through November 1986 disclosed a consistency in numbers called, minutes on the line, and locations from which the call was placed (normally telephone booths).

Each number repeatedly called was tracked, and the person to whom the number is billed identified. In each case, the person(s) identified are also suspects or convicted drug smugglers.

EXHIBIT 12-5

# CRIMINAL INTELLIGENCE REPORT—FIFTH PROGRESS: DRUG TRAFFICKING

## 1987, Re: Walter R. Seabrook III

Confidential Source 295 has come forward with affidavits and agreed to testify in a criminal trial about his knowledge of Seabrook's drug smuggling activities. Source has agreed to be identified and is Mr. Samuel Smith, employed by Seabrook as a bookkeeper during the past two years. During that time, Smith was cooperating with the ad hoc task force. As a result of Smith's affidavit, a search warrant was obtained for Seabrook's warehouse office and residence, where, according to Smith's affidavit, Seabrook maintained records.

After serving the search warrant and seizing all corporation and personal records, auditors from the FBI, U.S. Customs, and the IRS reviewed and audited all financial records and identified banks and audited their records regarding Seabrook. The audit revealed that during the period January 1984 through January 1987, Seabrook had a cash flow of about $9 million.

An assets search revealed that $8.2 million was invested in real estate, stocks, bonds, a rare coin and stamp collection, aircraft, motor vehicles, water craft, and personal effects. Cash totaling $670,000 was located in several safe deposit boxes.

Confidential Source 745 also made an affidavit and agreed to be identified and testify against Seabrook.

Sufficient evidence is available to open a criminal investigation. This intelligence case is closed.

### BASIS FOR INVESTIGATION:

Criminal Intelligence case # 000000000000.

### OFFENSES:

Drug trafficking (and multiple other offenses, involving Federal laws, several state statutes in a variety of states, and laws of foreign countries)

### SUSPECTS:

Walter R. Seabrook (address)

(and multiple other persons who were identified as participating in concert with Seabrook during his drug trafficking operations)

### SUMMARY OF INVESTIGATION:

During the period August 1975 through January 1987, in New England City, throughout Any State, several other states, Canada, Bahamas, Jamaica, and other areas, Walter R. Seabrook III trafficked in cocaine, marihuana, and heroin and received at least $9 million in cash from the illegal sale of drugs.

EXHIBIT 12-5

# CRIMINAL INTELLIGENCE REPORT—FIFTH PROGRESS: DRUG TRAFFICKING

## 1987, Re: Walter R. Seabrook III

**SUBSTANTIATION:**

Criminal intelligence operations detailed in CI case number 0000000000 revealed conclusive evidence to support the allegation that Seabrook is a long-term drug trafficker operating the illegal activity as a business and source of income.

Also, a listing of all confidential sources who agreed to be identified and provided affidavits of their knowledge.

**WITNESSES:**

Listing of all witnesses including law enforcement officers and agents who participated in the intelligence collection and development.

**EXHIBITS:**

A listing of each item of evidence, including a copy of each intelligence report and initial information reports.

Exhibit 12-5

# APPENDIX A

## High-Tech Information Management and Report Writing: Computers in Law Enforcement Applications

Computers are becoming as common as television sets; most people have at least one, and some households have more than one. Adults use computers to manage household activities and finances; children use computers to do their schoolwork and play video games. Schools across the country are integrating personal computers (PCs) into daily classroom activities, and colleges offer advance courses in programming. Even small businesses rely heavily on computer systems to keep records, control inventory, and determine profit and losses. Auditors, state agencies, and law enforcement are moving fast to use computers in ways that replace the typewriter and even the pen. Wherever we look, there's a computer.

## COMPUTERS FOR COLLECTING, MANAGING, AND WRITING INFORMATION

Computers are akin to electric lights and appliances; they're great when they work. It seems that any technology that makes our lives easier and more efficient can also make us more miserable when the machine malfunctions.

I'm not anticomputer—I have three, and although my trusty typewriter still occupies a prominent place in my office, it is rarely used. For law enforcement investigations, a computer brings a new dimension. Small departments can have sophisticated computer systems that fit into limited budgets. Information flows across the country in seconds, and more criminals are brought to justice because of the computer. Dispatchers and patrol officers alike use high-tech systems to create efficient response, saving time getting to a complainant and being able to return to duty faster.

However, there's a downside as well, and we have to confront both the pros and cons, so that we can design a backup system. Far too often, we become so high-tech that when a system fails, we're left without an alternative. However, our law enforcement responsibilities won't allow excuses for nonperformance.

Law enforcement departments across the country are managing information with either PCs or laptop systems; many are using or experimenting with both. Of course, large city departments develop mainframe systems with terminals similar to what many large newspa-

315

pers and publications use. Since a majority of law enforcement departments are small to mid-size, we'll concentrate on the possibilities at those levels.

## THE LAPTOP COMPUTER SYSTEM

There are over a hundred laptop computer systems on the market, designed by several manufacturers. Buying and using a laptop computer system isn't as simple as buying and using a typewriter, and prices vary. Although dollars are important, both for department and personal budgets, for the time being we'll set that consideration aside and look at capability and feasibility.

If your department doesn't have the funding to purchase laptop computer systems, seriously consider buying your own. As I mentioned early in this book, personalizing your equipment has distinct advantages. First, you're the only person using the equipment, and you are able to design what works best for you, not conform to what someone else thinks works best for you. That is rarely effective because although some areas are rightfully standardized, we all have our way of getting from point A to point B. How we do that is not as important as how good the outcome is. Don't be discouraged if your chief is still hooked on stubby pencils, pocket notebooks, fill-in-the-blanks forms, and ballpoint pens. Generally, that attitude comes from genuine fear of computer systems. My first experience with a computer was apprehensive (it's a lot easier to deal with things we're already comfortable with); however, once you become familiar with a computer, it becomes comfortable, too. Go out and buy your own laptop computer system, make payments if you must, and watch your capability and effectiveness increase. Your increased ability to write dynamic reports will amaze you.

### What to Look for When Shopping for a Laptop Computer System

The laptop, and actually all computer systems, is designed with the business world in mind. That's understandable, because it's the largest consistent market. In the same vein, computer salespersons are thinking business, not law enforcement, and most haven't any idea of how you can apply a computer to enhance your job performance. They may pretend to have the knowledge, but they probably don't. I don't mean to put down computer salespersons or specialists; I just want *you* to decide what works and not allow the salesperson to sell what he or she thinks will work best for you.

There are several features to consider when shopping for a laptop computer system. First, consider the screen and how it operates. Your screen must be compatible to the use intended and is one of the key components in the system. If you aren't able to see what you're telling the computer, the system is worthless. A good rule to remember is, the brighter and clearer the image on a screen, the more power it takes. That's not important on a PC that plugs in to an outlet or to your laptop if you have plug in capability an outlet to connect it to. However, in most situations, you'll be operating on battery power.

*LCD (liquid crystal display).* You can't use this kind of screen in dimly lit areas or in the dark, because the screen depends on light entering from the front. Without that light entering the screen, you are not able to see the images. It's not a good choice for a law enforcement application. However, there is an alternative LCD which does perform well.

*Backlit LCD.* This is nearly the same type of screen, but instead of requiring incoming light, which then reflects off the parts of the display not polarized, an electroluminescent light source is placed in the rear of the screen panel. It produces a blue glow and is very efficient (producing a lot of light for the amount of electricity consumed) and is the least expensive in comparison with plasma lit screens. Disadvantages include vulnerability to heat. Don't leave the screen in a car that's closed and sitting in the sun. When exposed to high levels of heat, the display can darken. It may correct itself as the temperature is lowered; however, the screen can also be damaged. In dark or poorly lit areas, the backlit LCD may also have some clarity problems. However, for all-around dependability, low battery drain, and reasonable versatility, it's a good screen for average law enforcement portable applications.

*Gas plasma display.* Unlike LCD, gas plasma screens generate light and can be used in dark or dimly lit areas. There are, however, two advantages and several disadvantages. Their major advantage is that they're bright, and that's necessary for the law enforcement officer working in all kinds of conditions, often in darkened areas or at night. However, if there's not enough power and voltage falls below a certain level, the light goes out. A second advantage is that the resolution or image clarity is high, not fuzzy as in some cases. That's especially important in dark areas and to preserve your calm attitude when writing. Another disadvantage, however, is that they are expensive, pushing up the cost of the computer system, dependent on the screen. Although they're a good screen, you're likely to be relying on battery power most if not all the time. For that reason, gas plasma is not a good choice because of its thirst for power, shutdown when power is insufficient, and fast drain consumption of your batteries.

Having settled on a backlit LCD screen, I'm now interested in a key question. How long will the batteries keep the computer operational? If I process five crime scenes back-to-back and each takes one to two hours, will a laptop be feasible?

First, you'll want to consider the type and application of batteries used with your laptop selection. Although the computer comes with standard batteries, it is often advantageous to replace them with a better type. Normally, you can work all that out with the dealer as your personal specifications. Be certain you select a computer that enables fast, easy battery changes; some do not. Remember, don't let the salesperson tell you what's best for a law enforcement officer; you tell him or her what you must have and go from there. Some batteries may only provide power for one hour, others two or three. The key to selecting batteries is to select those which provide an amp-hour rating 20 to 40 percent more than what you need to power up. Then buy a good charger and several battery packs. I like to have eight hours worth when I go out on a case, to obtain statements, or do other kinds of writing. It is an added expense, but that is a part of the cost of excellence.

Second, take good care of the batteries, making certain you use a good quality charger that puts in the right charge for the battery. Putting in a charge too fast will reduce the life of your batteries or damage them permanently. Store new batteries in the fresh food compartment of your refrigerator (not the freezer). Put them in a plastic bag to prevent contamination from possible leakage. Warm up the batteries at room temperature for several hours before using. Avoid using or storing batteries in temperatures above 75 or 80 degrees Fahrenheit. A good rule of thumb for ensuring that batteries have a long life is to remove them from your computer when not in use (for example, at the end of a shift), keep them charged, and on days off or vacations put them in separate plastic bags and store in the refrigerator.

With screen and batteries in mind, begin searching for a laptop computer that performs as you want it to perform. Chances are you won't find any single computer that does it all, unless you're willing to pay vast fortunes, a luxury most law enforcement officers don't have. However, there are a few important capabilities to look for, such as the following:

1. *Overall weight and size.* A rule of thumb in this category is: the heavier and bigger a portable computer system is, the more capability it will have. If, for example, you're a detective who works white-collar crimes, business crimes, or any area that

requires a variety of programs such as word processing, spreadsheets, databases, and maybe graphics, you'll need a computer with more capability than a detective who uses his or her computer to write reports, take statements, make affidavits, and the like. Maybe you investigate a number of vehicle collisions each week and want to use programs that are now available to draw detailed sketches, compute skid marks and other items, and write your report. All of these things are a factor when selecting a computer by weight and size. If you travel by air a great deal, you'll want a computer system that will fit in a briefcase or its own case of similar size to a briefcase. If you're using the computer for a patrol car or unmarked sedan, or traveling by automobile, a larger, heavier computer system isn't a problem.

2. *Capability*. Beware of systems that only run on their own programs. That limits your capability, and undoubtedly you'll regret the choice in a short time. Select a system that is IBM compatible for the greatest versatility and selection of programs. You won't be locked into buying expensive specialty programs, and chances are if your department has PCs, they're IBM compatible. If you're not familiar with computers, a word of clarification is needed here. The term *IBM compatible* refers not to IBM computers, although they have fine systems. It does refer to the kinds of programs a computer will accept; in other words, the internal configuration by which the system works. Even well-established systems once using only their own software or programs are slowly converting their systems to use either their own versions or IBM-compatible software. Another reason to select a system that is IBM compatible is that several excellent law enforcement information management programs are now available, with many more sure to be coming.

3. *Keyboards*. Most keyboards are standard insofar as placement of letters and numbers, like typewriters. However, they do vary considerably in the way their keys are set and spaced. Select a keyboard that works well for you, is comfortable, and enables you to type words at your best speed. If you hunt-and-peck type, any keyboard will do; however, if you're going to all the trouble of using a computer system, you should learn how to type properly, without looking at the keys. It is not only more comfortable, but will save you a lot of valuable time and frustration.

4. *Hard disk, floppies, or both*. I'm sure you've heard a lot about hard disks, floppies, 5 1/4" disks, 3 1/2" disks, and all the jargon, pros and cons; and if you're not a computer user now, it makes you hesitant to become one. The first rule to remember is that computer users, salespersons, and others will try to impress you with lots of words they know you don't understand. A hard disk is in easy-to-understand terms: a series of metal disks, stacked one on another, and encased in a container. It has the advantage of storing vast amounts of information, depending on its capacity, ranging from 10 to 100 megabytes and beyond. A hard disk adds convenience to the computer. Once a program is copied onto your hard disk, you don't have to keep inserting floppy disks (which come in two sizes, 5 1/4" or 3 1/2"). Other sizes are around, along with CDs, but stay away from them. The common disks will be around a long time, as long as your computer lasts. Most new model computer systems are using the 3 1/2" floppy disks because they are actually not floppy but encased in a hard plastic container, which provides better information storage protection; they're smaller and ironically store more information than the larger disks. Your best bet is to buy a system that accepts 3 1/2" disks. A hard disk is okay, but a couple of disadvantages are that (a) users have a tendency to become too reliant on hard disk storage and fail to make floppy disk backup copies. If the disk fails, and most do after two or more years, all the information on it is lost. Don't assume your hard disk will be fine for two years; anything mechanical or electronic is subject to defects. (b) A hard disk adds considerable expense to the overall cost of your system. Most hard disks add $350 and up to the price tag. In my opinion, a hard disk is

the way to go, since the benefits outweigh the risks. If important information is placed on a hard disk, back it up by copying the same information to a floppy and keep it in your file. Using the same program, on a compatible computer, you can continue to use the information.

Here's my recommendation for a laptop computer system:

1. Buy a backlit LCD screen.

2. Buy a system that allows you to change batteries easily and quickly. Buy rechargeable batteries with 20 to 40 percent more output than needed to run the computer.

3. Have enough battery sets to last eight hours of running time, and keep them fully charged.

4. Acquire a system that has a keyboard you're comfortable using.

5. Acquire a system that's IBM compatible.

6. Acquire a system that is equipped with at least a 20-megabyte hard disk and uses 3 1/2" floppy disks.

## SELECTING A PRINTER

A law enforcement computer system without a printer is like having a typewriter without a ribbon. You can type all day and never see or document what you've typed. Of course, you can see it on the computer screen, but you can't have a witness sign the screen or forward your report to a reader without a printer to transfer the information to a hard copy.

There's a couple of options with printers. You can plug into a printer used normally with an office PC. The problem with that procedure is that you are unable to use your laptop in the field to take statements and have them signed on the scene. Taking all your data back to the department and plugging into a printer there (assuming one is there), printing your statements, and then going back out to have them signed isn't feasible. If a witness decides to omit part of the statement, or wants to add something to it or change part of it, you'll have to fix it on the computer, then travel back to the department, print the new statement, and back to the witness. The time factors involved are not acceptable. What you need is a portable printer. Kodak makes an ink jet Model 150 that runs on batteries and provides an acceptable near-letter-quality print, fine for on-the-scene or in-the-field statement taking. Your report can also be printed on this printer, although it can also be printed at the department on a larger, plug-in printer.

## COST

You will be surprised how much costs vary for the same item. However, a portable computer system and printer will range from about $1,500 and up, depending on where you shop. If you add a hard drive, add another $350. In realistic figures, a total system will cost you about $2,000. Of course, those are the bare prices, and with more features (less weight, smaller size, better screens, and all the other amenities) prices can range up to $8,000.

There are some alternatives that cost far less and work effectively. Brother, Magnavox, and Smith Corona sell portable systems, but you have to use regular 110-volt power sources. I have a Brother, and although it's heavy, it has a small screen, comfortable keyboard, 3 1/2" disk storage, spell checker, spreadsheet capability, word processing, and an excellent but noisy daisy wheel printer built in. You can acquire one or the others for about $600, and sometimes less if you shop around.

Another alternative is a portable electronic typewriter system which has an LED display that allows correcting, spell checking, fairly good print, and runs off flashlight batteries. It will fit in a good-sized briefcase and is lightweight. Casio, Canon, and other companies make them, costing about $100.

The alternatives are like computers; they have chips, memories, and several amenities that help get the job done.

## SOFTWARE

A computer without software is no help at all. Word processing software is a must, along with filers, spreadsheet, and perhaps specialized programs that make your writing effective.

When selecting a word processing system, choose one that's as simple as possible, but include spell checking capability, to save some embarrassing moments. No matter how perfect you may think your spelling is, you'll be surprised that now and then you do make an error. The reason I suggest simplicity is that word processing programs are written with the business world in mind. Composing letters, merging information, cutting and pasting, and all the sophisticated possibilities of corporate operations get in your way. Most programs will do all that in any case, but simple-to-use software limits the amenities.

Some excellent software programs are available for several hundred dollars, and excellent programs which will meet all your needs are available for less than $50. Shop around; if it's inexpensive and has a spell checker, it should serve you well for your law enforcement applications.

# APPENDIX B

## How to Interview Suspects and Take Statements Legally

Throughout this book, I emphasize the importance of written statements, primarily from witnesses and victims. However, obtaining a written statement from a suspect is worth a great deal. I recall dozens of serious cases over the years which came to a successful conclusion because a suspect decided to confess the details of a crime. However, a written statement by a suspect can also be the downfall of an otherwise successful investigation during a trial. I strongly suggest you don't talk to a suspect until you've collected all the information possible through other means. If you're not careful, a confession and all that it led you to can be thrown out of court, leaving a prosecutor with no evidence to introduce. Avoid talking to a suspect until there's absolutely nothing else to be gained—and then, do it with considerable care. The idea is to write winning reports based on information management, not based on what the suspect told you. In other words, let the suspect have the opportunity to tell you what is already known and proved. If his or her confession is thrown out, all your hard-won evidence will still be in place and as strong as ever. Put icing on your cake with a confession, if possible, but do it within the letter of the law; more importantly, within the letter of how courts have interpreted the law.

This appendix discusses prominent court decisions which affect suspects' confessions. These quick reference guidelines should be reviewed from time to time, before you start talking to a suspect, and especially before you start taking his or her written statement. Don't be afraid to explain the law and decisions to suspects; often I've found they're more willing to have you write their confession when they're sure you're fair and want them to be certain of their rights.

The Constitution of the United States produces the law regarding a suspect's rights about talking to law enforcement officers about a crime. The courts interpret the Constitution, and those decisions affect what will be accepted as reasonable and fair in any court and what will not be accepted as admissible.

In the case of *Miranda v. Arizona*, 384 U.S. 436, 444 (1966), the Court said:

Prior to any questioning, the person must be warned that he has a right to remain silent, that any statement he does make may be used as evidence against him, and that he has the right to the presence of an attorney, either retained or appointed.

In the case of *Doyle v. Ohio*, 426 U.S. 610, 617 (1976), the Court said:

> The warnings, mandated by [Miranda] as a prophylactic means of safeguarding Fifth Amendment rights…require that a person taken into custody be advised immediately that he has the right to remain silent, that anything he says may be used against him, and that he has a right to retained or appointed counsel before submitting to interrogation.

*Note*: A key phrase in the *Doyle v. Ohio* decision is "person taken into custody"—and I'm certain you've heard prosecutors and trainers pointing that out in regard to confessions and written statements. They say that unless the person is arrested, no requirement of advising a person of their rights is present; that if they confess, it's a good confession. They base that advice on the landmark *Miranda v. Arizona* case primarily, and others such as *Doyle v. Ohio*. There's another consideration, however, just as prevalent as Miranda rules. A good defense attorney is going to argue a key point, and likely be successful, especially to a jury, about the suspect's perception of being in custody. If you are talking to a lawyer and he or she confesses to a crime, you'll probably be okay if his or her lawyer raises that question. But how often do we have lawyers as suspects of committing a crime? Most often, the suspect, in court, represented by his or her lawyer, will be completely ignorant of the requirements, will have no idea about his or her Constitutional rights, will be terrified of the law enforcement officer who took the confession, and is just a person the police brow-beat into confessing. No rights were given because you didn't make an arrest—you just sat down and talked to the suspect. But in court, the suspect's lawyer will contend the suspect didn't believe he or she could refuse to answer questions, or could get up anytime and leave the room, or could refuse to give you a written statement. It's a common defense used nearly every day in courtrooms across the country.

If you're going to talk to a person whom you believe is or may be a suspect, but you have no arrest warrant or any legal grounds to arrest the person, don't risk the aforementioned scenario—let the suspect know he or she isn't under arrest, and tell the suspect what his or her rights are. Use the following information to do this. I suggest you make a form containing this information and have the suspect sign it, just as you should if a suspect is under arrest.

In the case of *Berkemer v. McCarty*, 468 U.S. 420, 430, 433, 434 (1984), the Courts said in part:

> One of the principal advantages of the doctrine that suspects must be given warnings before being interrogated while in custody is the clarity of that rule. Miranda's holding has the virtue of informing police and prosecutors with specificity as to what they may do in conducting custodial interrogation, and of informing courts under what circumstances statements obtained during such interrogation are not admissible. This gain in specificity, which benefits the accused and the State alike, has been thought to outweigh the burdens that the decision in Miranda imposes on law enforcement agencies and the courts by requiring the suppression of trustworthy and highly probative evidence even though the confession might be voluntary under traditional Fifth Amendment analysis.

> [A] person subjected to custodial interrogation is entitled to the benefit of the procedural safeguards enunciated in Miranda, regardless of the nature or severity of the offense of which he is suspected or for which he was arrested.

> The purposes of the safeguards prescribed by Miranda are to ensure that the police do not coerce or trick captive suspects into confessing to relieve the inherently compelling pressures, generated by the custodial setting itself, which work to undermine the individual's will to resist, and as much as possible to free courts from the task of scrutinizing individual cases to try to determine, after the fact, whether

particular confessions were voluntary. Those purposes are implicated as much by in-custody questioning of persons suspected of misdemeanors as they are by questioning of persons suspected of felonies.

In the case *Orozco v. Texas*, 194 U.S. 324, 326 (1969), the Court handed down the following decision [in part]:

The admission of testimony...obtained in the absence of the required warnings was a flat violation of the Self-Incrimination Clause of the Fifth Amendment.

In the case of *Mathis v. United States*, 391 U.S. 1, 4 (1968), the Court decided in part:

Miranda...[is not] applicable only to questioning one who is "in custody" in connection with the very case under investigation. There is no substance to such a distinction and in effect it goes against the whole purpose of...Fifth Amendment rights.

In the case of *United States ex rel. Williams v. Twomey*, 467 F.2d 1248, 1250 (7th Cir. 1972), the Court said:

Miranda requires a clear and unequivocal warning to an accused of his constitutional rights, prior to the taking of any statement, whether exculpatory or inculpatory, during interrogation occurring after an accused is taken into custody.

In the case of *United States v. Mata-Abundiz*, 717 F.2d 1277, 1279, 1280 (9th Cir. 1983), the Court said:

Civil as well as criminal interrogation of in-custody defendants by INS investigators should generally be accompanied by the Miranda warnings.... Not all civil questioning constitutes interrogation.... We hold that in-custody questioning by INS investigators must be preceded by Miranda warnings, if the questioning is reasonably likely to elicit an incriminating response.

In the case of *United States v. Alderete-Deras*, 743 F.2d 645, 648 (9th Cir. 1984), the Court said:

A principal purpose of the Miranda warnings is to permit the suspect to make an intelligent decision as to whether to answer the government agent's questions.... In deportation proceedings, however—in light of the alien's burden of proof, the requirement that the alien answer non-incriminating questions, the potential adverse consequences to the alien of remaining silent, and the fact that an alien's statement is admissible in the deportation hearing despite his lack of counsel at the preliminary interrogation—Miranda warnings would be not only inappropriate but could also serve to mislead the alien.

In the landmark case of *Miranda v. Arizona*, 384 U.S. 436, 444 (1966), the Court said in part:

By custodial interrogation, we mean questioning initiated by law enforcement officers after a person has been taken into custody or otherwise deprived of his freedom of action in any significant way.

In the case of *Rhode Island v. Innis*, 446 U.S. 291, 300-02 (1980), the Court held:

The considerations calling for the accused to be warned prior to custodial interrogation apply with no less force to the pretrial psychiatric examination at issue here. Respondent was in custody...when the examination was ordered and when it was conducted. That respondent was questioned by a psychiatrist designated by the trial court to conduct a neutral competency examination, rather than by a police officer, government informant, or prosecuting attorney, is immaterial. When [the psychiatrist] went beyond simply reporting to the court on the issue of competence and testified for the prosecution at the penalty phase on the crucial issue of respondent's future dangerousness, his role changed and became essentially like that of an agent of the State recounting unwarned statements made in a post-arrest custodial setting.... [Defendant] was given no indication that the compulsory examination would be used to gather evidence necessary to decide whether, if convicted, he should be sentenced to death. He was not informed that, accordingly, he had a constitutional right not to answer the questions put to him.

In the case of *Berkemer v. McCarty*, 468 U.S. 420, 440 (1984), the Court said in part:

The similarly noncoercive aspect of ordinary traffic stops prompts us to hope that persons temporarily detained pursuant to such stops are not "in custody" for purposes of Miranda.

It is settled that the safeguards prescribed by Miranda become applicable as soon as a suspect's freedom of action is curtailed to a "degree associated with formal arrest."...if a motorist who has been detained pursuant to a traffic stop thereafter is subjected to treatment that renders him "in custody" for practical purposes, he will be entitled to the full panoply of protections prescribed by Miranda.

In the landmark case of *Miranda v. Arizona*, 384 U.S. 436, 478 (1966), the Court decided:

There is no requirement that police stop a person who enters a police station and states that he wishes to confess to a crime, or a person who calls the police to offer a confession or any other statement he desires to make. Volunteered statements of any kind are not barred by the Fifth Amendment and their admissibility is not affected by our holding today.

Investigation may include inquiry of persons not under restraint. General on-the-scene questioning as to facts surrounding a crime or other general questioning of citizens in the fact-finding process is not affected by our holding.

In the case *United States v. Castro*, 723 F.2d 1527, 1530, 1531 (11th Cir. 1984), the Court held:

There is a four-factor test for determining whether a declarant is in custody, to wit: (1) the existence of probable cause to arrest; (2) the subjective intent of the police; (3) the subjective belief of the Defendant; and (4) the focus of the investigation. ...The former Fifth Circuit...recognized a clear exception to the Miranda rule for voluntary unresponsive statements.

*Note*: Referring to the suggestion of noncustodial warnings of rights, note number (3) in this Court decision. Belief and/or perception of the person you're talking to is a key factor and not one that needs to be tested in court. The risk is removed with noncustodial warnings, not based on Miranda but on the Fifth Amendment and the interviewee's perception at the time; or more importantly, the perception the suspect's lawyer will tell the jury was present.

In the case of *United States v. Jackson*, 448 F.2d 963, 970 (9th Cir. 1971), cert. denied, 405 U.S. 924 (1972), the Court held:

No Miranda warning was necessary before the officers questioned defendants...as to their identity and places of residence. Disclosure of name and address is an essential neutral act. It identifies but does not by itself implicate anyone in criminal conduct.

In the case of *United States v. Pullen*, 721 F.2d 788, 790 (11th Cir. 1983), the Court held:

> While it is established that the Miranda safeguards come into play when an individual is in custody and subjected to interrogation, the Miranda safeguards are not applicable to private citizens who conduct an investigation unless they have some connection with the government.

In the case of *United States v. Crisco*, 725 F.2d 1228, 1231 (9th Cir.), cert. denied, 466 U.S. 977 (1984), the Court said:

> Miranda warnings are required only where there has been such a restriction on a person's freedom as to render him "in custody.... This circuit employs an objective reasonable person test in determining whether a person is in custody. Factors to be considered are the language used to summon the defendant, the physical surroundings, the extent to which the defendant is confronted with evidence of his guilt, and the pressure exerted to detain him.

*Note*: The following cases are of key importance to taking written statements from suspects or people who may be suspects. The Court decided, based on Miranda and subsequent cases, however, that this application is not only critical in your statement taking of persons in custody but supports the noncustodial advice provided earlier. A considerable weight can be brought to bear on the person's perception of being in custody, or what his or her attorney says the perception was.

*Waiver of rights*: Suspects may relinquish their constitutional rights, but the government must establish that the waiver is made voluntarily, knowingly, and intelligently. The following court decisions help define the waiver and problems you can avoid by understanding it fully, based on court precedence.

In the case of *Miranda v. Arizona*, 384 U.S. 436, 478, 479 (1966), the Court held:

> After...[the required] warnings have been given, and such opportunity [to exercise these rights] afforded him, the individual may knowingly and intelligently waive these rights and agree to answer questions or make a statement....Any statement given freely and voluntarily without any compelling influences is, of course, admissible in evidence.

> However, if the individual indicates in any manner, at any time prior to or during questioning, that he wishes to remain silent, the interrogation must cease...and, if the individual states that he wants an attorney, the interrogation must cease.

In the case of *Edwards v. Arizona*, 451 U.S. 477, 484-85 (1981), the Court decided:

> An accused, ...having expressed his desire to deal with the police only through counsel, is not subject to further interrogation by the authorities until counsel has been made available to him, unless the accused himself initiates further communication, exchanges or conversations with the police....It is inconsistent with Miranda and its progeny for the authorities, at their insistence, to reinterrogate an accused in custody if he has clearly asserted his right to counsel.

In the case of *Smith v. Illinois*, 469 U.S. 91 (1984), the Court said:

> An accused in custody, having expressed his desire to deal with the police only through counsel, is not subject to further interrogation by the authorities until counsel has been made available to him, unless he validly waives his earlier request for the assistance of counsel. This rigid prophylactic rule embodies two dis-

tinct inquiries. First, courts must determine whether the accused actually invoked his right to counsel. Second, if the accused invoked his right to counsel, courts may admit his responses to further questioning only on finding that he (a) initiated further discussions with the police, and (b) knowingly and intelligently waived the right he had invoked....Where nothing about the request for counsel or the circumstances leading up to the request would render it ambiguous, all questioning must cease. In these circumstances, an accused's subsequent statements are relevant only to the question of whether the accused waived the right he had invoked. Invocation and waiver are entirely distinct inquiries, and the two must not be blurred by merging them together.

In the case of *Oregon v. Bradshaw*, 462 U.S. 1039, 1045-46 (1983), the Court decided:

Although ambiguous, the respondent's question in this case as to what was going to happen to him evinced a willingness and a desire for a generalized discussion about the investigation; it was not merely a necessary inquiry arising out of the incidents of the custodial relationship....Since there was no violation of the Edwards rule in this case, the next inquiry was whether a valid waiver of the right to counsel and the right to silence had occurred, that is, whether the purported waiver was knowing and intelligent and found to be so under the totality of the circumstances, including the necessary fact that the accused, not the police, reopened the dialogue with the authorities.

In the case of *Miranda v. Arizona*, 384 U.S. 436, 475 (1966), the Court said:

If the interrogation continues without the presence of an attorney and a statement is taken, a heavy burden rests on the government to demonstrate that the defendant knowingly and intelligently waived his privilege against self-incrimination and his right to retained or appointed counsel.

In the case of *North Carolina v. Butler*, 441 U.S. 369, 373 (1979), the Court decided:

An express written or oral statement of waiver of the right to remain silent or of the right to counsel is usually strong proof of the validity of that waiver, but is not inevitably either necessary or sufficient to establish waiver. The question is not one of form, but rather whether the defendant in fact knowingly and voluntarily waived the rights delineated in...Miranda.... As was unequivocally said in Miranda, mere silence is not enough. That does not mean that the defendant's silence, coupled with an understanding of his rights and a course of conduct indicating waiver, may never support a conclusion that a defendant has waived his rights. The Courts must presume that a defendant did not waive his rights; the prosecution's burden is great; but in at least some cases waiver can be clearly inferred from the actions and words of the person interrogated.

In the case of *United States v. Charles*, 738 F.2d 686, 697-98 (5th Cir. 1984), the Court said:

The waiver of constitutional rights must be considered in light of the background, experience, and conduct of the accused. That defendants were police officers at the time their statements were given is therefore relevant to a determination of the voluntariness of their statements.

*Note*: The court decision excerpts shown on these pages are for your guidance and do not purport to be a complete compilation of all court cases on this subject. They are intended to heighten your awareness when you are obtaining or attempting to obtain written statements which will be used as evidence, implicating a person in criminal activity.

A good rule of thumb is, When in doubt, advise the person of his or her constitutional rights. If the person is under arrest or in custody, use the Miranda warning. If the person is not under arrest, use a noncustodial warning. When you're fair and proceed in strict legal procedures, you'll always be successful and on the winning team.

Exhibit B-1 shows an example of the Miranda warning. Exhibit B-2 shows an example of the noncustodial warning.

328

# ARKANSAS HIGHWAY POLICE

Arkansas State Highway and Transportation Department

## – YOUR RIGHTS –

(Before we ask you any questions, you must understand your rights.)

YOU HAVE THE RIGHT TO REMAIN SILENT.

(Response: _____ )

ANYTHING YOU SAY CAN BE USED AGAINST YOU IN COURT.

(Response: _____ )

YOU HAVE THE RIGHT TO TALK TO A LAWYER FOR ADVICE BEFORE WE ASK YOU ANY QUES-
TIONS, AND TO HAVE HIM PRESENT WITH YOU DURING QUESTIONING.

(Response: _____ )

IF YOU CANNOT AFFORD A LAWYER, ONE WILL BE APPOINTED FOR YOU BEFORE ANY QUES-
TIONING IF YOU WISH.

(Response: _____ )

IF YOU DECIDE TO ANSWER QUESTIONS NOW WITHOUT A LAWYER PRESENT, YOU WILL STILL
HAVE THE RIGHT TO STOP ANSWERING AT ANY TIME.   YOU ALSO HAVE THE RIGHT TO STOP
ANSWERING AT ANY TIME UNTIL YOU TALK TO A LAWYER.

(Response: _____ )

I have read this statement of my rights, and I understand what my rights are.   No promises or threats have
been made to me, and no pressure or coercion of any kind has been used against me.

Signed: _____

Date: _____

Witness: _____

_____

Date & Time: _____  Location: _____

| | |
|---|---|
| _____ | _____ |
| **INVESTIGATOR** | **REPORT NUMBER** |
| _____ | _____ |
| **DATE SUBMITTED** | **TYPE OF REPORT** |

A.H.P. FM 7

– FOR OFFICIAL USE ONLY –

EXHIBIT B-1

# NONCUSTODIAL STATEMENT OF RIGHTS UNDER THE FIFTH AMENDMENT TO THE CONSTITUTION OF THE UNITED STATES OF AMERICA

I am a law enforcement officer conducting a criminal investigation. I would like to ask you questions about a crime that I am now investigating and in which I regard you as a possible suspect; however I want to make certain you have a clear understanding about the following points:

1. That you are not under arrest.

    Initials ————————————

2. That the Fifth Amendment of the United States Constitution guarantees you cannot be made to answer any of my questions or submit any information which you feel might incriminate you in any way.

    Initials ————————————

3. That anything you do say and any documents you provide, or any written statements you sign, may be used against you in a criminal proceeding.

    Initials ————————————

4. That you may obtain the assistance and advice of an attorney before responding to any of my questions.

    Initials ————————————

5. That you do not have to answer any of my questions and you can discontinue this interview anytime you choose.

    Initials ————————————

6. That you are free to leave this room or this place anytime you wish; no effort will be made to stop you.

    Initials ————————————

Do you understand your rights as I have read them to you?

    Initials ————————————

Do you wish to contact an attorney at this time?

Write yes or no ————————————      Initials ————————————

# NONCUSTODIAL STATEMENT OF RIGHTS UNDER THE FIFTH AMENDMENT TO THE CONSTITUTION OF THE UNITED STATES OF AMERICA

Are you willing voluntarily to answer my questions and/or provide documents and/or sign a written statement summarizing your information to include questions and answers?

Write yes or no ———————————————    Initials ———————————————

I have read the above explanations and fully understand my rights as written here. I have initialed each applicable item above and placed my reply of "yes or no" as needed in my own hand. I willingly waive my right to call or consult with an attorney at this time and agree to answer questions, understanding I may stop anytime, leave anytime, select the questions I want to answer, and that I am not under arrest.

Signature ——————————————————————————————————

Printed Name ——————————————————————————————————

Place of Interview ——————————————————————————————

Time and Date ——————————————————————————————————

Law Enforcement Officer's Signature ————————————————————

Law Enforcement Officer's Printed Name ————————————————————

# Index

## A

Abbreviations, guidelines for, 270–272
Arkansas Highway Police Forms
    property receipt, example of, 39
    suspect rights warning, example of, 330
    suspect, description of, 39
    written statement, example of, 40
Armed Robbery Reporting, examples of, 102–110
Art of Taking Written Statements, 111–112
Attitudes, changing of, 95–96

## B

Basic Evidence Reminders, 58–59
Body Language, Uses of, 126–127

## C

Career Advantages, 1–2
Checklists
    beginning to write reports for, 5
    crime prevention inspection for, 252
    crime scene sketch for, 24, 137
    developing a, 13
    equipment component for, 75–80
    exhibits/evidence for, 26
    guides for reports of, 22–23
    identification of people for, 30–38
    information management for, 14
    personalized types of, 13
    physical evidence for, 60
    report writing for, 86
    vehicle collision sketch for, 213
City Block Sketch Form, 82
Collisions, Motor Vehicle
    classification of, 207
    essential elements of, 206
    factors of, 208
    glossary of terms for, 207

Collisions, Motor Vehicle (*cont'd*)
    information management of, 210
    investigation of, 206
    report writing about, 205–221
    reports of, 217
    sketches of, 213
    stages of, 209
    steps for making sketches of, 217
    supplemental reports of, 221
    vehicle reports of, 205
Computers, Report Writing Uses, 315
Conclusions, Writing of, 95
Containers, Use of
    field, in the 12
    personal files, for, 12
    types of, 12
Court Environment, the, 53
Craft of Writing, Intelligence Reports, 191
Crime Prevention
    model report of, 252
    writing inspection reports for, 251
    writing reports of, 239
Crime Scenes
    arrival at, 5
    searches of, 53–54, 61
Crimes, Model Reports of, 290–301
Criminal Intelligence
    closing cases with, 200–201
    converting to an investigation from, 200–201
    cycle of, 188
    data, dissemination of, 188–189
    differences of, 190–191
    information sources, managing for, 201
    managing report information for, 199–200
    public sources of information for, 201–204
    report examples of, 193–194, 197–198
    report writing systems for, 187
    report, model of, 301–314
    reports for, 191
    reports, craft of writing a, 191–192
    role of, 187
    strategic, 104

Criminal Intelligence (*cont'd*)
    terminology of, 189–190
    using progress reports in, 200
    versus information, 187–188
Criminal Investigation
    completed report for, 152–160
    definition of, 143
    eight step planning process for, 146–147
    first progress report for, 147–149
    information management for, 163
    investigative log for, 149–150
    investigator's statement for, 184–185
    objectives of, 144
    progress report system, 144–145
    quick reference guide for, 161
    reopening a closed, 167
    report examples of, 168–171
    report writing formats for, 142–143
    requirements of, 172
    second progress report for, 150
    statement examples for, 176–183
    statement taking tips for, 172–175
    subsequent progress reports for, 150–152
    supplemental reports for, 164
    third progress reports for, 152
    undeveloped leads reply for, 166
    undeveloped leads report for, 163–164
    undeveloped leads request for, 165
    visual network planning technique for, 145–146
    written statement benefits in a, 167
Critiques of Reports, 193

**E**

Equipment
    about your need for, 86–87
    component groups of, 74
    information management with, 6–8
    photographic kit of, 75
    requirements for, 6
    resource kit checklists of, 75–80
    tool box of, 6–8
Essential Elements of Crime, Importance of, 4
Essential Elements of Proof, Importance of, 60, 71
Evidence
    basic reminders for, 58–59
    categories of, 58–59
    collection kits for, 76–80
    collection of, 60–64
    court decisions about, 65–67
    definitions of, 60
    physical types of, 29, 58–59, 60–64, 65–67, 76–80
    preservation of, 60–64
    purpose of, 60–61

Exhibits, Identifying in Reports, 108
Exploded Room Sketch Form, 81
Expository Report Writing Style
    advantages of, 96
    example of, 91, 94–95
    important objectives of, 96
    reasons for, 91

**F**

FBI Laboratory, 62–64
Fingerprint, Latent Kit, 79
Fingerprints, 62–64

**G**

Grammar, Guidelines for, 261
Graph Paper Sketch Form, example of, 83
Guidelines
    assembling reports for, 139
    photographs for, 138
    report writing for, 96–99
Guideposts
    law enforcement investigations for, 57
    physical evidence categories of, 58–59

**H**

Heavy Writing, Examples of, 97–100

**I**

Information Management Techniques
    beginning the process of, 4
    beyond routine, 1
    collecting and managing, 2
    collection and, 1
    collection problems, 5
    effectively, 1
    equipment collection of, 8
    excellence of, 123
    focusing on, 4
    investigator's statement, writing of, 109
    kits for, 6
    management of, 1
    personalized checklists for, 13–14
    personalized worksheets with, 12–13
    personalized, 6
    physical evidence of, 29
    purposes of, 11–13
    reporting for, 1

Information Management Techniques (*cont'd*)
    systems, development of, 11
    technique systems, 11–13
    through hearing skills, 123–126
    tool box for, 6
    using containers for, 12
    using molds and casts for, 72
    using photographs and sketches for, 72
    using photographs for, 72, 136–137
    using written statements for, 71–72
    with a case file, 69, 139
    with equipment for, 86
    with essential elements considered first, 71
    with investigative resource kits for, 74–85
    with physical and trace evidence, 72
    with report-oriented sketches for, 127–136
    your approach to, 5
Investigative Question Guide, 92–93
Investigations, law enforcement, 57

**L**

Listening, Importance of
    essential actions of, 123–124
    evaluating information heard when, 125
    interpreting what you hear when, 125
    interruptions of, 124

**M**

Model Reports, 277–314

**N**

Narrative Report Styles
    examples of, 89–90
    versus expository style of, 89
Non-Custodial Rights Example, 330–331
Numbers, Guidelines for Writing of, 272–273

**O**

Organizing Techniques
    equipment needed for, 86
    professional image, a part of 73
Outlining Reports
    advantages of, 262
    benefits of, 261
    guidelines for, 261

**P**

Photographs
    advantages of, 136–137
    components kit for taking of, 75
    in court, use of, 215
    information collection advantages with, 72
    report exhibits using, 138
Photography, Nighttime Techniques, 215
Physical Evidence 72
Post Mortem Evidence Kit, example of, 78
Punctuation, Guidelines for Use of, 273–276

**Q**

Quick Reference Guides, Report Writing for, 9

**R**

Report Form Examples
    arrest for, 20
    complaints for, 18
    investigation and arrest for, 17
    investigations for, 16
    offense, 15
    supplementary, 19
Report Writing Techniques
    accuracy and speed of, 97
    breaking with tradition in, 95–96
    completed types, 152–160
    completeness of, 98–99
    examples of, 89–91, 102–103
    exhibit identification in, 108
    expository objectives of, 96
    first progress of, 147–149
    first supplemental of, 168–169
    formats of, 69
    guidelines for, 96–99
    high impact types of, 101
    including photographs, ways of, 138
    intelligence use of, 193–194
    investigator's statement, attaching to, 109
    reader's perception of, 4, 98
    second progress of, 150–152
    sketches, reasons for, 135–136
    structuring of, 104
    substantiating your, 104–106
    undeveloped leads for, 165–166
    vehicle collisions for, 4–5
    victims, listing of, 106–107
    witnesses, listing of in, 106–107

Report Writing Techniques (*cont'd*)
  writing of, 69, 73


## S

Sketch Templates, examples of, 230–231
Sketches, Aids for
  at the scene for, 127
  body diagram for, 84–85
  city block guide for, 82
  equipment for, 128–129, 131–132
  exploded room guide for, 81
  graph and legend guide for, 83
  information collection with, 72
  injury symbols for, 84–85
  report-oriented types of, 135–136
Sketches, examples of, 234–235
Sketches, Making of, 223–231
Sketching, Techniques of, 127–136
Spelling, Guidelines for, 261, 267
Style, Guidelines for, 261
Suspect Statements, Examples of, 182–183


## T

Task, Defining your, 8–9
Templates, Examples of, 128–129, 131–132, 230–231
Time Management
  best reason for, 1
  best way to implement, 1
  law enforcement use of, 2
  saving techniques of, 1
Tradition, Breaking with, 95–96
Traditions, 2–3
Traffic Accidents
[See also Collisions & Vehicle Collisions]
  128–129, 131–132, 230–231


## U

Using Written Statements, as notes, 112


## V

Vehicle Collisions
  classification of, 207
  effective reports about, 210
  essential elements of, 206

Vehicle Collisions (*cont'd*)
  factors of, 207–208
  forgone conclusions, dangers of, 205
  glossary of terms for, 207–208
  investigation of, 205
  report writing style, 206–207
  reports about, 205
  reports, how to write, 217
  sketches, making of, 223–231
  stages of, 207, 209
  supplemental reports, 221
  terminology for, 230


## W

Witnesses, Reporting
  identifying and, 107
  in your report, 106–107
  statement form examples, 176–181
  ways of listing, 107–108
Worksheets, Report Writing for
  crime scene for, 24, 27
  crime scene search for, 25, 133
  exhibits/evidence for, 26
  handout on-scene interviews for, 122
  investigation and complaint for, 21
  personalized for, 12–13
Writing, Techniques of
  accuracy of, 97
  completeness in, 98–99
  heavy styles, causes of, 99–100
  high impact, 101
  how readers perceive your, 98
  quickly accomplishing, 110
  style, guidelines for, 261
  with speed in, 97–98
Written Statements, Uses of
  art of taking, 111–112
  benefits of, 167–168
  examples of, 113–116
  how to use as notes, 112–113
  importance of, 167–168
  information collection with, 71–72
  investigator's by, 184–185
  listening as crucial steps for, 123–126
  myths about, 110–111
  standard form example, 121
  truth about, 110–111
  twelve tips about, 172–175
  voluntary form example of, 119–120
  witness form example of, 117–118